Great Jews in
SPORTS

To Drew,

What a wonderful heritage
to follow, for excellence in
both sports performance, and
Sportsmanship!

Best,
Bri & Betty Rysman

Great Jews in SPORTS

Robert Slater

INTRODUCTION BY

Red Auerbach

JONATHAN DAVID PUBLISHERS, INC.
Middle Village, New York 11379

GREAT JEWS IN SPORTS

Copyright © 2011
by
Robert Slater

Jonathan David Publishers, Inc.
68-22 Eliot Avenue
Middle Village, New York 11379

www.jdbooks.com

4 6 8 10 9 7 5 3

Library of Congress Cataloging in Publication Data

Slater, Robert
    Great Jews in sports / Robert Slater ; introduction by Red Auerbach. — Updated and rev. ed.
      p. cm.
    Includes index.
    ISBN 978-0-8246-0453-0
    1. Jewish athletes—Biography. 2. Jews—Biography. I. Title.

GV697.Al S53 2003
796'.092'3924—dc21

82-19953
CIP

Book design and composition by John Reinhardt Book Design

Printed in the United States of America

For my children
MIRIAM, SHIMI, ADAM, TAL, and RACHEL

Photo Credits

Acknowledgments and thanks are due to the following institutions and persons for having kindly permitted their photographs to be used in this book:

Professional Bowlers Association; Basketball Hall of Fame; Jewish Sports Hall of Fame, Netanya, Israel; *Ring Magazine*; Haskell Cohen; Israel Government Press Office; First Interstate Bank Athletic Foundation; Pittsburgh Pirates; Harold O. Zinman/Haskell Cohen; World Maccabi Union; Philadelphia Eagles; Marshall Goldberg; Uzi Keren; *Daily Mirror*; Marshall Goldberg; Pittsburgh Steelers; Victor Hershkowitz; City College of New York; New York Knickerbockers; New York Racing Association; American Bowling Congress; Temple University; Women's Professional Bowling Association; Angelica Rozeanu; Los Angeles Dodgers; United Press International; Baltimore Orioles; Pinky Danilowitz; New York Mets; Wingate Institute of Physical Education and Sport, Netanya, Israel; Danny Wachsberg; *Sport Tennis Magazine*; Leah Fishbein; Zvi Nishri Physical Education and Sport Archives of the Wingate Institute of Physical Education and Sport, Netanya; Ruth Kedar, Israel Tennis Center, Ramat Hasharon, Israel; Amy Alcott; Yossi Roth, *Yediot Aharonot*; Los Angeles Clippers; ABC Radio Networks; Craig Blankenhorn; Sid Gillman; Buffalo Bills; Montreal Canadiens; National Basketball Association; Israel Sports Federation; Eran Groumi; Lydia Hatuel; Marty Glickman; Dan Calichman; University of Southern California Sports Information Department.

Acknowledgments

Although the writing of *Great Jews in Sports* was done largely in Israel, where I have lived for over three decades, most of the research was carried out during numerous visits to the United States. During the initial preparation, no single facility was more valuable than the sports branch of the Time, Inc. Library, in New York's Time-Life Building. Bruce Liebman, a staff member at *Time*'s sports library, became my personal research aide; and I owe him a special debt of gratitude. His overall enthusiasm for the project, coupled with his skill at finding answers to my countless questions, made my work very much easier and contributed immeasurably to the success the book has enjoyed.

Sports Illustrated's main library has been described by its staff as the greatest sports library in the world, and it did indeed prove helpful in tracking down thousands of details. I am particularly indebted to Lester Annenberg, Peter Miller, and Harry Peckham, the magazine's research librarians, for giving so generously of their time. I also want to extend thanks to Linda Ronan, manager at the *Sports Illustrated* library, who graciously made the collection's files available to me during my research for the 1992 updated edition.

It was something of a joyful coincidence that the founders of the Jewish Sports Hall of Fame at the Wingate Institute, in Netanya, Israel, were launching their new enterprise just as I began research on this book. I wish to express appreciation to everyone connected with the Hall of Fame, both in Israel and the United States, for their cooperation. Special tribute must be paid to Dr. Uri Simri, then executive director of the Hall of Fame. Not only did he serve as an invaluable fount of general sports knowledge, but also came to be an informal advisor on which Jewish sports figures merited inclusion. Others at the Jewish Sports Hall of Fame also contributed significantly: Effi Yaacobi, director of the Department of Public Relations and External Affairs; Zipporah Zeidner, one-time public relations director at the Wingate Institute; Shlomo Korlandchik, archivist at the Wingate Institute; and the capable staff of the Wingate Institute sports library.

Few men are more knowledgeable about the subject of Jews in sports than Haskell Cohen, long-time sports editor of the Jewish Telegraphic Agency. Fortunately for me, he gave of his valuable time to assess and offer new perspectives on material gathered for the book. I am deeply grateful.

I am, of course, aware of the major contribution to the subject made by Bernard Postal, Jesse Silver, and Roy Silver with the publication of their *Encyclopedia of Jews in Sports* (New York: Bloch Publishing Company, 1963). Needless to say, it served as an invaluable reference. Also very helpful was *The Jewish Almanac* (New York: Bantam, 1989), which was compiled and edited by Richard Siegal and Carl Rheins. Its chapter on Jewish athletes is excellent.

In researching the section on Israeli sports figures, I relied heavily on the help of several people: Shmuel Lalkin, director-general of the Sports Federation of Israel; Uri Afek, first as deputy director of the Israel Government Sports Authority and later as head of the Israel Olympic Committee; Gilad Lustig, director of the Top-Level Sports Center at the Wingate Institute; and Israel Paz, former editor of *Hadashot Hasport*, the Israeli sports newspaper. I thank them all for giving of their time and expertise.

Many other individuals were instrumental in bringing this work to fruition. I am particularly grateful to Dorothy Resnik for her good-natured help in translating material from Hebrew to English, as well as for a host of other efforts that made my work easier; Jennifer Frey, for her technical assistance with the original manuscript; and Leslie Dickstein, of *Time Magazine*, who spent many hours at the *Sports Illustrated* library, culling magazine and newspaper articles. Without her faithful, diligent effort, the 1992 edition would not have been possible. My gratitude also goes to Jean Max, who tirelessly gathered material for the 2003 edition.

Other individuals and institutions deserving of thanks are: Andrea Schwartz, Israel Tennis Centers Association, New York; Ian Froman, executive director of the Israel Tennis Center, Ramat Hasharon, Israel; Blanche Blumberg, public relations, Israel Tennis Center, Ramat Hasharon; Lloyd Wagner, Office of Public Relations, City College of New York; Clifford Kachline, historian, National Basketball Hall of Fame, Cooperstown, New York; Pro Football Hall of Fame, Canton, Ohio; Bud Fisher, public relations director, Professional Bowlers Association, Akron, Ohio; Mary Anne Marenna, *Meriden Record-Journal*, Meriden, Connecticut;

Los Angeles County Sheriff's Department, Los Angeles, California; Meyer F. Steinglass, New York City; Mac DeMere, news department manager, Sports Car Club of America, Englewood, Colorado; Louis Geseltzer, World Maccabi Union, Kfar Maccabiah, Israel; Robert Spivak, chairman, Maccabi U.S.A./Sports for Israel; Suzie Adams, editor-in-chief, *World Tennis Magazine,* New York; Nat Lobet, former publisher and editor, *Ring Magazine*; Joseph Telecki, Haifa, Israel; Bruce Pluckhahn, curator, National Bowling Hall of Fame and Museum, Greendale, Wisconsin; Ray Nelson, press relations manager, American Bowling Congress, Greendale, Wisconsin; Bess Resnik; Dana Gilbert, Abbe Abboa-Offi, ABC Radio Network; Ephraim Shen, public relations department, Wingate Institute; Scott Berchtold; Dr. Herb Krickstein; Miriam Don, Israel Tennis Academy; Rifka Rabinowitz, director of the Pierre Gildesgame Maccabi Sports Museum, Ramat Gan, Israel; Joe Siegman; Alan Sherman; Elli Garshowitz; Marc G. Whitney, public relations office, Women's International Bowling Congress; Terry Lyons, *NBA News*; Claude Mouton, director of public relations, Montreal Canadiens; Rich Vach, Association of Tennis Professionals; Mark Gerbert, Professional Bowlers Association; Ed Oliva, New York Knicks administrative staff; Aryeh Rosenzweig, chairman, Organizing Committee of the 14th Maccabiah Games; Mrs. Loraine Jacobs; Susan Cohen; Brian Flinn; Alan Friedman; Lee Kolligian; David J. Kufeld; Steve Lippmann; Jim McManus; George N. Postolos; Riva Rabinovitch; Barry Schweid; Shel Wallman; David Eiger; and Asaf Stolarz.

I extend a special thanks to Michael Winick for his crucial contribution in helping me obtain hard-to-locate information for the original and updated versions of *Great Jews in Sports*.

I would also like to express my gratitude to the following sports figures with whom I had personal contact: Amy Alcott, Yael Arad, Barry Asher, Red Auerbach, Isaac Berger, Margarethe "Gretel" Bergmann, Mickey Berkowitz, Ron Blomberg, Shimshon Brockman, Tal Brody, Angela Buxton,

Dan Calichman, Pinky Danilowitz, Pierre Darmon, Eitan Friedlander, Benny Friedman, Sid Gillman, Pamela Glaser, Marty Glickman, Shlomo Glickstein, Marshall Goldberg, Brian Gottfried, Hank Greenberg, Ernie Grunfeld, Julie Heldman, Victor Hershkowitz, Ken Holtzman, Red Holzman, Agnes Keleti, Sandy Koufax, Lenny Krayzelburg, Aaron Krickstein, Shaul Ladany, Harry Litwack, Amos Mansdorf, Debra Turner Marcus, Tom Okker, Paulina Peisachov Peled, Zhanna Pintussevich, Al Rosen, Esther Roth, Angelica Rozeanu, Dick Savitt, Dolph Schayes, Mathieu Schneider, Mark Spitz, David Stern, Eva Szekely, Brian Teacher, and Henry Wittenberg.

The following were especially helpful in providing photographs: Michael P. Aronstein, president, TCMA Ltd., Amawalk, New York; W.R. "Bill" Schroeder, managing director, First Interstate Bank Athletic Foundation, Los Angeles, California; Israel Government Press Office, Jerusalem, Israel; Jewish Sports Hall of Fame, Netanya, Israel; June Harrison Steitz, library director, Naismith Memorial Basketball Hall of Fame, Springfield, Massachusetts; Lev Borodulin, Tel Aviv, Israel; Eli Hershkowitz, Jerusalem, Israel; Rich Eng, NYRA Photo Services; New York Racing Association, Jamaica, New York; Burt Sugar, *Ring Magazine*; Debbie Harmison, Sports Information Director, Old Dominion University, Norfolk, Virginia; and United Press International.

Special thanks to Adam Slater, Elinor Slater, Michael Winick, and Michael Fein for their assistance in preparing this 2011 edition of *Great Jews in Sports*. My gratitude also to Shimon Casspi, father of basketball star Omri Casspi; Nitzan Feraro, Maccabi Tel Aviv basketball executive; and Tom Marchesi, Communications Manager for the NBA in Europe, the Middle East and Africa. I also express sincere appreciation to Udi Zitiat for providing photographs of Omri Casspi and to Michael Ivins, Manager of Photography for the Boston Red Sox, for providing photographs of Kevin Youkilis.

Contents

MAJOR BIOGRAPHIES

THUMBNAIL SKETCHES

ISRAELI SPORTS FIGURES

Foreword
by Red Auerbach

A long two-handed set shot by Dolph Schayes. Eddie Gottlieb, lovable, ex-owner, schedule-maker, rules-maker, and a member of the Basketball Hall of Fame. And many other great players running with the best of the pros, I guess that's what a book like this is all about.

Great Jews in sports: Nat Holman, perhaps the greatest player of the original Celtics back in the '20s. Red Holzman did a fantastic job while coaching the New York Knicks. I remember the great track star and famous announcer, Marty Glickman, who represented the Jews in the confrontation with Hitler back in 1936. Those are the things that stick with me.

The question of just who are the greatest Jews in sports grows on you. Everybody knows Sandy Koufax, Mark Spitz, and Hank Greenberg. Anyone who's followed boxing knows Barney Ross and Benny Leonard. These were unquestionably athletes who ranked at the top of their sports. Jews, however, have been reaching the pinnacle in sports far more broadly than the mention of these few names would suggest.

As I leafed through the pages of *Great Jews in Sports*, I felt a sense of pride that Jews have had such an impact. It's people like the Hungarian ping-pong player, Victor Barna. Like the Hungarian swimmer, Eva Szekely. Like the British sprinter,

Harold Abrahams. Each of them has a wonderful story.

What makes this book distinctive is that it is not merely a review of sports statistics. The men and women whose stories comprise this volume lived lives filled with a mixture of heartbreak (Barney Ross toward the end of his life) and of poignancy (Gretel Bergmann losing out on a chance to compete in the 1936 Berlin Olympics because of Hitler), as well as the story of victory.

Of course, a major theme strikes the reader throughout the sketches of these athletes and coaches: for the parents of many of these men and women sports were a real taboo. Jews just didn't aspire to careers in athletics. A lawyer or a doctor or an engineer, yes. But not a bowler, a football player, or a ping pong player. Those were not the spheres in which Jews strove to excel.

But what the older generation couldn't realize was that sports was a passport to a better way of life for some of the people in this book. Sports gave them a chance to excel, to make a living. Furthermore, in some cases at least, like Benny Leonard or Sid Gordon, sports was all they ate, drank, and breathed. I know how the older generation must have felt, but I have to admit, that I side with their children, the ones who wanted to skip the three professions, to head for the tennis court, or the football stadium, or the boxing ring.

Of course, in some sports Jews have reached the heights, while in others they have not. In ping pong, handball, and even boxing, Jews have climbed to the top. But, they've had a difficult time in golf, and in tennis for that matter. And, of course, in my own sport, basketball, only a relative handful have made it big in college and in the pros. Moreover, while there were quite a number of Jews playing basketball, in the 1920s, 1930s and 1940s, that number has dwindled to only a few. I don't know why it's that way. It just is.

If this book has done one thing for me, it's aroused my interest in the whole subject of Jewish sportsmen. Like many others, I guess I had thought I knew who would naturally be in this book. Well, some of the sports figures included here I hadn't heard of, while some that I thought would belong really don't.

I'd like to think that youngsters, and oldsters for that matter, who read *Great Jews in Sports*, will find new heroes to emulate. These are, after all, men and women who have achieved a great deal, who have overcome intense pressures, great injustice here and there, and much physical wear and tear. They have made something of themselves, and if a youngster finds in one or more of them a worthy model, I believe he's making a good choice.

A Note from the Author

This marks the twenty-eighth anniversary of the original publication of *Great Jews in Sports*. When I undertook the project in the early 1980s, I was one of the first to treat the subject of Jewish athletes with any degree of seriousness. Others joked about the topic, mostly to remind us of how few stellar Jewish sports figures existed at the time. In 2011, such attempts at humor are heard far less frequently. Jewish athletes from Sandy Koufax to Mark Spitz now occupy a highly respected place in the constellation of legendary sports personalities.

The goal of each updated edition of *Great Jews in Sports* is to keep readers informed of what has happened to their favorite Jewish athletes of years past and to introduce them to the stars of the future. I continue to encounter readers who do not know me personally but know this book well. Frequently they offer suggestions as to specific personalities who ought to be included in forthcoming editions. I assure you that each suggestion is carefully considered.

Many thanks, readers, for keeping *Great Jews in Sports* an important part of Jewish life these many years.

Robert Slater
Jerusalem, Israel,
August 2011

Introduction

As a young boy, I had the same obsession with major league baseball as most American youngsters. But I also had a grandfather who, every time Sid Gordon (the great National Leaguer of the 1940s and 1950s) came to bat, reminded me that "Gordon is Jewish." I could not possibly have figured out—nor did I bother to ask my grandfather—how Sid's religious heritage could have been related to his socking the ball out of the park. I was mostly interested in the number of home runs Gordon hit that particular season. But my grandfather's "hang-up" about Gordon's Jewishness was the stimulus that started me in search of great Jews in sports.

Common knowledge has it that few Jews have had noteworthy sports careers. This may have been true for a long time. Indeed, Judaism traditionally eschewed a sports culture. In antiquity, sports were associated with pagan worship, and for centuries Jews did not regard sports as an area of life in which success should be sought. So Jewish parents encouraged their children to become lawyers, doctors, engineers, and teachers. The parents of many of the people in this book offered this traditional advice, but their sons and daughters still sought success and glory in the gym or on the playing field. Over the years, these "rebels" from the traditional Jewish pursuits have accumulated impressive records of achievements in sports.

The point is—and I'm certainly not the first to make it—that Jews have been doing quite well in the sports world dating back to the nineteenth century. Their achievements have not received the acclaim they deserve. Indeed, until the *Encyclopedia of Jews in Sports* appeared in 1965 (a book to which I am greatly indebted), no one had really focused on the Jew in sports. Since the *Encyclopedia*, Jews have continued to succeed in sports in even larger numbers than in the period before the 1960s.

So, now there is ample room for another look at Jewish sports figures. And, it seemed to me, there was good reason not to just attempt another encyclopedic look at the subject (*Encyclopedia* authors Bernard Postal, Jesse Silver, and Roy Silver did that quite well), but to pick 100 or so of the most interesting and most important Jewish athletes and coaches in history, to tell their stories, and by doing so, to demonstrate that Jews have triumphed in the world of sports time and time again.

Great Jews in Sports is designed to entertain and enlighten by telling some of the most heartwarming and fascinating stories of the best Jewish athletes ever. The reader may be surprised to discover that in several sports Jews have actually climbed to the top. One thinks not only of Mark Spitz, the Olympic swimmer who outdid almost every Olympian who had come before him. One also thinks of Sandy Koufax, the gutsy left-hander for the Brooklyn Dodgers, of Hank Greenberg, the famous baseball power-hitter of the 1930s and 1940s. And of Sid Luckman, the great pro football quarterback of the 1940s.

Some of the athletes in this book became known outside sports circles only after their personal stories were popularized. Harold Abrahams, the British track star at the 1924 Olympics, was probably known only to track enthusiasts until the 1981 movie *Chariots of Fire* recounted his story. Many boxing fans have been aware of Barney Ross, but the public at large came to know him when his autobiography, *Monkey on My Back*, was made into a film. And, there are those who have remained less well-known, but nonetheless reached the pinnacle in their sports—figures like Jimmy Jacobs and Victor Hershkowitz, the great handball players of the 1950s; Victor Barna, a Hungarian, and one of the greatest male table tennis players of all time; and Angelica Rozeanu, a Romanian who was unquestionably the greatest female table tennis player ever.

■ ■ ■

The roles played by Jews in sports reflect the change in the social and economic roles played by Jews in society in general. The 1920s and 1930s produced many Jewish boxers and 17 champions. As for other minority groups, boxing was a way to escape the slums. So Ted "Kid" Lewis, Battling Levinsky, Barney Ross, and others used their fists to get ahead. By the 1970s tennis, once a province of the elite, had become a sport in which Jews excelled. Though there have been some great Jewish baseball players (such as Hank Greenberg and Sandy Koufax), relatively speaking the number of Jews in that sport has never been large.

Some Jewish sports stars have been caught up in the history of their times. Gretel Bergmann might have won an Olympic gold medal if she had not been a victim of Nazi anti-Semitism in 1936. Elias Katz was killed fighting for the State of Israel in that country's War of Independence. Eva Szekely joined many of her fellow Hungarian athletes in

defecting after the 1956 Olympics (though she later returned). And Esther Roth reached the semifinals of the 100-meter race, but had to bow out when Palestinian Arab terrorists murdered eleven of her Israeli teammates at those Olympics in Munich in 1972.

Of course, anti-Semitism has always been experienced by Jews in sports as in other fields. Gretel Bergmann had to face the devastating anti-Semitic policies of the Nazis. Louis Rubenstein, the figure skater, had enormous difficulty trying to compete in the unofficial World Figure Skating Championships in Moscow in 1890. Tennis ace Angela Buxton, the only Jewish Wimbledon doubles finalist, had her application to join the All-England Club rejected for years. Dick Savitt, the Wimbledon champion of the early 1950s, was passed over for Davis Cup play. In each instance, anti-Semitism was thought to have played a role, major or minor.

Getting the stories of the greatest Jewish sports figures down on paper has been challenging. Perhaps my most difficult task was to determine which figures to include. I decided to enlist the aid of experts. Of course, each expert has his own biases, and I was offered many varying opinions. On occasion, I would discover that the person wasn't even Jewish! I realized fairly early that some criteria would have to be established to determine which "Jewish" athletes would be included in the book. If I were to limit the book to approximately 100 sports figures, then I would have to be fairly rigid about who is and who isn't a Jew. I chose to go along with the Orthodox definition of a Jew: A Jew is someone born of a Jewish mother. In only one case did an overriding consideration lead me to include someone who didn't fit that definition. Tennis star Tom Okker's mother is not Jewish but his father is. But because Okker has so clearly identified himself as a Jew, I felt he should be included.

By adhering to this definition, I felt compelled to exclude a number of athletes whom others have counted as Jewish or who are known as Jewish. I'm thinking of the great fighter of the 1930s, Max

Baer, considered Jewish by virtue of everything about him but his mother. He wore a Jewish Star of David on his boxing trunks, and he called himself a Jew. But, in fact, his closest Jewish relative was his paternal grandfather. Emil "Bux" Mosbacher, the yachting champion, was born a Jew but became a Christian.

I have chosen to exclude athletes who were born Jewish but did not identify themselves as Jewish throughout their lives. Thus I had to exclude a leading Princeton University football player of the early 1900s, Phil King, who turned to Christian Science later in life, as well as Peter Revson, the racing driver of the early 1960s, who was buried as a Christian. Then, there is the intriguing example of Rod Carew, a Panamanian baseball player (what a player!) who was married to a Jewish woman and who raised their children as Jews. But I've left Carew, a seven-time batting champion, off the list.

I expect that some sports lovers will take issue with which personalities I have chosen to include or exclude. To them I make the following comment: When limiting oneself to selecting 100 or so of the Jewish greats (the list could have easily grown much larger), there is no way to satisfy everyone. I regret if a favorite player or coach of yours has been excluded.

Another point. I've deliberately weighted the list toward the Americans. I have tried my best not to minimize the contributions of non-Americans, and a substantial number of these do appear. But the reader will quickly perceive that preference has been given to American sports and sportsmen. One reason is my feeling that most readers of this book would be more familiar with American sports and sports figures than with non-Americans.

In this volume, the baseball world is well represented, as is the world of football, basketball, and tennis. This is no accident. These are the sports where Jews have really made a mark. Still, I have included figures prominent in the lesser known sports with the intention of offering the reader information about athletes of whom he might have heard little and about whom he would like to know more.

I hope you, the reader, get as much enjoyment and satisfaction from reading these profiles as I did in researching and writing them.

Robert Slater
Jerusalem, Israel

Great Jews in
SPORTS

Harold Abrahams
A Chariot of Fire

ABRAHAMS, HAROLD MAURICE (born December 15, 1899, in Bedford, England; died January 14,1978) English sprinter. One of the leading sprinters in English track history. By winning the 100-meter dash in the 1924 Paris Olympics he became the first European to win an Olympic sprint title, as well as the first and only Briton to capture such a title. A lawyer by profession, Abrahams was admitted to the bar in 1924 and practiced until 1940. He also became one of England's most important sports administrators.

• • •

The product of a wealthy, athletic family, Harold Maurice Abrahams took up track at eight years of age. In 1911 he won his first 100-yard race. His time was 14.0 seconds. By age 19 he had won both the 100-yard dash and the long jump at the British public schools championships. A law student at Cambridge University from 1920 to 1923, he became one of the school's greatest athletes. The secret of his success in running, he once quipped, was being born with long legs.

But it was more than that, obviously. Abrahams competed in the 1920 Antwerp Olympics, managed to win his 100-meter heat in 11.0 seconds, but was eliminated in the next round. In the long jump, he came in 20th. After the Olympics, Abrahams decided to concentrate on sprinting.

Though he spoke little of the subject, Abrahams was conscious of the subtle discrimination against him because he was a Jew. Sprinting afforded him an opportunity to prove to those gentlemen who practiced anti-Semitism that he could beat them at their own sport. With this in mind, he took the then-unusual step of hiring a personal coach for the six months before the 1924 Olympics. Such a tactic, if not against the formal rules, was certainly against the unwritten code of amateur sport. The man he hired, Sam Mussabini, half-Arab, half-French, was considered to be the best sprinting coach in Britain.

Harold agreed with Sam that it was important to concentrate on the 100-meter dash at the Paris Olympics, and that the 200-meter race was secondary. Three times a week the two men went through a rigorous training schedule. Abrahams worked meticulously on perfecting the start, the arm action, the placing and digging of starting holes (there were no starting blocks in those days), and on controlling the accuracy of the first few strides. "I always carried a piece of string the length of the first stride," Abrahams once explained, "and marked the spot on the track at which I gazed intently when I first heard the word *set*."

The intense training had its side benefit when, on June 7, 1924, a month before Paris, Abrahams set the English long-jump record of 7.38 meters (24 feet, 2½ inches), a mark that stood for 32 years. That same afternoon he ran the 100-yard dash in 9.6 seconds, but the record was not submitted for recognition because the track was on a slight downgrade.

To his chagrin, Abrahams was selected to compete in the 100 meters, 200 meters, long jump, and relay in Paris. Unconventionally, he penned an anonymous letter to the *Daily Express* (signing it "A Famous International Athlete"), in which he suggested that it was "unfortunate" that Abrahams should have to compete in four events; he should have at least been allowed to drop out of the long jump. The "Famous International Athlete" added: "The authorities surely do not imagine that Abrahams can perform at long jumping at two o' clock and run 200 meters at 2:30 on the same afternoon." The letter, closing with a plea that Abrahams be permitted to focus on the 100 meters, had its intended effect: Harold was excused from long jumping.

With four American speedsters competing among the 75 entries for the 100-meter race in

tacle positively appalling in its grandeur." He had managed to get in an extra stride (46 instead of 45). Coupled with his now-famous "drop finish," this provided enough spurt for him to take the race by a full two yards in 10.6 seconds. It was the third time in 26 hours that Harold Abrahams had equaled the Olympic record! In Harold's view, his victory was not only a triumph for Britain, but also a fitting rebuttal to the anti-Semitism that he had discerned within the British establishment.

Harold was not as successful in the 200-meter race. He reached the finals after clocking a personal best of 22.0 seconds in a heat, but came in last in the final. He did, however, win a silver medal in the 4 x 100-meter relay.

Harold Abraham's track career came to an end prematurely. In May 1925, he broke his leg while long jumping. He would never compete again. The accident eliminated his chance of becoming Europe's first 25-footer in the long jump.

After his track days, Abrahams became an athletics administrator as well as a sportswriter. From 1925 to 1967, Abrahams was athletics correspondent for the *Sunday Times* and one of the BBC's first broadcasters. A 1955 profile of him in the *Sunday Times* described Abrahams as a prophet and hero to the younger generation.

Abrahams had a passion for Gilbert and Sullivan (he could quote passages from their plays at ease). He also had the unusual hobby of holding a stopwatch on anything that could be timed. He timed Wimbledon rallies, after-dinner speeches, concert applause, and moving stairways. He even admitted to having "been conceited enough" to time the applause for one of his own speeches.

He was one of the official timekeepers when British miler Roger Bannister ran his historic four-minute mile in 1954 (Harold later presented his Omega Chronometer, stopped at Bannister's record time of 3 minutes, 59.4 seconds, to Bannister).

Harold was something of a male chauvinist when it came to the issue of female participation in track and field competition. In 1928, he observed: "I do not consider that women are built for really

Paris on July 6, 1924, Abrahams thought little of his chances. But in his first round he breezed to an easy triumph in 11.0 seconds. Remarkably, in the second round he equaled the Olympic record of 10.6 seconds. Could he maintain his top form in the semifinals and finals the next day?

Settling in his holes for the semifinals at 3:15 P.M., July 6, 1924, Abrahams nearly lost the race at the outset. Noticing a runner on his right move slightly, he started badly, figuring there would be a recall. There wasn't. He still won the race in 10.6 seconds. Then he prepared for the final. For those next four hours, he felt "like a condemned man feels just before going to the scaffold."

At 7:05 P.M., Abrahams went to his mark for the final. An eyewitness, Bernard Darwin, described Abrahams in midcourse as "scudding along like some vast bird with outstretched wings, a spec-

violent exercise of the kind that is the essence of competition. One has only to see them practicing to realize how awkward they are on the running track . . ."

He was one of the most influential members of the British Amateur Athletics Board, serving as its treasurer from 1948 to 1968. The public and press came to regard Abrahams and secretary Jack Crump as the two men who virtually ran British athletics. Both came under heavy criticism for writing and broadcasting on athletics while holding the highest official posts. Abrahams served as chairman of the Board from 1968 to 1975. In November 1976, he fulfilled a life's ambition by being elected president of the AAA.

Harold Abrahams' only civil honor was awarded him for his work as a civil servant: from 1930 to 1963 he had been secretary of the National Parks Commission. In 1981, three years after his death, Abrahams was the subject of a major movie, *Chariots of Fire*, which portrayed the influence of religion on athletes.

Abrahams is a member of the Jewish Sports Hall of Fame in Israel.

Amy Alcott
On the Verge
of the Hall of Fame

ALCOTT, AMY (born February 22, 1956, in Kansas City, Missouri–) American golfer. She turned pro at 18 and won the 1975 Orange Blossom Classic, only her third tournament, a feat not equalled by any other woman pro golfer. In 1991, Amy Alcott won her 29th tournament, only one short of the total needed for automatic entry into the Women's Golf Hall of Fame. She was finally inducted in February 1999 when officials relaxed the rules.

● ● ●

Amy has lived in Santa Monica, California since she was six months old. Golf got into her blood at an early age. She was a tomboy with skinned knees who watched television on Saturdays with a bowl of ice cream by her side.

When girls her age were learning how to apply make-up and how to dress, she pretended that she was playing in the Masters or the U.S. Open. "I loved the click of the ball going into the hole. I marveled at the golf swing. However, as a little girl I thought all golfers were named Byron, Labron, or Lanny, and all were from Texas. I really wondered if any women played golf."

At the age of nine, Amy vacillated between tennis and golf. She chose golf and later called it one of the most important decisions of her life. She began taking lessons from Walter Keller, a well-known Los Angeles golf teacher, owner of a golf equipment shop. Zealous and intense, Amy hit golf balls into a net in the back of Keller's shop four hours a day. She also studied her swing in front of a mirror.

Amy turned her backyard at home into a miniature golf course, hitting balls six hours a day. She put soup cans in the ground for cups and cut the grass short enough so she could putt. She chipped over the hedges to the cups. "I dropped balls eight feet from the cup and would say to myself, 'This putt is for the Open Championship.' You'd be surprised how many I made."

She discovered however, that her home could not provide all the conditions needed to practice. She had a truckload of sand dumped under her bedroom window so that she could practice hitting out of sand. But blasting out of the bunker proved costly; she kept breaking her bedroom windows when the ball flew too far. But that did not deter her.

Fanatically, she put her entire life into her golf game. She felt guilty when she was not practicing. "I can remember watching TV back when I was still a kid and thinking I should be outside chipping about 1,000 balls."

She began playing on municipal golf courses but soon switched to the well-known Riviera Country Club, in Los Angeles. Going there every day after school, she entered a man's world which her mother Lea Alcott knew was unusual for a teen-aged girl: "She could have had art lessons, dancing lessons, anything the other children availed themselves of. But she chose this, and I went along with it. I never objected. Mr. Keller, her teacher, told me, 'Just watch her because she's going to be a race horse.'"

This was not a race horse that needed a mother's push. "She did it all on her own," Lea recalled. "Her goal is simple—she wants to be the best there is." Thanks to Riviera's small greens and deep bunkers, Amy's short game improved. She would average 220 to 230 yards off the tee and seldom got into serious trouble. Her chipping and putting became the strongest part of her game.

Freckle-faced, brown-haired, possessing strong arms and a powerful torso, she understood that her athletic prowess made her different. "Boys were more or less in awe of me," she recalled.

Her short amateur career was highlighted by winning the USGA Junior Girls title at the age of 17 in 1973. Before turning professional, Amy won the Los Angeles Girls' title three times, the L.A.

Women's Championship and the California Women's Amateur.

Amy Alcott made her second crucial life decision right after graduating from Pacific Palisades High School. She had to choose between going to college or pursuing golf full-time. Having won 150 junior golf tournaments by the time she was 18, Amy had an easy choice. "Amy," she said to herself, "you don't want to go to college, you want to go out and knock sticks down." Her self-confidence grew as she began to defeat an increasing number of professional women golfers. "Gee," she thought to herself, "I can beat these babes who are old enough to be my mother. Maybe this is my niche."

Briefly she examined the prospects of obtaining a college scholarship. She was offered the chance to play on the men's golf team at Dartmouth. When school officials asked her if she had taken advanced calculus, she began thinking that she did not in fact want to leave California "to play golf with a bunch of men in a place where it snowed half the time."

She also asked herself how she could take college courses like biology? "I don't give a damn about biology, and I'll be sitting there in class worrying about what I could be shooting that day."

So, when she finished high school in January 1975, she decided to join the Ladies' Professional Golf Association.

To get Amy started professionally, her mentor Walter Keller persuaded 15 people, most of them Riviera members, to put up $1,000 each to sponsor Amy Alcott's first year on the tour. In her first tournament in 1975 she came in 22nd and won only $350. But, by the time half the year had passed, her official earnings stood at $189,466, 12th on the money list; $2,000 more than any rookie had ever won in an entire year.

Amy won her first LPGA tournament at the 1975 Orange Blossom Classic. It was only her third tournament as a pro and she came in with a record nine-under-par 207 (68-68-71). Only Marlene Hagge, who took the Sarasota Open in

1952 at age 18, won an LPGA event at a younger age. Amy Alcott celebrated her 19th birthday on February 22 by firing a second-round 68.

For her efforts she picked up a $5,000 check. "No, I'm not surprised I won so early," she said at the time. "I won because I played the best. I had the confidence and desire to rip it up, and I did. People knew I was a contender the minute I teed up."

Amy Alcott was the hottest prospect on the tour in years. She averaged 73.52 strokes that first year. Walter Keller was thrilled that Amy had done well so quickly on the tour; most women golfers mature in their late 20s.

By the summer of 1980, a year filled with achievements, Amy had won 12 tournaments. She won the U.S. Women's Open in early July by nine strokes. She overcame oppressively hot 105 degree temperatures to set an Open record of four-under par 280. Her yearly average was 71.51, best of her career. She attributed much of her success to the fact that she lost weight the previous winter. For her achievements in 1980 she was *Golf* magazine's Player of the Year and won the Seagrams Seven Crown of Sports Award for golf.

In July 1980, Amy Alcott described what it was like to be a young, single, Jewish woman pro golfer. "These Jewish parents keep calling me up and telling me they want me to meet their sons. They say, 'You'll like him. He'll walk the course with you.' I guess I should be out trying to meet a doctor or a lawyer, but I'm having too much fun."

In 1983 Amy Alcott became the sixth LPGA player to win one million dollars, reaching that mark at the Chrysler-Plymouth Classic when she collected $8,750. That same year she won the YWCA Silver Achievement Award. A year later, 1984, she won the LPGA Good Samaritan Award.

During three seasons (1979, 1980, and 1984) she won four tournaments per season. She needed only to win the Mazda LPGA Championship to become the second player in LPGA history to win the four modern major championships. (Pat Bradley became the first in 1986.)

In 1985 Amy averaged 71.78 on the tour. The next year, 1986, she won the Mazda Hall of Fame Championship and the LPGA National Pro-Am. That same year she was awarded the Founders Cup, designed to recognize altruistic contributions to the betterment of society by an LPGA member. Her average in 1986 on the tour was 71.99.

She does not lack self-confidence. In early 1986 she observed: "I know in my heart I'm one of the best women golfers ever, not because I'm the biggest money winner, but because I've managed for 11 years to be consistent."

The year 1988 was her most successful season. She earned $292,349 and won the first major tournament of the year, the Nabisco Dinah Shore. When she won the $80,000 first place prize at the Nabisco Dinah Shore, she became the LPGA's third member to surpass the two million dollar mark in career earnings. In 1988 she had 15 top-10 finishes. Her average on the tour in 1988 was 71.71.

The year 1989 was her 11th consecutive season in which she earned more than $100,000. That same year she recorded six top-10 placings including a triumph at the Boston Five Classic. She was ranked 18 on the LPGA money list. Her average that year was 72.16.

In 1990 Amy played in 23 events and earned $99,208, the first time in 12 years she had not won $100,000 in single-season earnings. She had four top-10 finishes including second place at the Rochester International. Her other top-10 finishes were ties for fourth in the Boston Five Classic, ninth in the Orix Hawaiian Ladies Open and ninth in the U.S. Women's Open. The year 1990 marked the first time in her career that she was ranked outside the top 20 on the money list. Her average that year on the tour was 73.12.

In 1991 she won the Nabisco Dinah Shore for the third time, bringing her within one tournament victory of qualifying for the LPGA's Hall of Fame, one of sport's most formidable achievements. At the time, there were only three ways to get in: win 30 tournaments, including two different majors, win 35 tournaments with one major, or win 40 tournaments. Amy Alcott had been stuck on 29 since March 1991. She came close on many occasions with seven top-10 finishes. She tied for second at the Atlantic City Classic; finished third at the U.S. Women's Open; tied for fourth at the MBS LPGA Classic; tied for sixth at the Oldsmobile Classic; finished eighth at the JAL Big Apple Classic and tenth at the Mazda LPGA Championship. She played in 23 events that year and earned $258,269. Her average for the year was 72.43.

In the 16 tournaments she played in during the first half of 1992, Amy won $65,235. She described her results for that period as "nothing spectacular."

Known for her consistent game, (Amy uses a

short backswing, which she compares to Arnold Palmer's) she is one of the longest hitters among the women's pros.

The secret of her success? Amy suggests that "Learning to keep yourself totally under control is what separates the winners from the also-rans in golf. You don't shout out that bad word, no matter how much you want to. You have to save your frustrations for later, go home, and bite a tree or something."

She has served on the President's Council Against Drug Abuse and has been a *Golf Digest* playing editor. She has her own annual charity golf tournament to benefit the Multiple Sclerosis Society, called the Amy Alcott Pro-Am for MS. Amy's hobbies are gourmet cooking, dancing, and mimicry. She does a passable Howard Cosell and Cary Grant, and an impressive version of Edith Bunker singing "Those Were the Days."

Since 1983, Amy has worked part-time as a short order cook at the Westwood Butterfly Bakery in Los Angeles, finding it good therapy for the pressures of playing on the golf tour. "In the beginning, it was just something I did for myself. Nobody recognized me back there behind the counter. Now I'll be stepping up to the tee at a tournament and somebody will yell, 'Hold the mustard, no pickles!'" Then, she added: "The pressure of getting an order right is greater than sinking a putt," not making clear whether she was serious. "It gives you a thrill when you make the perfect sandwich, when the pickles are placed just perfectly on the plate."

Despite a busy life she found time to write *A Woman's Guide to Golf*, and to prepare her own golf instruction video for adults and juniors called "Winning at Golf." She is very proud of the thoroughbred horse named after her.

In 1994, Amy Alcott had four top-10 finishes, among them a fourth place in the Minnesota LPGA Classic and a tie for sixth place in the U.S. Women's Open. That same year, she crossed the $3 million mark in career earnings.

In 1995, her best finish was a tie for fifth at the PING/Welch's Championship in Tucson, Arizona. The following year, she played in 20 tournaments and earned $106,783, with her best tournament the Weetabix Women's British Open, where she finished second. In December of that year, she suffered a broken kneecap and was unable to return to compete until March 1997. As a result, she played in just 16 tournaments in 1997.

On November 6, 1997, Alcott was awarded the 1997 Sports and Law Award in Beverly Hills, California, along with basketball star Kareem Abdul Jabbar.

By the spring of 1998, she had still not managed that magical 30th triumph. However, her career earnings had climbed to $3,261,334.

In February 1999, she gained entry into the Golf Hall of Fame, when officials relaxed the rules, and she no longer required that elusive 30th win.

In 2002, Alcott tied for 21st at the Kellogg-Keebler Classic golf tournament, in Aurora, Illinois, earning $11,500. Continuing in active competition, she joined the Women's Senior Golf Tour, which showcases the talents of some of the greatest female golf stars of all time. Amy tied for fifth place at the 2002 HyVee Classic, in Johnston, Iowa, and for second place at the 2003 Hyvee Classic, in Des Moines, Iowa. Her career winnings total $3.4 million.

In July 2007, Alcott assumed the position of girls' golf coach at Harvard-Westlake School, in North Hollywood, California. By 2011, she had earned the reputation of being one of the top female golf-course architects

Mel Allen
The Famous Voice of the New York Yankees

ALLEN, MEL (born February 14, 1913, in Birmingham, Alabama; died June 16, 1996) American sports broadcaster. Famous as "The Voice of the New York Yankees." His career as a broadcaster of sports events began in 1939. He was on the air to describe Joe DiMaggio's 56-game hitting streak in 1941, Don Larsen's perfect game in the 1956 World Series, hundreds of Mickey Mantle's home runs, and Roger Maris' record-breaking 61st home run in 1961.

• • •

Mel Allen's parents Julius and Anna Leib Israel, immigrants from Russia, named their eldest son Melvin Allen Israel. Taking the suggestion of his employers, Allen used only his given names when he began to broadcast in New York. He legalized his name as Mel Allen when he entered the army in 1943.

During his childhood, Allen's family lived in Johns, Alabama, a small town near Birmingham, where Mel's father owned a general store. Mel graduated from grammar school when he was 11 and, at age 15, he graduated from Birmingham's Phillips High School in 1929.

Mel played high school basketball and football, and did well enough to win a letter in each sport. But his real love was baseball.

At age nine he played on a baseball team with boys older than himself, and at 12 was selling soft drinks at baseball games in Detroit so he could watch the games for free when visiting his Detroit relatives. At 13 he had a job working as a batboy for a minor league team in the Piedmont League in Greensboro, North Carolina.

At the University of Alabama, Allen was active in sports as a participant, but in his third year he turned to sportswriting and became a columnist for the campus newspaper. He majored in political science and obtained his Bachelor of Arts degree in 1932, after which he took up the study of law at the University. (He received his law degree in 1936.)

In 1935, while teaching speech at the University, Allen was appointed manager of the campus public address system and was assigned the task of announcing Alabama football games. "From then on," said one sportswriter, "the stage was set for the entrance of one of the best sportscasters in the field." When Alabama played Tulane that fall, a Columbia Broadcasting System executive heard Allen's commentary, and in January 1936 Mel joined that network as an announcer in New York.

His first assignment with CBS was as a disk jockey and news broadcaster. It was the keen competition between the CBS and NBC sports departments that created the circumstances which catapulted Mel into the limelight. In 1939, after NBC had scooped CBS with its coverage of the Poughkeepsie Regatta, the angry CBS team planned a double revenge. The following weekend Ted Husing was to cover the Drake Relays from a church steeple and Mel Allen was assigned to cover the Vanderbilt Cup races from an airplane. Allen carried out his assignment despite his fear of heights. When rain delayed the races, he ad libbed for a full hour. This performance won him a special CBS commendation.

By 1939 Allen started to cover major college basketball doubleheaders at New York's Madison Square Garden and to cover the World Series. In 1939, he handled the New York Yankees and New York Giants baseball broadcasts, first as assistant to veteran sportscaster Arch McDonald, and then, through 1943, as chief announcer. By 1941 he was earning the then-handsome annual sum of $30,000.

In 1943, Allen entered the U.S. army as a private in the infantry. After two years, he rose to the rank of staff sergeant and was then transferred to the armed forces radio service where he became a featured announcer on the *Army Hour* program.

Upon his discharge from the army in 1946, Allen became the radio voice of the New York Yankees. In 1949, Yankee star Joe DiMaggio hit four home runs during a three-game series against the Boston Red Sox, after having missed 65 games due to an injured heel. Every time DiMaggio belted one of those homers, Allen made his now-famous remark, "How about that!" Mel soon became known as "Mr. How About That."

Another Mel Allen expression, "Going, going, gone" was coined during a game at Yankee Stadium in 1946. As he watched a hard hit ball hang in the air before landing in the bleachers, he kept shouting, "It's going, it's going, it's going, it's gone." Mel thought he sounded like an auctioneer, but the expression stuck.

Radio broadcasting was always Allen's true love, but working on television broadcasting, said Allen, made it necessary for an announcer to know the game as well as a coach or a player. He liked to liven up coverage with a higher quality of English than was usually heard from sportscasters. Thus, the World Series was not only the "Series" but also the "Fall Classic." DiMaggio's swing was not just "good," it was "poetry in motion." But Mel Allen's great talent was summing up a game quickly for listeners who had tuned in late, and in being able, at all times, to fill in empty air space. Occasionally, his "filling in" would border on the embarrassing such as when he improvised that "International Falls is the coldest place in the U.S.," to which he had to add, "temperature-wise, that is."

One writer attributed Mel Allen's greatness to the "sheer delight he gets out of every event itself. Whenever there's a hot play, and the fans roar, Mel roars along with them." The famous Yankee catcher, Yogi Berra said of Mel Allen that he used "too many words."

Over the years, Mel broadcast 14 Rose Bowl games, two Orange Bowls, two Sugar Bowls, 20 World Series and 24 All-Star baseball games.

Mel listed his religion as Conservative Judaism. His favorite books were non-fiction and detective stories. He never married and shared his home in Westchester, New York, with his parents.

Reports appeared in the press that Mel's parents were disturbed by his giving up a law career for broadcast announcing or that they had always wanted him to become a cantor. But Mel insisted that all this was untrue, and that, in fact, his mother was especially pleased when he became a broadcaster.

Without explanation, the famous announcer was abruptly fired by the New York Yankees in the fall of 1964. He was replaced by former Yankee shortstop Phil Rizzuto.

In 1965, Allen began broadcasting games for the Milwaukee Braves, and in 1966 he was the announcer for the Cleveland Indians.

Mel also hosted the weekly 30-minute syndicated television program *This Week in Baseball* from 1977 to 1996 and the MSG (Madison Square Garden) regional cable television network show *Yankees Magazine* from 1986 to 1996. A sportswriter wrote in August 1990, "Mel Allen may be 78, but his voice is as resonant, mellifluous and invigorating as ever." To put together one program, Allen's staffers reviewed 250 hours of taped features and highlights.

In 1972, Allen was elected to the National Sportswriters and Broadcasters Hall of Fame. In 1978, his peers voted him and Red Barber, the Brooklyn Dodgers' broadcaster of the '40s and '50s, the first Ford C. Frick Award for broadcasting excellence. Their names were placed on a plaque in the Baseball Hall of Fame in Cooperstown, New York. Allen considered this the greatest honor of his life. He is also a member of the Jewish Sports Hall of Fame in Israel.

Mel Allen made a comeback in 1981, as announcer of the Yankee games on cable television for the next seven years. And whenever he appeared at ceremonies at Yankee Stadium, he was introduced as "The Voice of the New York Yankees."

On July 25, 1998, the Yankees dedicated a plaque in Allen's memory in Monument Park at the original Yankee Stadium. The plaque read "A YANKEE INSTITUTION, A NATIONAL TREASURE" and included his signature line, "HOW ABOUT THAT?"

Yael Arad
Israel's First Olympic Medalist

ARAD, YAEL (born May 1, 1967 in Tel Aviv, Israel–) Israeli women's judo champion. She won a silver medal at the Barcelona Olympics on July 30, 1992, the first Israeli ever to win an Olympic medal. She placed third in the 61-kilogram division at the World Championships in Barcelona in July 1991. She also won a gold medal in the women's 61-kilogram division at the French Open Judo Championships in February 1992. When in active competition, she was considered one of the world's top judoists."

■ ■ ■

Judo is not the sport of choice of most Israeli eight year-olds. It was, however, for Yael Arad largely because of the influence of her older brothers. "People thought I was crazy, a young girl getting up early to train," Yael recalled. Taken aback by the sight of a girl engaging in judo, boys challenged her to fights all the time. "They weren't used to seeing muscular women," Yael laughed. "'But look at me, I hardly look like a gorilla."

She does look strong, and compact—and quite capable of pulling an opponent off his feet at a second's notice. And yet she has a grace that comes from the hours she put in as a youngster in ballet and swimming. She found swimming dull, judo exciting. When her brother, Yuval, at age 11, took judo lessons in north Tel Aviv, eight year-old Yael tagged along. "I loved it," she said. "Judo is a very intelligent sport. If you're good at it, you sense it right away. And there's nothing more enjoyable for a child than to throw another child down." At first she trained twice a week, then four to six times a week, then every day.

Mostly, at that early stage, Yael was upending boys, not girls, though she found nothing odd about that. She grew up with three older brothers who are two, six, and eight years older than she. She also has a sister ten years younger. Yael's parents are journalists; her father Aryeh wrote about aviation and transportation for the now defunct Israeli newspaper *Davar*; her mother, Nurit, covers consumer topics for *Yediot Aharonot*, the most popular Israeli daily.

An early competitive experience in judo was almost Yael's last. She took "only" second place in an Israeli judo championship when she was nine years old. She was devastated. "I cried for three straight days and wouldn't leave home. I always wanted to win."

A year later, at age ten, she won the Israel judo championship in the 31-kilogram weight class, competing against children through age 14. She remained Israeli champion for the next six years.

The greatest influence on Yael Arad was her first coach, Moni Isaac. He coached her from age eight to 18. "He gave me self-discipline and sports values. He taught me to honor my rival, to shake hands before each match. He also taught that I must want more than just to take part, I must want to win." Training was hard. "If you were late, you were punished. You had to do 50 push-ups."

In 1983, at age 16, Yael was the runner-up in the 56-kilogram weight class for women in the German Open for Cadets, held near Hamburg. Again, she was shocked at taking only second place, "I cried in my room. I was very frustrated." And although Yael gave little thought to becoming world champion, her trips abroad convinced her that such a goal was not out of reach. She backed that conviction by increasing the number of hours she put into training.

Because Israeli judo was an underdeveloped and underfinanced sport, Israeli judokas were not routinely sent overseas to train or participate in tournaments. Yael was only able to travel to world and European championships, while her competitors abroad took part in eight competitions and two training camps a year.

Yael was convinced that the only way she would advance her career was to go abroad for training. Taking matters into her own hands, she wrote let-

was nice, intelligent, and a great judoist. I liked her style."

After completing service in the army, Yael faced a crisis. "I didn't know if I wanted to continue judo. There was no money to help sports people. Nobody was sending us abroad. I felt I was missing something. I had invested all this effort, but nobody was helping me."

At that point, additional encouragement came from Peter Seisenbacher, an Austrian who had been an Olympic judo champion in Los Angeles in 1980 and in Seoul in 1988. Seisenbacher not only urged Yael to train abroad, but advised her where to travel. "He made me understand that I could be a housewife or a student anytime of my life; but to be a world champion in judo, it was now or never. He gave me the final push."

Eager to step up her training, but being without funds, Yael turned to many institutions for sponsorship, without luck. She coached children in weightlifting at 6 A.M. and in judo in the afternoons, but found that it interfered with her efforts to train six hours a day.

To attain her goal of competing in the 1992 Barcelona Olympics, Yael needed even more financial support. Again she undertook a letter-writing campaign to Israeli authorities. As a result, the Israel Olympic Committee selected her for the special pre-Olympics program that entitled Yael to a monthly income of 1,500 Israeli shekels ($625 dollars). She also obtained sponsorship from the Israeli magazine *La-Isha* (For The Woman).

In the next few years, Yael steadily improved. In 1988, she took second place in the German Open. In 1989, Yael was third in her weight class at the European Championships. In 1990, she defeated the world No. 1 and No. 2 at a tournament in France, before losing in the final. She also took the silver medal at a tournament in Germany.

Her greatest leap forward came in the 12 months before Barcelona. In July 1991, she placed third in the 61-kilogram division at the World Championships in Barcelona. She was hailed at home as a heroine, which to Yael, was a dubious

ters to the Knesset (Parliament) Sports Committee and to national sports officials to drum up support for her sport.

Yael's own international accomplishments in judo forced the authorities to take notice of Israeli judokas. She began participating in national championships in Western Europe. When she was 18, six months after she began her two-year stint in the Israel Defense Forces, Yael traveled to the England Championships and stayed on to train with world judo champion Karen Briks of England. (The IDF permits the country's best athletes to train and compete on a limited basis). Strong encouragement also grew out of her friendship with Belgian-born world champion Ingrid Bergmans. "She was what I wanted to be," noted Yael. "She

distinction: "Many claimed that this exaggerated praise would ruin me because anything less than a place on the podium at any contest would be regarded as a failure."

Trying to overcome such pressure, she prepared for the French Open, scheduled for February 1992. After the World and European Championships, the French Open is the third most prestigious judo tournament. While at training camp in Austria the week before, she became ill, and spent four days fighting a high temperature. On the fifth day she traveled to Paris to join the other 21 contestants in her weight class.

In the opening rounds Yael bested the Cuban and Italian national champions and the European national youth title-holder, France's Catherine Petit. In the semifinals, before 6,000 fans, the Israeli judoka won on points in an evenly-matched contest. She was now poised to take the gold medal. "I have always been a bridesmaid and never a bride. I had made it many times to the finals, but somehow I always fell at the final hurdle. Maybe, I secretly doubted my own ability and stopped trying after I attained a place in the semifinals."

Not this time. Her triumph over Marika Januskova of Czechoslovakia was never in doubt. A knee injury, suffered during the tournament, did not mar Yael's performance. "The most exciting part," she said after capturing the gold medal, "was hearing 'Hatikvah' (Israel's national anthem) being played with the Israeli flag waving overhead."

Watching a videotape of her triumphant final match at the French Open, Yael noted that she has a whole battery of techniques to overcome an opponent. "Some have only one or two. I have five. A lot of judo is technique. But without strength you can't do the technique today, because judo is very sophisticated. Everyone today is strong. If you have enough strength you can combine strength and technique. I'm considered very strong, fast, and dynamic. Others are considered static. I work a lot on tactics."

Yael was named Sportswoman of the Year for 1991–1992. On June 14, 1992, Yael captured the gold medal in the 61-kilogram class at the Austrian Open Judo Championships, winning all five of her contests.

Having put judo on the map in Israel, Yael no longer had to worry about obtaining adequate financial support. She traveled to Japan once a year and to Europe several times a year for training because there were not enough strong opponents in Israel. Her dream was to be the best in the world, and she came close when at the 1992 Barcelona Olympics she won the silver medal, losing only in the finals to France's Catherine Fluery.

Yael dedicated her medal to the victims of the 1972 Munich Olympics massacre.

Following a year's layoff because of recurring back pains, Arad announced in early 1995 that she planned to start training for the 1996 Atlanta Olympics. Her goals were still to win either an Olympic gold medal or a world championship— or, better still, both. Yet, she earned only a fifth place at the World Championships in 1995. A year later she grew optimistic about securing part or all of her dreams when she earned a bronze medal in her first tournament of the year in the Moscow Open Championships.

In late 1995, Yael Arad married Lior Kahane.

On the eve of the Atlanta Olympics in 1996, Yael Arad had been Israeli champion 16 times and had competed in 49 international competitions, winning 24 medals: seven gold, eight silver, and nine bronze.

Although she had been suffering from a prolonged viral infection, Arad decided to compete for a medal at Atlanta, but failed. Asked by a reporter what her post-Olympic plans were, she replied almost automatically, "Babies."

Yael Arad was one of sixteen Israeli sports figures chosen to participate in Israel's fifty-sixth Independence Day torchlighting ceremony, held on April 26, 2004. Yael continues her involvement with the sport she loves by coaching young Israeli judokas. The mother of two, she is the CEO of PMI, a marketing company.

Barry Asher

The Best Unknown Bowler in the Country

ASHER, BARRY (born July 14, 1946 in Costa Mesa, California–) American bowler. In 1976, he became the 15th man in the history of the Professional Bowlers Association tour to win 10 or more titles. His most successful year was 1973 when he won two PBA tournaments and $57,196 in prize money.

. . .

Barry took up bowling at age eight when a friend volunteered to pay Barry's way if he would bowl with him. At age 10 Barry was averaging 170, and at age 11, 180.

His father died in 1958. "His last words to me," said Barry, "were about bowling. From that time on, I devoted my life to becoming a pro bowler." Barry and his mother—who had become his biggest fan—moved to Santa Ana, California.

Bowling in adult competitions at age 14, Asher averaged 200 for the first time in 1959 at the Orange County (California) Open League. He continued to average 200 that year, considered quite respectable even for a pro. "By then," said the Californian, "I thought I knew all there was to know about bowling." But at age 15, he fared poorly in some tournaments: "It could have been the best thing that happened to me, I then knew what I didn't know."

By age 16, he was back in form, and he produced the first of three career 300 games at Maple Lanes in Garden Groves, California.

He turned professional in 1964, at 18, the earliest age possible for pro status. He became the youngest person ever to win a PBA-sponsored tournament when he won the Pacific Coast PBA Open in January 1965, in Santa Ana, California. Barry then went on the summer tour without much luck, but in 1966 his fortunes changed: "All of a sudden I got the right help and won. I guess I had the right conditions. I didn't average much to win, but I beat some great bowlers. It just happened."

He won the tenth time he bowled on the PBA circuit. That was in Encino, California, in 1966. That same year he took a second PBA title in New Orleans. Joining the pro tour full-time in 1968, he did moderately well: in 1969, he won $12,635; in 1970, $17,710; and in 1971, his first really successful year, $34,528.

In 1971, Barry Asher assured a place for himself in the record books when he won the PBA tournament at the Chippewa Lanes in South Bend, Indiana. There, on September 13, he won the highest-scoring championship in PBA history with a record 247 average for 42 games. That record stood for ten years. In his first six games in the South Bend tournament he scored an incredible 264 average. He also rolled one of the 11 perfect games recorded in the tournament.

Three weeks later, in St. Louis, Missouri, Barry won another PBA title.

In 1972, he won two more PBA titles, the Japan Gold Cup, and the Cranston, Rhode Island, tournament. Financially, his best year was 1973, when he was second on the winnings list with $57,196. He won PBA titles that year in Las Vegas, Nevada, and Tucson, Arizona.

In 1974, Asher's career went into a slump that he attributed to pressure, tension, and possibly a loss of ambition. The slump was most conspicuous on his approach, where he consistently balked. Instead of taking the usual smooth steps to the line, he would often hesitate, stumble and draw back. In the spring of that year, Asher acknowledged that he was seeking the help of a hypnotist in the Los Angeles area. His winnings that year totalled only $16,773, and he won no PBA titles.

The following year was only slightly better. Asher did win a PBA tournament in Alameda, California, his first since his excellent 1973 year. He also finished second in the Firestone Tournament of Champions. But he bowled in only 15 tournaments and earned $29,310.

In 1976, Barry cut down further on his PBA tour activity. He did bowl in Tucson, Arizona, near his home in Costa Mesa, California, and took the tournament for the tenth PBA title of his career. Winning there depressed him as much as it excited him, for few people around the country would know about his feat since bowling was not brought via TV into the homes of millions of Americans.

Asher recalled how he felt after the Tucson victory: "Mark (Roth) and Joe (Berardi) were with me and we drove all night to make a practice session for the Best Ball Doubles the next day. At one point, Mark was sleeping in the back seat and Joey was driving and I was thinking about the fact that only a few hours earlier I was the best bowler in the country, yet nobody was going to know it because it was only on Home Box Office TV." He made $25,000 on the tour in 1976.

After 1976, Barry stopped his membership in the PBA, and the curly-haired bowler said he has few regrets: "I liked bowling on the tour. But the tour itself is just one big, constant hassle." Added Barry: "I wonder what would have happened if I had listened to my mother and been a nice Jewish boy and gone to college. At my present age, I'd probably be a CPA or a lawyer and be making $40,000 or $50,000 a year. So there's pros and cons to bowling as a career. I made my bed and I'm sleeping in it."

In the late 1970s, Asher partnered with Dick and Diane Braasch to form Braascher Distributors, a clothing apparel business. Clothing had always been important to Asher. He had been known for his sartorial elegance as a bowler. In 1970, his fellow players voted him one of the "best-dressed players" on the tour. He wore custom-made pants with lightning streaks, bowling pins and bowling balls as part of the decorative scheme.

"Often," Barry noted in 1970, "especially when my game is off and I'm feeling low, I dress for dinner. Dressed up, I feel better. It's like a tonic. It peps me up and I come back for the night [bowling] ac-

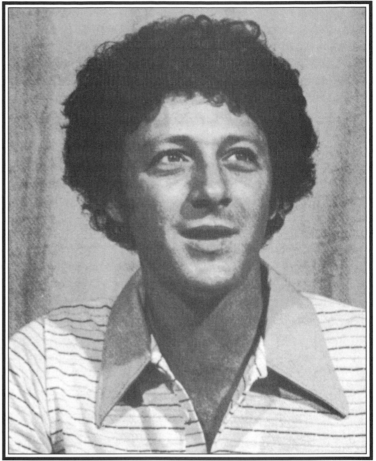

tion a new man." His wardrobe was one of the most extensive and expensive of any athlete. His specially-designed slacks cost almost $500 for three pairs.

In 1982, Barry opened a bowling pro shop in Anaheim, California. Four years later, in Costa Mesa, he founded a business that specialized in computerized embroidery for shirts, caps, and jackets.

In 1985, Asher won the All-Events American Bowling Congress, and from 1995 to 2003 he won 19 events as part of the West Coast Senior Tour. In 1988, he was elected to the PBA Hall of Fame in the Veterans category. Eleven years later, in 1999, he was inducted into the Hebrew University's Jewish Sports Hall of Fame, and the following year he was elected to the Southern California Jewish Sports Hall of Fame.

Barry Asher is married and the father of a daughter.

Abe Attell
San Francisco's Little Champ

ATTELL, ABE "THE LITTLE CHAMP" (born February 22, 1884, in San Francisco, California; died February 6, 1969) American boxer. World featherweight champion from 1901 to 1912. Damon Runyon called Abe one of the five best fighters of all time. Nat Fleischer said he was the third best ever in his class. Attell's career record: 167 pro bouts, 91 wins (47 by knockout), 10 losses, 17 draws, and 49 no decisions.

■ ■ ■

Attell was born Albert Knoehr on George Washington's birthday but was named Abe for Abraham Lincoln. A poor boy from a large San Francisco family, he learned to fight at an early age. "We were Jews living in an Irish neighborhood," he recalled. "You can guess the rest. I used to fight three, four, five, 10 times a day." On the street, in the vacant lots, on the docks, a little of Abie's blood stained every street in Frisco.

But then he learned that he could get paid for fighting, and so he quickly gave up the streets and went over to the "amateur" clubs. He was only 5 feet 4 inches and weighed 122 pounds, but he was a hard hitter. "When I started I was only 16 years old," Abe observed, "and I thought the easy way was to knock 'em out." That's exactly what he did. He enjoyed the work at the clubs because he could trade the medals he won for cash from the club promoters: a winner's medal was then worth $15, a hefty sum for a poor 16-year-old at the turn of the twentieth century.

Abe turned pro when he was almost 17. In his first pro fight he received $100 for fighting a 10-round draw with one Jockey Bozeman. Attell was working as a Western Union delivery boy at the time. His mother had been against his fighting, and demanded that he give up the ring for good.

When he brought home $15 from one fight and showed it to her, she relented, becoming his number-one fan. A nice Jewish boy had no business mixing with the boxing game, but the Attell family could certainly use the handsome sums Abe started bringing in.

Abe's career began with an incredible number of knockouts. He won the first 24 of his 29 fights by felling his opponents for the count of 10. "I was a conceited fighter," acknowledged Attell. "I thought I could lick anybody. For a long time, I was right."

But the price for the knockouts was high; Abe was constantly being injured. He admired the way James J. Corbett and George Dixon boxed: skipping, blocking, ducking, and sidestepping punches. Abe realized there was more to boxing than just trying to knock one opponent out and getting injured far too often in the process. "The light dawned," noted Attell. "A fellow could be a prizefighter and not get hurt, provided he was smart enough. I learned that lesson way back in 1900 and I remembered it until I quit boxing in 1915."

His first important triumph was a 20-round decision over Jack Dempsey in Pueblo, Colorado, in September 1901. He reported the win to his mother with a wire: "Dear Mother, win in 20 rounds easy. Abe." Instead of telegraphing his punches, he was telegraphing his victories.

Attell won the featherweight title the next month, surviving a four-man elimination contest for the crown; he defeated George Dixon in a 15-round decision in St. Louis to take the prize.

He successfully defended his title 12 times over the next 10 years until he finally lost to Johnny Kilbane in 20 rounds on February 22, 1912, in Vernon, California. The setback occurred on Abe's 28th birthday. For losing that bout he received $15,500, the biggest purse of his career.

Attell claimed that his greatest thrill was in defeating Battling Nelson, though the record books (for reasons that have not been properly explained) indicate that the fight, held in San Francisco in 1908, ended in a draw after 125 rounds. It may well be that Abe convinced himself thereafter that he should have won the match—and subsequently tried to rewrite history ever so slightly.

Attell's name was mentioned frequently during the probe that followed the infamous 1919 Chicago White Sox World Series baseball scandal. Attell was first linked to the scandal when a magazine story described him as sitting in the bar of a Cincinnati hotel with a bale of hundred dollar bills on his lap, trying to bet on the Cincinnati Reds—against the White Sox in the World Series.

He was indicted in Chicago on a conspiracy charge in connection with allegations that ball players and gamblers had conspired to fix the World Series. But because of insufficient evidence, he was exonerated. Abe called the charges against him lies.

Abe was indeed a gambling man. He had spent his free time at racetracks, dice games, sporting events—anywhere a bet could be made. "I have always gambled and I'm no angel," he said after the scandal, "but I was born on Washington's birthday and have tried to live up to the reputation of the father of our country where truth and honesty are concerned."

Attell's business life and his private life were not successful. His first marriage ended in divorce. During the long spells between title bouts, Abe fought six-round bouts in small cities, offering $100 to any local youngster who could stay the distance. It brought in the crowds and filled his pockets with some cash.

Abe's business fortunes improved after 1939 with his marriage to the former Mae O'Brien who helped him manage a tavern on the East Side of New York. Though long retired from boxing, he was a regular figure at Madison Square Garden

bouts until he had to enter a nursing home. During those years he liked to refer to himself as "the oldest living ex-champion."

Abe Attell was inducted into the Jewish Sports Hall of Fame in the spring of 1983. In 1990, he was inducted into the International Boxing Hall of Fame as a member of its original class.

Arnold Auerbach

Legendary Basketball Coach of the 1950s and 1960s

AUERBACH, ARNOLD J. "RED" (born September 20, 1917, in Brooklyn, New York; died October 28, 2006) American basketball coach. Coach and later general manager and president of the Boston Celtics of the National Basketball Association. He was, in his time, the most successful basketball coach in history, establishing the Celtics as one of the greatest sports organizations. As Celtics' head coach between 1950 and 1966, Auerbach led his team to nine NBA titles (eight in succession) and 11 division titles. His overall coaching record of 938 wins wasn't surpassed until it was bested by Lenny Wilkins and Bill Fitch in the late 1990s.

. . .

Auerbach's father, Hyman, was a Russian immigrant and his mother, Marie, American-born. Red began playing basketball at P.S. 122 in the Williamsburg section of Brooklyn, and became a guard for the Eastern District High School varsity team. As a senior he captained the team and made All-Scholastic second team. He also captained the handball team.

In February 1936, Red entered Seth Low Junior College on an athletic scholarship. The school was the Brooklyn branch of Columbia University. In 1937, he went on to George Washington University and was a star basketball player there until 1940. In his last year, Red was the leading college scorer in the Washington, D.C. area, averaging 10.6 points per game. His major field of study was physical education with a biology minor.

After college, Auerbach coached St. Albans Prep School and Roosevelt High School in Washington, D.C. In 1941, he married Dorothy Lewis and received his M.A. from George Washington Univer-

sity. His thesis was on physical education programs for junior high schools. From 1943 to 1946, he served in the U.S. Navy. As an ensign he directed intramural sports at the Norfolk, Virginia naval base. Later, promoted to lieutenant, Auerbach served as rehabilitation officer at the Bethesda, Maryland Naval Hospital.

When Mike Uline, owner of the Washington, D.C. Arena, decided to create a Washington-based pro basketball club in 1946, Auerbach successfully persuaded the owner to hire him as a founding coach. "It cost me less than $500 in phone calls to assemble that club," Auerbach recalled with a smile. In their first three seasons, the Washington Capitals won 115 and lost 53. Ironically, one of Auerbach's first decisions as coach was to pass over a popular All-American guard from Holy Cross named Bob Cousy. The Capitals' head coach felt that he had to build up his team so he acquired three players instead of taking only Cousy. Cousy ended up playing for the Boston Celtics.

In 1946–47, Red's team finished in first place in the Eastern division of the Basketball Association of America (the forerunner of the NBA). His 49-11 record was the best won-lost percentage in the league's history. After three successful seasons with the Capitals, Auerbach moved to the Tri-City (Moline and Rock Island, Illinois, and Davenport, Iowa) Blackhawks as coach. The team, a member of the new NBA, was 28-29 for the 1949–50 season, the only year an Auerbach team lost more than it won. The Blackhawks' owner made a trade without informing Auerbach, a trade Auerbach opposed, and he quit in protest. Mutual friends brought Auerbach and the Boston Celtics owner Walter Brown together. Auerbach agreed to move to Boston, and an historic association began. Brown gave his new coach free rein to choose his players. In April 1950, Red replaced Alvin Julian as head coach of the Celtics.

Auerbach had his work cut out for him: the Celtics had finished last in the Eastern Division the previous season, with the third worst record in NBA history. Things changed under Auerbach. In his first six seasons, the team finished second in the Eastern Division four times. Then in 1956–57, with Bill Russell added to the lineup, the Celtics won their first NBA title.

The next season they lost to St. Louis in the NBA Championship final, but then the Celtics went on to a winning spree unprecedented in NBA history. With Russell, Bob Cousy, Bill Sharman, Frank Ramsey, Tom Heinsohn, John Havlecek, and the Jones boys—K.C. and Sam— the Celtics won the league eight straight times— from 1959 to 1966. Auerbach built a team, not just individual players—the sixth man could start if necessary. Red was not a good loser: "Show me a good loser," he liked to say, "and I'll show you a loser."

His coaching techniques included fining players for every minute they were late for practice. "I have a $.25 fine for every minute a guy's late. If (Bill) Russell comes in at 10:10 A.M., it costs him $2.50. I'd rather fine the big guys. Hell, anybody can fine a rookie."

Instinct guided his coaching technique as much as anything else. He would know when to substitute, when a player had soured. He could get more from players than other coaches. "You take a washed-up guy," he once said, "and if you instill in him his pride again and create desire, you can squeeze a good year or two out of him."

He infuriated the opposition when he complained about bad calls, and was often pounded with eggs and vegetables. He was assessed $17,000 in fines during his career. His practice of lighting a cigar when victory appeared infuriated the opposition.

He was ahead of his time on the racial issue. He brought the first black player, Chuck Cooper, into the NBA and in 1966 he made Bill Russell the Boston Celtic coach.

He has given basketball clinics around the world, including Eastern Europe. In 1964, for example, he took a pro All-Star team, which included Oscar Robertson, Bob Cousy, and Bill Russell, on a visit to Egypt, Romania, and Poland.

When Walter Brown, co-owner of the Celtics, died in 1964, Auerbach succeeded him as vice president and general manager. Lou Pieri, co-owner, remained in the presidency. In 1965, Auerbach was named NBA Coach of the Year, an honor voted him for the first time only after winning eight NBA titles. One complaint against him was that anyone could have won with Bill Russell, a charge many thought unfair.

When Red retired from coaching in 1966, he had led his team to division and world titles in nine of his last ten seasons. As general manager of the Celtics between 1966 and 1984, Auerbach presided over Celtic teams which won another six NBA titles. In 1968, Red was elected to the Basketball Hall of Fame, and in 1981 he was chosen NBA Executive of the Year.

Bill Russell pointed out the greatness of his coach and mentor in his autobiography, *Second Wind*.

"Red would never let things get very far out of focus. He thought about winning more than I thought about eating when I was little. He ached when he didn't win: his whole body would be thrown out of whack when he lost. He didn't care about a player's statistics or reputation in the newspapers: all he thought about was the final score and who had helped put it on the board. He was our gyroscope, programmed solely for winning, and it was difficult for any of us to deviate from the course he set for us."

In the fall of 1991 Auerbach wrote a book called *Red Auerbach MBA: Management Tips from the Leader of One of America's Most Successful Organizations*. One piece of advice for executives was how to deal with the media. Be upfront, counseled Auerbach. Bad news should be reported quickly. "If you are lucky," he wrote, "[the story] will come out on the same day Russia drops Communism and enters a team in the NBA."

In June 1990, Auerbach explained why he was turning over more and more responsibility to others in the Celtics organization: "I'll be 73 soon. Your body gets tired, you know? It's not that I've lost any toughness. I just don't have that old zing. I'm lucky that I still have all my senses—really."

Recalling that he had quit coaching when he was only 48 years old in 1966, Auerbach noted how hard he had worked then: "We have eight people doing what I used to do by myself then. . . . When we used to play games on Wednesdays and Fridays, I'd hold practice Thursday morning, then take a plane down to New York or Philly to scout some game, then catch the midnight train so I could be back the next day to work with the team. I didn't have any assistants, scouts, no traveling secretary. Now, everything has changed."

In 1993, Auerbach had heart bypass surgery, and his physicians told him to smoke no more than three cigars a day. In 1997, by then vice chairman of his beloved Celtics, Auerbach, nearly 80 years old, was still conducting summer clinics at Brandeis University, which had renamed its gym after him. In 2003, his 53rd year with the Celtics, Auerbach served as the organization's president. In October 2004, Auerbach published his memoirs, *Let Me Tell You a Story: A Lifetime in the Game*, written in collaboration with author John Feinstein.

The 2004–2005 season marked Red Auerbach's fifty-fifth year as a member of the Boston Celtics organization, of which he continued to serve as president until a heart attack claimed his life in Washington, D.C., on October 28, 2006. He was a member of the Jewish Sports Hall of Fame in Israel.

BARNA, GYOZO VICTOR (born August 24, 1911, in Budapest, Hungary; died February 28, 1972) Hungarian table tennis player. Barna won 16 world championships, including five singles titles. He accumulated more than 1,000 prizes and won nearly every national championship. Ivor Montagu, president of the International Table Tennis Federation from 1926 to 1966, called Victor "the greatest table tennis player who ever lived."

• • •

Victor came upon table tennis—or as he called it, "Tisch tennis"—as a youngster when his friend (and subsequent rival) Laszio "Laci" Bellak discovered a ping-pong table among his Bar Mitzvah presents. The two boys practiced with one another frequently. "The very first time I took a bat (paddle) in my hand," recalled Victor, "I knew that this was the game for me."

Two events helped make table tennis Victor Barna's game. The first occurred when he watched the two top table tennis clubs in Budapest play. "There's nothing to it," the young Victor told himself. "You can do it just as well."

The second event happened while he was playing football (soccer) for a local sports club, even though youngsters were barred from membership in such clubs. If a youngster was caught playing for a club, he risked expulsion from school. Although Victor played under an assumed name, he was nevertheless discovered and, to avoid being expelled, promised the school authorities that he would never play football again.

From that time on Barna concentrated on his "bat" and the little, celluloid ball. He played in his first table tennis tournament on December 25, 1925, coming in third and receiving a small bronze plaque which he carried with him for a long time thereafter. For his 15th birthday he was given a ping-pong table, and 16 months later—December 26, 1927—Victor enjoyed his first tournament triumph by winning the Hungarian Junior National Championship.

In 1929, Barna was a member of the Hungarian team which won the Swaythling Cup, symbolic of the men's world championship. (The Cup was donated by Lady Swaythling, mother of table tennis administrator Ivor Montagu.) The following season he won the first of his five world singles championships in Berlin.

In Budapest the next year (1931), he lost in the finals of the world singles championship. But he won the title back in 1932 in Prague, and kept it for the next three years. The year 1932 was a great disappointment for Barna. Though he won both the world singles and men's doubles, his Hungarian team lost the Swaythling Cup competition to Czechoslovakia. Victor was convinced his teammates could have done better.

Afterwards in the dressing room, speaking to them, he had some simple advice: "Forget the crowd, even your opponent, his style and even yours. All you see is the ball as it leaves your opponent's bat, and then return it. Place it so that it is out of his reach. It is all very simple; you have to keep the ball in play just one more hit than the other fellow does."

He himself tried to increase his own power of concentration: the results were impressive. He won the singles titles and the men's doubles title in 1933, 1934, and 1935. Victor also helped his Hungarian teammates gain the Swaythling Cup team championship. (He was the men's double champion each year from 1929 to 1935.)

Barna's greatest performance came in February 1935, when during the world championships at the Empire Pool and Sports Stadium in Wembley, England, he took the world singles, doubles, and mixed doubles. His native Hungary also retained the Swaythling Cup that year.

Victor Barna was small, fleet-footed, and wiry, returning almost impossible shots with ease. His backhand was especially effective, and he played nine out of every ten strokes backhand. Victor and his Jewish colleagues played all over Europe in the early 1930s, helping to popularize a sport that was then little-known. In 1933, he and another Hungarian Jew, Sandor Glancz, joined to win the world doubles title. As a result, the following year the two were invited to tour the United States for four weeks, becoming the first foreign table tennis players ever to reach the U.S. In Chicago, they played before an enthusiastic crowd of 4,000.

Unfortunately, an accident cost Victor Barna the chance to continue his championship play. On May 10, 1935, he was injured in an auto crash in France, where he had been living for a year. His right arm, the one he used in table tennis, was so badly injured that the doctors could repair the fracture only by implanting in his arm a silver plate, held by four screws. Those same doctors told him he would never play the game again. Barna did play, however, though the caliber of his singles game was seriously affected.

On April 22, 1939, he married the former Susie Arany, and he and his wife had some success in a few mixed doubles tournaments. They were semi-finalists in a Wembley open tournament in 1940, and runner-up in the East India Open Championship in Calcutta in 1949, as well as in the Irish Open in 1950.

Victor retired from singles competition in 1949, and five years later, he quit competitive doubles as well. Until the end of his career, Barna had the experts mesmerized. Table tennis administrator Montagu wrote that Barna's "backhand was so spectacular that few spectators appreciated that the winning rally position had often been opened by his forehand. His positioning was so perfect that with the slightest change of foot angle and body balance his flick could instantly and invisibly alter the direction of the kill from diagonal to straight or vice versa . . ."

During World War II, Victor gave table tennis exhibitions for the British Red Cross and the troops. He also joined the British army's commando unit.

In 1946, Barna joined the Dunlop Sports Company, helping this major sports equipment firm market its own line of table tennis equipment, including tables, nets, and a "Barna Super Ball." Barna eventually became head of all Dunlop sporting equipment for the international market.

In 1947, he became a British national.

Barna suffered a fatal heart attack on one of his frequent overseas tours promoting Dunlop Sports equipment in Lima, Peru in 1972.

Gyozo Barna is a member of the Jewish Sports Hall of Fame in Israel.

Herman Barron
The Greatest Jewish Golfer

BARRON, HERMAN (born December 23, 1909, in Port Chester, New York; died June 9, 1976) American golfer. Considered the greatest Jewish golfer ever. His greatest years of accomplishment were the 1930s and 1940s, after which he retired to become a teaching pro.

• • •

Herman Barron was a member of the U.S. Ryder Cup team in 1947 and won a number of major tournaments, including the Goodall Round Robin (1948) and the Professional Golf Association Seniors and World Seniors in February 1963. In 1963, he also captured the unofficial senior championship of the world at St. Anne's, England.

He grew up in Port Chester, New York, and was introduced to golf as a caddie, toting his first golf bag at the Port Chester Country Club when he was only nine. Herman, along with the other caddies, got a chance to hit a few when the greens were unoccupied.

Barron's talent was noticeable at an early age. At 11, he astounded the golfing world by shooting a 70 to break the Port Chester course record. The local *Port Chester Daily Item* ran his picture and the story on page one. A few weeks later, he won his first tournament—the Metropolitan Caddie Championship.

At age 13, Herman had a strong aversion to mathematics, and was expelled from school for missing mathematics classes. On the same day that his formal education ended, he was named assistant pro at the Port Chester Club. There he began instructing his elders in the fine points of the game.

The next year, playing at the Lakeville Club in Flushing, New York, Barron captured the Metro-politan Assistant-Pro Championship. He became head pro at Port Chester at age 15.

In 1934, the young protégé won his first major tournament, the Philadelphia Open. On each of the first three days of the tournament, Barron equaled the competitive course record of 60 for the Philmont Club Course.

In 1935, Barron became the pro at the Fenway Golf Club in White Plains, New York, and began alternating his time between Fenway and Palm Beach (Florida) Country Club where he spent his winters as a golf host.

In 1946, Barron earned $30,000 in prize money and Ben Hogan was the only golfer to win more. In one three-week span, Herman took the rich *Philadelphia Inquirer* tournament, lost the National Open by one stroke, and captured Chicago's All-American pro championship at the Tam O'Shanter

Country Club. The highlight of his career was being named to the U.S. Ryder Cup team in 1947, the year in which the Americans totally overwhelmed the British.

Herman attributed his achievements to a key decision taken in the early part of the 1930s: "Success came when I discarded the whippy shafts I had used for so many years and switched to stiff-shafted clubs. The more powerful clubs stepped up my distance off the tee. I used to be a short driver, though pretty straight. Back in the early '30s they argued that direction was more important than distance off the tee, but, brother, you can't get anywhere in golf today unless you're long off the tee."

Barron is proud of being the first Jewish golfer to do well. Once Byron Nelson, the great golf pro, advised Herman to "advertise the fact that you are Jewish. Cash in on being the first great Jewish golfer. There's money in it for you." Nelson then pointed to other Jewish sports stars: Hank Greenberg, Sid Luckman, Benny Leonard, and Nat Holman. "You can earn the same sort of (moral) support from Jewish folks who yearn for a golf champion." Barron took this advice, practiced twice as much, sought solid coaching, and became determined to do well in the sport so that Jewish fans would have something to follow.

Among the other major crowns Herman won are the Canadian Open, the Western Open, the Metropolitan PGA, and the Westchester PGA. He rated Byron Nelson as the greatest player he ever faced, with Ben Hogan a close second. Nelson said of Herman: "He had one of the finest short games in the business."

Herman Barron gave up the winter competitive pro tour in 1948 after four bouts with pneumonia. Had Herman not quit, he might have gone on to dizzying heights. But he never regretted doing so and going into teaching: "There is as much satisfaction in that as I ever enjoyed in competition," he noted.

In November 1964, Barron scored his 11th hole-in-one. His best score in competition was 64. In 1975, he retired from his job at Fenway to live in Palm Beach, Florida, with his wife Carla, a former model. When he died in 1976, he had been a golf pro for over 50 years.

Morris Berg
The Best Educated Major Leaguer

BERG, MORRIS "MOE" (born March 2, 1902, in New York City; died May 30, 1972) American baseball player. He was considered the best educated man ever to play in the major leagues. Moe was a catcher for the Brooklyn Dodgers in 1923, the Chicago White Sox from 1926 to 1930, the Cleveland Indians in 1931 and 1934, the Washington Senators in 1932 and 1934, and the Boston Red Sox from 1935 to 1939. In 663 games he had a career batting average of .243. The classic remark, "good field, no hit," was coined by scout Mike Gonzales in assessing Berg.

. . .

Moe was born on East 121st Street in New York City in a cold-water tenement, the second son of immigrants from the Ukraine. His father, a pharmacist, decided to move from New York City to Newark, New Jersey because he thought the environment was better.

At the age of three, Moe displayed athletic tendencies. Sometimes he would squat down, like a catcher, behind a manhole cover which served as home plate while a policeman on the beat would throw to him. Moe caught everything thrown his way, and soon crowds began to gather to watch.

At the age of seven, Moe caught the attention of Newark's Rose Methodist baseball team. The team's coaches wanted Moe to play for them, but for obvious reasons wanted him to change his name. Moe agreed, and played for Rose Methodist as Runt Wolfe. In 1909, Moe's pseudonym was mentioned for the first time in the *Newark Evening News* sports section.

Moe's father was upset over his son's devotion to baseball. He preferred that he devote himself to schoolwork and help in the family pharmacy.

Moe did well in his studies at South Eighth Street Public School. The only criticism of his schoolwork, duly noted in his report card, was that he sang off key. After school, Moe ran off to play ball, seldom returning home before dark. Baseball continued to cause tension in the Berg home, and once Moe even ran away. However, he didn't stay away long. In a few hours he trudged home, his bat slung over his shoulder.

At Newark's Barringer High School, Moe's athletic prowess received some public attention. He played third base for the high school baseball team and was its star. In 1920, upon graduation, he enrolled at Princeton University and played baseball with a Princeton team acclaimed the greatest in its history. He was a crack shortstop on the team which won 19 games in a row, a record that stood for many years.

After graduating in 1923, Princeton offered Berg a teaching position, but he wanted to study romance languages at the Sorbonne in Paris. When Moe received an offer to join the Brooklyn Dodgers, he did the practical thing: he signed with the Dodgers and managed to sandwich in his schooling during the baseball off-season. In 1925, he went to Columbia Law School where he received his law degree in 1928.

In 1926, Berg became a catcher with the Chicago White Sox. He broke into the lineup by accident. His manager Ray Shalk, also a catcher, broke a finger and so did the second-string catcher. Shalk yelled to his road secretary, "Call a Class D club and get us a catcher, quick." Moe Berg turned to Shalk and said, "What do you mean, get a catcher? We have a catcher on this bench."

"Okay," said Shalk, "get in and catch, wise guy." Moe Berg then made his debut as a major league catcher. "The funniest thing about it," Berg said later, "is that when I said we had a catcher, I didn't mean myself. Earl Sheely, a first baseman, was a pretty good backstop and I had him in mind."

In 1931, playing for the Cleveland Indians, Berg

batted .350 and played errorless ball. Walter Johnson, one of the major league's greatest pitchers, thought Moe was one of the major league's better catchers. Later, Moe played for the Boston Red Sox. Joe Cronin, captain of the team, said, "Book sense and baseball sense don't always go together, but this fellow's got more than his share of both."

Moe Berg knew more languages than any other ball player: French, Spanish, Latin, Portuguese, Italian, Russian, Yiddish, Japanese, and Greek, among others. The total number was actually 12. Yet he was sensitive about publicity that portrayed him as a scholar: "I don't want to be known as a ball player who reads a book."

Reminiscing about the game, Moe said, "In baseball, a player stands on his own feet, and the fact that he can talk in five or six languages avails him nothing when he is up there at the plate with the bases filled and two out."

In 1941, he was appointed "good will ambassasador" to South America by Nelson Rockefeller, then coordinator of Inter-American affairs. During World War II, Berg broadcast to the Japanese and became a counterintelligence agent in Europe.

Much of his life after World War II has been cloaked in mystery, and the suspicion that he had remained within the counterintelligence community has remained strong. In 1951, he officially reentered government service. The government had asked him to confer with European scientists at a time when reports of dramatic Soviet scientific advances were current. According to a biography of Berg (*Moe Berg: Athlete, Scholar* by Louis Kaufman, Barbara Fitzgerald, and Tom Sewall, 1974), he had a contractual relationship with the CIA at the time.

After the Soviets launched Sputnik I in 1957, Berg agreed to accept a role in the NATO defense structure, joining the staff of the head of NATO's advisory group for aeronautical research and development. He worked with scientists and military personnel of other nations to determine where NATO's missile-launching base should be centered.

In February 1963, Berg was invited to the White House to attend an award ceremony for his boss at the NATO advisory group. "Moe," President John F. Kennedy had said, "baseball hasn't been the same without you." To which Moe replied, "Thank you, Mr. President. I'd like to think that was true."

Berg worked little during the last seven years of his life. An occasional law case provided pocket money. He would rise early and walk to various newsstands to buy newspapers. In 1972, he was taken to Clara Mass Hospital in Newark, New Jersey, after suffering injuries in a fall at home. He was 70 years old. Minutes before he died he turned to a nurse and spoke his last words: "How did the [New York] Mets do today?"

Fascination with Berg continued long after his passing. Nicholas Dawidoff's incisive biography, *The Catcher Was a Spy: The Mysterious Life of Moe Berg*, was published in 1994. In 1998, American singer-songwriter Chuck Brodsky released "Moe Berg: The Song" on his album *Radio*.

Isaac Berger

First Featherweight to Lift 800 Pounds

BERGER, ISAAC "IKE" (born November 13, 1936 in Jerusalem, Palestine–) American weightlifter. He won three Olympic medals in the featherweight class: a gold in 1956 and silver in 1960 and 1964. Berger was the first featherweight to lift over 800 pounds and the first to press double his body weight. His 1964 Olympic record of 336 pounds in the jerk at a body weight of 130 pounds made him pound-for-pound the strongest man in the world, a record that stood for nine years. His 1958 victories over Russian opponents won him recognition as the finest weightlifter in the world at the time.

∎ ∎ ∎

Isaac lived in Jerusalem until age 12 where he attended a yeshiva (Jewish religious school.) His father, a deeply religious man, was a rabbi and a diamond setter. During the 1948 Israeli War of Independence, Isaac recalled that he would go out each day to get food for his family and the neighbors. He had to walk about three miles each way and had to contend with occasional artillery shelling and snipers. Once he was nicked in the back by shrapnel. And another time when he returned three hours late, his mother was certain that she would find him in the morgue.

With his family, Isaac emigrated to the United States in 1949, when he was 13 years old. They settled in New York City. In 1952 Ike Berger, as he was called, started lifting weights at Shaffer's gym in Brooklyn, New York. He studied auto mechanics for three years at East New York Vocational School, and later also studied voice and trained to be a cantor in a synagogue.

When Isaac began lifting weights he was small.

He weighed 102 pounds, and was 4 feet, 11 inches tall which made him a target for bullies. This bothered him quite a bit. One afternoon as he was standing in front of the Adonis Health Club, he noticed some girls admiring the pictures of muscular, good-looking men. Berger decided then and there to start lifting weights.

Isaac was always a competitive lifter, never a body builder. Eventually he developed what some called the most perfect proportionate form for all weightlifters, except for his slightly large 16½-inch neck. His chest measured 40 inches; his waist, 28½ inches; and his hips, 36 inches. Part of his training included tumbling and hand balancing. As a youngster, Ike spent considerable time in playgrounds, doing acrobatics, playing softball, basketball, and even getting in some boxing at the Hebrew Educational Alliance in New York.

In 1955, Berger, then 19, won the Senior United States weightlifting title, a feat he repeated the next two years. At the end of that year he became an American citizen. Berger represented his adopted country at the 1956 Melbourne Olympics and won a gold medal by lifting a total of 777 pounds. At age 18, he was the youngest competitor at the games. He returned to his native country for the 1957 Maccabiah Games. There he broke the world featherweight record for the press. It was the first world record established in Israel. Ike pressed 258 pounds (117.1 kilograms.) In doing this, he became the first man ever to press double his body weight. David Ben-Gurion, Israel's prime minister at the time, was among the spectators. The crowd watched silently as Berger lifted the bar to his chest. His groans were audible as he strained to raise the weight over his head. A deafening roar erupted when the judges raised white flags to indicate Ike Berger had succeeded.

Over the course of the next year, Berger defeated the Russian weightlifters on all four occasions that he met them: in Chicago, Detroit, and New York and at the world championships at Stockholm. At Stockholm, Berger won the featherweight title with a recordbreaking performance. He broke the world

mark with a total lift of 804.7 pounds and then bettered that record with 821.2 pounds for the press, snatch, and jerk. He also established a world standard for the jerk with a lift of 335.1 pounds.

In October 1958, *The New York Times* noted that "this 21-year-old package of puissance is the major stumbling block to Soviet domination of the weightlifting field." At that point, Berger had beaten the Russians five out of five times in international competition. At one of those events, in Stockholm, one of the Russian coaches, a Jew, confided to Berger in Yiddish, "You're the only one [of the weightlifters] who's given us trouble. And you happen to be Jewish." In other words, the coach was delighted that at least it had taken one Jew to beat another Jew (the coach). That, at least, was how Berger interpreted the coach's remark. During this period, to earn his living, he worked in the food distribution section of Olympic coach Bob Hoffman's York, Pennsylvania, barbell firm.

Berger spent relatively little time training. He worked out for 90 minutes at a time three times a week. He was not overly careful about his diet. He would consume as many hot dogs, hamburgers, and milkshakes as any Coney Island youngster. Before a match, he was moody and jittery. Some believed a weightlifter should avoid sex before competing. "That was silly," noted Berger. "I didn't. I needed it to relax me." He thought of the weights as the enemies he had to defeat. Lifting them was his conquest. Once he had accomplished the feat and heard the applause, the weights became his friends again.

Berger thinks that weightlifters are more relaxed than other athletes. He feels that all weightlifters are well-adjusted extroverts who never take more than five minutes to fall asleep at night. He has had to suffer a certain amount of unexpected abuse from the opposite sex. He noted that women may stare and make derogatory comments about lifters and body builders and consider them dull, vain, and horrible. But, he has also noticed that women will date the athletes they criticize.

Overconfidence cost Berger the featherweight title in the 1960 Rome Olympics. Four days before the Games he broke four world records: in the press (264 pounds), the snatch (253 pounds), the clean and jerk (336 pounds), and the total (853 pounds). As a result, he hurt his muscles and received only a silver medal behind Eugene Miniev of the Soviet Union (Miniev had won the silver medal in 1956.)

Berger admitted that he should have concentrated more on the Olympics and less on breaking the world records, but he had been certain that he could win at both. He partially avenged his Rome defeat by whipping Miniev in the 1961 World Championships in Vienna. Berger retired in 1962 but returned the following year. In the 1964 Olympics he captured a silver medal lifting 841½ pounds. His U.S. Olympic teammates nicknamed him Mighty Mouse.

Ike Berger retired from weightlifting after the Tokyo Olympics in 1964. That year he began a mail-order firm in New York, selling an exerciser that promised to help people lose weight. The following year, 1965, he invented a product called Waste-a-Way, a belt for losing weight, that was marketed quite successfully.

Ike was inducted into the United States Weight-lifters Hall of Fame in 1965. And in that same year he began a three-year training period at the New York College of Music to become a cantor. Since then he has officiated in synagogues in Florida, Missouri, and New York.

In 1970 Ike started to concentrate his attention on a business venture (called Ike Berger Enterprises) which was devoted largely to the sale of weightlifting and exercise products.

Ike Berger is a member of the Jewish Sports Hall of Fame in Israel.

Margarethe "Gretel" Bergmann

An Outstanding Athlete Crushed by the Nazis

BERGMANN, MARGARETHE "GRETEL" (born April 12, 1914, in Lauphein, Germany–). German high jumper. Forced off the 1936 German Olympic team by the Nazi government, she never received the rewards she merited. In 1980 the Jewish Sports Hall of Fame honored her with a commemorative award.

. . .

As a youngster, Gretel (the diminutive of Margarethe) loved sports and all physical activities. She was the only girl in her class in Lauphein, and for the first nine years of her schooling she played soccer and field-handball on the boys' teams.

She loved winter sports, particularly skiing. She even went shopping on ice skates.

In 1930, when she began her secondary education in Ulm, Gretel joined the town's athletic club. With the improved coaching available, she excelled in track and field and sometimes won six different events in one day. Her specialty was the high jump.

In the spring of 1933, shortly after Hitler had come to power, she completed her studies at Ulm. She wanted to become a physical education teacher and was accepted by the university in Berlin. But immediately thereafter, when it learned that she was Jewish, she was advised not to attend classes until the political situation changed. During that same spring, the UFV club (the Ulm Soccer Club) where she had won many medals, notified her that she was no longer welcome.

As the Nazis intensified their discrimination against the Jews of Germany, Jews formed their own social and athletic clubs. In Gretel's hometown, she and her Jewish friends leveled a potato field to play soccer. Gretel was the coach and the only female member.

Realizing that there was no future for her in Germany, Gretel and her parents decided that she should go to England to pursue a degree in physical education. Gretel hoped that she might qualify to represent England at the 1936 Olympics, which were to be held in Berlin. In England she found no suitable school in her chosen field so instead she enrolled in the London Polytechnic to study English.

In June 1934, competing for her school, Gretel won the British high jump championship. Her father was in England at the time on what his daughter believed to be a business trip. After Gretel won in the competition, her father took her aside and informed her that he was actually in England to deliver an important message: she was to return to Germany to try out for the German Olympic team. If she refused, not only would her family in Germany suffer the consequences, but all the Jewish athletes in Germany would also suffer. Gretel had no alternative and returned to Germany.

In America, a groundswell of protest against American participation in the 1936 Olympics had arisen. The American Olympic Committee had sought assurances that everyone, no matter what his religion, could participate in the 1936 Games. But in 1933 Germany had decreed that Jews would be excluded from joining. Fearful that the United States might boycott the Berlin games, the Nazis announced in June 1934, that 21 Jews, including Gretel, had been nominated to attend German Olympic training camp.

On Gretel's return to Germany, she was placed on the so-called Olympic nucleus team from which the three best for every event would be chosen. Gretel later noted ironically that at a time when Jews were not permitted in restaurants, resorts, movies, or concerts, she was being considered for a place on the German Olympic team!

Gretel was sent with the rest of the nucleus team to training camp twice a year. She experienced no overt anti-Semitism from her fellow athletes (although the officials were not so restrained) and was grateful for the opportunity to train properly. But she was not permitted to compete with her non-Jewish German teammates at the same meets. The reason: She was not a member of the German Track and Field Association. Still, she often achieved results as good as or better than those teammates.

Gretel's roommate at the training sessions was Doro Ratjen. Gretel later noted that she doubted Ratjen's femininity, but dared not voice these thoughts outside her family circle. (Ratjen competed in the Olympics but did not win a medal. Years later Ratjen was barred from all women's competition and in 1966 emerged as Hermann Ratjen, confessing that he had been forced to pose as a female during those years in the hope of winning an Olympic medal.) Putting the two together served the Nazis' purpose: Gretel could not afford to betray Ratjen and "she" dared not make advances toward Gretel as Aryan men could be severely punished for cavorting with a Jewish woman.

In June 1935, Gretel and a group of Jewish athletes began training at Baden. Of the entire group, Gretel was the only one who measured up to Olympic standards. There, Gretel met her future husband, Bruno Lambert.

As the fall of 1935 approached, the American Olympic Committee's membership still appeared ready to stay away from Berlin. To offset the possibility, the Nazis invited Gretel and one other Jew, Helene Mayer, to join the Olympic team. Mayer was a winner of a gold medal in fencing (foil) at the 1928 Olympics and a silver one in the 1932 Los Angeles Olympic Games.

The admission of the two Jewish athletes to the German team tipped the scales in favor of having the American team go to Berlin.

On June 30, 1936, Gretel equaled the German high-jump record with a mark of 5 feet 3 inches, an

achievement that would have sufficed to win either a gold or silver medal that summer in Berlin. But on July 16th, she received a letter from the German sports authorities informing her that her achievements were inadequate. She was terribly disappointed because participating in the Olympics had been extremely important to her. She had been eager to refute Nazi caricatures of the Jew as "fat, bowlegged, and miserable."

Helene Mayer did participate in those 1936 Games. She won a silver medal in fencing. During the medal award ceremony, Helene wore a swastika on her sweater and raised an arm in Nazi salute.

Gretel arrived in New York in May 1937, with $10 in her pocket, all the money she had been permitted to take. She began using the American version of her name, Margaret. At first she worked as a maid for $10 a week and later as a masseuse. But soon thereafter she earned $100 a month, and she began to feel rich.

Bruno Lambert, whom Gretel had met in 1935, joined her in August 1938. He had been studying medicine in Switzerland, because the Germans would not let him take his state boards in Germany. They were married in 1939. That fall, Bruno became the first foreign intern to be accepted at Wyckoff Heights Hospital in Brooklyn, New York. He received no salary, so the couple had to live on Gretel's salary.

In the late 1930s, she began training again at the private athletic club she had joined: the Park Central Athletic Association. Weighing only 112 pounds she managed to win the American championship in the high jump and shot put.

In 1938 Gretel again won the American championship in the high jump. The following year, she had already begun to prepare for another championship try, but decided against it when the war broke out. Her family was still in Europe and she could no longer concentrate on sports. When her husband joined the U.S. Army, she moved with him to the various army posts where he was stationed. They returned to New York when the war was over, where Dr. Lambert, an internist, reestablished his private practice.

In February 1980, Gretel Bergmann was given a special commemorative award by the Jewish Sports Hall of Fame in Israel.

In August 1995, the German Sports Federation dedicated a sports arena in Bergmann's name in the Berlin district of Wilmersdorf. Standing by her decision never to visit Germany again, Gretel did not attend the dedication ceremony.

However, in the summer of 1996, she softened her stance somewhat toward the Germans when the German National Olympic Committee, hoping to make amends for not selecting Begmann for the 1936 Olympic team, invited her to be guest of honor at the 1996 Atlanta Olympics. On the eve of Atlanta, she was 82 years old and living in New York.

She told a reporter: "I don't hate all Germans any more, though I did for a long time. I'm aware of many Germans trying to make up for wrongs. The young people of Germany should not be held responsible for what their elders did so I decided to accept the invitation.... I thought that going to Atlanta...would be good for my mental outlook. It will make the ghosts of the past a little less unfriendly."

During the Atlanta Olympics, Bergmann's experience nearly 60 years earlier was featured at an exhibit at the U.S. Holocaust Memorial Museum in Washington, D.C. "I think it should be known what can happen if a maniac like Hitler comes to power," said Bergmann.

After a 62-year absence, Bergmann finally agreed to visit Germany at the age of 85 in November 1999. Only after the Opal Automobile Company honored her as one of "Twelve Silent Victors" did she decide to visit her homeland.

In July 2004, HBO aired *Hitler's Pawn*, a documentary about the little-known chapter in Olympic history involving Bergmann. The program featured moving interviews with the former high jumper at age 90 and a tearful reunion between her and Elfriede Kaun, the only one of Bergmann's German teammates to treat her with kindness.

In September 2009, a movie about Gretel Bergmann's life, entitled *Berlin 36*, debuted in German theaters. On November 23, 2009, her national record from June 1936 was officially restored by the German Track and Field Association, which also requested that she be admitted to the German Sports Hall of Fame. Well into her nineties, she continues to live in Queens, New York, relishing her vindication.

Ron Blomberg
A New York Yankee Jewish Hero

BLOMBERG, RONALD MARK (born August 23, 1948, in Atlanta, Georgia–) American baseball player. A major leaguer for eight years, mostly in the 1970s. He was baseball's number-one draft pick in 1967. Blomberg became a Jewish sports hero in New York while playing for the New York Yankees in 1969, and again from 1971 to 1976. He played for the Chicago White Sox in 1978. In 1973, he was the first designated hitter. In 461 games, Blomberg had 391 hits, 52 home runs, and a career batting average of .293.

■ ■ ■

In high school, Ron not only won four letters in both baseball and basketball, he also earned four letters in track, excelling in the sprints. To make money as a youngster he collected returnable bottles, sold Kool-Aid, and had a newspaper route. Ron began playing Little League baseball at the relatively late age of 12, and claims that he began his basketball career two years later, when he picked up a basketball and dunked it in a ninth-grade physical education class.

After graduating from Druid Hills High School in Atlanta, Georgia, in 1967, Ron spurned numerous college basketball scholarships to play baseball. He enrolled in DeKalb Junior College in Atlanta that year (attending the school for another two years), but devoted himself principally to his baseball career.

The 205-pound athlete was the Yankees' number-one selection in the 1967 free-agent draft. He broke into pro baseball in 1967 in the Yankee farm chain with Johnson City of the Appalachian League, hitting 10 home runs in 66 games, with a .297 average. In 1968, playing for Kingston in the Carolina League, he hit only .251 in 105 games, with seven homers. But in 1969 he hit .284 and 19

homers for Manchester in the Eastern League and was brought up to the Yankees very briefly that season. He played only four games and had three hits in six at bats. In 1970, he played for Syracuse in the International League, the highest level minor league. In 92 games, he hit .273, with 10 home runs and 38 runs batted in.

The following year, 1971, Blomberg hit .326 and six homers in 48 games for Syracuse before being brought up again to the Yankees, this time for good. In 64 games for the Yankees that season, he hit .322 with seven homers.

While playing for the Yankees, Blomberg resumed his college studies, majoring in psychology at Fairleigh Dickinson University in Teaneck, New Jersey.

Ron Blomberg had some excellent years with the Yankees. In 1972, he slammed 14 homers in 107 games, though he hit only .268 as a first baseman and an outfielder. In 1973, in 100 games, he batted .329 with 12 homers and 57 runs batted in. In 1974, he hit .311 and 10 homers in 90 games. Then the injury jinx struck him.

His problems began in 1975 with a shoulder injury. He went to bat only 106 times in 1975, only twice in 1976, and not at all in 1977. Blomberg in-

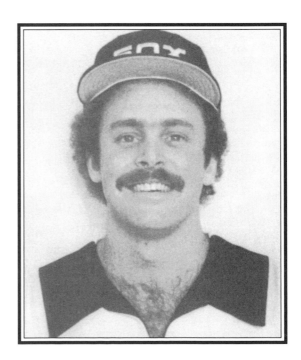

jured his knee running into a fence in pursuit of a fly ball in 1977 spring training and that kept him out for the entire season. He played in only 35 games between 1975 and 1977 because of injuries. He had two operations, one in 1976 to redirect tendons in his shoulder and one in 1977 to reassemble his shattered knee.

Blomberg remembers his playing days in New York fondly. New York's Jewish fans dubbed him the Messiah. He liked to succeed for them just as black and Hispanic players like to be heroes for their people.

His attitude toward playing on Jewish High Holidays seemed ambiguous. He once said he would not play on Jewish High Holidays because Jewish fans would have difficulty understanding such behavior. But when reminded that this would have caused him to miss the World Series opener in 1978 if the White Sox were playing, he observed: "In that case, I've talked to a couple of rabbis who say they'll pray for me at the ballpark." The White Sox, however, did not make the World Series.

Blomberg received his nickname of "Boomer" when he hit a towering home run on his third trip to the plate in his first major league game—and the name stuck.

Blomberg's last team—the Chicago White Sox—obtained him through the reentry draft in 1978. Six teams had picked him in the free-agent draft but the White Sox offered him the security of a four-year guaranteed contract in which he was to receive $600,000 over four years. On opening day of 1978 he hit a home run to help the White Sox beat the Boston Red Sox. But injury again marred that season. In August, he pulled a groin muscle and played in only 61 games that year. He managed to hit only .231 with five home runs. Blomberg had been a designated hitter that year.

He was released by the White Sox in March 1979.

Later that year, Ron and his wife Beth moved to Atlanta where he worked as a public relations representative for a firm run by the former New York Giant quarterback, Fran Tarkenton; the firm provided advice to Atlanta-based industries.

Blomberg frequently addresses synagogue and men's groups on topics that include being a Jew in sports and combating drugs. He has a son Adam, and daughter Chelsey.

In the spring of 1995, Blomberg established the Ron Blomberg Championship Baseball Program, a series of comprehensive clinics for children between the ages of five and 17. He turned down an offer from the Yankees to return as a coach so that he could remain in Atlanta and create the program.

Blomberg's autobiography, *Designated Hebrew: The Ron Blomberg Story*, was published in April 2006. Even with the passage of years, fans fondly remember him as baseball's first designated hitter.

In 2007, Blomberg managed the Bet Shemesh Blue Sox in the inaugural (and only!) season of the Israel Baseball League, attaining a 29–12 league-leading record as well as the IBL championship. By the finish of the 2010 season, Blomberg ranked seventh all-time in career batting average among Jewish major league baseball players.

Tal Brody

American-born Israeli Basketball Player

BRODY, TAL (born August 30, 1943, in Trenton, New Jersey–) American-born Israeli basketball player. An All-American basketball star in the 1960s at the University of Illinois, Brody emigrated to Israel and captained Maccabi Tel Aviv to Israel's first European basketball title in 1977. He is credited with introducing fast-paced American-style basketball into the Israeli game.

■ ■ ■

At age 10, Brody played basketball at the Trenton, New Jersey Jewish Community Center. He graduated from Trenton Central High School in 1961, as a member of the undefeated state champions. Brody was selected for the All-State team. He continued to show talent at the University of Illinois where, between 1961 and 1965, the 6-foot 1½-inch guard won All-America, All-Academic, and All Big-Ten honors.

In the summer of 1965, Tal went to Israel for the Maccabiah Games and helped the United States win a gold medal in basketball. He was approached by the Israeli Ministry of Education and the managers of the Tel Aviv Maccabi basketball team about living in Israel and playing basketball for Maccabi. "I liked what I saw," Brody said later. "They hit just the right note." He was asked to return to Israel to set up sports programs.

But first he returned to Illinois, earned his masters (in 1966) in educational psychology and turned down a chance to play with the Baltimore Bullets. He was the 13th player picked in the 1965 NBA draft, a time when there were only nine NBA teams. In 1966, Brody returned to Israel: "They approached me with the challenge of helping to build basketball and sports in the country."

Tal's family was no stranger to Israel. Earlier, Tal's father had spent two years in Palestine en route from Eastern Europe to the United States and one of Tal's grandfathers had helped to build an electric station and an airfield in Palestine.

After completing his studies, Tal returned to Israel and played for Maccabi Tel Aviv from 1966 to 1968. In 1967, he nearly led the team (runner-up that year) to the European title, and was named Israel's Sportsman of the Year.

Though he had decided to settle in Israel permanently, Brody returned to the United States in 1968 to fulfill his military obligation. For the next two years, while serving in the U.S. army, he played for the Armed Forces All-Star teams in national and international competitions. The army team for which he played also represented the U.S. in the World Championships in Belgrade, Yugoslavia, in 1970, and came in third.

Brody returned to Israel late in 1970, becoming an instructor at the Wingate Institute of Physical Education in Netanya. He established a sporting goods business and married Ronit, an Israeli. His guest of honor at the wedding was Moshe Dayan, then Minister of Defense, who was an enthusiastic basketball fan. That same year, Tal rejoined the Maccabi Tel Aviv club. He became an Israeli citizen and served for a time in the Israeli Defense Forces.

One wintry evening in 1977, in Vitron, a small Belgian town, Brody led Maccabi Tel Aviv in a game against the mighty Red Army team of Moscow. The winner would play in the European Cup finals. In a startling upset, Maccabi won 91-79, and Brody, as team captain, was carried shoulder-high from the court by ecstatic fans. It was then that he made his now-famous remark, "We are on the map. We are staying on the map, not only in sport, but in everything." He succeeded because of a combination of excellent playmaking, shooting, and aggressive defense.

Later that same year, Maccabi Tel Aviv went on to win the European Cup, a tournament matching 23 national champion club teams. To everyone's

(Right) Brody shakes hands with the late Moshe Dayan at the Yad Eliahu (Maccabi Tel Aviv's home court) on January 16, 1975. Dayan, former Israeli Defense Minister (1967–1974), rarely missed a Maccabi Tel Aviv home game. (Below left) Tal Brody, holding ball, playing for Maccabi Tel Aviv on January 9, 1975. (Below right) Tal Brody, holding European Cup won three days earlier by Maccabi Tel Aviv. Photo was taken on April 10, 1977. Brody was team captain. Maccabi Tel Aviv won first European Cup ever for an Israeli basketball team.

surprise, on April 7, 1977, Maccabi defeated Mobil Girgi of Varese, Italy, 78-77 in Belgrade, Yugoslavia, for the title.

Soon thereafter, Brody retired from basketball when, as he put it, "I realized that I was running on the court with guys half my age." He declared that he would continue to coach and establish sports programs for Israeli youth. In keeping with that, he reached out to some 200,000 Israeli youngsters by giving basketball clinics in schools, development towns, and in the army.

He has twice been named Israeli basketball player of the year. Sporting goods dealers who used to sell six soccer balls to one basketball now say that this ratio has been reversed, and they credit Tal Brody largely for the turnabout.

Brody had come to Israel, as he said, to make a contribution. "Since I was Jewish, I thought I'd take a year out of my life and see what was going on in the world. One year turned out to be 26." He knew that he could have had a good life in the U.S., "but I felt that in Israel I could do something special."

Brody spent a lot of time giving lectures to overseas Jewish groups—Israel Bonds, the United Jewish Appeal, etc.—to try to encourage businessmen and others to get involved in Israel. In 1979, President Yitzhak Navon of Israel awarded Brody the nation's highest honor: the Israel Prize, in recognition of his contribution to youth and sportsmanship.

In 1980, Brody sold his sporting goods business to his partner and opened his own life insurance agency which gave him more free time to devote to his great love: basketball. Each year since then he has qualified as a member of the "Million-Dollar Round Table" comprised of Israel's life insurance industry's greatest performers. He served as assistant coach for Maccabi Tel Aviv from 1981 to 1983.

In 1983, he and his wife, Ronit, were divorced.

In 1985, Brody formed Bnei Herzylia, a city-run basketball program that by the year 2003 had grown to 1,100 youngsters ages 5 to 18. Organized around 14 town centers in Herzylia, the program sends its top players to Maccabi Tel Aviv, the country's best basketball team.

Starting in October 1988, Brody has also served as a liaison between the National Basketball Association and Maccabi Tel Aviv. He has organized games between an NBA team and Maccabi Tel Aviv. Thus far, the Israeli team has played against the Philadelphia 76ers, the Miami Heat, the Los Angeles Lakers, and the Los Angeles Clippers.

During the early 1990s Brody worked for Israel Television as a commentator for Maccabi Tel Aviv's games.

During the late 1990s, Brody gained a number of honors. In February 1996, the University of Illinois selected him as "Man of the Year," a distinction given to an Illinois graduate athlete every year for his efforts both in and out of sports.

In the summer of 1997, Brody joined a newly formed 12-member board of directors for Spirit of Israel, an Israeli supplemental arm of the United Jewish Appeal, a fund-raising enterprise securing funds from Israelis for Israeli projects.

In April 1998, the Israeli newspaper *Ma'ariv* conducted a poll, timed for the country's 50th anniversary celebrations, which ranked Brody as the Israeli sports figure who most influenced sport in Israel. Another *Ma'ariv* poll, conducted at the same time, placed Brody among the top five Israeli basketball players of all time.

Brody continues to be actively involved in the Tal Brody Insurance Agency, which is located in Ramat Gan and managed by his second wife, Tirtza. He also represents Mitsubishi, C. I. Co., Ltd., in its search for Israeli products that will appeal to Japanese consumers.

In December 2008 Brody, seeking a Knesset seat, ran unsuccessfully in the Likud primaries. In July 2010, he became the first Israeli to serve in the newly-created post of Goodwill Ambassador for Israel, the mission of which is to help Israel's international diplomacy. In that role Brody speaks to audiences outside Israel about the nation's culture, sports, and myriad achievements.

Larry Brown

A Highly-Successful Basketball Coach

BROWN, LARRY (born September 14, 1940, in Brooklyn, New York–) American basketball coach. More famous for coaching than playing, Brown played basketball for the University of North Carolina in the early 1960s and was then an ABA All-Star for three years. He was ABA Coach of the Year in 1974–75. In 1988, he coached the University of Kansas to an NCAA championship. Brown coached the Detroit Pistons to the 2004 NBA Championship. A stint with the New York Knicks in 2005–2006 culminated in his termination. In 2009, he assumed a coaching position with the Charlotte Bobcats. By the end of the 2008–2009 season, with 1,045 wins, Brown was the fifth most winning coach in NBA history.

■ ■ ■

Larry Brown was only seven years old when his father died of a heart attack. The youngster grew up in a Long Island apartment above his immigrant grandfather's bakery, Hittelman's, which was famous for its cakes and rolls. Larry played on an outdoor basketball court until his mother ended her day at the bakery and called him home for the night.

Always small for his age, Brown made up for that disadvantage by being a superb athlete. His long-time friend, actor Billy Crystal, recalled, "The first basketball game I ever saw Larry in, he scored 44 points. In our little town of 8,000 people, he was the guy. Larry was 5' 9" and for me being 5' 7" and a little bit less, he was my hero. There were two things you could hear in Long Beach at night, the waves hitting the shore and Larry Brown dribbling the ball."

Though far better known as a basketball coach than a player, Brown played college basketball for the University of North Carolina between 1959 and 1963, averaging 11.8 points in 56 varsity games. During a five-year career in the ABA starting in 1967, he played for New Orleans, Oakland, Washington, Virginia, and Denver. In 376 ABA games, he averaged 11.3 points per game. In 47 playoff games, he averaged 14.3 points per game. He was an ABA All-Star guard for three years.

Brown began coaching in the ABA in 1972. His first team, the Cougars, finished first that year and third the next. His record with the Cougars was 104-64. Between 1974 and 1976, he coached the Denver Nuggets, finishing first in the division twice, and in the league once. In 1974–75, Brown was voted ABA Coach of the Year.

From 1976 to 1979 he coached Denver in the NBA and his three-year record was 126-91. His record during the five seasons he coached Denver, ABA and NBA, was 251-134. He won the division titles in the first four seasons and reached the ABA finals in 1976.

In 1979–80, he coached UCLA to a 22-10 season, and the team was ranked fourth in the country. UCLA lost to Louisville in the 1980 NCAA finals. In 1980-81, UCLA had a 20-7 season and was ranked third nationally. Brown returned to the NBA in 1981-82 to coach the New Jersey Nets. His 44-38 record, third in the division, was the Nets' best in six NBA seasons. They lost 0-2 in the opening round of the playoffs to Washington. From 1981-83 Brown's record was 91-67; he reached the playoffs in 1982, then quit the playoff-bound Nets with six games left in 1983 to become head basketball coach at the University of Kansas. Between 1983 and 1988 his record at Kansas was 129-44; he won the NCAA championship in 1988. Danny Manning was the star of that team.

Of utmost importance, says Brown, is gaining the players' trust. "I want to be able to walk into that dressing room and have the players look at me and say to themselves, 'everything that man tells me, it's because he wants me to get better. He treats me with respect and he cares about me as a player. And he can help me do what I want to do.'"

For three and a half seasons—from 1988 to early 1992—Brown coached the NBA San Antonio Spurs with a record of 153-131. He won two division titles, but was fired on January 21, 1992, the first time that had happened to him. Brown found it "pretty damaging" to his pride and dignity.

He was hired by the Los Angeles Clippers of the NBA on February 6, 1992 and signed a five-year contract. Coaching his seventh team, Brown was assailed by one sportswriter who called him a "high-priced itinerant." He disliked the accusation. "I'm proud of the jobs we've done . . . and I'm disappointed that people keep perceiving me as someone who's got to move on."

His arrival gave the Clippers an immediate boost. Ticket sales jumped 20 percent. Brown's work was cut out for him: the Clippers had not won more than 32 games since moving to Los Angeles in 1984. One of Brown's Clippers was former Kansas star Danny Manning whom Brown described as being "like a son" to him.

The Clippers, who had difficulty getting along with coaches in previous years, responded positively to Larry Brown. They respected him for his proven record of turning losing teams into winning ones, and they liked his willingness to let everyone play. It was not unusual for Brown to put nine Clipper players into the game in the first quarter.

"Win or lose, I like this coach, and I mean that," said Clipper owner Donald Sterling. "And I think he'll be with us for a decade."

The Clippers finished the 1991-92 season with a 45-37 record, winding up in fifth place in the Pacific Division of the NBA's Western Conference, good enough to earn a playoff place for the first time in 16 seasons. They were ousted in the first round. He coached the Clippers to a disappointing 41-41 regular-season record in 1992–93, and again they went out in the first round of the playoffs. Brown resigned on May 20, 1993 and three weeks later signed a five-year agreement with the Indiana Pacers, a team that had enjoyed only three winning seasons and had never advanced past the first play-

off round in six appearances since joining the NBA in 1976.

Heeding Brown's defense-first strategy, the team wound up the 1993–94 season at 47-35 before sweeping past the favored Orlando Magic in the playoffs' first round and then ousting the Atlanta Hawks in the Eastern Conference finals; it marked Brown's first second-round playoff triumph since becoming an NBA coach. The Pacers lost to the New York Knicks in the Eastern Conference finals in seven games.

In the 1994–95 season, the Pacers won their first Central Division crown with a 52-30 record and eliminated the Knicks in seven games in the postseason's second round, only to lose to the Orlando Magic in seven games in the Conference finals.

He invariably left a team in better shape than before his arrival. Paul Attner wrote in *The Sporting*

News on May 30, 1994: "He's one of the last of a generation of coaches who yell and prod and provoke, who consider winning, not the feelings of players, to be most important, who have established rules and expect them to be followed without exception, who target their stars for the most verbal abuse."

In the 1995–96 season, the Pacers were again 52-30 but were eliminated by the Atlanta Hawks in five games in the first round of playoffs.

In the 1996–97 season, the Pacers had a lackluster 39-43 record, only the second time in Brown's 25 years of coaching that his team had finished below .500. He resigned as coach on April 30, 1997, after posting a 190-138 record over four seasons for the Pacers.

Five days later Brown was named head coach of the Philadelphia 76ers. In the 2000–2001 season, he led the 76ers to the NBA Finals for the first time in 18 years and was named NBA Coach of the Year. In seven seasons coaching the 76ers, ending in the spring of 2003, Brown posted a 255-205 record along with 26-30 in the playoffs.

Brown resigned from his job with the 76ers on May 26, 2003, and a week later he became head coach of the Detroit Pistons.

Brown has posted a winning record in 28 of his 32 seasons as a professional head coach or collegiate head coach, and he has compiled a 1,285-853 (.601) career record. In twenty-one NBA seasons he has a record of 933-713 (.567), ranking seventh in all-time victories among NBA coaches and second among active coaches.

A highlight of Larry Brown's career came in June 2004, when his Detroit Pistons captured the NBA title against the Los Angeles Lakers. He thus became the first coach to win both a college national championship and the NBA crown. And, at age 63, Brown became the oldest coach to win an NBA title. He also earned the distinction of taking longer than any coach in NBA history, twenty-two years, to capture an NBA championship, easily outpacing Red Auerbach (1957) and Bill Fitch (1981).

The luster of Brown's 2004 season was badly tarnished when the U.S. men's basketball team, which he coached at the Athens Olympics that summer, gained only a bronze medal, tying its worst finish since basketball's Olympic debut in 1936. More tarnish fell on Brown in November 2004, when his team clashed with the Indiana Pacers in the worst brawl in NBA history. "I'm not really excited about doing my job right now," Brown acknowledged soon after the incident.

In 2005, with great optimism, he was appointed head coach of the New York Knicks. But in June 2006, after accumulating a dismal 23–59 record—the second worst in the NBA and equal to the most season losses in the club's history—Brown was fired and replaced with president and general manager Isiah Thomas. During the 2008–2009 season, assuming his ninth NBA coaching job, Brown brought his twenty-three years of experience as a head coach to the Charlotte Bobcats. As of the middle of the 2009–2010 season, Brown had a career total of 1,862 games won and 1,031 games lost, for a .554 percentage.

On December 22, 2010, after Charlotte went 9–19 in the 2010–2011 season, Brown ended his coaching stint with the team—some reporting that he resigned, others that he was fired. Brown's NBA career coaching record was 1,098 wins and 904 losses; his overall career record, including his ABA coaching, was 1,327–1,011.

Angela Buxton

1956 Wimbledon Doubles Champion

BUXTON, ANGELA (born August 16,1934, in Liverpool, England–) British tennis player. The first British woman to reach a Wimbledon final since 1939. In 1956 she was Wimbledon doubles champion (with Althea Gibson).

• • •

Both of Angela's parents were born in Britain. In 1940, during World War II, Angela, then six years old, was evacuated from England, to Capetown, South Africa, together with her mother and brother; her father remained behind. Angela attended a convent school in Johannesburg for four years and while there, at age eight, began playing tennis. She played every day on the convent's tennis courts, instructed by a visiting coach.

When she returned to England in 1946, at age 12, she discovered that she was a far better player than her English contemporaries who, because of the war, had missed out on tennis altogether. Her parents divorced shortly after the war, and Angela and her mother moved to Llandudno, North Wales, where her maternal grandparents were living.

At the school she attended in Llandudno, opportunities to play tennis barely existed. Tennis lessons were given to a few select pupils, Angela included, but only for a half hour a week. But the tennis instructor recognized Angela's potential and advised her parents to enter the youngster in tournaments. Mrs. Buxton asked if he meant Wimbledon. The instructor laughed and suggested starting with lesser tournaments.

Although her father couldn't even score a tennis match, he offered to finance Angela's tennis career.

The first step was to help Angela and her mother move to London in 1950. Angela worked at her tennis and in 1952, she studied for one year at the Polytechnic in London, specializing in domestic science.

Angela played in her first Wimbledon tournament in the spring of 1952. She was one of two players to win a lottery permitting her to play in Wimbledon. The lottery was drawn from players who had lost in the final qualifying round and therefore became known as the "Lucky Loser" lottery. Angela went out in the first round. But she managed to reach the quarterfinals of the Plate event for first-round losers.

Realizing that she needed to improve, Angela convinced her father to send her and her mother to California for six months. The two women chose an apartment overlooking the Los Angeles Tennis Club, but Angela was surprised to find that the club would not permit her to play. She blamed it on anti-Semitism. So, mornings, she played at the La Cienega public courts; afternoons, she worked in Arzy's tennis shop; and nights, she attended typing courses at Fairfax High School. She was coached by Bill Tilden, the great American star, during the last months of his life. Buxton played in a few tournaments, doing well in some. In March 1953, expecting to begin a brilliant career, she returned to England.

In April 1953 she played in the Bournemouth Hardcourt Championships and lost to Doris Hart, the 1952 Wimbledon champion, 6-0, 6-0. She was utterly crushed and felt she had wasted all of her father's money. In the Bournemouth clubhouse, she came upon *Daily Mirror* sportswriter Jimmy Jones, who cautioned her not to read the newspapers the next day. He offered to help her with her tennis, but she declined, figuring he may have had other motives.

Angela had decided to play out the 1953 season and then go into dress designing. By the end of 1953, she obtained a degree in dress designing from the Katinka Dress Designing School of London.

Despite her humiliation at Bournemouth, she

tennis lessons of which he had spoken. The lessons took place at two courts at Lincolns Inns Field behind Cheshire House, where Jones had an office. Jones also ran a tennis magazine. Jones introduced Angela to the psychology of tennis and its tactics (elements of the game she had never considered before). Until then, she had learned only that one had to return the ball over the net.

In December 1953, two months after the lessons began, Angela was defeating opponents whom she had never defeated before. In 1954 she improved so much that she managed to achieve the No. 4 ranking in England by the year's end. No one ever before had come from such total obscurity to so high a rank in so short a time. In 1954 and 1955 she represented Britain in the Wightman Cup matches against the United States. She did not do well in either year, and the U.S. won both times. In 1955 she reached the quarterfinals of the Wimbledon singles, and was ranked No. 9 in the world.

Angela's best year was 1956. She won the English Indoor and Grass championships, as well as the hardcourt doubles title (with Darlene Hard). She also won the doubles (with Althea Gibson) of both Wimbledon and the French Open. Her crowning achievement was reaching the singles final at Wimbledon that year, but she lost the match to the American, Shirley Fry, in the finals.

Wimbledon singles winners have automatically been invited to join the All-England Lawn Tennis Club (Wimbledon), and doubles winners, when they applied, were usually accepted. But Angela's application was refused. She applied in August 1956, and reapplied years later, but was told to wait patiently. Trying to uncover the real answer why she had not been asked, she came up with the conclusion: anti-Semitism.

In June of 1981, on *Nationwide* an English TV program, Angela was asked why she had never been admitted to the club: "I'm Jewish; it's as simple as that." When the chairman of the club was asked the same question, he replied that he did not know and that he had never really looked into the matter. (She again applied for club mem-

worked on improving her tennis. In October 1953, she traveled to Israel for the Maccabiah Games in what she was sure would be her "swan song" (her own phrase) in tennis. To everyone's surprise, Angela defeated Anita Kanter, of California, then ranked eighth in the world, 6-2, 6-3 in the finals. (Kanter had just beaten Doris Hart.) Buxton picked up a second gold medal by winning the Maccabiah doubles.

Sailing back to Europe on the *Artza*, Angela decided that she would look up Jimmy Jones for the

bership in 1996, and again she was turned down.)

In 1956, with great tennis potential in her future, Angela was forced to curtail her playing career prematurely. In August of that year, while playing in a tournament in New Jersey, the wrist on her right (playing) hand suddenly swelled up and had to be placed in a cast for six weeks. She thought she would be able to return to her previous level when she recovered, but discovered that after practicing more than two or three times a week, the injury recurred. In 1957 she did manage to win the coveted French court title, and that same year she won the Maccabiah singles event easily.

Even before her wrist problems began, Buxton had worked for Lillywhites, the famous English sports shop located at Picadilly Circus in London. She worked for them between 1954 and 1958, first as a typist, then as a receptionist. Afterwards, she worked in the shop's tennis department, and later represented the store in India and the U.S.

In February 1959, Buxton married Donald Silk, an attorney. They have three children: Benjamin, Joseph, and Rebecca.

From 1960 to 1967, Angela was involved in dress designing.

Angela Buxton went to Israel after the 1967 Six-Day War, and spent six months there. She considered settling there and setting up a tennis school. But when she returned to England in early 1968, she discovered that her husband, who had been an ardent Zionist until then, did not want to leave England. (She separated from him in 1970.) So she and Jones began the Angela Buxton Center, a tennis school in London's Hampstead section.

Though Angela sold the school in 1988, it retains its original name. She devotes her time to lecturing and feature-writing on tennis. Two favorite lecture topics have been "What It's Like to Play on Center Court at Wimbledon," and "Living on a Kibbutz." She bases that latter talk on her four-month stay at Kibbutz Amiad in the northern Galilee after the 1967 war.

In a newspaper interview in 1997, Angela Buxton recalled how controversial and difficult it had been for her to team up with African-American Althea Gibson during the 1956 Wimbledon doubles tournament. Many Americans, she observed, passed up the opportunity to play for the doubles title rather than partner with an African-American. That worked out fine for Buxton: "Since Althea was black, she was having a difficult time getting a doubles partner in America," Buxton said. "And since I was Jewish, I was having a similar problem in England. So we just hooked up."

In 2004, continuing to serve as a tennis consultant to young players, the 69-year-old Angela Buxton spent half of her time in Florida and the remaining time in London and Cheshire. That same year, in *The Match*, American writer Bruce Schoenfeld told the story of two women—one Jewish (Buxton), one black (Gibson)—both victims of prejudice, who went on to develop a poignant friendship and on-court partnership.

Dan Calichman
Outstanding Defender in Major League Soccer

CALICHMAN, DAN (born February 21, 1968, in Flushing, New York -) American soccer player. An All-American soccer player at Williams College, Dan Calichman traveled to Japan in 1990, where he played professional soccer in Hiroshima for four years. In 1996, he joined the Los Angeles Galaxy, one of the ten teams in the brand-new league called Major League Soccer and became one of the league's best defenders. A broken leg in May 1998 forced him out of play for a substantial part of his third season. He ended his professional soccer career in 2001 and began coaching at a men's college.

• • •

Soccer, far more popular in Europe and other parts of the world than in the United Sates, gained recognition as a professional sport in America in the 1990s. Dan Calichman, born in Flushing, New York, in 1968 and raised in Huntington Station, New York, has become one of America's top soccer stars.

Friends of Dan's parents decided to encourage their children to play soccer. The sport had just gained some popularity at the Huntington YMCA. Dan, who was six years old at the time, wanted to play as many sports as possible. "I started with soccer but grew up with a baseball mitt in my hands," he said in an interview. His earliest days in soccer were with the Long Island Junior Soccer League.

At Walt Whitman High School in South Huntington, New York, he was captain of three teams—soccer, basketball, and lacrosse. In his senior year, he was all-Long Island in soccer.

Dan played the central midfielder position, from which he could play offense or defense. He enjoyed the position "because that's where the most action is all the time."

In the fall of 1986, he entered Williams College, where he majored in history and played soccer and lacrosse, captaining both teams. In his final three years at the school, he was first-team All-American in soccer. In his sophomore and junior years, Williams won the East Coast Athletic Conference title. Though he was certainly talented enough to become a pro soccer player, Dan entertained few thoughts of playing pro soccer.

Yet, in the spring of 1990, as he was finishing his senior year of college, he jumped at an opportunity to play in a professional soccer league in Japan. At the time, the one American professional soccer league would not have afforded him a decent living.

Dan's brother Richard, who had been living in Japan, had met the coach of a professional Japanese soccer team. The coach was permitted to use three non-Japanese players on his team. Phoning his brother, Richard asked Dan if he wanted to play pro soccer in Japan. Thrilled at the prospect, Dan visited Japan for two weeks. He was offered a very generous one-year contract to begin playing that summer for the Mazda soccer club in Hiroshima, Japan. Graduating from Williams in June, Dan was off to Hiroshima a month later. He noted, "The pay was excellent for a 22-year-old kid just out of college. At Williams, students were getting $10,000 as signing bonuses to become investment bankers, and what I was paid dwarfed what they got."

He remained in Japan for four years. For the first two years, 1990 and 1991, he played for the Mazda team. Faring well that first season, the team was promoted from the second to first division. The following year, Mazda came in fifth in the ten-member league and was elevated to the new J League of Japanese soccer.

In Calichman's third and fourth years in Japan, 1992 and 1993, he played for the Hiroshima San Frecce Football team, coming in fifth place in the ten-team league.

The only American to play in the J League until then, he became quite popular in Hiroshima. "They made me a Brazilian. I was called simply 'Danny.'" He recalled that interest in Japanese soccer grew dramatically during his four years there. At first only 500 people showed up for the games, but by Calichman's final season, 50,000 were attending on weekends, 20,000 on weekdays.

Thrilled to be playing professional soccer, Calichman enjoyed the Japanese experience. "It didn't matter where I was. I loved the lifestyle of training and playing. Getting paid to play soccer was unbelievable."

At the start of his fourth year, he announced to the San Frecce coach that he planned to return to the United States at the season's end. He had accomplished what he had set out to do—play professional soccer. He had built up a nice nest egg, and so he felt it was time to focus on the non-soccer aspects of his life, which he had put on hold while in Japan. He thought about studying to become a veterinarian and regretted not having taken a course in biol-

ogy, even though its afternoon lab sessions would have kept him from soccer practice.

Returning to the United States in early 1994, Calichman was aware of plans to organize the new Major League Soccer, but no one had contacted him about joining the league. He traveled to England and remained for two weeks in the hope of playing soccer there. When he failed to obtain a working visa, he moved on to Sweden but was too late to participate, as the Swedes were just completing their soccer season.

Again returning to the United States, he at-

tended Harvard's summer school, taking that biology course that he hoped would get him accepted to veterinarian school. Meanwhile, he attended some World Cup soccer games played in Foxboro, Massachusetts, near Boston.

The following spring and summer of 1995, he began playing for the New York Centaurs in the eight-member pro soccer A League. The Centaurs finished in last place in the leagues, but it provided Dan with a chance to gain some exposure throughout the United States as an up-and-coming professional soccer player. After all, because he had played in Japan, American coaches didn't know how well he actually played.

One of the A League coaches, Lothar Osiander, coach of the Atlanta Ruckus, took notice of Calichman. At season's end, September 1995, Osiander became head coach of the Los Angeles Galaxy in the newly created Major League Soccer, set to begin in early 1996. In December 1995, Osiander sought out Calichman and asked him to play for the Galaxy. Calichman agreed and was signed to a three-year contract.

He began playing for the team in January 1996 and was chosen captain. In that first season, the team went on a 12-0 opening run. By the time the season was over, it had won the five-team Western Conference, with a record of 19-11. Winning the playoffs, the Galaxy lost the championship game in October 1996 to the Washington, D.C. United, 3-2, in Foxboro. Ironically, Calichman was barred from the championship game, as he had too many yellow (penalty) cards during the playoffs. He was named to the Major League All-Star team for the Western Conference, and *USA Today* voted him the best defender in the MLS for 1996.

Calichman's Galaxy got off to a poor start in its second season in January 1997 with a 3-11 run; but it came first in the league, winning its final six games. The season ended for Calichman's team when it was knocked out of the playoffs by the Dallas Burn. In that year, Dan played six times for the American national team.

The third season began in January 1998 and was much better for the Galaxy as it embarked on an 8-0 streak. Calichman, however, broke his right leg in the eighth game in May 1998 and was out for much of the season. Three months later, in August 1998, he married Ruth Ksarjian. They have two children.

Playing for the New England Revolution in the 1999–2000 season, Dan Calichman was voted by fans the team's best defender and MVP. In May 2000, he was traded to the San Jose Earthquakes, playing for that team in 2000 and 2001. In 2001, happy to return to a league in which he had played earlier, Calichman spent his last active soccer season with the Charleston Battery in the A League.

Dan embarked upon a career as coach of men's college soccer in 2004 at California's Claremont McKenna College. Since 2007, he has also been the Director of Player Development for the Los Angeles Futbol Club Chelsea (LAFC), a soccer organization that seeks to guide young people of all races and economic stations to a brighter future.

Omri Casspi

The First Israeli to Play in the NBA

CASSPI, OMRI (born June 22, 1988, in Holon, Israel–) Israeli basketball player. Drafted by the Sacramento Kings in June 2009, Casspi became the first Israeli to play in the National Basketball Association. In the first half of his inaugural season, 2009–2010, Casspi was one of the top NBA rookies, averaging 12.5 points per game.

. . .

In 1990, two-year-old Omri and the rest of the Casspi family moved to Lima, Peru, where father Shimon, a private investigator, had accepted employment. The Casspis returned to Holon in 1992 and moved to the Israeli town of Yavne a year later.

Omri's first sport was karate, but the aggressive five-year-old kept hitting and hurting his friends, so Shimon and his wife, Ilana, a high school teacher, decided to be prudent and switch their son to basketball. As a youngster, Omri played for Maccabi basketball teams, first in Yavne, then in Rishon LeZion. He played with the Upper Galilee Maccabi team for one year, displaying uncommon talent. When Omri was but twelve years old, his father predicted that one day he would play in the NBA.

The elder Casspi tried unsuccessfully to secure a spot for his son on the Maccabi Tel Aviv basketball team. Despite the rejection, Shimon assured Omri that eventually he would reverse that fortune. And so he did. The 6-foot 9-inch, 222-pound Israeli played in the Euroleague with Maccabi Tel Aviv for four years, 2005–2009. In May 2009, Omri contributed to Maccabi Tel Aviv's triumphant win over Maccabi Haifa for the Basketball Super League title.

Many Israeli basketball stars have dreamed of playing in the NBA, and some have come close. In 1979, Mickey Berkowitz (page 311) was invited to play for the Atlanta Hawks, which would have made him Israel's first NBA player. But that dream was dashed when Maccabi Tel Aviv refused to release him from his contract. Nadav Heneman and Doron Sheffer appeared NBA-bound, but they fell short. Oded Katash agreed to terms with the New York Knicks in the summer of 1998, but the lengthy NBA lockout prevented him from joining the team.

Omri Casspi first impressed the Sacramento Kings with his intelligence and athleticism when playing for the World Select Team at the 2007 Nike Hoop Summit, in Memphis, Tennessee. But not until completing his obligatory three-year

with the Kings guarantees an annual salary of $1.2 million.

Sacramento selected Casspi twenty-third in the 2009 draft, making him the first Israeli ever to be picked in the first round and virtually assuring his becoming the first Israeli to play in the NBA. Sitting in his parents' living room in Yavne, watching the draft on television, Omri wept when he heard NBA Commissioner David Stern call his name. Stern's smile seemed broader than usual, perhaps because Stern himself is Jewish (see page 269). The next day Omri flew to Sacramento.

Some of Omri's fellow Israelis were irked at his departure for the United States. The media labeled him selfish for abandoning his country's national team. Former coaches and basketball analysts predicted that Omri would fail at Sacramento because his was not an NBA game, that he was not ready for the best league in the world. Those critics seemed prescient when, playing in the Las Vegas summer league in July 2009, Omri shot only 29.5 percent from the field, hardly the performance of a promising NBA player.

When Casspi first hit the court in Sacramento in October 2009, fans waved Israeli flags and held Hebrew signs aloft. Spurred on by the reception and determined to prove that he belonged in the league, Casspi shot an impressive 7 of 8 from the field in the team's first two preseason games, averaging 8 points in 13 minutes. In his first official game with the Kings, Omri scored 15 points.

Omri Casspi got his first start in the NBA on December 16, 2009, scoring a career-high 22 points; he also had five rebounds and put in a crucial late-game three-pointer, the difference in the Kings' 112–109 victory. From December 16, 2009 to January 6, 2010, he averaged 17.5 points per game and raised his season average from 11.1 to 13.2 points per game.

On December 31, 2009, *The Jerusalem Post* named Omri Casspi its Israeli Sports Personality of 2009.

service in the Israel Defense Forces could he even contemplate playing for the NBA. His release from the IDF came just before the NBA's June 2009 draft.

Word surfaced that Omri had been a sniper in the Israeli army, prompting Kings scouting director Scotty Sterling to comment: "So how much pressure can be on him now? . . . He wasn't in combat, but he said they taught him to shoot a rifle. But he said he'd rather shoot a basketball than a rifle." Casspi quickly corrected the record: "I don't know where that rumor started. I wasn't a sniper. . . . I was in basic training. But I did hold a gun, and I shot a lot."

At one point, Omri was offered to play in Europe for $3.5 million a year, but his father urged him to say no, suggesting that he would make ten times that amount in the NBA. "The NBA is your dream," Shimon reminded his son. "Go for your dream. The money will come." Omri's contract

On February 15, 2010, two days after scoring 13 points to help the NBA rookie All-Star team defeat the sophomore team 140–128, Casspi described his NBA experience: "It's a good feeling, but it was never a goal to be the first Israeli player. Since I was young, I dreamt about the NBA. There is a lot of responsibility to being the first. I am not only representing myself, but I am representing basketball in Israel, my country, and the Jewish people in the States. Now the [Israeli] kids can dream about playing in the NBA, because we've got somebody over here."

During Casspi's early days in Sacaramento, close relatives could often be seen rooting him on from the stands: brother Eitan, sister Aviv, father Shimon, mother Ilana, grandfather Eli, grandmother Mati. Two Israeli flags flew high above, as they would at every Sacramento Kings home game at Shimon Casspi's request. Noting that Omri was wearing the number 18 for *chai*, the family glowed with pride.

Casspi's critics were proved wrong when Omri surpassed his Euroleague career-highs in many categories in the first half of the 2009–2010 season. "I didn't come [to the NBA] to fail and sit on the bench," he said. "If I didn't believe I could do well, I wouldn't have bothered coming here." How does he explain doing better in the NBA than in the EuroLeague? "I'm just 21 and am improving all the time."

Acknowledging that the NBA presented him with new challenges, Casspi noted that "the NBA courts are larger, which was different for me at first, but I got used to it." The biggest challenge, though, has been the NBA schedule. "I used to play about 15 games in a European season, so I would have a lot of time to prepare compared to the 82-game season in the NBA. You've got to make adjustments very quickly, because one day you go up against LeBron James, and then Kobe Bryant a few days later. You don't get a whole week to prepare for a single game, but that's life here and you get used to it."

Another difference is the fans: "NBA fans come to see a show and get a family experience: jerseys thrown to the stands, posing with basketball stars for photos, mascots and halftime spectacles. And Sacramento fans are the best in the NBA. In Maccabi, the fans come for a war."

How does a Jewish rookie in the NBA practice his religion? "It's tough with all the travel and games, but Sacramento has a very good Jewish community, as does almost every city we travel to. My family came here for Chanukah, and we celebrated with the community. We lit the Chanukah candles together even though it wasn't easy to be away from Israel."

In his second season (2010–2011), Casspi started 27 games for Sacramento, averaging 8.6 points and 4.3 rebounds for the entire season. In his two seasons with Sacramento, he averaged 9.5 points and 4.4 rebounds. In June 2011, he was traded to the Cleveland Cavaliers.

Howard Cosell
The Most Famous Talker in America

COSELL, HOWARD (born March 25, 1918, in Winston-Salem, North Carolina; died April 23, 1995) American sports broadcaster. A sportscaster for ABC from 1956 until 1985, Cosell revolutionized the profession by going beyond simple play-by-play to render strong opinions on players and issues. Described as "the most dominant sportscasting personality of his time," Cosell has also been dubbed the most famous talker in America.

. . .

Born Howard William Cohen, he changed his last name to Cosell. Howard grew up in Brooklyn, where his father, Isadore Cohen, a Jewish immigrant from Poland, was an accountant for a chain of clothing stores.

Howard hoped to become a newspaper reporter but his parents urged him to enter law school. He attended New York University, became Phi Beta Kappa and editor of the *Law Review*, and graduated in 1940. He began to practice law but in December 1941 enlisted in the U. S. Army as a private.

Cosell spent the war commuting by subway to the New York Port of Embarkation on the Brooklyn docks where he was in charge of a manpower pool of 50,000 soldiers. In 1944, he married Mary Edith Abrams, a WAC sergeant. They had two daughters: Jill and Hillary. Discharged from the army in 1946, Cosell had little interest in returning to the law, but with no better choice, he spent the next eight years as an attorney.

In 1953, an ABC program manager asked him to provide a panel of youngsters who were to interview athletes for a weekly series of coast-to-coast programs over WABC Radio. Asked to serve with-

out pay as a moderator of "All League Clubhouse," he jumped at the chance. To lure baseball players on to the show, Cosell staked out hotel lobbies, buttonholing the stars and tempting them with free lunches. "We made news with that show," Cosell later said. "Out of the mouths of babes came words of wisdom and depth!" Once, under Cosell's careful prodding, the youngsters pressured New York Yankee outfielder Hank Bauer into scolding his own manager Casey Stengel for not playing him enough. One panelist was future sportscaster Marv Albert. He remembered Cosell calling Albert's home to make sure he would appear for the program.

Three years later, in 1956, ABC offered Cosell $250 to do ten five-minute sports broadcasts each weekend. Bored by the slow pace of his law practice, Cosell decided to take up broadcasting full-time. "My disposition," he told his wife, "demands the immediacy of translation of effort into result." His wife advised him, "So, go translate."

By the early 1960s, Howard Cosell sought to gain greater recognition as a broadcaster. Moderating pre-game and post-game shows over ABC during the first two seasons of the then-hapless New York Mets, he campaigned for the dismissal of manager Casey Stengel. ABC eventually chose to drop the Mets. "We didn't want to be identified with a loser," explained Cosell.

Thanks to the vocal support he gave to controversial heavyweight boxer Cassius Clay in the 1960s, Howard Cosell gained substantial public notice—as well as condemnation. Not everyone took Clay seriously when, after turning Muslim, he changed his name to Muhammed Ali. Cosell did, allowing Ali to gain respect at a crucial point in the fighter's life.

When Cosell draped his arm around the boxer and agreed to refer to him as Muhammed Ali, some of Cosell's more conservative audience bristled. A northern newspaper referred to Howard as a "White Muslim," and white supremacists and parents of servicemen penned nasty letters to the broadcaster. Moreover, Cosell became Ali's most vocal defender when in 1967 the boxer was stripped of his heavyweight title for refusing to be inducted into the U.S. Army during the Vietnam war.

Cosell insisted that he covered Ali fairly, not overlooking his flaws. After all, it had been he who had assailed Ali's Muslim followers for their rudeness; and it had been Cosell who had cut off the heavyweight champion in mid-sentence during one of Ali's eulogies to his teacher, Elijah. "Awright," Cosell broke in, "we've been through that."

Their relationship cooled after Ali's fight with Ernie Terrell. On *Wide World of Sports*, Ali insisted that Cosell defend him against accusations that he had taunted and fouled Terrell. Cosell refused, shouting at Ali. Letter writers then accused Howard of picking on Ali and of being anti-black!

The sportscaster did not refrain from delivering his opinions over the air. He championed Curt Flood's case against Major League Baseball's reserve clause; he lashed out at boxing for being brutal and corrupt; he assailed college sports for cheating and academic abuse; and he argued that the Olympics had become commercialized. "I'm a man of causes," he wrote in his book, *I Never Played the Game*, published in 1985. "My real fulfillment in broadcasting has always come from crusading journalism, fighting for the rights of people."

In the mid-70s, he taught a course at Yale University called "Big Time Sports in Contemporary America." The subjects ranged from "Do Sociological Realities Confirm Jean Paul Sartre's Views of Sport?" to "The Louisiana Superdome and Municipal Funding of Stadiums."

In 1970, Howard Cosell became the outspoken commentator on ABC-TV's *Monday Night Football*, a job he kept for the next 14 years. Because of Cosell, *Monday Night Football* became a major factor in popularizing the National Football League. Cosell seemed all wrong for television, "overeducated, odd in appearance, a nasal voice. Yet with that staccato delivery, he demanded the audience's attention," is how sportswriter Norman Chad put it.

Cosell was the first sportscaster to take athletes seriously. Brash, even insolent, at news conferences he asked the sharpest questions. "There is no way you will ever hear me saying"—he lowered his voice to a whisper, mimicking golf broadcasters—'This is Howard Cosell on the 16th green . . . 420 yards to the pin, with a dogleg to the left.'" Howard did not whisper while on the air. "I've brought to this business, the direct, honest and total reporting that previously has been the sole province of the press." Yet, he was a sensitive man. He refused, for instance, to give out ball scores the day after Robert F. Kennedy was assassinated in June 1968.

He believed that his sportscasting had "made" athletes into television stars—and sometimes he told them so. Once, he needed Los Angeles Dodger pitching star Sandy Koufax to redo an interview because of a technical hitch. Koufax refused until Howard reminded him: "You were a little nothing sitting in the corner of the Brooklyn dugout when I used to come around and talk to you." And,

former heavyweight boxing champion Sonny Liston turned to Cosell, after hearing the broadcaster describe him on the air as a congenital thug, and barked, "You ain't my friend." Cosell replied that he was correct!

Never working from a script, Cosell ad libbed, exhibiting great self-confidence. "I really believe I'm the best. My relationship with the men who play the games—all games—is probably unparalleled in this country." He had few kind words for sports broadcasting: "There are two professions in which one can be hired with little experience," he said in November 1978. "One is prostitution. The other is sportscasting. Too frequently, they become the same." Sportscasters, in his view, too often gave the public "pabulum." Howard believed they did not work hard enough at getting at the news in sports and they did not tell it like it is—as did Howard.

During the 1980s, Cosell lost respect for some of the sports he had covered. In 1982, he ceased doing boxing commentary, disgusted with what he called "the hypocrisy and sleaziness of the boxing scene." When he left *Monday Night Football* in 1984 he said: "Pro football has become a stagnant bore."

Angered and upset by the 1972 terrorist slaying of 11 Israeli athletes at the Munich Olympics, Cosell stepped up his efforts on behalf of Israel, and, specifically, Jerusalem's Hebrew University.

In 1986, the Hebrew University's Center for Physical Education was named after Cosell and his wife Mary Edith.

During the summer of 1991, he had two operations to remove a malignant tumor from his chest. Retiring in February 1992, he gave up his daily show for ABC Radio, "Speaking of Sports," a two-minute program broadcast daily over 200 stations. He also gave up his weekly interview program, "Speaking of Everything," a half-hour program over 100 stations.

Upon his retirement *Time* magazine described him as "one of the most liked—and disliked—sports journalists in the U.S." *People* magazine called him "irascible" and "incurably polysyllabic."

Sportswriter Robert Lipsyte of *The New York Times* wrote: "Unlike most sports journalists who disdain athletes as 'jimbos,' air-headed men to be rubbed up until they're rubbed out, Cosell took athletes seriously, expected them to be responsible, and asked them intelligent questions…He was smarter, worked harder, and was luckier than most everyone else…Cosell was symbol, know-it-all uncle, stern coach, comic relief."

When Cosell was asked if there was anyone to whom he could pass the torch, he glared and said he did not think anyone could cover the range of topics he had covered with the same intelligence or morality.

In its September 1994 issue, *Sports Illustrated* voted Cosell the 22nd most important sports figure (out of 40) of the previous 40 years. He was the sole Jewish sports figure on the list. Howard Cosell died at the age of 77 on April 23, 1995.

On January 30, 2009, David J. Halberstam, a former broadcaster and Executive Vice President of Westwood One Sports, chose Cosell as number one on his list of the Top 50 All-Time Network Television Sports Announcers on Yahoo! Sports.

Harry Danning

The New York Giants Outstanding Jewish Player

DANNING, HARRY "THE HORSE" (born September 6, 1911, in Los Angeles, California–) American baseball player. Considered to be the best Jewish player to play for the New York Giants. In 890 games, he hit .285.

. . .

Harry's older brother Ike was an inspiration to him. Ike played as a catcher for the St. Louis Browns in only two games in 1928, but it was enough to encourage Harry to be a catcher.

For a while, Danning was a rug salesman. His baseball interest was sparked when his brother Ike was doing well at semipro baseball in Mexico. Harry decided that he, too, would play there, and he did so successfully.

In 1931, Harry got into organized ball in the United States by signing with the Bridgeport team in the Eastern League where he hit .324. The following year (1932) he got off to a quick start, hitting .320. In midseason, he moved to Winston-Salem (North Carolina) of the Piedmont League. There, he became the regular catcher and finished the season at .313.

In 1933 Harry moved up to the International League and became the starting catcher for the Buffalo Bisons, hitting .349 for half a season's play. He reached the major leagues midway through the 1933 season, playing for the New York Giants.

For the rest of the 1933 season, Danning was on the bench, where he watched the Giants participate in the World Series. The National League pennant-winning Giants of 1933 had two veteran catchers, Gus Mancuso and Paul Richards, and

Harry couldn't displace either of them. In 1934 he was used, but only sparingly. In 53 games, he hit .330.

When the next two years followed the same pattern, Harry grew unhappy playing second-string catcher to Mancuso. In 1937, Danning asked Giants' manager, Bill Terry, for a chance to catch. Terry's Giants had failed to win pennants in 1934 or 1935, and Danning was a stronger hitter than Mancuso, so Terry relented. The Giants' pitching staff at that time had such stars as Hal Schumacher, Fred Fitzsimmons, and Carl Hubbell.

On June 9, 1937, Danning hit a two-run homer to help the Giants defeat the St. Louis Cardinals in New York's Polo Grounds. That homer gave Harry the chance to play regularly. On July 13, he hit a homer in each game of a doubleheader, showing his power. By July 24, he had become a regular, catching the next 35 games in a row.

In the 1937 World Series against the New York Yankees, Harry split the catching chores with Mancuso. Harry was the batting star of the fourth game, going three for four to help beat the Yankees. (The Yankees won the Series four games to one.) The following season, Danning became the team's number-one catcher.

For the next four years (1938 to1941) Harry caught at least 120 games each season. In 1938, he hit .306; in 1939, .313; and in 1940, .300. In one game on June 15, 1940, he hit a single, double, triple, and home run.

Danning served in the U.S. Army during World War II, and when he was discharged, announced that he was retiring from baseball.

It was sports announcer Ted Husing, a reader of Damon Runyon, who created the character named "Harry the Horse." Husing, thinking of the Runyon character, gave the nickname to Harry, and it stuck.

After retirement, Harry Danning went into the automobile business in Los Angeles, his hometown. One of the oldest living Jewish athletes, Danning was living in Valparaiso, Indiana, in 2004.

Al Davis

Mastermind of the Los Angeles Raiders

DAVIS, AL (born July 4, 1929, in Brockton, Massachusetts–) American football coach and owner. Starting in 1963, and lasting for two decades, Davis built the Oakland Raiders into a football powerhouse that had won more games and lost less than any other team in professional football up to that time. They garnered three Super Bowl championships (1977, 1981, 1984) and emerged victorious in more than 70 percent of their games. After moving to Los Angeles, the Raiders had some triumphant years, including a 1983 Super Bowl victory, and some mediocre ones, especially during the late 1980s.

∎ ∎ ∎

Al Davis' career began in Brooklyn, New York. His father, Louis Davis, owned a clothing store and other businesses. Al considered his father a brilliant, competitive, and politically conservative man. He was pleased that his father always encouraged him to think for himself.

Growing up in Brooklyn was not without difficulties. Davis had to cope with street gang fights, and he learned early that it is much better to win than to be beaten up.

At Erasmus High School in Brooklyn, Davis played football, baseball, and basketball and was chosen the most popular boy in his senior class (1947). Upon graduation, he attended Wittenberg College in Ohio on an athletic scholarship, but then transferred to Syracuse University in upstate New York where he played football, basketball, and baseball. He graduated in 1950.

Al's family wanted him to go into business, but Al wanted to be a football coach. So at age 21, in the fall of 1950, he joined the football staff at Adelphi University, in Garden City, New York. He distinguished himself there by becoming the first coach to advocate a four-man line in football. His idea was not readily acceptable at that time, but since then it has become widely accepted.

In addition to coaching, Al published technical articles in coaching magazines which gained attention from other coaches.

Davis joined the U.S. army in 1952 and was assigned to organize a football team at Fort Belvoir, Virginia. His team was so good, it beat the national college champion, University of Maryland, in a practice game.

In the years that followed, Al scouted for the Baltimore Colts of the National Football League and served as coach at The Citadel, a college in Charleston, South Carolina. In 1957, he moved to the University of Southern California where he became assistant coach responsible for the line.

Davis was a fanatic about studying game films, and often could be seen with a film projector under his arm on his way to study the replay of a game. He remained with USC until 1959.

In 1960, the American Football League, financed by millionaire Lamar Hunt, began its first season. Sid Gillman, coach of the Los Angeles Chargers, hired Davis as offensive coach.

During the early 1960s, the Oakland Raiders were not having much success. They won only two games in 1961 and in 1962 won one and lost 13. In an attempt to turn this around, Davis was brought in from the Chargers to become head coach of the Raiders. He insisted on full control, which meant becoming general manager as well. He was given full reign, and overnight the Raiders shocked their fans by posting a 10-4 record, second only to San Diego's 11-3 record that season.

For the next 18 years, except for the first year, the Raiders suffered only one losing season (in 1964). And even in that year, when they failed to win in their first six games, it was because of injuries, with the Raiders bouncing back to win five of their last eight games.

Davis reacted to the 1964 season by signing eight of his first 10 draft choices, thereby helping the club return to a respectable 8-5-1 record in 1965, again coming in second to San Diego.

In April 1966, Davis became commissioner of the American Football League (which had been founded in 1959). For six years a bitter struggle ensued between the fledgling AFL and NFL as they competed for players. Davis was particularly interested in wooing star quarterbacks from the NFL. When the AFL owners negotiated a merger of the two leagues, Pete Rozelle, the NFL commissioner, not Davis, was named commissioner of the newly-formed National Football League. Davis returned to Oakland in his former roles of coach and general manager. Some have argued that Davis has never been satisfied with the merger, wishing that the AFL were still independent.

In 1968, the Oakland Raiders lost to the Green Bay Packers 33-14 in the Super Bowl game at the Orange Bowl in Miami, Florida. For six years in the 1970s (1970, 1972, 1973, 1974, 1975, and 1976), Oakland won the Western Division, but lost in the playoffs. But, in 1977, the jinx was finally broken and Oakland finally won its first Super Bowl, defeating the Minnesota Vikings 32-14 at the Rose Bowl, in Pasadena, California.

First as head coach and general manager and then as principal owner of the Raiders (he holds 25 percent of the stock) Davis built Raider teams that were aggressive and physical, violent, as well as technically sophisticated.

Davis developed what he calls "pressure football," which includes a solid running game that focuses mostly on the long pass. He pioneered the use of the "bump and run" by receivers. He also developed such strong-armed quarterbacks as Tom Flores, Frank Davidson, Daryle Lamonica, George Blanda, and Kenny Stabler.

He is sensitive about aspersions that he interferes with the day-to-day running of the team. When an article appeared in a Miami newspaper in January 1968, which suggested that Davis was undermining the authority of his coach, Johnny Rauch, Davis sent a messenger to buy up all the newspapers on the stand so Rauch wouldn't see it.

Davis, who believes in taking castoffs and building these players into a winning team, claims that he got the idea by reading Theodore Dreiser, especially *Sister Carrie*. He believes that people respond to the pressures of their environment and change in keeping with their surroundings. In *Sister Carrie* a wealthy businessman who fell on hard times was rejected by his poor girlfriend who had become wealthy. Davis reflected that the girl rejected the man because his environment had changed. Similarly, football players can fare poorly on one team (not get along with a coach, develop an image of being lazy or a troublemaker), but when their environment is changed, Davis says, and players join a new team with a new coach, they often become self-confident again and even Super Bowl heroes.

The Davis record at Oakland is a story of triumph after triumph. In 20 years, Al's teams have had only two losing seasons. His overall record (through the 1982 season) had been 194-78-11. In 1982, the Raiders led the American Football Conference at 8-1, but then lost the conference semifinal playoff to the New York Jets 17-14.

Davis had tried to move his team from Oakland to Los Angeles where the potential pay-TV market for professional football was thought to be enormous. (He wanted to play in the Los Angeles Memorial Coliseum which the Los Angeles Rams had vacated in 1979.) The NFL objected to Davis' plans suggesting that chaos would result if individual owners could simply move teams wherever and whenever they wanted. The dispute went to the courts. There was a mistrial in 1981. But, on May 7, 1982, a Federal District Court in Los Angeles, retrying the case, sided with Davis, ruling that the NFL had no right to keep the Raiders from moving to Los Angeles. On August 29, the Oakland Raiders became the Los Angeles Raiders.

In 1983, the Raiders were 12-4, and won the Super Bowl on January 22, 1984, defeating the Washington Redskins 38-9. In 1984, Davis and the Raiders had another good year, 11-5; Los Angeles lost to Seattle in the AFC Wildcard Playoff 13-7. And again in 1985, the Raiders had an excellent season, finishing 12-4 and winning the Western Division before losing to New England 27-20 in the AFC playoffs.

Starting in 1986, however, the Davis magic began to fade. The Raiders were 8-8 that year, 5-10 in 1987, 7-9 in 1988, and 8-9 in 1989. A revival occurred in 1990 as the Raiders completed the season at 12-4, winning the AFC playoff by defeating Cincinnati 20-10 before losing to Buffalo 51-3 for the AFC Championship. The Raiders were 9-7 in 1991.

In early 1992, Davis was elected to the Pro Football Hall of Fame, one of five Jews to be so honored. The others are Sid Gillman, Sid Luckman, Ronald Mix, and Marv Levy. "I said many times that it should have happened a long time ago," Davis said after hearing of the decision to admit him.

Davis left football only once: when his wife Carol had a massive heart attack in 1979 and went into a coma. He moved into the hospital during that football season and turned the team over to coach Tom Flores. After she recovered, Davis reminded her that he had once told her that only a matter of life and death would take him away from football, but he had not expected her to put him to the test.

In 1992, Davis was inducted into the Pro Sports Hall of Fame.

In the mid and late 1990s, Davis' Raiders teams have had mixed results. The Los Angeles Raiders were 7-9 in 1992; 10-6 in 1993, losing to the Buffalo Bills in the AFC Division Playoffs; and 9-7 in 1994. Having moved back to Oakland for the 1995 season, the Raiders were 8-8 that year, but 7-9 in 1996 and only 4-12 in 1997.

In 1997, Davis sued the Oakland-Alameda County Coliseum for $1 billion for allegedly luring him from Los Angeles back to Oakland by falsely promising packed stadiums. He finally testified in the court case in June 2003, and deliberations were ongoing as of August of that year.

In January 2003, despite the fact that his Raiders lost to the Tampa Bay Buccaneers in the Super Bowl, Davis retained his status as one of professional football's most successful leaders, with three Super Bowl championships and the best winning percentage in pro football since 1963. Ironically, in the 2004 season Oakland had a miserable 4-12 record, the worst ever collapse by a team that had reached the Super Bowl the previous year. In their first nine games of the 2004 season, the Raiders were 3-6.

In 2007, eighty-year-old Davis sold a minority stake in the Raiders for $150 million and stated that he would not retire until he wins two more Super Bowls or dies.

Barney Dreyfuss
A Great Innovative Baseball Executive

DREYFUSS, BARNEY (born February 23, 1865, in Freiberg, Germany; died February 5, 1932) American baseball executive. Owner of the Pittsburgh Pirates from 1900 to 1932, creator of the modern World Series, and builder of the major leagues' first stadium. At the time of his death he was vice president of the National League as well as Pirates' owner.

• • •

The slightly-built Dreyfuss was born in Germany, but his father was an American citizen. To avoid being conscripted into the German army, Barney came to the U.S. when he was 16, settling in Paducah, Kentucky. Finding work at the Bernheim whiskey distillery there, he cleaned whiskey barrels at first. Soon, his innate intelligence was recognized and he was assigned an office position. In time, he became the distillery's head bookkeeper.

Dreyfuss worked nine hours a day, and then studied English and other subjects until midnight. He soon suffered from headaches, poor digestion, and a generally run-down condition. A doctor, concerned about the new immigrant's poor health, suggested that Dreyfuss take up outdoor activity. Barney chose baseball and soon organized a semi-pro team and played second base.

In 1900, the distillery moved to Louisville, Kentucky, and so did Barney Dreyfuss. He obtained part ownership of the American Association team, the Louisville Colonels, then a major league club. He was elected treasurer of the club in 1890 and became its president nine years later.

In 1899, Dreyfuss acquired the Pittsburgh Pirates and served as owner and general manager of the team until his death. From Louisville, he brought such great baseball stars as Honus Wagner, Fred Clarke, and Rube Waddell, all Hall-of-Famers, to Pittsburgh.

Dreyfuss ran the Pirates without delegating much authority. He was his own scout. He carried with him a little black book filled with the names of minor league players and their statistics—at least those whom he considered potential players for his Pittsburgh team. Dreyfuss was considered the best judge of baseball talent at the time.

By nature, Dreyfuss had little tolerance for losing. "We are a first-division town," he would say, "and I'm a first-division club owner." More often than not he was right. In his 32 years as Pirates owner, his clubs finished in the first division 26 times and landed in the second division (which he considered a sin) only six times. Before he came to Pittsburgh in 1900, the Pirates had never won a National League pennant.

Barney soon changed that. Under his stewardship, the Pirates won six National League pennants—in 1901, 1902, 1903, 1909, 1925, and 1927. They also won the World Series twice: in 1909 and 1925.

In 1903, Dreyfuss arranged the first modern World Series. The Boston Pilgrims, the American League champions, accepted his challenge to meet the National League champion team in a post-season tournament. Boston won that first eight-game Series (it is now seven games), but the Pirate players earned more money than their rivals. In addition to receiving their players' shares for participating in the Series, they were given an extra amount which Dreyfuss contributed from the club's own receipts. Hence, each Pirate wound up with the sum of $1,316 against the Boston share of $1,182 per man.

In 1909, Dreyfuss built Forbes Field which could seat 25,000 spectators. It was the first of the modern triple-tier ballparks. Construction started March 1st and the first game was played June 30th. The stadium was located in Pittsburgh's choice

Oakland neighborhood. Barney faced cynicism at first. "When I first selected the Forbes Field site for a new ballpark," he recalled, "people laughed at me. They said I'd never fill our 25,000 seats, but I knew better. One friend bet me a $150 suit that the park would never be filled, but he was wrong." On opening day, 30,338 fans packed the stadium (extra room had to be found by blocking off part of the outfield with rope). In the first five weeks, the park was filled another four times.

Dreyfuss forbade advertisements inside the ballpark to preserve the stadium's beauty. However, during World War I, he yielded to pressure from the government and allowed war-bond posters to be mounted. Hating what he called "cheap homers," Barney had left field extended in 1918. To do this, he had to lease land from the City of Pittsburgh and blast out the concrete wall which had been put up in 1909.

Barney Dreyfuss was also a pioneer in pro football. He was the co-owner and manager of the Pittsburgh Athletic Club which captured pro football's championship in 1898. Pro football was only four years old at the time.

Dreyfuss groomed his son to inherit ownership of the Pirates. In 1930, the elder Dreyfuss stepped down as the owner, turning the reins over to his son, Sam. But in February 1931, the son died unexpect- edly of pneumonia. Barney, having no other choice, resumed command of the Pirates, but he never re- covered from the shock of his son's death. Barney Dreyfuss also died of pneumonia, just a year later. At the time of his death, the *Sporting News* called him "the last of the generation of history makers." He is a member of the Jewish Sports Hall of Fame at the Wingate Institute in Israel.

Charlotte Epstein

Mother of Women's Swimming in America

EPSTEIN, CHARLOTTE "EPPY" (born September, 1884, in New York City; died August 27, 1938) American swimming administrator. Considered the mother of American women's swimming, Charlotte Epstein established women's swimming as a sport in the United States, and was largely responsible for the inclusion of the first American women's swimming team in the Olympics when a delegation participated in the Antwerp Games in 1920.

• • •

Shortly after the 1912 Stockholm Olympics in which women competed in swimming events for the first time, Charlotte developed an interest in competitive swimming although she herself was not a particularly strong swimmer.

In 1914, she founded the National Women's Life Saving League, which provided a place for women to meet and swim; it offered competitive swimming as well as lessons. In the autumn of that year, Charlotte persuaded the Board of Directors of the Amateur Athletic Union to permit women for the first time to register as athletes with the AAU (as swimmers only). This led to a large increase in local and national swimming events for women.

In October, 1919, Charlotte's League became the New York Women's Swimming Association. This tiny group of businesswomen built the WSA into the world's greatest swimming organization.

Charlotte's first great coup was to get women's swimming recognized as an international sport. She successfully pushed for its inclusion in the 1920 Antwerp Olympics. The true beginning of American female participation in the Olympics was in Antwerp. Other than the appearance of women archers and golfers in 1900 and 1904, this

marked the first time American women were truly involved in competitive athletics at the Olympic Games. The difference this time was that swimming, unlike archery and golf, counted as a major sport in the eyes of the International Olympic Committee.

At the 1920 Olympics, U.S. women swimmers won an unprecedented four out of five races; they also finished first, second, and third in three events and set two world and Olympic records (many of these women were Charlotte Epstein's WSA swimmers).

The success of the 1920 Olympic experiment led to the inclusion of track and field and other sports for American women in future Olympic Games.

Charlotte did not actually coach the women at the Olympics. She had been appointed head of the women's team largely on the strength of being chief executive of the WSA. She again headed the women's Olympic team at the 1924 Paris games and at the 1932 Los Angeles games. (She was

present at the 1928 Amsterdam games in an unofficial capacity.) American female swimmers dominated the Olympic swimming events during all of these Olympics.

Among Charlotte's protégées were Gertrude Ederle, Aileen Riggin, and Eleanor Holm. Ederle was the first woman to swim the English Channel, doing so on August 6, 1926, in a time (14 hours and 39 minutes) that was faster than any male swimmer had achieved to that point. Aileen Riggin won the springboard diving competition at the 1920 Olympics. Eleanor Holm won a gold medal in the 100-meter backstroke at the 1932 Olympic Games.

In 1935, Charlotte Epstein served as chairman of the swimming committee in charge of the trials and selection of teams for the second Maccabiah Games, to be held in Tel Aviv.

During her 22 years with the Women's Swimming Association, Charlotte's swimmers held 51 world records and put together 30 national champion relay teams. By profession, Charlotte Epstein was a court stenographer and legal secretary. She had been a court stenographer for 10 years prior to the illness that led to her death in 1938. She never married. Her last assignment was at the Court of Domestic Relations in Brooklyn.

Charlotte Epstein is a member of the Jewish Sports Hall of Fame in Israel.

Jackie Fields

One of the Youngest Athletes to Win an Olympic Gold Medal

FIELDS, JACKIE (born February 9, 1908, in Chicago, Illinois; died June 3, 1987) American boxer. One of the youngest athletes to win an Olympic gold medal. He won 51 out of 54 amateur bouts, including the gold medal in the 1924 Paris Olympics, and held the welterweight title twice: 1929-30 and 1932-33. Jack Kearns, Fields' fight manager, said of him: "The best all-around battler in the United States, and he never received credit for the champion he was." His career record in 84 bouts was: 70 wins (28 by knockout), nine losses (one by knockout), two draws, two no-decisions, one no-contest.

. . .

Born Jacob Finkelstein, Fields grew up in a Jewish neighborhood in Chicago. "Being in the ghetto," he once recalled, "you had to fight." Fields' father was a butcher who had contracted tuberculosis and was forced to move to a warmer climate. The family moved to Los Angeles when Jackie was 14. There his father tried his luck in the restaurant business, but the venture was not particularly successful.

A pro fighter named Irving Glazer who had befriended Jackie introduced him to boxing. He advised the youngster to approach George Blake at the Los Angeles Athletic Club for boxing lessons. Fields lied his way through the interview with Blake by telling him he had fought previously in the Chicago Athletic Club. Blake, having been a boxing instructor there, knew that Jackie was lying, but still gave him a chance.

The lessons began in September 1921. Soon thereafter, Fields fought Fidel LaBarba, the Pacific Coast Flyweight Champion, and the newcomer was soundly beaten in a three-round decision. In 1924 Fields competed in the pre-Olympic AAU Nationals in Boston and, despite a broken hand, won the preliminaries, reaching the semifinals. Still, he earned a place on the Olympic team as an alternate.

During the voyage to the Paris Olympics, Jackie fought another alternate and defeated him, but it still appeared unlikely that he would fight in Paris. However, at the Paris training camp, Fields impressed the coaches by defeating another Olympic candidate, Harry Wallach. Jackie was therefore chosen as one of the two entrants (along with National AAU champ Joe Salas).

He and Salas reached the finals. The two men dressed for the fight in the same room. "When they knocked on the door to call us to fight," Salas recalled, "we looked at each other and started to cry and we hugged. Ten minutes later we were beating each other up." Fields, then only 16 years old, won the fight and the gold medal. He was now the Olympic featherweight champion! "When they started to play the national anthem I burst out crying," Jackie recalled.

Joe Salas remained convinced that he should have won in Paris. Bearing a grudge, he challenged Fields to another fight in the U.S. Fields agreed, but only on the condition that the promoter pay him (Jackie) the then-huge sum of $500. Fields was victorious again and, according to Jackie, that fight "just broke his [Salas'] heart." Salas refused to talk to Fields ever again.

Upon his return to the United States, Fields decided to turn professional. He was not yet 17 years old. His first pro fight, for which he earned $5,000, was held in February, 1925. He was not only badly beaten, but suffered a broken jaw.

He returned home to a surprise: his mother administered a spanking to Jackie for fighting in the ring. "You know how Jewish mothers are," Fields explained. Acceding to his mother's wishes, he announced that he would hang up his gloves, but when his friends taunted him, saying that he lacked guts, he decided to return to the ring.

Fields wanted to fight Mushy Callahan, the reigning junior welterweight champion, and offered him a large sum (about $25,000) to contend for Callahan's title. It was billed as the Jewish Championship of Boyle Heights and Central Avenue (Callahan was born Jewish, but converted to Catholicism). Fields later recalled: "I kicked the hell out of him. That was the first time I ever bet on myself and we won it. He never spoke to me for years afterward."

Fields' next fight was against Sammy Baker in Los Angeles. In the second round, coming out of a clinch, Fields landed a left hook: "I caught him on the chin and he dropped. I didn't walk to the corner; I ran to the corner. When they started to count and they got up to four and five, I started to pray. I really did." Baker stayed down for the count of 10.

On March 25, Fields won the National Boxing Association welterweight title from Jack Thompson. Then, four months later, on July 29th, Jackie fought Joe Dundee—then recognized in New York as the title holder—for the world championship. Dundee was clearly losing the fight until the second round when he fouled Fields with a blow to the genitals, knocking him out. When Jackie woke up in the dressing room, he was informed that he was champion. Fields believed later that Dundee had fouled him deliberately so that his manager and friends would not lose a $50,000 bet placed on Dundee. Since Dundee lost on a foul (and not by a knockout or decision), all bets were considered off.

On May 9, 1930, Fields lost the welterweight title to Young Jack Thompson by a decision in Detroit. Fields explained: "It was one of those nights when I was overtrained. I couldn't lift my hands up." So, Fields retired—again. But his manager Jack Kearns encouraged him to challenge Thompson one more time for the title. Meanwhile, Thompson lost the title to Lou Brouillard. Trying to earn back his self-respect, Fields prepared well for the match and beat Brouillard in Chicago on January 28, 1932, in 10 rounds. Thus Jackie Fields became welterweight champion for the second time.

In 1932 Jackie was involved in an automobile accident in Hammond, Indiana, on a trip from Louisville, Kentucky. He lost sight in one eye but told no one about it.

On February 22, 1933, Fields lost the world crown by losing a 10-round decision to Young Corbett III in San Francisco. When the referee, Jack Kennedy, raised Corbett's hand at the end of the fight, Fields and many others were amazed. In the dressing room after the fight Kennedy admitted to Fields' manager, "I made a mistake." The referee said he had raised the wrong hand. Kearns hit Kennedy, sending him to the floor.

Fields fought once more, winning a decision over Young Peter Jackson on May 2, 1933, in Los Angeles. He retired after that triumph mainly because his eye injury was becoming too troublesome.

Jackie's prizefighting encounters with Joe Salas during the 1924 Olympics and afterward were made into a 1939 movie entitled, *The Crowd Roars*.

Fields worked for Twentieth Century Fox as an assistant unit manager and then as a film editor for MGM from 1934 to 1940. Following this he became the distributor for Wurlitzer jukeboxes in Pennsylvania from 1940 to 1949.

In the early 1950s, he represented the J & B Scotch Whiskey Company in the Chicago area. Then, in 1957, he became part-owner of the Tropicana Hotel in Las Vegas. He later sold his interest and became the hotel's public relations director.

In 1965, Jackie coached the U.S. boxing team at the Maccabiah games in Israel. In 1972 he was elected to the United Savings-Helms Athletic Foundation Boxing Hall of Fame. Five years later, Fields was named to the Boxing Hall of Fame.

Jackie Fields is a member of the Jewish Sports Hall of Fame in Israel. He was inducted as well into the International Boxing Hall of Fame in 2004.

Harry Fisher
Outstanding Basketball Coach

FISHER, HARRY A. (born February 6, 1882, in New York City; died December 29, 1967). An All-American basketball player at Columbia University in the early 1900s, and later an outstanding basketball coach at Columbia, and the United States Military Academy at West Point.

• • •

At Columbia University, Fisher was the team leader and scoring star from 1902 to 1905. Early in his career he set the field-goal record of 13, a record which stayed on the books for 48 years. During his final two years as a player, the team lost only twice, and he was one of the players named All-American in 1905. In that same year he was appointed to a committee established to rewrite the rules of college basketball.

While serving as coach at Columbia University (from 1906 to 1916), he guided the team to three Eastern Invitational League titles, two of which were the reward for undefeated seasons. His overall record was a sensational 101 wins and 39 losses. From 1911 to 1917, Fisher also served as graduate manager of athletics at Columbia.

Fisher retired from Columbia and athletics in 1917, but five years later General Douglas MacArthur convinced him to become head basketball coach at the Military Academy at West Point. The 1922 and 1923 seasons were outstanding and closed out a great period of his career. In those two seasons he won 46 of 51 games.

Army defeated Navy in each of those years.

Harry Fisher is a member of the College Basketball Hall of Fame.

Herbert Flam

Outstanding Tennis Player of the 1950s

FLAM, HERBERT (born November 7, 1928, in New York City; died November 25, 1980) American tennis player. One of the outstanding American tennis players in the early 1950s, he was the first Jewish netman to reach the finals of the United States Nationals at Forest Hills when he lost to Art Larsen in 1950. No other Jewish player had as high a world ranking as Herb Flam until that time.

. . .

Flam began to play tennis at age 10 and won his first tournament two years later. With his father as his coach, Herb earned his reputation in California as a junior player. In 1948 he came to prominence in national tennis when, as an unseeded player, he reached the semifinals of the National singles competition. On the way he knocked out the third-seed, Gardner Mulloy, and the sixth, Harry Likas. Flam was ranked No. 9 in the U.S. that year.

Herb reached the quarterfinals in six national singles championships. In 1951, he was a semi-finalist at the first Wimbledon tournament he played. He won his quarterfinal match in that tournament against Frank Sedgman after losing the first two sets. Flam was ranked No. 6 in the world that year.

Flam was American Clay Court champion in singles in 1950 and 1956 and Clay Court doubles champion in 1950. He played 14 Davis Cup rubbers for the U.S. from 1951 to 1957, winning 12.

In 1952, Herb reached the semifinals at Wimbledon and was ranked No. 10 in the world. He reached the last eight at Wimbledon three times in all. He was ranked No. 7 in the world in 1956 and No. 5 in 1957.

Flam's style of play has been labeled "retriever" with negative implications. A "retriever" in this sense is a tennis player who plays defensively, simply returning the ball without acting aggressively to try to win the point. Flam was not thrilled with that label. He contended that he did rush the net more than others. He realized that he didn't hit the ball that hard but played subtly, for control, to get his opponent off balance. He tried to work into position to win the point.

Flam acknowledged that he started using the "retriever" style because of his small size as a youngster. As a teenager he grew to be 6 feet tall.

After Herb Flam retired from active tennis he attempted several businesses in Los Angeles with little success. Intermittently he gave private tennis lessons.

Flam was inducted into the University of California at Los Angeles Hall of Fame in 2006.

Alfred Flatow

Member of the Berlin Gymnasts Club

FLATOW, ALFRED (born born October 3, 1869, in Gdansk, Poland; died December 28, 1942) German gymnast. He won the parallel bars competition in the 1896 Athens Olympics and was awarded a silver medal (gold medals were not given then). He also placed second on the horizontal bars (no medal was given for this in 1896).

■ ■ ■

Alfred Flatow became involved in athletics at the age of eight when he joined the Youth Department of the German Athletics Club, and 10 years later he became a member of its Adult Department.

In 1890 Alfred passed the examination required to qualify as teacher of athletics, and at 21, he was the youngest person to hold that position in Germany at the time. Flatow served as a volunteer soldier in the 66th Infantry regiment in Magdeburg in 1893 and 1894.

The following year, Flatow was a member of the gymnast delegation from the German Athletic Union that participated in the Italian Athletic Federation Festival in Rome. Flatow came in second in the general competition.

In 1896, Flatow was one of the 10 Germans chosen to represent his country in athletics at the Athens Olympics. He did well, but not nearly as well as some present-day records indicate. He is listed as having won the equivalent of three gold medals in the parallel bars and placed second in the horizontal bars. Another member of the delegation, Gustav Felix Flatow, has often been described as Alfred's brother, but they were not related.

At about this time Alfred began writing articles for the *Berliner Zeitung*. He gained a reputation as a gifted writer, and continued to write for the same newspaper for 40 years.

In 1898, at the Ninth Athletic Festival of German Athletes in Hamburg, Flatow won the Twelve Rounds competition, a series of gymnastic events. He considered this victory as important as his Olympics accomplishment.

Flatow was also a champion in 1899 at the Markisch Kreis Athletic Festival in Guben, Germany. The next two years he supervised athletic activities in Berlin.

He belonged to the elite of German gymnasts, and became an honorary member of the Deutsche Turnerschaft, the Union of German Gymnasts. Until World War I erupted in 1914, Flatow was active in athletics and even at the age of 50 he was still working out on the parallel bars. To earn a living he ran a bicycle shop in Berlin.

Three years after Hitler came to power, Flatow was the subject of a sympathetic newspaper article in the *Berliner Tageblatt* (April 18, 1936). The article read in part: "We met Alfred Flatow at his home in the first floor of an old house on Alexandrinen

Street. The door led directly into a large room which served both as a storeroom for bicycle parts and an office. Flatow has lived here for over three decades. The 66-year-old man invited the guests into his semi-office. Numerous diplomas, some framed, others in glass cases, decorated the walls. Among these are some precious pieces."

When he came to power, Hitler moved against the Berlin Gymnasts Club, whose most famous member was Alfred Flatow. The Jewish club members were politely asked to resign. They were bitter but no one dared protest. Rupert Naumann, chairman of the Berlin Gymnasts Club, had expressed support for Flatow. But Flatow was unable to resist Hitler and, on October 20, 1936, wrote to Naumann: "After receiving your letter of October 18, 1936, I reported my announcement of resignation from the organization of German gymnasts to Adolf Sengebusch [secretary of the German Turnerscheft]. For your expressions of your private feelings, I thank you very much. Concerning my own feelings and thoughts I prefer to keep silent."

Flatow was sent to the Theresienstadt concentration camp. He died either there or in another death camp during World War II.

Alfred Flatow is a member of the Jewish Sports Hall of Fame in Israel.

Nat Fleischer

Founder and editor of *Ring* magazine

FLEISCHER, NATHANIEL STANLEY "Nat" (born November 3, 1887, in New York City; died June 25, 1972) American boxing promoter and editor. One of the major pioneers of modern boxing, Nat Fleischer became its outstanding promoter and authority. Founder and editor of the influential boxing magazine, *Ring*.

. . .

Nat Fleischer grew up on the Lower East Side of New York. The exact date of his birth is unknown. (When he was 21, he selected November 3 as his birthday because he wanted to vote in that year's election.) While at P.S. 15 in New York City, he became interested in journalism and became editor of the school's monthly newspaper.

Nat's interest in boxing was first sparked when his father gave him photographs of fighters which came with packages of cigarettes. Nat watched his first world championship fight at the age of 12 in Tuckahoe, New York, when Terrible Terry McGovern knocked out Pedlar Palmer for the bantamweight title. The photographs and the title fight hooked Fleischer on boxing, a passion which never left him.

Two weeks after Nat watched that title fight, he took up boxing and became, in time, captain of the boxing team as well as president of the Oregon Athletic Club in New York City. He also played first base and catcher on the Oregon AC baseball team.

Nat desperately wanted to be a prizefighter, but, at age 15, and weighing in at 122 pounds, he was flattened in the first round of an amateur match at the Boys Club of New York. It was his first important bout, and it turned out to be the last time he put on boxing gloves.

Nat did better at sprinting. He became the Public School Athletic League 220-yard sprint champion. After graduating from Townsend Harris High School in New York, he entered City College of New York (CCNY) in the fall of 1904. He and Dan Daniel, who went on to become a famous New York sportswriter, founded the first CCNY intercollegiate basketball team. It was at CCNY that Nat got his first taste of serious writing, becoming the campus correspondent for two New York dailies and working on the sports desk of the *New York Press*.

In 1908, Nat graduated from CCNY with a bachelor of science degree in botany and chemistry. While working on the *Press* at night, he passed the teachers' examination and began teaching sixth-grade girls' botany at New York City's P.S. 7. His new vocation did not agree with him.

He decided next to take a graduate course in commercial chemistry at New York University. But in a few months his course of study came to an abrupt end. Arriving at the lab one day, sleepy following a long, hectic night at the *Press*, Nat mixed the wrong solutions and blew up part of the lab. He was promptly dismissed from the course.

Fleischer followed this scholastic experience with a new one at Yale University where he enrolled in a forestry course. This too did not last long, and he decided to become a full-time journalist, investing all his energies in his work at the *Press*. He went on to become sports editor of the *Press*. When the *Press* later merged with the *Morning Sun*, Fleischer became an assistant to the new sports editor.

In 1914, Nat became sports editor of the *Sun Press*. Over the next 13 years, he was sports editor at the *Morning Herald*, the *Mail-Telegram*, and the *Evening Telegram*. Then, in 1927, Scripps-Howard bought the *Telegram* and Fleischer was fired. He decided to devote all of his time to *Ring* magazine, which he and three associates had founded five

promoter he insisted on rigorous physical examinations for boxers before a fight was staged, and better care for those seriously hurt during a fight. He also protected spectators from questionable promotional gimmicks. In addition, he advocated closed-circuit television coverage and home viewing of fights, to encourage and maintain public interest in boxing. Despite threats on his life by vested interests who were being hurt by his progressiveness, he persevered.

Fleischer initiated boxing's rating system, and awarded handsome belts to world boxing champions. He also helped establish boxing commissions around the world.

Nat refereed and judged more than 1,000 fights. His career as a boxing official, however, was not without its brushes with danger. In 1939, he was to referee a bout between the American fighter Joey Archibald, the featherweight champion, and Simon Chavez, in Caracas, Venezuela. The night before the fight, two men entered Nat's room while he sat in his pajamas. Throwing a good deal of money on his bed and brandishing a gun, they informed him tersely that they had bet heavily on Chavez and "you know what you're going to do." Brushing the money to the floor, Nat barked orders to the men: "Put that gun away. I am going to call police headquarters the moment you leave the room." The men, obviously surprised by his reaction, promptly left the room.

The fight went on under heavy guard, and Chavez won. Before the fight, Fleischer had asked Joey Archibald to make a special effort to win on a knockout, but the high altitude had sapped his strength. After the match, Nat explained to the defeated fighter why he had encouraged him so much. "Gee, Nat," said Archibald, "I just thought you wanted me to put the U.S. on top of the heap."

years earlier, in 1922. Several years later, Nat acquired full ownership of the magazine. The magazine provided the only comprehensive coverage of boxing in the world. Its ratings of fighters were accepted as authoritative.

Fleischer was a small man (5 feet, 2 inches) who frequently wore a brown hat with the brim curled up at the sides. While serving as editor, sportswriter, and referee, he could not help but notice that boxing was plagued with questionable promoters who had foisted much impropriety on fans and participants. Nat vowed to free boxing of these promoters. Fleischer wanted to protect boxers against mismatches and give the fans the quality fight they had paid to see.

Nat's influence on boxing is unmatched. As a

Another time, when Nat was refereeing the Harry Jeffra-Spider Armstrong featherweight title bout in Baltimore on July 29, 1940, Fleischer had to put up with 102-degree heat at ringside. After the eleventh round, he took off his tie; after the twelfth, he unbuttoned his shirt; after the thirteenth, he pulled his shirt off; came the fourteenth round, and off came Nat's undershirt; came the fifteenth, he held up Jeffra's hand and slumped against the ropes, unable to move.

Just then, a lady who obviously had taken Fleischer's preaching of morality in boxing (as espoused in *Ring* magazine) seriously, approached him and said: "So you're the Nat Fleischer who preaches morals in *Ring*. You should be ashamed of yourself, taking off your underwear in public!"

Nat Fleischer wrote 60 books on boxing. His first, *Training for Boxers*, came at the prompting of his wife. It was written immediately after the bank in which he had deposited his money collapsed in 1929. The book sold almost a million copies at $1 each. In 1942 he published the first edition of the annual *Ring Record Book*, still considered the authoritative source book in the sport.

A nonstop author, Nat once wrote a 30-chapter biography of the famous Jim Corbett in 36 hours shortly after the boxer had died in 1933. One estimate has it that Nat wrote 40 million words in his life.

"Mr. Boxing," as Nat Fleischer came to be called, gave boxing a respectability it did not possess before his time.

Sidney Franklin
The First Jewish Bullfighter

FRANKLIN, SIDNEY (born June 11, 1903, in Brooklyn, New York; died April 26, 1976) American bullfighter. Not the first American to step into the ring, but most certainly the first Jew to take up the sport. He became one of Spain's leading matadors, reaching the zenith of his career in the early 1930s.

． ． ．

His real surname was Frumkin, but he took the name Franklin out of admiration for Ben Franklin. Sidney's parents were Russian Jewish immigrants and he was the fifth of their 10 children. His father was a policeman. The future bullfighter, intimidated by other children, shied away from them. At age 13, he won a first prize offered by Wanamaker's Department Store for beaded embroidery.

Franklin's ambition was to become an actor. For a while he appeared in the Peter Rabbit Annual Shows at the Globe Theatre and was a member of a theatrical stock company.

After three years at Brooklyn's Commercial High School, Sidney studied Spanish at Columbia University's Extension Department. In 1922 after an argument with his father, he sailed for Mexico and told friends that he was making the journey to study Mayan art.

Once there, be began a poster business which featured artwork for bullfight impresarios. To check whether the sketches he was selling were accurate, he attended a bullfight and got caught up in the excitement.

Some Mexican acquaintances argued that no American, including Sidney Franklin, could learn the sport. Franklin took up the challenge. He had watched bullfights carefully and had been over-whelmed by the precision and grace with which the matadors handled the cape. The slim, sandy-haired Franklin sought out Rodolfo Gaona, the great Mexican matador, and asked for instruction.

After several weeks of strenuous training, Sidney Franklin entered the ring for the first time on September 20, 1923. He lost his balance twice but killed his bull. "If you've got guts," he once said, "you can do anything." In fact, Franklin's debut that autumn day was made possible by a local promoter who believed that the spectacle of a "gringo" pursued around the ring by a fighting bull would be a superb amusement for the crowd. He never bargained for Franklin becoming a great star.

After some years in Mexico, Franklin went to Spain in 1939 and became the first American to engage in bullfighting there. He became a drawing card not only throughout Spain, but also in Portugal, Mexico, and other parts of South America, earning as much as $100,000 a year. In a March 1930 fight in Madrid, he was gored so badly that he could not fight for a number of years. About the risk of being injured in the ring, Franklin once said, "It is part of the game and makes no difference to any of us."

Sidney Franklin's performances in the ring were impressive. His costume and highly decorative cape cost $1,000—an extravagant sum at the time. The costume weighed 50 pounds and it took him an hour to dress for the fight.

Naturally righthanded, Sidney taught himself to be ambidextrous so that he could handle the seven-pound sword with either hand. He was highly superstitious, and would never pick up a salt shaker to hand to someone. Instead, he always slid it along the table. He also knocked on iron for good luck.

In 1945, Franklin reached the pinnacle of his profession when he became the headliner in Madrid Plaza de Toros. "I didn't have the gracefulness or art of the Spaniards," he said later, "but I was brave and that made me famous."

Ernest Hemingway, one of Sidney's close friends, described Franklin in *Death in the Afternoon*: "Sidney Franklin is brave with a cold, serene, and intelligent valor. No history of bullfighting that is ever written can be complete unless it gives him the space he is entitled to."

Franklin had hoped to introduce bullfighting in the United States, but his plan to hold a bloodless bull-dodging contest in Newark, New Jersey, was barred in 1930. His only opportunity to show his prowess to his former Brooklyn neighbors occurred during the 1939 New York World's Fair when he put on a series of bull-dodging exhibitions with the approval of the Society for the Prevention of Cruelty to Animals.

Sidney managed a cafe in Seville, Spain, in the 1950s, and also had the cafeteria concession at the American Strategic Air Command base at nearby Moro de la Frontera at the same time. He wrote his autobiography in 1952, *The Bullfighter from Brooklyn*. After that he fought only intermittently, devoting most of his time to running a school for bullfighters at Alcaia de Guerdaira, near Seville.

In 1957, Franklin was fined and jailed for illegally keeping an automobile in Spain. After serving nine months of his 25-month sentence, he was pardoned, and returned to the U.S.

Franklin tried to make a comeback in June 1958, but did not do well. In May 1959, in Juarez, Mexico, he suffered a serious injury which ended his career.

In the years that followed, his love for the sport did not wane. "The pleasurable thing about bullfighting," he said once, "is the thrill of matching one's agility and wits against those of an active opponent who can kill you if he catches you."

He became an authority on the history of bullfighting. The article on the subject in the *Encyclopedia Britanica* was written by Franklin.

Franklin died in 1976 while residing at the Village Nursing Home in New York where he had lived since 1970. His obituary in *The New York Times* included this terse statement: "Sidney Franklin was the only matador ever born at 14 Jackson Place in the Park Slope section of Brooklyn."

Benny Friedman

The Quarterback Who Had Never Made a Mistake

FRIEDMAN, BENNY (born March 18, 1905, in Cleveland, Ohio; died November 23, 1982) American football player. Football's first great passer, and one of the greatest Jewish football players in history. A true popularizer of the game, he added imagination to football and was once described by coach Fielding Yost as "the quarterback who never makes a mistake." Red Grange, the legendary runner, called Friedman the best quarterback he had ever seen.

• • •

Friedman was an all-around athlete in high school. Upon enrolling in the University of Michigan in 1923, he immediately made the freshman football team. The next year he was invited to try out for the varsity and made it.

For the first half of the football season Benny was a benchwarmer, and he felt that the coach was not favorably inclined toward Jews. Later that season, when Friedman was given a chance to play toward the end of one game, he performed so well that from then on he was a starter.

In 1925, Benny Friedman became Michigan's starting quarterback, enjoying a great year and becoming a first-team All-American choice. He passed for 11 touchdowns and did all the place kicking. The Wolverines were 7-1 that year winning the Western Conference Championship. Largely because of Benny Friedman, Michigan's 1925 team was one of football's greatest. The Wolverines scored a total of 227 points while allowing their opposition only three. Friedman's most spectacular performance that season was in the game against Indiana: he ran 55 yards to score one touchdown, threw another five touchdown passes,

and kicked eight extra points. Friedman was personally responsible for 44 of Michigan's 63 points that day. Final score: Michigan 63, Indiana 0.

In 1926 Friedman was Michigan's captain and he enjoyed another marvelous season. The team again was 7-1 and again he was first team All-America selection. He was also chosen Most Valuable Player in the Western Conference.

Friedman was one of the pioneers who helped change football from a contest of brawn to one of intelligence. Fiercely competitive, he was one of the first quarterbacks to dare to pass from behind his own goal line. Friedman had a toughness and durability that helped him avoid injury through 10 years of rugged football. In those days, good players like Benny Friedman played 60 minutes each game.

Benny encountered little anti-Jewish feelings in his college days, In fact, as a superstar on campus, he was, for the most part, immune from whatever anti-Semitism might have lain under the surface. He wrote: "There were times when I thought the grade was made harder for me on account of racial prejudice. I soon found out that was bunk. The fact that I was a Jew didn't preclude social recognition for me on the campus."

In a letter to the author (written December 23, 1981), Friedman provided this illustration of his family's Jewish faith as it related to his football career. "We had an Orthodox home and on the kitchen wall was a *pushke* (charity box). I noticed when I was a high school player, mother would go over to the box after serving me brunch and drop some coins in the box. I would see her lips moving as though she was saying a prayer. I asked what she was doing and she said she was protecting me by putting 18 cents in the *pushke*. I asked why. She told me that 18 in Hebrew stands for *chai* which means life.

"Mother would come out to the game and watch. In the course of a game on occasion someone would be hurt or laid out. She never worried that it was I, because she had taken care of me through her faith. I never was hurt and throughout my high school and college career mother continued her vigil. I never questioned her whether it was my ability that kept me aloof from injury; I let it go that it was *chai* working for me."

When the 5-foot, 8-inch Friedman began playing pro football, he seemed somewhat concerned about the large size of the pros facing him. Once, out from nowhere during a game, he heard someone say in Yiddish, "Keep your chin up, Benny. It's a nice, friendly game." Wondering who this fellow-Jew was, Benny looked over at the rival team's line and saw a hefty tackle grinning from ear to ear. "What's your name and where are you from?" asked Friedman. The large-framed tackle replied with the same grin, "O'Donnell of Notre Dame."

Friedman joined the pros in 1927 and played for the next seven years, making All-Pro each of his first four years. He played first with the Cleveland Bulldogs. In 1928 he was with the Detroit Wolverines, and from 1929 to 1931 with the New York Giants. He concluded his pro career by playing with the Brooklyn Dodgers football team between 1932 and 1934.

Until Friedman arrived on the scene, the pass had been used on third down as a weapon of desperation in long yardage situations—or when the team was far behind. The Chicago Bears' owner, George Halas, called Friedman the first pro quarterback "to exploit the strategic possibilities of the pass." Halas noted that "Benny demonstrated that the pass could be mixed with the running plays as an integral part of the offense."

Because of Benny Friedman's innovative use of the forward pass, the professional rules committee slenderized the football, one more major step in the evolution of pro football from a purely straightforward running game into the passing-and-running game it eventually became.

Friedman retired from football in 1934, not without a measure of bitterness at having become a pro football player rather than the stockbroker he had desired to be. "For the past six years," he wrote later, "I've made $10,000 a year at pro football. It's been fun, hard-earned fun. But where has

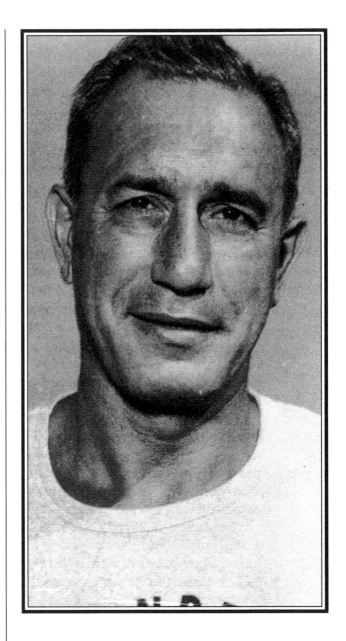

it got me?" Still, he was not prepared to advise others against pursuing a pro football career.

In 1934 Friedman returned to collegiate football as head coach of the City College of New York, a job he held until 1941. In that year he joined the U.S. Navy and became an officer assigned to aircraft carriers. Between 1949 and 1963 he served as head football coach and athletic director at Brandeis University, the Jewish supported and sponsored school in Waltham, Massachusetts. He also ran a summer camp for boys and at the end of the summer a special camp for quarterbacks, both in Kohut, Maine.

In April, 1963, Friedman resigned as athletic director at Brandeis, citing the growing responsibilities heaped upon him by his outside business interests and his summer camp in Maine. Another factor in his decision was the university's new athletic policy which dropped intercollegiate football as an activity.

In February 1976, Friedman wrote a letter of protest to the sports editor of *The New York Times*. He felt that he had been denied the ultimate recognition due him. He recounted his exploits, calling himself "the highest-priced and yet the least-expensive player of the game." By least-expensive he explained that he had always played 60 minutes, never had to be taken out of a game due to injuries, and always was ready for the next game: "I not only ran the ball and passed, but also did all the place kicking." What grieved Friedman was that while he is a member of the Citizens Savings Hall of Fame and the National Football Foundation Hall of Fame, as well as the Jewish Sports Hall of Fame, he had been skipped over by the Pro Football Hall of Fame in Canton, Ohio.

Friedman died on November 23, 1982 in his East Side apartment in New York City of what the police described as a self-inflicted gunshot wound.

Despite his impressive record, Friedman did not become a member of the Pro Football Hall of Fame until 2005. Some attribute the delay to Friedman's incessant campaigning for induction, considered bad form at the time. He is also a member of the College Football Hall of Fame and the International Jewish Sports Hall of Fame.

Max Friedman
A Pioneer of Basketball

FRIEDMAN, MAX "MARTY" (born July 12, 1889, in New York City; died January 1, 1986) American basketball player. Considered a great defensive star and team leader, he was a pioneer of basketball. One of the "Heavenly Twins," he was chosen on Nat Holman's All-Time Pro Team in 1922 and named to an All-Time Pro Second Team in 1941.

. . .

Friedman attended the Hebrew Technical Institute, a vocational high school in New York, graduating in 1908. At the same time, he was playing with the University Settlement House team on New York's Lower East Side. He turned pro in 1910 when the Hudson River League of New York was formed.

In 1914 he played on the Utica, New York, basketball team in the Hudson River League. The following year Friedman played with Carbondale in the Pennsylvania-Intercounty League, where his team set a record of 45 straight wins. Carbondale beat the competing Penn State League winners that year.

From 1915 to 1917, Friedman played with the Philadelphia Jaspers of the Eastern League. The team reached the championship finals in 1917. Max then enlisted in the army, went to Officers Training School, and qualified as a pilot. He was sent to France but never saw combat.

While overseas, Friedman organized an athletic program for troops who stayed in Europe, and he organized and captained the basketball team that took the American Expeditionary Forces title. In 1919, he captained the team that beat the French and Italians for the championship in the Interallied Games.

On his return to the U.S., Friedman joined the

championship Albany, New York team which won the New York State League in 1920. That year he began playing for one of the greatest pro teams ever, the New York Whirlwinds. His teammates were Barney Sedran and Nat Holman. Marty Friedman and Barney Sedran became known as the "Heavenly Twins," an indication of how well the two of them played together.

Friedman was part of two championship teams in 1921: Albany and Easthampton of the Interstate League. He played for two teams in 1922: Albany and the Brooklyn Dodgers of the Metropolitan League.

An injured knee and shoulder kept Friedman out of action for most of the next year. He then joined the Cleveland Rosenblums and captained them from 1925 to 1927. In 1927 the team lost the American League title to the New York Celtics.

After the 1927 season, Friedman retired from playing, but in 1939 he was back in basketball as coach of the American League's Troy Haymakers. Then he went into the garage business with his playing partner, Barney Sedran, and stayed in the business until retiring in 1958. Friedman died on January 1, 1986, at the age of 96.

Brad Gilbert
Greatest Jewish Tennis Player of the 1990s

GILBERT, BRAD (born August 9, 1961, in Oakland, California–) American tennis player. His best career world rank was four on January 1, 1990. His career earnings came to $5,509,060. He had been in the top 20 every year from 1985 to 1991 except for 1986 when he was ranked 21. Gilbert won 20 career titles.

■ ■ ■

W e're family," observed Brad Gilbert's father Barry. "We're a close-knit Jewish family." Add to that, a tennis-playing family. Brad's sister Dana played for the UCLA women's tennis team, and then joined the pro tour for five years. In 1978, when Brad was 17, Dana won the U.S. Clay Court Championship. Brad's brother Barry Jr. played on the tennis team for the University of South Carolina.

Brad picked up his first tennis racquet at the age of four. He played continuously, but by the time he reached his teens, bigger, stronger and more talented players gave him trouble on the court. He considered giving up tennis because he could not handle losing. Defeat was an agony for him, and he reacted with temper tantrums. "He was a little tyrant," the late tennis star Arthur Ashe remembered.

Gilbert explained that the tantrums had nothing to do with his attitude toward tennis rivals or referees. "I'm not mad at other people. I'm mad at myself. I'm a perfectionist. It bothers me when I let someone else take advantage of a situation I should have taken advantage of." Gilbert's striving for perfection led to his meteoric rise on the tennis tour. In 1981, at the age of 20, he ranked 282 and only four years later climbed to No. 18.

Brad's climb up the tennis ladder was propelled by physical maturity. When he graduated from high school, Brad was only 5 foot 8 inches and 135 pounds, but in his late teens he grew to 6 foot 1½ inches and 175 pounds.

Brad played for two years (1980-82) at Foothill Junior College in Los Altos, California under tennis coach Tom Chivington, who remained his coach for the next decade. Gilbert credits his later success to Chivington. Brad won the California Junior College singles championship and the U.S. Amateur Hardcourt Championship at Cleveland, Ohio, while at Foothill. And in 1981, he was a member of the American Junior Davis Cup team and a member of the U.S. team at the Maccabiah Games in Israel where he won the doubles title with partner Jon Levine.

In 1982, he transferred to Pepperdine University and played under Allen Fox, who had ranked among the top ten and played in the Davis Cup. Gilbert became an All-American and reached the finals of the 1982 NCAA championship, runner-up to Mike Leach. He helped Pepperdine achieve a 23-5 record that year.

Following his junior year at Pepperdine in June 1982, Gilbert turned pro. He captured his first title in Taipei that year at the age of 21. Playing well, and defeating such stars as Eliot Teltscher and Vitas Gerulaitis, Gilbert ended 1982 with a world rank of 54. A year later, in 1983, he had dropped back to No. 62.

Bouncing back in 1984, Gilbert played in 25 tournaments, winning two Grand Prix events in Columbus and Taipei. He closed the year with a world ranking of 23.

During 1985, Brad won tour events at Livingston, Cleveland, and Tel Aviv and was a finalist at Stuttgart and Johannesburg. Brad moved into the top 15 for the first time in 1985 and completed the year ranked 18 in the world.

Gilbert began 1986 with a surprise triumph over John McEnroe in January at the Grand Prix Masters tournament at Madison Square Garden in New York City. Gilbert's 5-7, 6-4, 6-1 pasting of his opponent left McEnroe shaking his head in disbe-

lief, and put the 24-year old Brad into the quarter-finals. That accomplishment helped Gilbert land a berth on the American Davis Cup team.

Highly disciplined about tennis, Gilbert keeps diaries and charts on his matches. The discipline worked. He kept improving, finishing the next year, 1986, at No. 11. He earned $308,492 in 1986, defeating Jimmy Connors and Stefan Edberg to win the U.S. Indoor crown in Memphis; adding Grand Prix titles in Livingston, Tel Aviv, and Vienna; and reaching the final 16 at Wimbledon.

Though he won only one tournament in 1987—in Scottsdale, Arizona—Gilbert reached the finals at the Paris Indoor, the South African Open, Tel Aviv, and Washington. His prize money in 1987 came to $507,187, bringing his six-year total to $1.4 million. He ended the year ranked at No. 13 in the world.

An injury in early 1988 forced Gilbert to miss the first six months of the year. He underwent sur-gery on his left ankle on April 27. Still, after recu-peration, he managed to win a bronze medal for the United States at the 1988 Olympics in Seoul. He won his first tournament of the year that fall in Tel Aviv. He reached the finals at the Paris Open and the semifinals in three other tournaments. He finished 1988 with a world ranking of 21.

Gilbert came into his own in 1989, compiling a career-best 17-match winning streak. In the pro-cess, he won three consecutive tournaments, the first time anyone had accomplished that since Boris Becker in 1986. "Sometimes," he said after-ward, "you get on a winning streak like that. Even if you're not playing that well, you feel you can al-ways find a way to win."

Called in at the last minute to replace John McEnroe on the U.S. Davis Cup team in its match against Germany in Munich in July, Gilbert played excellently, winning both matches against Carl-Ube Steeb and Patrik Kuhnen.

When Gilbert showed up for work in 1989, he almost always did well, reaching the quarterfinals or better in 17 of 20 tournaments. Even the best players had little chance against him. In August, he beat top-10 players Michael Chang, Boris Becker, and Stefan Edberg to take the tournament in Cincinnati.

Although he is regarded as having a poor second serve and an ineffective lob, Gilbert worked around them. He calls it "winning ugly." Some players win by overpowering the ball, Gilbert notes, and that naturally excites the crowds. "People see me," he told *The New York Times*, "and I don't hit the ball that hard. They say, 'How's he winning?' I do a lot of things well, but I don't do anything overpowering."

Agreeing, Arthur Ashe explained that Gilbert "doesn't have strokes you'd want to write home about. But he's fast." Indeed, Brad's feet are said to be the fastest, most nimble in the game, and his greatest asset. "Anybody who covers the court that well," said Ashe, "is scary." He does possess a good return of serve, accurate passing shots, and a strong forehand approach shot. To which Gilbert adds, "I'm a real fighter. I never give up."

"Winning ugly" and using those deceptively quick feet helped Brad close that magnificent year of 1989 with a 60-17 match record and a No. 6 world ranking. Winning his fifth title at San Francisco by defeating Anders Jarryd, helped him accumulate a career high of $900, 848.

On January 1, 1990 Gilbert attained a career high ranking of four. He won titles in Rotterdam, Orlando, and Brisbane. That same year, he was a runner-up at Cincinnati, losing to Stefan Edberg in the finals. He was also a semifinalist at the Toronto Indoor, the Japan Open, and Washington. He was a quarterfinalist at Wimbledon, Long Island, and Stockholm. He closed 1990 at No. 10 in the world.

Though Gilbert did not win a title in 1991 for the first time since 1983, he reached three finals. He was runner-up at San Francisco, losing to Darren Cahill; a semifinalist at Philadelphia; and a quarterfinalist at Orlando. His Davis Cup play remained exceptional as he gained two wins over Mexico in the first round. From April to June he fell into a slump, winning just six of 15 matches. He recovered, however, compiling a 10-5 record in the previous six weeks of the year. His world ranking at the end of 1991 was 19, marking the sixth time in the previous seven seasons that he finished in the top 20. Only Gilbert, Stefan Edberg, and Ivan Lendl finished in the top 25 each year from 1984 to 1991.

Gilbert has been Boris Becker's biggest nemesis, beating the German tennis star four times, including twice in a row in Washington and then in a dramatic five-set victory in the third round of the U.S. Open. Gilbert is one of only three players (the other two are Ivan Lendl and Stefan Edberg) to beat Becker, the three-time Wimbledon champion, at least three times.

Off the court, Gilbert loved sports. "I'm a junkie for anything on the scoreboard page. Just this morning I got a *USA Today* and I was studying the archery results." He is an enthusiastic basketball fan, attending pro basketball games, and imagining himself "being 6-7 and having a 40-inch leap."

Brad got off to a good start in 1992. He finished in the finals at Scottsdale; the semifinals at San Francisco, Philadelphia, and Hong Kong; and the quarterfinals at Tokyo. As of July, 1992, he was ranked 15th in the world.

In 1994, Gilbert began coaching tennis star André Agassi, who over the next eight years won six Grand Slam titles and became No. 1 in the world. In January 2002, Gilbert and Agassi parted ways amicably. In June 2003, Gilbert began to work his coaching magic on American tennis star Andy Roddick, turning him into a No. 1 ranked player and the 2003 U.S. Open champion. In 2006 and 2007, Brad worked intensively with British tennis star Andy Murray, but shortly thereafter the two parted company.

In 2011, Gilbert continued to coach up-and-coming tennis players as well as serve as a tennis analyst.

Sidney Gillman

One of Pro Football's Great Innovators

GILLMAN, SIDNEY (born October 26, 1911, in Minneapolis, Minnesota; died January 4, 2003) American football player and coach. He played for Ohio State in the early 1930s and was an All-American honorable mention end in 1932 and 1933. But Gillman is best known as the coach of the Los Angeles Rams between 1955 and 1959 and then of the Los Angeles and San Diego Chargers, of the fledgling American Football League, between 1960 and 1971.

• • •

Gillman grew up in Minneapolis. He attended Ohio State from 1931 to 1933 and was co-captain of the 1932 football team. In a 1933 game against Northwestern he recovered a fumble and ran 54 yards for a touchdown.

Sid intended to pursue a law career, but coaching was his real love. He began his career in 1934 as assistant coach at his alma mater Ohio State. He had his heart set on winning the job of Ohio State head football coach, but the offer never came.

From 1935 to 1937 he was assistant coach at Denison University in Granville, Ohio, and returned to Ohio State as assistant coach from 1938 to 1940. In 1941 he went back to Denison as assistant coach. In 1942 and 1943 he was assistant coach at Miami of Ohio (located in Oxford), and head coach from 1944 until 1947.

In 1944, his first season at Miami's helm, Gillman's team was 8-1-0, and from that year on, his college teams never failed to post a winning season. After an 8-0-1 mark in the 1947 season, his Miami team won the Sun Bowl against Texas Tech. His overall four year record at Miami was 30-6-1. In 1948 he became an assistant coach at West

Point. Red Blaik, Army's coach, observed that "there are few brilliant thinkers left in football. Sid is one of them."

From 1949 to 1954, Gillman was head coach at the University of Cincinnati where he succeeded in establishing a career record of 49-12-1.

In 20 seasons of coaching in the Midwest, Gillman never saw his teams win fewer than seven games in a season. Despite his impressive record, he failed to obtain that coveted job of head coach at Ohio State. Sid always suspected that his being Jewish was a factor, so he went to the pros.

In 1955, Gillman became head coach of the National Football League Los Angeles Rams and in his very first year he led the team to a Western Division title. (The Rams team that year had Bob Waterfield, Norm Van Brocklin, Tank Younger, Elroy Hirsch, and Tom Fears.) The Rams lost the 1955 NFL championship to the Cleveland Browns, 38-14. Gillman's overall Rams record between 1955 and 1959 was 38-35-1.

Sid was considered one of football's great innovators. He was a strong advocate of frequent use of the forward pass and was responsible for its wide usage in the NFL. He was the first to put the names of players on their jerseys. He is credited with being one of those who introduced the two-platoon system. And, in 1956, he was the first to begin filming practice sessions, and the first to cut game films and organize them according to plays.

Gillman sometimes watched films for 18 hours a day. The whole exercise came naturally to him: "I had the advantage of my family being in the movie business (in Minneapolis in the '20s and '30s). I used to be able to get newsreels in the old days, when we had *Paramount News* and *Fox News*. I'd clip the football parts off." He was once asked how he had been able to do so well in pro football, to which he replied: "The movie projector. You've gotta get your butt behind a movie projector, constantly test your theories, examine your ideas to see where they hold up, to get better ideas."

When the American Football League was founded in 1960, Sid accepted the dual post of head coach and general manager of the Los Angeles Chargers. He led the club to the Western Division title, but lost the playoff to Houston. The Chargers moved from Los Angeles to San Diego in 1961, and Gillman, general manager and head coach, organized their move.

In 1963, when San Diego won the AFL title, Gillman advocated a revolutionary idea, a "super bowl" between the AFL and NFL title winner. The Chicago Bears owner George Halas and NFL Commissioner Pete Rozelle would hear nothing of the idea. At the time of Pope John XXIII's Ecumenical Council in the early '60s, Gillman wired Rozelle: "Pope John was a great man because he recognized the other league." Rozelle wired back: "Yes, but it took a thousand years."

Gillman's Chargers that year were regarded by some observers as the greatest offensive team in pro football history. They averaged an incredible 29 points per game, had an 11-3 record, and crushed the Boston Patriots in the AFL title game, 51-10. Sid himself called the team the best ever produced in the AFL.

In 1964, Gillman's team won the Western Division but lost the title game to Buffalo, 20-7. In all, he won five division titles: 1960, 1961, 1963, 1964 and 1965. His overall record with the Chargers: 86-53-9.

Gillman's teams won because they used the forward pass: "We had to throw the ball. Nobody had any great defenses. I thought that the AFL, from that standpoint, had a slight advantage. You start something new, people want to see the ball. They don't care where it goes, as long as you put it in the air." His teams always did just that.

A duodenal ulcer and hiatal hernia forced his premature retirement in November 1969. But he returned to guide the Chargers in 1971. Sid and millionaire owner Gene Klein did not get along. Bitter disputes ensued; some said over money, some said over Klein's desire to dictate which players to use. Klein dismissed Gillman in midseason.

Between November 1971, when he left the Chargers, and 1973, Gillman enjoyed a brief retire-

ment. For a time he served as an aide to Dallas Cowboy coach Tom Landry. Then the opportunity arose to take over the Houston Oilers.

In 1973 he was hired as executive vice president and general manager with orders to rebuild the Oilers. They had not had a winning season since 1967. In 1972, the year before Gillman joined the organization, the Oilers had been 1-13.

Five games into Gillman's first season (1973), Oiler coach Bill Peterson had led the club to a dismal 0-5 record. Gillman decided to become his own head coach; he put jobs on the line, imposed curfew fines, and bed checks, and added hours of hard work to the training schedule. By the end of 1973, the Oilers were still losing (they wound up 1-13), but they had become competitive. The dramatic change came in 1974, when Houston finished 7-7. "It was like winning the Super Bowl," recalled Sid.

Gillman had problems with Oiler owner J.C. (Bud) Adams, who felt Sid was extravagant. "I'm a believer that you have to have an edge to win," observed Gillman, "and that takes money. You

have to try things the other teams aren't trying. Adams didn't want to hear any of that." He fired Gillman. Soon thereafter, Sid was named Coach of the Year for 1974.

Gillman wrote a column for a syndicated newspaper supplement called *Inside Football Report*, and beginning in 1977 he spent a year as offensive coordinator for the Chicago Bears. The Bears made the playoffs that season for the first time in 14 years. But, eventually he felt his ideas were not getting through to anyone, so, in disgust, he quit.

For 18 months (1978-79) Gillman was athletic director at the United States International University in San Diego, California, near his home in La Costa. He hoped to upgrade football there, but when he got a call from Philadelphia Eagle head coach Dick Vermeil in April 1979, asking him to join the Eagles as an assistant, he quickly agreed. "Pro football is my life," Sid explained.

In July of that year, Sid had a six-way bypass heart operation and he recovered well from it. His title for the Eagles was special assistant in charge of research and quality control. Gillman's major contribution was turning Eagle quarterback Ron Jaworski into a first-class quarterback. "He's the guy who turned us around offensively, as far as being innovative," said Ron of "Coach Sid." Sid taught the Eagles how to use the entire 53⅓ yard-width of the football field on their passing plays.

At the close of the 1980 season, Gillman retired to his La Costa, California, home, with its football-shaped swimming pool. His home was alongside the first fairway of the La Costa Country Club golf course near San Diego. But he could not bow out of football completely. He lectured the Green Bay Packer coaching staff on passing offense and then ran a camp for 10 to 15 year-olds in La Jolla.

When the 1981 season rolled around, Gillman was still in retirement in California. He missed the action: "You wouldn't believe how badly," he admitted. So he came back to the Eagles in March 1982, in his old job of assistant coach in charge of quarterbacks.

In February 1983, he was elected to the Pro Football Hall of Fame; he is also a member of the National College Football Hall of Fame and the Jewish Sports Hall of Fame in Israel.

Gillman joined the United States Football League in 1983 and 1984, first as general manager of the Oklahoma Outlaws, then as a special assistant with the L.A. Express. He was back with the Philadelphia Eagles in 1985 as quarterback coach. He served as an unpaid consultant for the University of Pittsburgh Panthers in 1987. The Panthers gave him the game ball after they upset Notre Dame 30-22 on the way to an 8-3 season.

In 1991, at age 80, Gillman was busy putting together what *Sports Illustrated* called "history's greatest study of offensive football." Using 200 cans of film, Gillman was splicing together raw footage of the best quarterbacks in history, in order to evaluate the current crop of quarterbacks. Though he played golf regularly, it was the time he spent talking with coaches about quarterbacks and showing his film library to friends that appealed to Gillman the most.

Sid Gillman died on January 4, 2003, at the age of 91. In the spring of that year, he was ranked 19th among NFL coaches for most career victories (123). At the end of the 2007 season, according to Actionheroreviews.com, Gillman was 25th in the ranking of all-time winning NFL coaches.

Marty Glickman

The Sprinter Whom Hitler Wouldn't Allow to Compete in the Olympics

GLICKMAN, MARTY (born August 14, 1917 in the Bronx, New York; died January 3, 2001) American sprinter/sportscaster. One of Brooklyn's greatest schoolboy athletes, he earned the right to run a leg for the powerful U.S. relay team in the 1936 Berlin Olympics but was forced to relinquish his place on the team because of Hitler's influence. He became a broadcaster and was best known as the voice of football's New York Giants, basketball's New York Knicks, and later the pro football New York Jets.

• • •

Born in the Bronx, Marty Glickman, while a youngster, never thought of becoming a great athlete, yet he knew that he had one advantage over the other children: from the time he was a five years old, he was always the fastest kid on the block. He remembers racing youngsters around his neighborhood and always winning by half a block. His speed gave him an edge over everyone in all the sports he would later play, and he became one of Brooklyn's greatest schoolboy athletes.

He also gave no thought to becoming a sportscaster, in part because as a youngster he had a lisp and even took remedial courses in grade school. (By the time he began his sportscasting, the lisp was gone, but he noted, "I still had a hard time pronouncing the name of [NBA star] Max Zaslofsky, so I called him Max or Zas.")

Entering Syracuse University, he began a premed program, but when he took a chemistry course he quickly realized that "I would never be a doctor." So he switched to a political science major with the hope of becoming a city manager.

At the age of 18, Marty earned the right to run a leg for the powerful American relay team at the 1936 Berlin Olympics. The Americans were a heavy favorite to win the race, and Glickman seemed assured of winning a gold medal. But at the last minute he and teammate Sam Stoller, also Jewish, were told they would not run in the race—and that the great track star Jesse Owens would take their place. Their coaches gave a reason that to Glickman sounded lame and phony—that the American team had to be strengthened even more because of rumors that the Germans had some powerful sprinters they were hiding. So Glickman and Stoller did not run, and the American team won the gold. The Germans had not produced any secret weapons, finishing in fourth place. Glickman would always suspect that the American track coaches, at the urging of Avery Brundage, president of the United States Olympic Committee, dropped Glickman and Sam Stoller to spare the Nazis the embarrassment of losing a prestigious race to a half-Jewish team.

Two years later, Marty Glickman became a broadcaster. He began by assisting two of the most famous sports announcers of the day, Ted Husing and Bill Stern. Glickman's first broadcast was of the Melrose Games at Madison Square Garden in 1940, an event he had run in himself on previous occasions.

He was best known as the voice of three New York professional teams—the football Giants, the NBA's New York Knicks, and pro football's New York Jets.

Glickman, who became famous for his quick speech delivery, recalled that he "never had a particularly good voice, but I could speak rapidly after I mastered the s. Temperamentally, as a sprinter, you have to be quick. Your mind has to be agile." He found, though, that during his years of announcing basketball games, he had to slow his speaking down. "People who worked with me as statisticians told me, 'We can hear everything you say, but we can't absorb it.' I could speak as rapidly as I think."

The secret of his success as a broadcaster, he liked to say, was his love of the game, almost any game. He announced everything from the New York City marble-shooting championships in the early 1950s to professional basketball and football. "When I broadcast a game, it was as if I were playing the game. So I 'played' football to the age of 75. When Y. A. Tittle or Frank Gifford [both of the New York Giants] scored a touchdown, I scored a touchdown." He enjoyed broadcasting football more than other sports "because every time the ball is snapped so many things can happen."

He coined the phrase "Good, like Nedicks" in describing someone scoring a basket in a basketball game.

In 1972, Marty, as the new sports director, helped the fledgling cable station Home Box Office get off the ground by doing the play-by-play for New York Rangers hockey games at Madison Square Garden.

One sportswriter in 1988 gave Marty the ultimate compliment: "For some of us, the game of football was never as perfect in person as when Glickman was describing it for our ears."

Glickman recalled how the advent of television had changed the way sportscasters worked. "For those of us who started in radio, we had a rapid fire delivery and painted a word picture so you could see the event and see the individual. On television, the broadcaster supplements the picture. He doesn't tell you the obvious, that the man is dribbling up the court. He gives you some background on the player dribbling. I always thought television was much easier; I could sit back and enjoy the game. In radio you're the whole show."

As for his Jewishness, Glickman noted that his parents, both born in Rumania, did not keep a kosher home, but his grandparents did. He himself had a Bar Mitzvah at a summer camp near Glen Wild, New York. "The one thing I don't do in regard to my Jewishness—I will not broadcast on Yom Kippur just as Hank Greenberg and Sandy Koufax wouldn't play on that day."

By far his most challenging broadcasts were those he did from 1989 to 1991 over closed-circuit radio to an audience of blind children. "How do you describe a trapeze performance, an elephant, or a clown's antics, to a blind person?" His first attempt was "brutal" and exhausted him mentally. In time, however, he began describing what he saw in terms blind people could understand—an elephant was "about two flights in the air," or an elephant was "the size of a big dog."

He and his wife, Marjorie, whom he met in high school, have four children: Nancy, David, John, and Elizabeth.

In the spring of 1982, Marty did weekend sports reporting on the six o'clock news for New York's Channel 4.

Starting in 1986 he did radio broadcasts of the NFL's New York Jets games. He was still at the mike for the Jets games in the fall of 1992, at 75, making him one of the oldest play-by-play broadcasters in sports.

He ended his broadcasting career by announcing the final game of the New York Jets season in December 1992. He had broadcast the Jets games for 11 seasons, the New York Knicks for 20, and the New York Giants for 23.

Glickman then embarked on a new career: coaching other broadcasters. That included a weekly seminar for undergraduate sportscasters at New York's Fordham University radio station WSFU-FM. He also coached sportscasters for the Madison Square Garden cable television network and was a consultant on sports to the HBO cable network.

In 1996, the U.S. Holocaust Museum in Washington, D.C., opened an exhibit on the 1936 Berlin Olympics and invited Glickman to speak at the opening. Since then, the exhibit has been taken to four other American cities, and Glickman has been on hand to speak at each of those openings.

In March 1998, the United States Olympic Committee decided to apologize to him for the injustice done him at the 1936 Berlin Olympics. He had always been embittered at being deprived of a gold medal, at being unable to show his children and grandchildren his gold medal. In place of the gold medal, the USOC's president, William Hybl, presented Glickman with the General Douglas MacArthur Award during induction ceremonies for the New York Jewish Sports Hall of Fame in Commack, Long Island.

Throughout the year 2000, Marty Glickman wrote a series of sports columns for GenerationA.com, a Website devoted to the over-fifty generation. He died on January 3, 2001, at the age of 83.

Shlomo Glickstein

Israeli Tennis Star
of the 1970s and 1980s

GLICKSTEIN, SHLOMO (born January 6, 1958, in Rehovot, Israel–) Israeli tennis player. In November 1982, he was ranked 22nd in the world, his highest ever. He concluded the 1981 pro circuit with a ranking of 33rd in the world, compared with his standing of 57 at the end of 1980, and 153 at the end of 1979. In 1981 he was 35th on the list of money-winners among the pros, earning $93,112. Glickstein is one of the greatest tennis players Israel has produced. He has defeated many of the top stars, including Australian Peter McNamara, ranked eighth in the world. Glickstein's best tournament win was the South Orange, New Jersey, $75,000 Grand Prix, held in August 1981. Glickstein's 1982 world rank was 38; in 1983, he fell to 43. His career prize money came to $588,880. He retired from active tennis in early 1988.

● ● ●

Shlomo began playing tennis when he was 10. He played at a small club near his home in Ashkelon about twice a week until the age of 16. An excellent athlete, Shlomo played basketball and soccer as a child, but he gave them up to concentrate on tennis. One major problem he faced was the lack of courts in Israel. "We had to move from one club to another to practice on different days every week," recalled Glickstein. "It was really tough." No club would accept the national team (of which Shlomo was a member) and allow them to practice because members wanted to use the courts for themselves.

By age 12, Shlomo had made enough progress to catch the eye of the national coach Ron Steele. "Shlomo was undoubtedly the best tennis prospect in Israel," recalled Steele. "I used to go down to Ashkelon on Saturdays especially to train him." During the 1975 and 1976 seasons, Shlomo competed in a number of international tournaments, doing rather well in general. "By the time he finished the juniors," noted Steele, "Shlomo was one of the top ten juniors in the world."

But an obstacle awaited him: the Israel Defense Forces. Like all Israeli males, Shlomo Glickstein had to serve three years in the Israeli army, beginning at age 18. Though the army gave him special consideration (he was based close to the Israel Tennis Center in Ramat Hasharon outside Tel Aviv), there is no denying that military service took three years out of his life at the most productive time in a young tennis player's career. Shlomo did manage to play on Israel's Davis Cup team from 1976 to 1980, despite his army service. His job in the army was to work with youngsters who, because of their social backgrounds, had little motivation to take the army seriously.

For a time, Glickstein wavered in his commitment to tennis. Then in 1978, his father, Moshe, a former chairman of the Israel Tennis Association's Youth committee, died. Shlomo told Ron Steele at the time, "I've made my decision: I'm going to be a tennis player. I want to honor my father's name in tennis." From then on he dedicated himself completely to the game.

Glickstein joined the professional tour in May 1979, shortly after his release from the army. That year he won his third straight Israeli national championship. Then came a turning point in his career. At the Tel Aviv Grand Prix that October he reached the quarterfinals, but more importantly, coach Ron Steele, arguing that he was still not aggressive enough, advised him to play in Sweden and in Australia. "Shlomo was instructed to attack, attack, attack." said Steele.

In November 1979, Glickstein managed to stretch John McEnroe to three sets in the first round of the Stockholm Grand Prix after losing the first set 6-0 in five minutes. "Shlomo realized," noted Steele, "that the giants of the game were only human." Glickstein learned that aggressiveness pays off.

In January 1980, Glickstein won the Australian Hard Courts Championship in Hobart, a victory which brought him $8,750 and enabled him to advance a full 200 places in the ATP rankings within three months. His second major success was also won below the equator as he climbed to the quarterfinals of the Sigma Open in Johannesburg, South Africa. Returning to the American circuit, Glickstein defeated Bill Scanlon to reach the semifinals at the Stowe Grand Prix in Vermont.

But, it was a first-round upset win at Wimbledon in 1980 that won Glickstein instant international recognition. He defeated Raul Ramirez (then ranked 35). Britain's mass circulation *Daily Express* carried a banner headline which read: "Shlo-motion." The subhead announced: "Ramirez Rocked by Israeli Hero." Israeli journalists, noting that Glickstein had grown up in Ashkelon, compared him with the biblical Samson, another native of that seacoast town.

In the second round at Wimbledon, Shlomo faced Bjorn Borg. The Swede triumphed on his way to his fifth Wimbledon championship, but the loss was tempered by Borg's kind words for Shlomo: "He has been doing very well. After all, he's been on the circuit only one year." Glickstein won the Wimbledon Plate, the consolation tournament, that year.

Then Shlomo defeated the world's No. 11 player, Brian Gottfried, at the Stockholm Open, and made it to the quarterfinals there. He also got into the finals of the British Hardcourt championships in Bournemouth. His biggest financial reward that year came in December when he earned $20,000 in prize money at the World Championship of Tennis Challenge Cup in Montreal, coming in fifth in the eight-participant tournament which included some major figures in international tennis.

In 1981 Glickstein continued to improve, and he won the South Orange, New Jersey, Grand Prix, the first time an Israeli had won a tennis grand prix. He reached the semifinals of the South African and Canadian Opens and the quarters of the Australian Championship. He also reached the

SHLOMO GLICKSTEIN

quarterfinals in another five Grand Prix meets. During that year Glickstein defeated Harold Solomon and Eliot Teltscher, ranked 9 and 10 on the ATP computer. In doubles, he was runner-up at South Orange, with his Davis Cup teammate Dave Schneider, and he reached the semifinals in two other Grand Prix standings. He was ranked twenty-fourth at the end of 1981: he had been thirty-eighth at the end of 1980.

Ivan Lendl, the Czech tennis star, commented on Shlomo in the summer of 1981: "He has great anticipation. He always waits for the ball where the ball is coming. He looks as if he's going to move very slow, but he is really very fast. He always does the right thing. He has great shots, especially passing shots on the backhand down the line. He has a great touch."

On his own performance in 1981, Glickstein noted, "My game is now steadier and I am not making so many unforced errors. I believe I am capable of beating any player on the circuit, except perhaps the top six."

He has one gripe: the media. "They quote me and that makes me nervous. They write all sorts of things about my personal life outside tennis."

In May, 1982, Glickstein achieved one of his most impressive wins, taking the eight-man Tennis Classic in Tulsa, Oklahoma. He picked up $25,000 for the triumph, but, unfortunately for him, no ATP points to improve his ranking, since the tournament was outside the Grand Prix circuit. The following August, he reached the semifinals of the South Orange, New Jersey, Grand Prix tournament, which he had won the previous year.

His best career win came in April 1983 when, ranked 43, he defeated Ivan Lendl, then ranked No. 1, in three sets in the first round of the Monte Carlo Open. Glickstein subsequently lost in the quarterfinals to Mel Purcell. Glickstein slipped to a world ranking of 82 in 1984; and to 167 in 1985.

Glickstein contributed his share to the Israeli Davis Cup team, winning 70 percent of his 65 matches between 1976 and 1988. Though ranked only 350 in 1986, Glickstein helped Israel conquer the European Zone Davis Cup competition, with wins over Belgium, Holland, and Switzerland.

Retiring from the tour in early 1988, Shlomo became director of the Israel Tennis Academy in Ramat Hasharon. The Academy provides coaching to Israel's most promising tennis players. Since 1988, he has been captain of his country's Davis Cup team.

In March 1992, Glickstein noted how far Israel had come in developing top-flight tennis players: "Now our program is fully professional. We have good coaches. Everyone has enough chance to practice. The improved facilities have made it easier on the players in the past 10 years. But maybe it's too good. When I was playing, we developed independently. We had to fight for everything."

Glickstein retired as director of the Israel Tennis Academy in 1996, but he continued to work with the Israel Davis Cup team, which he had been coaching since 1986. During various periods in the 1990s and early 2000s, he also coached the women's Federation Cup team. He curtailed that involvement in 2001, and since 2002 has been running a new "dream team" program at the Israel Tennis Center, the goal of which is to develop young tennis players in a team format. On August 31, 2005, at a ceremony in Tel Aviv, Glickstein was one of twenty Israelis honored with a lifetime achievement award by the Sports Veterans Association.

Shlomo Glickstein is married and the father of two daughters and one son.

Marshall Goldberg

All-Pro Defensive
Football Player

GOLDBERG, MARSHALL "BIGGIE," "MAD MAR-SHALL" (born October 24, 1917, in Elkins, West Virginia; died April 6, 2006) American football player. One of football's most powerful runners. He played for the University of Pittsburgh from 1936 to 1938 in the backfield. Twice chosen All-American. Played for the Chicago Cardinals from 1939 to 1943 and from 1946 to 1948. At Pittsburgh, in 29 games, he gained 2,231 yards and scored 18 touchdowns. An excellent defensive player in the pros, he led the National Football League in interceptions (7) in 1941. He was on the All-Pro defensive team in 1946, 1947, and 1948.

. . .

Marshall and his family were heroes in Elkins, West Virginia, a small town of 7,500. Marshall's father, Sol, a Russian immigrant, gained prominence in the town because three of his five sons were football stars with the local Davis-Elkins High School team. Marshall was chosen as the student "most likely to succeed." In 1934 and 1935 he was on the All-State basketball team and he captained the State Championship basketball team in 1935. He was All-State in football in 1934 and a member and captain of the track and basketball teams as well during his senior (1935) year of high school.

Marshall earned the nickname "Biggie" because he could play football with boys much older than he. He was 5 foot, 11 inches tall and weighed 183 pounds when he entered the University of Pittsburgh in 1935.

Marshall's effectiveness in college was hampered because he never did learn how to pass well; nevertheless his college career was studded with marvelous feats of running.

Goldberg broke into the Pittsburgh varsity lineup as a sophomore in 1936 and contributed significantly to the team's being chosen to play that year's Rose Bowl. He scored two touchdowns in the first game of the 1936 season. In the fifth game against Notre Dame, he carried the ball 22 times for 117 yards, scored a touchdown, passed for another, and set up a third. He was a national hero. New York reporters, impressed with his speed, called him "Glittering Goldberg." He was also described by sportswriters as "the finest ball carrier since Red Grange." Pitt was 7-1-1 in 1936; the team went on to beat Washington in the Rose Bowl 21-0. Goldberg had scored six touchdowns that season. He received an honorable mention for the All-American team.

The story is told of Marshall's father breaking the tension before the Pitt-Washington game on New Year's Day, 1937. With all the excitement surrounding the Rose Bowl, the Pitt team had a bad case of jitters before the game. In the dressing room, the coach, Doc Sutherland, read a telegram from Marshall's father:

"Dear doctor, bring home the bacon. And you know how I hate pork!"

Laughter erupted, and the team went on to beat Washington 21-0. When Sol Goldberg was not watching the team from the Pitt bench, he was back home running his movie theater. When a competing movie theater showed Marshall Goldberg playing in the Rose Bowl, Sol wrote to Fox Movietone's News Department: "When you have any more Goldberg pictures, for God's sake, send them to Goldberg!"

Marshall Goldberg's first great year was 1937 when he made the All-America first team, picking up 701 yards in 10 games and scoring five touchdowns. He was fifth in rushing in the nation. Pitt was undefeated, 9-0-1 and college national champion. In selecting Marshall Goldberg All-American in 1937, the Associated Press wrote: "Coaches say that he is the fastest man they have observed in years. But "Biggie" is not only a hard-driving, deceptive runner, especially dangerous off the tackles

or around the ends. He is a good blocker, hard-hitting on the defensive, and plays the safety spot."

In 1938 he was switched from halfback to fullback. He scored seven touchdowns and picked up 375 yards as the Pittsburgh Panthers were 8-2. Again, he was an All-American selection, one of the few players to become an All-American twice and in two different positions. After Goldberg helped Pitt destroy Temple, 38-6, one sports reporter wrote: "Goldberg had to be seen to be believed. He slashed at the tackles, swept the ends, ripped on reverses, pummeled the middle."

In 1939, Goldberg began his pro career, playing with the Chicago Cardinals. He was less impressive than in college because the pros relied more on passing than running, the latter being Marshall's real talent. In addition, the Cardinals were, quite simply, a poor team. From 1939 to 1946 (with two years out for navy service) Goldberg played on teams which compiled a 15-47-3 record.

Besides leading the NFL in interceptions with seven for 54 yards in 1941, he was also NFL kickoff return leader with a 24.2 yard average, 12 for 290 yards. In 1942 his kickoff return average jumped to 26.2, with 15 for 393 yards.

In 1947 the Cardinals finally had a championship team, but Goldberg hurt his knee in the ninth game of the season and he finished the year playing only defense. After Chicago won the title game, Goldberg wanted to retire but decided to try one more season. In 1948, he limited himself to defense, helping the Cardinals win a second straight Western Conference title. (They lost to the Philadelphia Eagles in the title game, 7-0) At the time, Goldberg was considered the league's best defensive back.

"Football," Goldberg once noted, "taught me to look for and expect only victory. It also taught me singleness of purpose, poise, competitiveness, the ability to get along with others and the ability to sacrifice."

Following retirement, Goldberg became involved in several businesses related to used machinery and machine tools. He sought to downplay his athletic career. "I don't like to live in the past and talk about my athletic accomplishments all the time," he said. "I prefer to live in the present. I'm more proud of my accomplishments off the field. To me, playing sports should be a stepping stone to a career. It's not an end in itself."

In 1987, when the University of Pittsburgh marked its 200th anniversary, Goldberg was presented with a Bicentennial Medallion for his lifelong contributions to the school. In December 1999, when *Sports Illustrated* named the 50 greatest sports figures of the century from each state, Goldberg ranked 31 on the West Virginia list.

A member of the Jewish Sports Hall of Fame in Israel, Marshall Goldberg died on April 6, 2006, at the age of 88.

Following his death, family members set up The Marshall Goldberg Traumatic Brain Injury Fund at the University of Illinois. Concussions sustained during Goldberg's career had made his post-football life difficult. The fund focused attention on the problem of head injuries among athletes, a topic of intense debate among National Football League personnel.

Sidney Gordon

A Talented and Well-Liked Baseball Player

GORDON, SIDNEY (born August 13, 1918, in Brooklyn, New York; died June 16, 1975) American baseball player. One of the most popular New York Giants. He played 13 years in the major leagues. In 1,475 games, he had 1,415 hits, 202 home runs, 805 runs batted in, and a career batting average of .283. A power hitter, he hit two homers in one inning in 1949, and four with the bases loaded in 1950.

• • •

Sid Gordon was a typical Jewish kid from Brooklyn whose ambition was to become a major league baseball player when he grew up. At Samuel Tilden High School, Gordon developed into a fine hitter, but since their school team played only twice a week, Sid had time to play semipro ball for the Bushwicks and the Brooklyn Pirates. In the summer, he drove his father's coal truck and hauled coal which helped develop his muscles.

In 1936, Gordon almost had his first break in baseball after his high school graduation. Casey Stengel, the Brooklyn Dodgers' manager, had an eye on him and told the youngster that he would have a place in the Dodger farm system at the first opportunity. But Stengel was fired, and Gordon missed his chance.

The following year Gordon was playing with the Queens Alliance League when he was spotted by a New York Giant scout. The scout offered Gordon a tryout with a Giant farm club in Milford, Delaware, on condition that Sid pay his own way. He would be reimbursed for the trip if he made the team. As he was getting ready to leave for the Milford tryout, his father died. Gordon believed he

should stay home to run the family coal business, but his mother insisted that her son travel to Milford. She gave him $32.00 for the trip and the gamble paid off.

Earning $17.32 a week playing for Milford (a minor league team in the Eastern Shore League), Sid won the league batting title in 1938 with a .352 average in 112 games. He played third base, hit 25 homers and led the league in total hits with 145. He was promoted to Clinton in the Three-I League, and by the end of the 1938 season, was moved farther up—to the Jersey City Giants. Two seasons later (by this time he was married to Mary Goldberg), he had done well enough for a chance at the majors. In the 1941 season, he got his chance.

Gordon was switched to the outfield. In his first game, he caught eight fly balls and hit a triple and a single. He finished that first season with a .304 batting average. That season the Giants had four Jewish players on the squad: Gordon and Morrie Arnovich playing the outfield, Harry Feldman pitching, and Harry Danning catching. In 1942, Gordon started at third base for the Giants, but he was sent back to Jersey City in the minor leagues where he hit .300 for the rest of the year. Gordon returned to the Giants in 1943 and remained with them through the 1940s except for 1944 and 1945 when he served in the armed forces.

Gordon's best seasons were after World War II. In 1947, he hit .272 with 13 home runs, a big improvement over the mere five he had hit the year before. In 1948, Giants' coach Red Kress advised Sid to change his batting stance so that Gordon could take advantage of the short leftfield wall at the Polo Grounds. The advice worked. That year Gordon reached his peak: he belted 30 home runs, hit .299, and drove in 197 runs.

In 1949, Gordon played the outfield, first base, and third base, hitting .284, with 26 home runs. During the winter of 1949 he was traded to the Boston Braves, and the next year—one of his best—Sid hit .304, with 27 homers, and 103 runs batted in. He also tied a major league record for most home runs (four) with the bases loaded in one season.

Even though the Braves slumped in 1951 and 1952, Gordon still did well, hitting .287 in 1951 and .289 in 1952. In 1953 his batting average was .274, with 19 homers and 75 RBI. Sid ended his career with the Pittsburgh Pirates, playing for them in 1954 and 1955.

Gordon was one of the most respectable and well-liked players. When some of the St. Louis Cardinals made derogatory anti-Semitic comments to him from the bench during a June 1949 game, New York's newspapers rushed to his defense. Sid refused public comment.

He always played well in Ebbets Field, home of the Brooklyn Dodgers, during his career. He had a simple explanation: "If 30,000 fans were in the park, I knew 25,000 of them."

In 1956, he became a player-coach for the Miami Marlin team, then the newest entry in the International League (minor league). After his connection with baseball ended, he was employed as a life insurance underwriter with Mutual of New York.

Brian Gottfried

One of the World's Best Male Tennis Players

GOTTFRIED, BRIAN (born January 27, 1952, in Baltimore, Maryland–) American tennis player. Semifinalist at Wimbledon in 1980. Best year on the circuit was 1977, when he won five tournaments and reached the finals in 15. In 1982 he was ranked fifteenth best tennis player in the world.

. . .

Brian, the son of a land development construction executive, began hitting balls across the net as an undersized seven-year-old in North Miami, Florida. When he was nine, his family hosted some Japanese youngsters who were participating in the junior circuit's prestigious Orange Bowl tennis tournament. The visitors provided the inspiration for his taking the game seriously. A year later, he was playing well enough to get an occasional free racquet from the local Wilson racquet agent.

Then a stroke of luck befell Brian in the person of Nick Bollettieri, a veteran teaching pro. Bollettieri spotted Gottfried practicing one day, liked what he saw, and agreed to take him on as a pupil.

For the next six summers, Brian was on the court by seven o'clock every morning for intense drills. "It constructed the entire foundation of my game," Gottfried recalled.

Brian won the national 12-and-under doubles championship (with partner Jimmy Connors) in 1962. The following year, Brian and Dick Stockton won the doubles title, and in 1964 Brian won the under-12 singles. For this last performance, *Sports Illustrated* focused on him in its "Face in the Crowd" section suggesting that he was a young tennis player with a bright future.

Brian spent the last two years of high school at the Baylor School, a military academy in Chattanooga, Tennessee. He went there because of the school's excellent tennis complex (where tennis could be played all year round), and because of the tennis coach, Jerry Evert (tennis star Chris' uncle). One of Brian's classmates was Roscoe Tanner, another tennis star. Gottfried and Tanner soon became close friends and later rivals on the court. In Brian's junior year, Baylor placed second in the National Interscholastics and in his senior year, first.

But life at Baylor had difficult aspects for Brian. He recoiled at Baylor's strict military regimen. "My whole life had been spent in a warm, liberal-thinking closely-knit Jewish family pattern where nothing was especially structured and an atmosphere of relaxed enjoyment prevailed. Now, suddenly, here's all this Mickey Mouse stuff coming at me. I found it hard to cope."

When Brian was 16, he discovered the opposite sex. Before that he had never dated. "How could I? I was always on a tennis court." He also developed a fondness for liquor, particularly rum and cokes.

Brian entered Trinity University in San Antonio, Texas, with a full tennis scholarship, but on academic probation due to his high school antics. Brian admitted to having little interest in academic life. "Truthfully, ever since my younger years in Florida, my Bar Mitzvah and all that—I'd lost interest in academics." His choice of college was based on the opportunities offered to improve his tennis.

Troubled by Gottfried's drinking, Trinity tennis coach Clarence Mabry minced no words when lecturing Gottfried in his office one day. Mabry told Brian that he could easily fritter away his talent on the court by too much carousing. "The choice is simple," said the coach. "Either play around or learn to play this game half decently." After that, Gottfried never took another drink.

The results were impressive. As an 18-year-old freshman, he won the 1970 National Junior Outdoors title (beating Jimmy Connors in the final). Gottfried was ranked as Trinity's No. 2 player after

Dick Stockton. Together, they led the university to the NCAA title. While in school, Brian had won 14 national junior titles. In 1972, he was runner-up in both the singles and doubles in the NCAA championships. Gottfried left college after three years; the lure of the profits in professional tennis was too tempting.

In 1973, his first full year as a pro, Brian won $90,000 and was named rookie of the year by *Tennis* magazine. He won the distinction largely because he was the only newcomer to win a major international tournament, namely the Alan King Classic held at Caesar's Palace in Las Vegas, Nevada. That triumph earned him $30,000 and a $6,000 car, making the Classic the most rewarding tennis tournament in history. The undersized kid had become a 6 foot, 170 pound champion. Brian's response to his victory was restrained, which caused his wife, Windy, to scream: "Get happy, will you!" *Sports Illustrated* concurred when it wrote of Brian, "He has eyes about the color of har-tru, his scraggly hair reminiscent of a net, his expression revealing all the emotion of a baseline."

Sandy Mayer, a tennis colleague who has played with Gottfried since they were nine years old, explained Brian's passive reaction: "Brian just always wanted to be a purist. He could put the ball where he wanted to anytime, anywhere, and it really didn't matter so much to him whether he won or lost." Purist and perfectionist.

From 1976 to 1978, Gottfried was a member of the U.S. Davis Cup team. Until 1977, he was regarded largely as a great doubles player, teaming up with his close friend and partner, Raul Ramirez. But his singles record is excellent as well. In 1976, he ranked sixth in the U.S. and tenth in the ATP rankings. A crucial turning point in his career was the U.S. Open in 1976. He was leading Bjorn Borg two sets to none in the quarterfinals when he came apart and the match eventually went to the Swede. "I could have beaten him," Brian said afterward, remorsefully. "I found out today that I can play those top guys and I can win. I'm sure of it."

He was right. In April 1977, *Newsweek* called him "simply the best male tennis player in the world at the moment." That year he won four tournaments and almost $100,000, and lost only three matches. On June 19, he attained his best career rank: No. 3. He was a runner-up at the French Open in 1977, reached the quarters of the U.S. Open in 1978, and was a semifinalist at Wimbledon in 1980.

Gottfried thrived on practice. On his wedding day, he managed to practice for a few hours in the morning, and then took the afternoon off to get married. To atone for those missed hours, he put in double sessions the next day. Says Brian: "I wouldn't like to believe I lost a match because I wasn't in shape or well prepared."

He won 25 singles titles, the last in Vienna in 1983; and 54 doubles titles, the last in North

Conway in New Hampshire in 1984 with Tomas Smid of Czechoslovakia. Brian Gottfried received the ATP Sportsmanship award in 1984.

He served as president of ATP in 1986–87, and again from 1987 to 1989. On the ATP Senior tour, Gottfried won the singles title in 1995 in Cincinnati and the doubles title with Ilie Nastase in 1994 in Geneva. In March 2003, with 25 titles, he was ranked 19th among the top 50 all-time open era singles title leaders. In May 2006, having earned $2,782,514, Brian Gottfried ranked 144 on the list of all-time prizewinners.

As of the spring of 2010, Gottfried was residing in Ponte Vedra, Florida, working with the ATP tour and playing on the senior circuit. He also was on the staff of the Harold Solomon International Tennis Academy, in Fort Lauderdale.

Eddie Gottlieb

Founder of the National Basketball Association

GOTTLIEB, EDDIE (born September 15, 1898, in Kiev, Ukraine; died December 7, 1979). American basketball coach and basketball administrator. One of the founders of the National Basketball Association, and one of the pioneers who held pro basketball together during its early decades. He coached the Philadelphia Warriors from 1947 to 1956, piloting the team to its first NBA championship in 1947. Gottlieb's 263-318 coaching record with the Warriors belies his true ability as a coach.

• • •

Eddie's family lived in New York when he was a youngster. There, he would hitch rides on the back of ice trucks to get to the Polo Grounds to watch the New York Giants play baseball. Baseball was his first love. As a player he was quite average. "Two things were wrong with me as a catcher," he said. "I couldn't hit very well, and I couldn't throw very well. But I was an A-1 receiver."

When he was nine, his family moved to Philadelphia. He graduated from South Philadelphia High School in 1916, and two years later from the Philadelphia School of Pedagogy. In 1918, he organized and coached the Philadelphia SPHAs (South Philadelphia Hebrew Association) basketball team.

In those days basketball was so underdeveloped that it was only a prelude to dances. On Saturday nights, one could enter the Grand Ballroom of the Broadwood Hotel in Philadelphia (65 cents for men, 35 cents for women), dance, and watch the SPHAs play. "After such a game," Gottlieb recalled, "one of the players named Gil Fitch would get out

of his uniform, shower, get into a suit, climb onto the stage and lead his band as the dancing began. In those days many of the Jewish people wouldn't let their daughters go to an ordinary dance except when the SPHAs were in action before the dance."

The team reached its peak in the 1925-26 season when it defeated the Original Celtics and the New York Rens in a special series. In the 1930s the SPHAs dominated the Eastern and American leagues with 11 championships. Eddie managed the quintet to American Basketball League titles in 1934, 1936, 1940, and 1945.

In 1946, Gottlieb assisted in organizing the Basketball Association of America which later became the NBA. He coached the Philadelphia Warriors from 1947 to 1955 until illness forced him to resign. His two greatest players were Joe Fulks and Wilt Chamberlain.

In 1952, Eddie purchased the Warriors for $25,000, thus keeping a pro basketball team in Philadelphia. The club went on to win its second NBA championship in 1956. In 1962, Eddie sold the Warriors for the then-record-price of $850,000

and stayed on as general manager when the team moved to San Francisco. In 1964, after serving in that role for only two years, he returned to Philadelphia.

Gottlieb was involved in another sports activity: he made up the season schedules for teams. He once said that he felt as though he had been making schedules "since I was born." From 1952 until 1970 it was Eddie who drew up the schedules of all NBA teams.

Gottlieb was called the "mogul" because, as *The New York Times* wrote upon his death, "his mental powers were extraordinary and his memory almost faultless. He remembered the scores of games, the gate receipts, the attendance, and even the weather. His only difficulty was often pinpointing the exact year." Gottlieb, when told that he was like a mogul, agreed, saying, "a mogul is a top banana."

Gottlieb is a member of the Basketball Hall of Fame and the Jewish Sports Hall of Fame in Israel.

Shawn Green

The Greatest Jewish Baseball Player of the 1990s and Early 2000s

GREEN, SHAWN (Born November 10, 1972 in Des Plaines, Illinois–). Playing in the Minor Leagues for a number of years, in 1993 Shawn Green finally reached the majors, but remained buried on the bench for five years. Only in 1998, when he was allowed to play regularly, did he show the signs of becoming a great baseball player. In 1999, he made the All-Star team and had his best year to date when he hit .309, blasted 42 home runs and drove in 123 runs.

. . .

Shawn's father Ira worked in sales. The family moved from Illinois to New Jersey, then to San José, California when Shawn was a year old. The Greens stayed on in San José until Shawn was 12, moving to Irvine, California. Playing catch with his father often, enjoying his first baseball game at Candlestick Park when he was seven, Shawn had a passion for baseball. His parents purchased a batting cage and pitching machine for him. In love with hitting, he would hit as many as 200 balls daily.

In 1986, at the age of 13, Shawn placed his foot on the railing of Angels Stadium and prepared to jump on to the field to celebrate the Angels eliminating Boston in Game 5 of the American League Championship Series. "I was one of the first kids there in the seventh inning. By the ninth there were thousands and I was worried about being crushed." The experience encouraged him to try to become a Major Leaguer.

In San José, Shawn joined the Little League, then moved on to Pony League ball. In Irvine, he attended Tustin High School where he excelled in

baseball, tying the California Interscholastic Federation hit record with 147 during his senior year. He was a first team selection to the 1991 *USA Today* All-USA high school team.

That year, Shawn earned a baseball scholarship to Stanford University and was drafted by the Toronto Blue Jays. Undecided whether to seek a major league career or attend college, he enrolled at Stanford in the fall of 1991. He reached a compromise with the Blue Jays: he would play baseball in the minor leagues during the summer and attend school during the off season.

Upon watching Shawn Green play for the first time in 1991, Blue Jays scout Moose Johnson filed a report: "Good looking, tall, left-handed hitter. Long neck. Has the resemblance in size, stature and swing to Ted Williams." It was quite a complement, and quite a burden for a young man to shoulder as he was beginning his baseball career.

Receiving one of the highest signing bonuses at the time, Shawn earmarked part of that sum for the Metropolitan Toronto Housing Authority Breakfast Club that provides breakfast for children who might otherwise go hungry.

In 1992, his first professional season, Shawn played 106 games as an outfielder for Dunedin of the Florida State League, hitting in 18 straight games at one point. The following year he played only 99 games for the Knoxville Smokies AA club of the Southern League due to a broken right thumb; he did get 102 hits and was regarded as a top outfield prospect for the majors.

On September 23, 1993, Shawn was called up to play for the Toronto Blue Jays. Playing in just three games, he had one hit in six at bats. Just 20 years old, he earned a World Series ring though he never played in the Series that the Blue Jays won.

Not long after Shawn Green had donned a Blue Jay uniform, Arthur Richman, a senior advisor to the New York Yankees, suggested to Yankee owner George Steinbrenner that he acquire Green.

"He's a Jewish boy, and because of the heavy Jewish population in New York, he could attract a lot of fans."

You don't learn much by having things come easy."

He became the ninth player in American League history (and the first Jew) to hit 30 home runs and steal 30 bases in one season. He was also the fifth player in club history to generate 100 runs and 100 RBI in a season. In that 1998 season, he had a .278 batting average, with 35 homers and 100 runs batted in. Always a good spray hitter, Shawn worked hard to show that he could hit for power. He began to extend his arms through each swing which enabled him to drive the ball greater distances.

"How could a Jewish boy be named Shawn?" asked Steinbrenner.

"It does happen," Richman replied.

Steinbrenner did seek a deal for Green, but it didn't work.

Green spent most of the 1994 season playing for the Syracuse Chiefs in the International League where he won the League's Most Valuable Player and Rookie of the Year awards for winning the batting title with a .344 average. Called up to the Blue Jays in June, he hit only .091 in 13 games and was quickly sent back to the minors for more polishing.

During the 1995 season, playing for Toronto throughout, he turned in a respectable .288 batting average, and yet the top brass seemed eager to trade him away since he could not hit left-handed pitchers. For the next few seasons, Shawn remained on the bench.

It was in 1998 that Shawn Green began to play regularly and the move lifted his game and morale immensely. "Playing every day has made the biggest difference. Adversity is something I've learned about. Being through a lot of tough times the first few years means now I can work through things.

In the 1999 season, Green had a wonderful year, hitting .309, belting 42 home runs and driving in 123 runs. He also stole 20 bases. He was a member of the 1999 All-Star team and was named a contestant in the home run derby. He managed only two homers, finishing fifth of ten. In the game he got an infield hit in his only at-bat. The real highlight for him was meeting his baseball hero, Ted Williams, on that day. Williams gave Green some hitting advice: try to drive the ball up the middle. Shawn said he would never forget the moment.

In one of the great turnarounds in baseball, Shawn Green began heading toward stardom. Talk show host Larry King described Shawn as "the game's next great superstar" in his *USA Today* column. The out-of-town media preferred a quote from Shawn to any other Blue Jay. On eBay, the cyberspace auction house, Green's Topps Stadium Club rookie card, in mint condition, was selling for $155. On becoming a super-star, Green said modestly during the summer of 1999: "This is the first time I've heard things like that. It's so early in the season, but it's very flattering. This year has been a big improvement. I have accomplished a lot of things I wanted to, but a lot of it has to do with our team."

The Blue Jays hoped to sign Green to a multiyear contract and were prepared to pay him $48 million for five years. But he informed the team that he really wanted to play in a major American city with a large Jewish population. One option appeared to be New York. But Shawn wanted to play near the place where he grew up: "It always feels good being in California: the way the weather feels; the grass smells a little different; the cool night air. Being in the stadium reminds me of being a kid again."

In November 1999 the Los Angeles Dodgers acquired Shawn Green from Toronto and signed him to the second highest-paid player contract ever with a six-year deal that averages $14 million a year.

"It's nice to be one of the more recognized Jewish players in the game," says Shawn Green. "There are not that many." In fact, in 1998 there were only five Jewish players, out of a total of 750.

As a Dodger, Green hit 24 home runs in 2000; then, in 2001, he set a team record with 49 home runs, his highest homer output in a season to date. He became only the fifth player ever to hit 40 home runs in a season in both leagues.

On September 26, 2001, the Dodgers were in a fierce battle for the pennant. Nonetheless, in observance of Yom Kippur, Green sat out a game against the San Francisco Giants.

He tied a major league record on May 23, 2002, slamming four home runs in one game, and equaled another record the following month by hitting four homers in four consecutive at bats. Shawn's season home-run total for 2003 was 19.

In September 2004, as had happened two years earlier, the Los Angeles Dodgers were locked in a close National League West pennant race with the San Francisco Giants. Once again Green was confronted with the difficult decision of whether to play baseball on Yom Kippur, and this time he

reached a compromise: he would play on Friday night, Yom Kippur eve, but refrain from playing the next afternoon, Yom Kippur day. He explained his decision as follows: "I'm committed to getting to the postseason and winning. At the same time, I'm committed to my religion and what I've stood for in the past. I wish there were an easy solution, but there's not."

Green and his dilemma attracted widespread attention. Some rabbis criticized the athlete for trying to have it both ways and for failing to fully observe the most sacred day in the Jewish calendar. But others, finding themselves in the same predicament of having to choose between devotion to their religion and obligations to their employer, respected Green's solution.

During the 2004 season, Shawn hit 28 home runs. That was his final year with the Dodgers, for on June 10, 2005, he was traded to the Arizona Diamondbacks. Green finished his debut year in Arizona with 22 home runs, for a career total of 270. Playing for the Diamondbacks through August 22, 2006, he hit .283, with 11 homers and 53 runs batted in.

On August 23, 2006, Shawn was traded to the New York Mets. Considered the best Jewish baseball player since Sandy Koufax, Green was welcomed warmly by New York baseball fans. "The Messiah has arrived," read one poster held aloft in the stands on the day of Green's debut.

Green retired from baseball in February 2008 with a career batting average of .283, 328 home runs, and 2,070 runs batted in. Two of Shawn's bats—the first used on May 23, 2002, to hit 4 homers against the Milwaukee Brewers; the second used to hit a grand slam on May 21, 2000, one of a record six grand-slam homers hit that day—are on display in the National Baseball Hall of Fame.

Henry "Hank" Greenberg

The Baseball Hero
John McGraw Refused to Hire

GREENBERG, HENRY BENJAMIN "HANK" (born January 1, 1911, in New York City; died September 4, 1986) American baseball player. One of baseball's greatest right-handed hitters. In baseball's first century (1839-1939), Greenberg is generally regarded as the best Jewish player. He played for the Detroit Tigers from 1933 to 1947 and the Pittsburgh Pirates in 1947. His career batting average was .313 in 1,394 games. He had 1,628 hits in 5,191 at-bats, with 331 home runs (including 11 grand-slam homers) and 1,276 runs batted in.

• • •

Greenberg was the first National Leaguer to earn $100,000 a year. He was Most Valuable Player in 1935 and 1940, and was selected to the All-Star teams from 1937 to 1940. He led the American League four times in home runs and runs batted in.

Hank Greenberg was the son of Orthodox Jewish parents from Romania. He attended James Monroe High School in the Bronx and won letters in four sports. He began playing baseball for the Bay Parkways in New York. One day, Paul Kirchell, a New York Yankee scout, was present when Greenberg hit three homers in one game. The youngster was offered $1,000 down and $500 a year while he attended college, but he did not accept it. Instead he entered New York University on an athletic scholarship.

In July 1929, while playing baseball with a team in East Douglas, Massachusetts, Hank was noticed by Washington Senators scout Joe Engel, who of-

fered him a $10,000 bonus plus salary of $800 a month if he would agree to play immediately in the Washington chain. Greenberg again refused. Detroit made a more attractive offer: a bonus of $9,000—$3,000 immediately and the rest after he graduated from NYU. The Detroit offer allowed him to stay in college and guaranteed him a job in baseball afterward. Hank agreed. But Hank became restless as spring training was nearing. After one semester at NYU, Hank wired the Tigers that he wanted to join them at once. He was given the remaining $6,000 of his bonus, and began receiving $500 a month to play with the Tigers' minor league farm team in Raleigh, North Carolina. That year, 1931, Greenberg hit .314.

At that very time, John McGraw, the famous New York Giants manager, wanted to buy or develop a great Jewish player. But McGraw overlooked Hank. Later, Greenberg enjoyed recounting how his father had once spent three hours waiting to see John McGraw to convince him to add Hank to the Giants' roster. When McGraw finally met with the elder Greenberg, the manager told him that his scouts had reported adversely on Hank and had concluded that he would never make the major leagues.

In 1932, playing with Beaumont in the Texas League, Greenberg drove in 131 runs, hit 39 homers, and was voted the league's most valuable player. In 1933 he joined the Detroit Tigers. He had problems that first season and moved to third base, because the Tigers already had a first baseman (Harry Davis, who had cost the club $50,000). Not an outstanding third baseman, Hank looked ahead and practiced in the mornings to improve his glovework at first base. Meanwhile, he hit .301 in 117 games, had 12 homers, and 87 RBI. By 1934, the Tigers sold Davis and moved Greenberg to first base. That year he batted .339 and led the league in doubles (63) and homers (26), and runs batted in (139).

As the season neared its autumn finale, Detroit was in a tight pennant race. The concern among fans grew that if Hank did not play on Yom Kippur, the Jewish Day of Atonement, the team's chances of winning the pennant might be hurt. To compound matters, the Tigers infield, of which Greenberg was a part, had played all season without a substitution. When Yom Kippur came, Hank refused to play and the Tigers did indeed lose that game. But Hank had won the city's respect. The Tigers went on to win the pennant (but lost the World Series).

Edgar Guest, America's most popular poet at the time, wrote a poem in homage to Greenberg:

> Come Yom Kippur—holy fast day world wide over to the Jew—and Hank Greenberg to his teaching and the old tradition true, spent the day among his people and he didn't come to play. Said Murphy to Mulrooney, "We shall lose the game today! We shall miss him in the infield and shall miss him at the bat. But he's true to his religion—and I honor him for that!"

In 1935, Greenberg was voted Most Valuable Player in the American League after hitting .328, leading the league with homers (36), and batting in 170 runs. He also collected more than 200 hits. In 1936, when the season was only 12 games old, Greenberg broke his wrist in a collision near first base, and was unable to return to play that year. But he returned in 1937 and drove in 183 runs, second highest in the history of the American League at the time, and batted .337. From then on, Greenberg was considered one of the best right-handed sluggers in the game.

In 1938 he set the major league season record for the most games in which a player hit two home runs in one game—11. He also tied two major league records that year, for most home runs by a right-handed hitter (58) and for home runs in consecutive appearances in two games (four).

Greenberg spent the All-Star break that season trying to improve his hitting: he paid semipro pitchers $10 and $20 to pitch to him all day long. He refused to attend the All-Star game, because the year before he had traveled all night on a Detroit-Washington train only to sit on the bench the entire game. After hitting four consecutive home runs on July 26 and 27, giving him 33, he realized that he was ahead of Babe Ruth's record-setting pace, so he began aiming for the fences.

When Greenberg hit his 58th home run, with five games left in the season, his mother offered to make him 61 baseball-shaped gefilte fish portions if he would break Ruth's 1927 record of 60 homers in one season.

In the final game of the season, with a slim chance to break Ruth's record, he hit three singles before the game was called due to darkness in the seventh inning. "It's just as well," Greenberg said much later. "There was no way I could have eaten all that gefilte fish."

In 1940 Hank moved to the outfield to allow the slower Rudy York to take over at first base. The move was not easy since Greenberg had been an All-Star first baseman. In 1941, he was earning $55,000 a year, a huge sum in those days. But with America's approaching involvement in World War II, Greenberg was drafted into the army after the nineteenth game of the season. Because he was nearing the age limit for military service, he was released from the service in December, two days before Pearl Harbor, only seven months after he had been inducted.

When war was declared against Japan, he immediately reenlisted, became an officer, and was sent to the China-Burma-India Theater where he was in charge of a B-29 squadron of the 20th Bomber Command. In July 1945, he was discharged as an air force captain. He returned to baseball to help the Tigers win the pennant and the World Series that year. Although he played only half a season, and was somewhat out of practice, he still hit 13 home runs and ended the season with a .311 average.

Hank was traded to the Pittsburgh Pirates on January 18, 1947. So loyal to the Tigers was Greenberg that he considered retiring, but he did play for Pittsburgh for one season.

In 1948, Bill Veeck, Cleveland Indian owner, hired Greenberg to work on the administrative side of the ball club. He traveled around the country studying Cleveland farm teams to improve their overall organization, and was paid $15,000. His suggestion to establish a central training camp was accepted by Veeck.

Shortly thereafter he became general manager of the Cleveland Indians, and in 1955, became a part owner. In 1956 Greenberg became the first Jewish major leaguer to be elected to the Baseball Hall of Fame. (He and Sandy Koufax are the only two Jewish major league players who have received that honor.)

Greenberg joined the Chicago White Sox in late 1958 as part-owner and moved to New York the following year. In 1959, the White Sox won their first pennant in 40 years (but Chicago lost to the Los Angeles Dodgers in the World Series, four games to two). Hank sold his interest in the club in 1961 and devoted himself full-time to the management of his personal investments.

He had married department store heiress Carol Gimbel in 1946 and they had three children. Greenberg divorced her in 1958, and, in 1966, married actress Mary Jo Tarola.

In 1974, Greenberg moved to Beverly Hills, where he took an active interest in managing his personal investments, He was also an avid tennis player. In the early 1980s he began work on his memoirs. He died on September 4, 1986.

Hank Greenberg: The Story of My Life, was published posthumously in 1989. Ira Berkow, *New York Times* sports columnist, edited Greenberg's tapes and completed the late ballplayer's literary effort. Berkow wrote in the introduction: "Green-

berg didn't change his name. And though he didn't flaunt his Jewishness, he didn't hide it, either."

In 1999, Greenberg was ranked Number 37 on the *Sporting News'* list of the 100 Greatest Baseball Players; he was also nominated as a finalist for the Major League Baseball All-Century Team.

Randy Grossman

The Football Player Who Was Called "Rabbi"

GROSSMAN, RANDY (born September 20, 1952, in Philadelphia, Pennsylvania–) American football player. All-American in his senior year at Temple University; later an outstanding receiver for the Pittsburgh Steelers of the National Football League. His best year as a pro was 1978 when he caught more passes (37) than any Steeler tight end since 1966.

■ ■ ■

Randy Grossman began his football career at Haverford High School in Philadelphia during the late 1960s. He was also a member of the high school wrestling team. Two schools recruited him: Temple and Xavier, a Roman Catholic uni-

versity in Cincinnati, Ohio. Xavier's interest in him was puzzling. "Maybe," said Grossman jokingly, "they figured I was a prime prospect for conversion." The school had not been known for recruiting Jewish football players.

At Temple, Randy Grossman vindicated the University's interest in him, doing well on a team that didn't pass that often. During the three years he played (1971-74), Randy had a career record of 89 pass receptions for 1,505 yards and 10 touchdowns. In his senior year Randy was named All-East, All-Pennsylvania, and All-American. Said Wayne Hardin, Temple's football coach: "He can catch anything in nine countries. He's a really super player—quick as a cat, superquick, tough, durable."

Randy has acknowledged that he owed his chance to play both college and professional football to Steve Joachim, the quarterback who passed to him in high school and college. College scouts, watching films of Joachim in their high school games, spotted Grossman by chance. The same thing happened when pro scouts watched films of Joachim in their college games: they noticed Randy!

Grossman was one of 14 rookies to make the Pittsburgh Steelers in 1974. He was signed as a free agent, making the team only because a players' strike prompted the league to increase rosters to 47 players. The Steelers decided to keep three tight ends, including Grossman.

Randy managed to make a few razzle-dazzle plays in his early years as a Steeler. He helped the team win the Super Bowl in his first season. In 1975, he caught four passes in the American Football Conference championship contest and scored the team's first touchdown in the Super Bowl against Dallas. Still, he was seldom a starter or a star.

In their sixth game of the 1978 season, Bennie Cunningham hurt his knee and Grossman replaced him. That was Grossman's best year. He started the final 10 regular season games and three post-season games. He caught a total of 37 passes during the season and added three more in the playoffs, including three in the Super Bowl victory over the Dallas Cowboys. By the end of the 1979 season, Grossman had pulled in nearly 100 passes for more than 1,000 yards gained. Noted for his quickness, he enjoyed the reputation of being able to pluck out a bullet-speed pass in midair. But what gave him his greatest thrill as a Steeler was seeing his picture on a bubble-gum card for the first time.

After the 1978 season, Grossman played somewhat fewer games because of Cunningham's recovery. In 1980 he started 15 games and caught 23 passes (12.7 yards per catch). In the 1981 season his playing time was limited to short yardage situations as a tight end and to the punt and kickoff return teams.

Grossman was nicknamed "The Rabbi" by the other Steelers. But, laughed Randy, "They didn't come to me for spiritual advice." When he grew a beard, he admitted that he "looked like a Hassidic rabbi." A reporter once asked him at a Super Bowl, what a nice Jewish boy was doing in a place like this. Grossman replied: "They called me some pretty bad names when I was on the high school wrestling team. Here they just call me Rabbi." He was once asked if he practiced on Rosh Hashanah, the Jewish New Year: "Why yes," he said, "the Gentiles have to practice on their new year, so I practice on mine."

February 2006 saw Randy Grossman working as a financial adviser. One of his hobbies is flying an airplane. "I do a lot of things," joked Grossman, "but I'm the master of none." Unusual for a football player, Randy also has a passion for knitting. In fact, in February 2006 he and daughter Sarah conducted a class at the Pittsburgh Knitting Festival.

Ernie Grunfeld

Romanian-Born
American Basketball Star

GRUNFELD, ERNEST (born April 24, 1955, in Satu-Mare, Romania–) American basketball player. He played for the University of Tennessee from 1973 to 1977, averaging 22.3 points per game and making the *Sporting News* All-America second team in 1977. He began playing pro basketball in 1977 with the Milwaukee Bucks. Grunfeld was traded to the Kansas City Kings in 1979 and signed to play with the New York Knickerbockers in 1982.

• • •

Ernie lived in Satu-Mare, his birthplace behind the Iron Curtain, until he was nine years old. His father, Alex, had been torn between table tennis and soccer as a youngster. By 1952, the elder Grunfeld was ranked 16th in the world in table tennis.

But as a child, Ernie concentrated on soccer, playing goalie fairly well. It was the only game he knew. His parents, sensing that Jews were not able to get fair opportunities in Romania, decided to emigrate. At first they considered moving to Israel. But in 1964 Grunfeld decided to take his family to New York, where he opened a fabric shop similar to the one he had in Romania.

Ernie grew up in Forest Hills, New York, learning basketball in the schoolyard and playground courts. There he developed a competitive streak that he carried into college and professional ball. On the courts at Russell Sage Junior High School, the team that lost had to stop playing and wait before it got to play again. The winning team kept on playing. The rule had an important effect on Ernie: he hated to lose!

From Russell Sage he went on to a record-breaking career at Forest Hills High School. Ernie was All-American and All-City in his senior year, averaging 25.4 points and 16.6 rebounds per game. He was 6 feet, 6 inches and weighed 215 pounds. In addition, he was selected as the outstanding student-athlete in New York City.

In the summer of 1973, Grunfeld earned one of his greatest honors: He was selected to play on the American team for the Maccabiah Games, the only high school student on the starting five. He led the team in scoring with a 20-point average, but unfortunately Israel defeated the U.S. in the final, 86-80.

Some 200 colleges pursued him. He rejected such major basketball powers as Marquette and Notre Dame, and picked the University of Tennessee because he liked the facilities, the schedule, and the chance it afforded him to become a college star.

In his first season's opening game at Knoxville, Tennessee, Ernie scored 28 points, leading his school to a victory over North Texas State. His best offensive move was the drive from the wing, either down the baseline or up the foul lane. He was especially strong on the offensive boards. Grunfeld was unusual for a freshman. DePaul's veteran coach Ray Meyer noted that Ernie was "like a bull in a china shop, but slick along with it."

Teamed with center Bernard King, Grunfeld helped Tennessee achieve success. (They were later to call it "The Bernie and Ernie Show.") As a freshman he averaged 17.4 points per game. But the following year, Ernie broke his wrist in a pre-season scrimmage against Western Kentucky and was forced to miss six games. Still, he managed to average 23.8 points per game that season. Pro scouts rated him equal—or perhaps superior—to King because he was so rugged.

The elder Grunfeld insisted that his son not work during the college's summer vacation periods so that he could refine his basketball skills. Ernie repaid his father's interest with diligence. In high school, he was a 58 percent free-throw shooter; as a Tennessee freshman, he increased it to 73 percent. Then, in his sophomore year, he hit 81 percent, 80 percent in his junior year, and 79 percent in his senior year. Ernie wore out countless nets to achieve these results.

Grunfeld played for America's gold medal-winning team in the Pan-American Games in the fall of 1975. But his biggest moment in sports came in the summer of 1976 when he helped the U.S. team win the gold medal in the Olympic Games at Montreal. In July of that year Ernie obtained his American citizenship.

His performance at Tennessee was impressive enough to warrant the careful scrutiny of the professional teams. In his sophomore year he had averaged 23.8 points per game; in his junior year, 25.3; and in his senior year, 23.8.

Grunfeld turned pro with the Milwaukee Bucks in 1977. His shooting average dropped considerably, but he was always a steady ballplayer and held his own in the NBA. He averaged 6.9 points in 1977–78, and 10.3 points per game in 1978–79, with Milwaukee. In 1979–80, playing with Kansas City, he had a 5.9 point per game average; and in 1980–81, a 7.5 point per game average. In the 1980–81 playoffs he averaged 16.8 points per game.

Playing for Kansas City, Ernie was put in the guard position, an unusual choice for a player with his build. His coach, Cotton Fitzsimmons, recognized that the move seemed improbable. He acknowledged that Ernie looked like the "first Clydesdale pulling the Budweiser wagon." But the

coach was confident that Grunfeld would do well, and he was proven right.

Grunfeld played with the New York Knicker-bockers briefly in the early 1980s. He remained connected to the Knicks as a television commentator, and then became their assistant coach. In November 1990, he was appointed the team's director of administration. Grunfeld's duties included serving as liaison between the Knicks and the league. In April 1991, Grunfeld was named the Knicks' vice president of player personnel.

He was elevated to vice president and general manager on July 21, 1993 and on February 23, 1996 was promoted to president and general manager of the team.

Grunfeld's 17-year relationship with the Knicks was severed on July 2, 1999, following his troubled relationship with Knicks coach Jeff Van Gundy. Ousted as president and general manager of the Knicks, Grunfeld bounced back and on August 13 of that summer was named general manager of the NBA's Milwaukee Bucks.

On June 30, 2003, Ernie Grunfeld was released from his contract with the Bucks, and a day later he became the president of basketball operations for the Washington Wizards, assuming the position that had been held by Michael Jordan during the previous two seasons. Less than two years after Grunfeld joined the Wizards, the team won a playoff series for the first time in more than two decades. Only in 2005–2006 did the Wizards have a winning record (42–40). In 2009, they were a dismal 19–63, coming in fifth in the Southeast Division.

In the 2009–2010 season, the Wizards were 26–56, fifth in the Southeast Division. In the 2010–2011 season, they were 23–59, once again fifth in the Southeast.

Grunfeld's number 22 jersey, which he wore while at Tennessee, was retired in 2008, making him only the second Tennessee men's basketball player to have a jersey number retired, the first having been teammate Bernard King.

Alfred Hajos-Guttman

Recipient of Olympic Medal for Swimming and Architecture

HAJOS-GUTTMANN, ALFRED (born February 1, 1878, in Budapest, Hungary; died November 12, 1955) Hungarian swimmer. The first Olympic swimming champion and the first Hungarian Olympic gold medal winner. Winner of the medal for architecture at the 1924 Olympics.

. . .

Born Alfred Guttmann, he took the name "Hajos" for his sports career because it was a Hungarian name. Alfred began swimming at the age of four. His father entrusted him to a swimming teacher who in a few short weeks had the child swimming better than his friends or his father.

Despite his swimming ability, Alfred remained a thin, weak boy. He was unable to climb a pole in one physical education class and was therefore excluded from the exercise in the future. As a result he began doing physical exercises to strengthen himself.

In school, Alfred paid little attention to geometry or drawing at first. His gym teacher reproached him for not taking these subjects seriously. Alfred became more serious about his studies, and one day when he showed the geometry teacher his homework, the teacher was so convinced that a professional draftsman had done the work for him that he was severely reprimanded. Later, realizing his mistake, the teacher predicted that Alfred would succeed as an architect.

Alfred was noticed during the Hungarian Swimming Association's first international meet in 1895 in Siofok, Hungary. He won the 100-meter freestyle, and desperately wanted to travel to Vienna to enter the European Championships, but his mother would not permit him to go unless he was accompanied by an adult. In addition, he could not afford the trip since he would have to cover his own expenses. He tried to convince his family that the potential victory in Vienna would bring them fame and help his future career, but to no avail.

Despite their opposition, he went on his own, hoping that some Vienna sports enthusiasts would give him room and board. Alfred's faith in himself was justified as he became European champion, winning the 100-meter freestyle in Vienna. In 1896 he again was European champion in the 100-meter freestyle.

When the first modern Olympic Games were to convene in Athens in 1896, Alfred Hajos was a first-year student of architecture at the Budapest Polytechnical University. He was one of Budapest's best known swimmers. Hajos asked the dean of his faculty, Lajos Llosvay, a chemistry professor, for permission to take a four-week leave of absence to allow him to train for the Olympics. The dean responded very coolly: "Only frivolous people practice sport instead of studying. It can't lead to an honest path." In the end, however, the dean grudgingly permitted Hajos to take the leave of absence.

Training for the Olympics was difficult. Hajos practiced at a pool 23 meters long, six of which were too shallow for swimming. He had to walk four kilometers to the pool each day, pay the equivalent of a 20 cent entrance fee and $10 for 50 training sessions. Alfred had no money, and he persuaded the pool director, Istvan Sad, to let him train without paying the fees.

At the first Games held in Athens, Hajos won the 100-meter and 1200-meter freestyle swimming events. He swam 100 meters in 1:22.2, a time far inferior to the 61.4 of England's Jack Typers when he won the 100-yard title in England that same year. But Typers did not compete in Athens.

However, the Hungarian's 18:22.2 time for 1200 meters was definitely superior to the performance of contemporary English distance swimmers. Alfred joined the other Olympic prize winners at a festive dinner with the King of Greece. The King asked Hajos where he had learned to swim so well. Alfred replied wryly, "In the water." The Greek newspaper *Akropolis* nicknamed Hajos the "Hungarian Dolphin."

On his return to Budapest, Alfred proudly went to Professor Llosvay, who was indifferent to his student's medals: "I'm just impatient to hear your reply to your next exam." Two months later, Hajos took the exams and he was concerned that he would not do well. Hajos was questioned orally by the dean himself. Afterwards, when Alfred passed the exams, Llosvay congratulated him on winning at Athens. He wished his student the same success in architecture as he had achieved in sports.

Hajos excelled in other sports as well as swim-

ming. In 1898 he became Hungary's junior champion in the 100-meter sprint and national champion in the 400-meter hurdles as well as the discus. Hajos was also a pioneer in Hungarian football (soccer). In 1901, 1902, and 1903 he played on several national championship teams in the position of forward. For the next few years he worked in football administration. At one stage he was managing director of the Hungarian Football Union. Between 1902 and 1904 he edited a sports newspaper called *Sport Vilag* (The World of Sport), and also wrote a sports column for Budapest's important daily newspaper *Pesti Naplo*.

In 1899 Hajos completed his studies and received his degree in architecture from the Budapest Polytechnical University.

At that time, fields of endeavor other than sport were included in the Olympics competition. At the 1924 Paris Olympics, a quarter of a century after he completed his degree, Hajos entered the art competition with a design for a stadium, drawn in collaboration with Dezso Lauber, an equally famous Hungarian athlete. Hajos defeated 13 other entrants for the silver medal. Hajos did not get the gold medal (it was not given to anyone that year) because the French did not want to give it to a non-Frenchman, and especially not to a Hungarian since Franco-Hungarian relations had been cool since World War I.

In 1929, Hajos won the Hungarian architects and engineers Grand Prix with a swimming pool study. The next year he created his masterpiece, the Margaret Island National Sports Hall, in Budapest, with a 3,000-seat capacity. That same year (1930) the Hungarian Architects Federation awarded him the title of Master for his "extraordinary creations."

In 50 years of work, Alfred Hajos-Guttmann created a variety of sports facilities as well as hotels, banks, factories, churches, and theaters. When he was 75, the International Olympic Committee awarded him the Olympic diploma of merit. Hajos had achieved the same success in architecture that he had in swimming.

He wrote a short book, *How I Became an Olympic Champion*, in his later years. But he died at the age of 78, a poor man, a few days after delivering the manuscript to the publisher. The book appeared a year after his death (in 1956) on the 60th anniversary of his first winning an Olympic gold medal.

He is a member of the Jewish Sports Hall of Fame in Israel.

HARRIS, SIGMUND (born July 2, 1883, in Dubuque, Iowa; died November 8, 1964) American football player. One of the great quarterbacks of his day. Selected quarterback on Knute Rockne's All-Time Jewish Football Team. In 1903, Harris was first team Fielding Yost All-America, and in 1904, third-team Camp All-America.

• • •

Sig's father was Polish, his mother a Chicagoan. When Sig was a boy, the family moved from Dubuque to Minneapolis, Minnesota. His parents raised him to feel a strong tie with Judaism, and he was sent to *cheder* (Hebrew school).

Harris made the Minneapolis Central High School football team in 1899. The following year, playing an exhibition game against Minnesota University at the start of the football season, he helped to hold the Gophers to a scoreless tie.

In 1901, Harris enrolled at the Minnesota College of Engineering and Mechanical Arts and became second-string varsity quarterback in his freshman year. When the regular quarterback left the next year, Harris took over. He was 5 feet, 5½ inches, and weighed only 140 pounds. During the 1902 season, Sig led Minnesota to a 10-2-1 record. The *Minnesota Alumni Weekly* of December 1, 1902, noted: "Harris has played a wonderful and consistent game all the season, and deserves credit for his work."

The following year (1903), Minnesota was undefeated (14-0-1) and scored 656 points while its opponents managed to score only 12 points. The 1903 Minnesota backfield, with Sig Harris as quarterback, has been rated one of the best in history. In 1904 the Gophers again had a dazzling season record: they were undefeated in 13 games and they scored 725 points while holding their opponents to a meager 12.

After his graduation in 1904, Harris served as assistant football coach at Minnesota, a post he held until 1920. For the next six years he worked in a Minneapolis machine business. In 1926, he returned to fill the job as assistant coach, but left again to return to his business. After three years, he was back as assistant head coach at Minnesota, and this time remained until 1941.

From 1941 until his death he was engaged in his machinery business. Aware that it was odd that he had never been offered a head coaching job, Harris refused to attribute it to anti-Semitism: "I never felt any anti-Semitism in my long contact with college football," he observed.

Julie Heldman

One of America's Best Tennis Players

HELDMAN, JULIE (born December 8, 1945, in Berkeley, California–) American tennis player. One of the finest women tennis players in the United States in the late 1960s and early 1970s. She was ranked No. 2 in the U.S. in both 1968 and 1969. She was ranked No. 5 in the world in 1969, her highest world ranking.

. . .

Julie came from a family steeped in tennis. Her father, Julius Heldman, had won the National Junior Championships in 1936. Her mother, Gladys, was Texas state champion in the early 1950s and founder of *World Tennis* magazine in the summer of 1953.

From Berkeley, where Julie was born, the family moved to Long Beach, California, in the late 1940s for a short time and then (also in the late 1940s) to Houston because Julie's father was working for the Shell Oil Company there. He was transferred to New York in the summer of 1953, and the family moved again.

Julie began playing tennis in the summer of 1954 when, as an eight year-old, she was sent to the United States' first tennis camp, the Hoxie Tennis Camp in Hamtramck, Michigan (located in the Greater Detroit area). At Hoxie the emphasis was on being competitive. Winning was all that mattered. Julie attended Hoxie for the next seven summers.

By her third summer she was winning some local tournaments. Julie's first major victory was the Canadian Junior Championships (for age 18 and under) in Ottawa in August 1958, and her next major achievement was winning the U.S. National

tournament in the summer of 1960 in Ohio (for ages 15 and under).

Julie attended private schools from eighth through twelfth grades, first at the Walt Whitman School and later at the Dalton school, both in New York City. She had skipped two grades while in grammar school and as a result graduated from high school at age 16.

To get far away from home and in order to play tennis, she enrolled in Stanford (California) in September 1962.

In August 1963, at the end of her first college year, she won the National Junior (18 and under) tournament, held that year in Philadelphia. To win this tournament was a "life's goal" because she wanted to match her father's achievement in 1936.

She spent part of her third college year studying in Tours, France, as part of a Stanford program. When the spring season ended in March 1965, Heldman played in a number of European tournaments, reaching the semifinals in the Italian Open in May, her greatest achievement until then. Later that year she played in her first Wimbledon, and got to the final 16 before being eliminated.

In May 1966, she played for the American team in the Federation Cup competition, a woman's team championship held in Turin, Italy. Playing No. 2 for the U.S., she swept all five of her matches in the five-nation tournament won by the U.S.

The pressures of the tennis circuit grew more and more burdensome until they became overwhelming. Heldman graduated from Stanford as a history major in December 1966, quit tennis, and went off to live in a hippie commune in Woodside, California, near Stanford.

Within a few months she tired of the unstructured commune life and, early in 1967, left for New York City where she found work in the art department of an advertising agency. That job lasted three months. She then returned to California where she obtained a job teaching at a summer tennis camp at the Berkeley Tennis Club.

Toward the end of the summer, Heldman returned to the tennis circuit and played in several

California tournaments, reaching the quarterfinals in one and defeating Billie Jean King in the opening round of another. Heldman realized that playing tennis could be a passport to the good life.

In 1968, playing for the Olympics Demonstration Tennis tournament in Guadalajara, Mexico, she came in second in the doubles (with "Peaches" Bartkowicz), and third in the singles. Two weeks later, she won the South American mixed doubles tournament (with Herb Fitzgibbon) in Buenos Aires, Argentina. She was ranked No. 2 in the U.S. that year, and No. 11 in the world.

In May 1969, Julie won the Italian Open. Then in August she traveled to Israel where she won the singles, doubles (with Marilyn Aschner) and mixed (with Ed Rubinoff) in the Maccabiah Games. That same month she played No. 1 for the U.S. in the Wightman Cup competition held in Cleveland, Ohio, winning two singles and a doubles match. She was named the outstanding player in the tournament. In 1969 she was ranked No. 2 in the U.S. and No. 5 in the world, her highest world ranking.

Heldman never experienced any blatant anti-Semitism on the tennis tour, although she did acknowledge feeling uncomfortable when playing tournaments at East Coast tennis clubs which excluded Jews and blacks from membership.

Julie was forced to quit tennis for six months in the summer of 1970, when she injured her elbow. In the fall of 1970, her mother, Gladys, was the key organizer of the Virginia Slims Tennis Circuit, the first all-women's tennis circuit. Gladys wanted Billie Jean King and other women tennis players who helped form the new circuit to separate women's professional tennis from the men's, to achieve parallel status for the women. Julie served as a liaison between her mother and the players.

Julie returned to active tennis in early 1971,

but didn't play well. She hurt her knee in August of that year, while playing at the Wightman Cup in Cleveland. In March, 1972, she underwent surgery in London for torn cartilage in her knee.

Toward the end of 1973, Heldman came under the tutelage of Angela Buxton, the great tennis star of the 1950s, and Jimmy Jones, Buxton's teaching partner. Heldman lost most of her good strokes because she tended to favor her injured knee, but Buxton and Jones helped restore her game. The next year, 1974, was Julie's second best of her career. In 1974, she reached the semifinals of the U.S. Open in Forest Hills (losing to Billie Jean King), and she reached the finals of the Virginia Slims tournament in Sarasota, Florida.

Fellow-players consider Julie Heldman one of the toughest competitors the game has known.

the toughest competitors the game has known. She was a hard and accurate hitter from the baseline, and her serves were soft, carefully-placed slices. She rarely went to the net. Heldman would usually win, not because of raw talent, but because of tactical superiority. Her strokes were never perfectly smooth, but she hit the right spots at the right time. Mixing up forehands and backhands with off-speed drop shots and lobs, Heldman used the tennis court like a large chess board. She also had an unorthodox forehand—a snappy undercut delivered with an oddly-cocked elbow. Although Heldman admitted that her stroke looked odd, it helped her get better topspin control. Her trademark was a floppy brimmed cap.

During Julie's tennis career, which ended in 1975 because of a shoulder injury, she carried on a second career in writing, radio, and television. She wrote tennis articles for *World Tennis* magazine and provided commentary for matches broadcast on TV. Between 1973 and 1975 she covered the U.S. Open on CBS-TV. Between 1975 and 1977 she helped cover Wimbledon for NBC. In 1976 she was the first woman to comment on a men's tennis tournament—the Avis Challenge Cup in Hawaii.

In August 1978, she entered UCLA Law School and graduated in May 1981. That same month she married Bernard Weiss, a businessman with two sons, Seth and Darren, from a previous marriage.

Heldman practiced law between 1981 and 1985 and then joined her husband in running USA Optical Distributors, Inc., a Los Angeles firm that sells eyeglass frames to optical retailers. She and her husband began a new venture in 1991 called Signature Eyewear, Inc., which has exclusive licenses to import, sell and promote Wimbledon and Laura Ashley eyeglass frames in the U.S. and Canada.

Julie resigned as president of Signature Eyewear on June 14, 2000. Nearly three years later, on April 25, 2003, her husband retired as Chairman of the Board and CEO of the same company. Signature's Laura Ashley Eyewear line has been the most successful women's eyewear collection in America.

Victor Hershkowitz
A Legendary American Handball Player

HERSHKOWITZ, VICTOR (born October 5, 1918; in Brooklyn, New York; died June 23, 2008) American handball player. The *United States Handball Association Magazine* rated him best all-around handball player in history. Few athletes have won as many championships as he did. Beginning in 1942, he accumulated 43 titles, including nine straight three-wall championships from 1950 to 1958, which no other player has repeated. "I don't know why," Vic said in 1974, "but people considered me a legend."

• • •

Victor Hershkowitz, born in the Williamsburg section of Brooklyn, was the youngest of seven children of an immigrant baker from Hungary. He went to Alexander Hamilton and Eastern District high schools. He was captain of the sixth-year high school intramural team in baseball, for which he played outfield and catcher, but could never make the high school handball team. One of the high school handball team's members was Red Auerbach, who later became the great basketball coach of the Boston Celtics.

It is quite likely that, had he wished, Vic could have carved out a career for himself in pro baseball. Vic explained it this way: "The late Sid Gordon of the New York Giants and Carl Erskine of the Brooklyn Dodgers used to tell me that. But I started playing handball. And anyone who plays handball gets addicted. It's like a disease—once you're exposed to it, it's got you."

Out of school in the depression year of 1936, Vic took whatever jobs were available, mostly in the shipping departments at various stores. He started playing handball in 1936 at the Lafayette and Marcy playground in Brooklyn. Compact and powerful-ly built, Vic entered his first tournament at the Washington Baths in Coney Island that same year and won. He entered his first national tournament two years later, losing in the finals of the one-wall tournament. But he continued to practice and improve his game. "I got to be good at handball and played it more than other sports," he said. "The fact is," he admitted, "I was unemployed and that's why I was playing ball."

He married in June 1941, and the couple had two boys and a girl. By 1942 he teamed with Moe Ornstein to capture the National One-Wall Championship. He then entered the service (in 1944) and did not play handball again until 1946. He was released from the armed forces in November 1945, and became a postman in 1947, remaining one for the next three years, and playing handball in his spare time.

His handball record was impressive. He won national titles each year from 1947 to 1967, except for 1959. "That's a tough record to beat in any sport," Hershkowitz wrote in 1982. In National AAU competition, he won the one-wall doubles in 1942, 1948, and 1956. He was one-wall champion in 1947, 1948, 1950, 1952, and 1953, and singles champ in 1949 and 1952. Hershkowitz was international three-wall champion every year from 1950 to 1955; he won the National YMCA singles title in 1953. In 1954, he won the National American Handball Association singles crown and the doubles in 1961. During this time he represented the Brooklyn, New York, YMCA.

Until 1947, he was strictly a one-wall player but then he defeated Angelo Trulio, the defending national four-wall champion, in a New York state tournament (which Vic went on to lose). In 1949 Hershkowitz won the national four-wall and one-wall tournaments.

Hershkowitz was one of the few players who played all year round, four-wall in the winter, one-wall at the beaches in the summer.

In April 1950, he became a fireman and remained one until July 1973. He had no special duties as he explained: "I just put out the fires." He liked his new profession because his work schedule fit in well with his playing: He worked two days from 9 A.M. to 6 P.M., then two nights from 6 P.M. to 9 P.M., and he was off for 72 hours. Thus, he was able to play at least three times a week. He usually played doubles when not participating in actual tournaments.

Harold Rosenthal, writing of Hershkowitz in *The New York Times* in 1948, said: "The report is that the Brooklyn champion has no obvious weaknesses. He can kill off either hand, is as tireless as an eight-day clock. He can pick the little black ball off the back wall with an almost unbelievable deftness."

In 1952 he gave his greatest performance on the courts, winning the four-wall, three-wall, and one-wall titles. At the time he was the only player who could accomplish that feat. Vic was nominated for the Hickok Belt as the Athlete of the Year but, as Hershkowitz recalled, "Handball being such a minor sport, I didn't get enough votes. But that doesn't bother me. When you talk about handball to someone who knows about handball, just mention my name. Everyone has heard of me. And that's a nice thing, you know."

In 1953, he tied Sam Atchinson's national record of 14 championships by adding the YMCA laurels to his collection. The following year he won his 15th, making handball history.

His strong points were his service and being able to hit hard with both hands: "I've got a good opposite (left) hand," he said. The secret of his success was putting pressure on when it was needed: "You force the other guy by speeding up the tempo. If you go for a kill, you hit a kill, and don't go for a foot above it to make sure you don't miss. You see an opening, you go for it. You don't lose your confidence. Will to win is the difference."

Hershkowitz contended that handball is "the toughest sport there is. There's no rest—you've got to go all the way. It's timing, accuracy, stamina, and no coasting."

His Judaism matters to him. "I've always felt that being a Jew made me play and try harder to defeat my adversaries. My Jewishness had to show the nation in this sport that I was proud of being a Jew."

"Vic," observed Sid Belinsky, a handball aficionado, "is the Babe Ruth of the sport. He has that certain something that is far above an ordinary player. He is colorful, graceful, has legs like springs, and he hooks with either hand. He would be a terrific athlete in any game." Because he adapted himself to four-wall and three-wall games after starting with one-wall, Hershkowitz got Belinsky's vote as the greatest handball player of all time. The others were outstanding in four-wall play only. Vic's achievements earned him a spot in the Helms Athletic Hall of Fame in 1957.

In addition to being a fireman, Hershkowitz has been a salesman of business forms.

Vic was asked on March 8, 1969, what, as a sports star, was the height of his ambition. His answer: "To live as long as the old biblical characters lived, well beyond 100. My pop is 95. My mom 90. With parents like that, I stand a pretty good chance of realizing my ambition. That's about all. I have everything else I want in life."

Vic Hershkowitz moved to Florida upon his retirement as a fireman in July 1973. In March 1974, he said that he continued to play handball once or twice a week, but other than that, "I do nothing. I'm retired. I'm supposed to do nothing."

He was inducted into the Jewish Sports Hall of Fame in Israel on December 1, 1990.

In October 1994, he was inducted into the Chicago-based National YMCA Hall of Fame. On March 29, 1998, he was inducted into the New York Jewish Sports Hall of Fame. Even in his late 80s, Hershkowitz played handball once a week at a local Jewish community center. He died on June 23, 2008, at the age of 89.

Art Heyman
College Basketball Hero of 1963

HEYMAN, ART (born June 24, 1942, in Rockville Centre, New York–) American basketball player. A three-time All-American (1961, 1962, and 1963) at Duke University, he was their highest scorer, averaging 25.1 points per game, with 1,984 total points. Art later played four years in the NBA and three in the ABA. In 147 NBA games he averaged 10.3 points per game. In the ABA he averaged 15.4 points. He was voted 1963 college basketball player of the year by the *Associated Press* and *The Sporting News*.

. . .

Heyman had always been interested in playing basketball. At age 10, growing up in Rockville Centre on Long Island, he would constantly dribble a basketball in the playgrounds, as well as in the school corridors.

Once, at age 12, he put tape over the lock on the gym door of his elementary school so that he could slip inside on Sundays to practice. Sometimes he would shoot alone, but more often, being tall for his age, he would be invited by older boys to play in a pickup game. He thus learned to be aggressive at an early age. He said that the most important thing he learned was not to shy away from the basket.

In his three years at Oceanside High School, from 1957 to 1959, Heyman scored 1,405 points, setting a Long Island record for most points scored in a high school basketball career, a record which stood until 1992 when Fred Lyson broke it with 1,580 career points. As a senior in high school, Art averaged over 30 points a game as well as 15 rebounds. The team won the Nassau County championship and Oceanside coach Frank Januszewski complimented his star by noting that "Artie was the team."

Art was also an outstanding soccer goalie on Oceanside High School's undefeated team, and received scholarship offers for both soccer and basketball.

In all, Heyman was offered nearly 100 scholarships. Adolph Rupp, Kentucky's great basketball coach, even showed up at Art's house one day to urge the basketball star's mother to send her son to the best basketball school in the nation and be coached by the best basketball coach.

Meanwhile, Vic Bubas, the new coach of Duke University, sat in the Playbill Restaurant of New York's Manhattan Hotel to discourage Art from following other New York basketball players to the rival University of North Carolina, then a basketball powerhouse. In the end, Art chose Duke, because his father was in favor and because Art thought it was academically superior.

The summer after his high school graduation, 1959, Heyman played summer league basketball, often with some of the best college basketball players. Some of those he played with were eventually involved in the college game-fixing scandals in 1961 in the New York area. But the fixers, Art suspected, never approached him because he was too affluent; they probably figured he did not need the money. When he arrived at Duke in the fall of 1959, Art had already played more basketball, against faster competition, than any Duke senior.

Heyman made a brilliant start. He was soon scoring 30 points a game for Duke in his freshman year. The Duke-North Carolina rivalry flared bitterly during one game that year. When a North Carolina player became angry during a scuffle, Heyman was knocked out by a roundhouse right to the jaw which needed five stitches.

In his sophomore year, he joined a team made up entirely of seniors. In the first 10 seconds of his first home game against Louisiana State University, he took a rebound and dribbled the entire length of the court, evading four opponents and driving over a fifth for a basket. That year, his 629 points led Duke to a 22-6 record. Duke was ranked tenth in the country.

In his junior year, Heyman scored 608 points and helped Duke finish with a 20-5 record and a national ranking of tenth again. In his senior year, he scored 747 points for a national ranking of second. He was All-American in his sophomore, junior, and senior years. Duke had a 69-14 record during Heyman's three years.

Art's coach, Vic Bubas, said that aggressiveness and strength were what set Heyman apart from other players. He was a great driver. Beyond that, he was fast for his size. He was so strong that it was impossible to take the ball from him.

Heyman was not overly modest about his prowess. He once said, "I was the biggest thing that ever happened to Duke." He was certainly one of the most controversial. Heyman was involved in violent incidents both on and off court. Once, after he and a premed student were exchanging insults in the TEP fraternity house, Heyman hit the student and damaged his retina. (Heyman insists that the student began the fracas.) The student lost the lawsuit he brought against Heyman. During Art's sophomore year, he was accused of assaulting a male cheerleader from North Carolina. The charges were dismissed but Heyman was suspended for involvement in a fight later in that game.

At Duke, a Methodist university that did not admit blacks until 1966, no one was particularly aware of Heyman's Jewishness. Many thought

Heyman was a Protestant from Connecticut. Heyman discovered that southerners with whom he came into contact could not comprehend a Jew being a great athlete. He received letters of praise from organizations like The Fellowship of Christian Athletes. A man in Alabama named Horace Shelton regularly sent Heyman telegrams urging him to continue to uphold the principles of white Christian supremacy. Once, Shelton, head of the Ku Klux Klan, offered Art membership in the Klan. Heyman ignored the invitation.

A hero at Duke, Heyman became less heroic after joining the pros. He was the number one draft choice in the NBA and was picked by the New York Knicks in May 1963. He received a large bonus for signing with the team. He played for the Knicks for two years—1963–64 and 1964–65—averaging 15.4 points per game that first year, the highest rookie average for a Knick until that time. In his second year, he fell to 5.7 points per game. In 1965,

Heyman was traded to the San Francisco Warriors for cash and one player.

In all, Heyman played six seasons of pro basketball (1963 to 1970) with seven teams in the NBA and the ABA. In 1967–68 he played for the New Jersey Nets and the Pittsburgh Pipers in the ABA, averaging 18.5 points per game. In 1968–69, he joined the Minnesota ABA team, averaging 14.4 points per game. In his final year, 1969–70, he was traded to the Miami Floridians of the ABA with whom he averaged 7.4 points per game.

He played a total of 310 games in the NBA and ABA and scored 4,030 points for a 13.0 average per game.

During the last 1970 season, he suffered from a bad back, and he would need a spinal fusion if he hoped to continue playing basketball.

Since leaving basketball in 1972, Heyman has owned and run restaurants in New York City. In 2003, he operated the Tracy J's restaurant in the city's Gramercy Park section.

In 2002, *The Sporting News* named Heyman one of the top 100 college basketball players of all time. As part of the 50th anniversary celebrations of the Atlantic Coast Conference, held in 2003, Heyman was named one of the top 10 Conference players of all time.

Marshall Holman

A Bowler Who Has Won More Than 20 Professional Championships

HOLMAN, MARSHALL (born September 29, 1954, in San Francisco, California–) American bowler. Winner of 21 National Tour championships, including the 1976 Firestone Tournament of Champions and the 1985 Kodak Invitational. Elected to *Bowling Magazine's* All-America first team in 1977, 1978, and 1979. He was Bowler of the Year in 1987 and was inducted into the Bowling Hall of Fame in 1990.

■ ■ ■

Marshall Holman's family moved from San Francisco to Medford, Oregon, where Marshall's father, Phillip, was a disk jockey for radio station KFHA. After Phil did a show from the top of a flagpole in the early 1950s, he was known as "Holman the Poleman." Marshall contended that he inherited a tendency to be a "ham" (his own phrase) from his father.

Marshall took up bowling at age 12 and was only fair at the beginning averaging 99 in his first year. In 1971, at age 17, he joined a pro bowling tour, but succeeded in winning only $500. For the next few years he bowled nearly every day, playing at least twenty practice games.

In 1974, Holman felt his game had improved considerably and he joined a summer tour. In his fourth tournament, in Tucson, Arizona, he predicted that he would win the whole thing, but instead finished fifth. In the championship round telecast on cable television, Holman rolled a lowly 149. His earnings for the year totaled only $4,845.

Marshall Holman's first PBA tournament victory came in Fresno, California, in 1975, during his second year on tour. He also won a tournament that year in Hawaii, and his yearly earnings climbed to $27,543. The next year he had one of his biggest tournament triumphs, the Firestone Tournament of Champions in Akron, Ohio. He was the youngest bowler ever to win this highly-prestigious tournament. That year, Holman won $48,630. His yearly winnings climbed to $71,350 in 1977, thanks in part to victories in the Brunswick World Open in Chicago and in the PBA Doubles Classic in San Jose, California, in which he was teamed with Mark Roth.

Despite winning only the Ford Open, in Alameda, California, and a tournament in Cleveland in 1978, he still earned $70,160 for the year. However, the following year Holman won the Quaker State Open, the Columbia-PBA Doubles Classic with Mark Roth, the Seattle Open, and the Brunswick Memorial World Open in Chicago. It was his most successful year; he earned $107,255 and thereby became only the third player to win over $100,000 in one year.

Holman has become famous—and controversial—for his mannerisms on the bowling alley. He wiggles, squirms, and leaps after almost every bowling toss. He talks, swears, and shouts at the pins. "It's not that I'm in another world," he says by way of defense, "but I get pumped up in big matches and most of what I do is the natural outlet for that extra energy." At times, his gestures have been called obscene, though he denies any such intention.

After a 1979 Seattle tournament he was put on probation for six months for kicking a chair and a ball rack, and then throwing pencils when the match was going against him. Then in 1980 at the Showboat Tournament in Las Vegas, Nevada, there was another outburst. Holman needed a tenth frame strike to put him and his partner in a position to win the tournament. When Marshall failed to make that particular score, he kicked a protruding foul light on a lane. He was fined $2,500 and received the longest suspension in PBA history: ten tournaments.

Holman managed to make a successful comeback after the incident. Although he earned only $46,035 in 1980, the year of the suspension, the next year, 1981, he enjoyed his best season. He won the Quaker State Open, the BPAA U.S. Open, and the King Louis Open, with winnings of $122,880 for the year.

He won no tournaments in 1982, but collected $74,023 in prize money. In 1983, he won the Venice (Florida) Open with a 290 in the title game. He collected $110,935 in prize money that year. He fired a 280 to defeat Mark Roth in the 1984 Brunswick Memorial World Open, but dropped his next match to finish third.

He captured his 19th PBA title, the Kodak Invitational, in Rochester, New York in the fall of 1985. He ended the 1986 winter tour by winning his second Firestone Tournament of Champions and the largest check in PBA history, $50,000. That took him over the $1 million mark in earnings, only the third player in PBA history to reach that plateau. (Mark Roth and Earl Anthony were the other two.) This, his 20th PBA title, put him in an elite group of six players—including Earl Anthony, Mark Roth, Dick Weber, Don Johnson, and Dick Ritger—who had won 20 or more PBA titles.

In 1987, though he did not win a tournament, Marshall Holman earned the coveted PBA Player of the Year Award. He also won the George Young High Average Award for the third time, leading the Tour in average with a 216.8 per game. He took that award in 1982 and 1984 as well.

Holman won his 21st PBA title at the Galaxy Lanes in the 1988 *Bowlers Journal* Florida Open in 1988. He demolished Ron Bell, 275-211 for the championship.

In 1990, Marshall Holman was inducted into the PBA Hall of Fame in recognition of his 21

PBA titles and the $1.4 million he had won in his career, more than any other PBA bowler. As of the spring of 1998, he had won 22 bowling titles, with career earnings of $1,690,745.

Holman served as a color analyst at the 2007 United States Bowling Congress Queens tournament and was a broadcaster for ESPN's coverage of the 2007 and 2008 U.S. Women's Open events. He also provided commentary for the 2009 U.S. Women's Open telecasts.

Nat Holman

The American Coach Taught Israelis How to Play Basketball

HOLMAN, NAT (born October 18, 1896, in New York City; died February 12, 1995) American basketball player and coach. A master teacher and innovator, and the brains behind the Original Celtics. Holman is considered one of the greatest basketball players of all time. He coached City College of New York from 1920 to 1953, and again in 1955–56, 1957–58, and 1959–60. His career coaching record: 422-188.

. . .

Nat Holman learned to play basketball in the parks, playgrounds, and settlement houses of New York's Lower East Side. An all-around athlete at Commerce High School, he played four sports there.

Nat, 5 feet, 11 inches tall, chose a career as a pro basketball player in 1916 while attending the Savage School of Physical Education at New York University. He turned down an offer to play baseball with the Cincinnati Reds.

Having graduated from the Savage School, Nat was appointed instructor of hygiene at the City College of New York in 1917, with extra duties that included coaching soccer and freshman basketball. After serving one year in the U.S. Navy during World War I, he returned to CCNY and was named head basketball coach for the 1919–20 season. At 23, Holman was the youngest college coach in the country. Asked how he managed to get so far at so young an age, he joked: "I think my older brother, Morris, put in a good word for me."

While continuing to coach at CCNY, Holman played pro basketball on weekends with the New York Whirlwinds in 1920 and early in 1921. He joined the Original Celtics toward the end of the 1921 season and remained with them until 1929. The Celtics rarely lost with Holman. They were 192-11 in 1922–23; 204-11 in 1923–24; and 134-6 in 1924–25. In 1926–27, the Celtics joined the American Basketball League where they were nearly unbeatable and no team could put up a decent fight between them. After a few seasons the team decided that it made no sense for the players to remain together, a move that strikes any observer of professional basketball of the 1980s and 1990s, with its high salaries for the players, as quite odd. Still, in 1929, the Original Celtics disbanded. In 1933, Nat retired as an active player.

Holman was regarded as the finest ball handler, playmaker, and set-shot artist of his day. While with the Celtics, he devised the pivot play, one of the most important plays in the game. It revolutionized basketball, and college coaches flocked to watch Holman feint an opponent out of position and run him into the pivot or post. He would then cut by him, receive a short give-and-go-pass, and lay up an easy basket.

At CCNY, he was slender and dapper, appearing at games with neatly combed hair and freshly shined shoes. The winning teams he turned out at CCNY were unique because his players were not there on athletic scholarships. "They were all boys who entered CCNY," said Holman, "because of their academic achievements. Yet, they, too, found in basketball the things that spurred me on. They, too, brought to the game a dedication and skill that enabled CCNY to rise to basketball prominence during the years I was there." He believed that winning required a positive mental approach as well as finely-honed skills. Once, after a team loss that he could not figure out, he said to his players, "You need a psychiatrist, not a coach."

Nat Holman's most successful season was 1949–50, when his CCNY Beavers won the "grand slam" of college basketball: the National Invitation Tournament and the NCAA playoffs. No other coach had accomplished that feat. Sadly, however, most of the players who won that "grand slam" were part of a point-fixing scandal the next year (though there had been no reported evidence that the team's players had point-fixed during the year of the "grand slam"). Nat himself was suspended from the physical education department of CCNY, but was eventually (after two years) cleared of all wrongdoing and reinstated as coach.

Holman has always been a proud Jew: "Some of what I heard and learned sitting next to my father in the synagogue rubbed off on me," he once said. He was a member of the committee that helped send the first American team to the Maccabiah Games in Palestine in 1932. And, he was the first American coach to go to Israel in 1949 to teach Israelis to play basketball.

Asked about his relationship with non-Jews, he observed, "I experienced no anti-Semitism from my opponents during my pro career. Occasionally, there would be some nasty remarks from the sidelines. But on the whole I had very little of it." There was one highly publicized incident in 1946 in Madison Square Garden: CCNY was playing Wyoming. When CCNY took a quick lead, Wyoming's coach directed some anti-Semitic remarks against Holman's players. Leaping from the bench, Holman had to be held back from going after the coach, who eventually apologized.

In 1967, Holman was elected to the Basketball Hall of Fame. In 1973 he became the president of the American Committee for Sport in Israel.

Three years later, Nat was named the greatest New York City athlete in basketball by the Boys' Athletic League. In 1977, CCNY's new gym was named after him and the following year the Wingate Institute in Israel dedicated the Nat Holman School for Coaches and Instructors. He was inducted into the Jewish Sports Hall of Fame in Israel in July of 1981.

A few years later, he acknowledged that he would have had trouble coaching against the new

crop of tall basketball players. "My 6-feet-5 players would be midgets now."

When he was in his 90s, Holman lived in the Hebrew Home for the Aged in the Riverdale section of the Bronx and still watched basketball on television. In the fall of 1991, when several people from the Hebrew Home asked him to show them some basketball techniques at a nearby court, Holman was happy to accommodate them. "You can zip it like this, across your body, or you can duck and throw it over your head, or bounce it behind your back to a receiver," he explained as he gestured. It was as if he were back with the Original Celtics.

He died of natural causes at the age of 98 on February 12, 1995.

Ken Holtzman

An Outstanding American League Pitcher

HOLTZMAN, KENNETH (born November 3, 1945, in St. Louis, Missouri–) American baseball player. Major league pitcher from 1966 to 1979 with a career won-lost record of 174-150. He helped the Oakland Athletics win three straight World Series between 1972 and 1974. Holtzman was named *The Sporting News* left-handed pitcher of the year in the American League.

• • •

Ken attended the University of Illinois and was awarded a Bachelor of Arts degree in Business Administration in 1965. That same year he was signed to a bonus contract by the Chicago Cubs. The major highlight of his first major league season (1966) was his triumph over his boyhood idol, Sandy Koufax. Ironically, the two Jewish pitchers played against one another because of Yom Kippur. Holtzman was to pitch on the day after Yom Kippur while the Dodger southpaw was scheduled to pitch on the holy day itself but asked to skip his turn. So the following day the two men faced each other at Wrigley Field in Chicago.

For seven innings Holtzman preserved a no-hitter and allowed only two hits in the end. Koufax allowed only four hits, but lost the game 2-1. It was Sandy's last loss in regular-season play as he retired the next year. Holtzman had been regarded as another Sandy Koufax: he threw hard like Sandy, was left-handed like Sandy and was Jewish.

With the Chicago Cubs between 1966 and 1971, Holtzman pitched two no-hitters, one in 1969, the other in 1971. He had a 74-69 won-lost

record for those years. After the 1971 season, he asked to be traded, and was sent to Oakland. In 1973 he won 21 games, lost 13, and was chosen best left-hander of the year in the league.

Holtzman won two American League playoff games and had four World Series wins for Oakland. In all, he recorded 67 victories between 1972 and 1975, years when the Athletics finished in first place.

Ken went to Baltimore in 1976 where he won five games while losing four in 13 starts. He next played for the New York Yankees from 1976 to 1978 but did not get along with Yankees' manager Billy Martin. The problem began when Holtzman was kept on the bench during the 1976 playoffs and World Series. Martin, it seemed, had a low opinion of Holtzman's pitching, and Ken didn't

pitch often while with the Yankees. In 1977 he was 2-3; in 1978, 1-0. Holtzman pitched only 90 innings altogether in those two seasons.

Holtzman was the New York Yankee player representative—the ball player who represented the Major League Players' Association, the ball players' union, on the team. Each team has one such player representative. Holtzman was eventually traded (on June 11, 1978) back to the Chicago Cubs. He had been 0-1 with the Yankees up until that point in 1978, and was 0-3 with the Cubs for the duration of the season.

In 1979 Ken pitched 118 innings and was 6-9. He decided to quit after the 1979 season.

Holtzman had talents and interests outside of baseball. He could speed-read an entire paperback while sitting in an airport terminal waiting for a flight. Holtzman was a member of a national telephone chess league and an excellent duplicate bridge player.

Ken has always been proud of his Jewish heritage. He has publicly stated that he believed in Jewish values and religion. He tried to observe Jewish customs as much as life on the road would allow. At home he observes Jewish dietary laws and he never pitched on a Jewish holiday.

Following his retirement from baseball, Ken Holtzman settled in Chicago and then, in the late 1990s, moved to his hometown of St. Louis. In 2002, he coached children's baseball teams at the Jewish Community Center in Chesterfield. In the inaugural 2007 season of the Israel Baseball League, Ken managed the Petach Tikva Pioneers. The team finished the season in last place (9–32) and lost to the Modi'in Miracle in the quarterfinals of the 2007 championship.

William "Red" Holzman

The Basketball Coach Who Was a Great Communicator

HOLZMAN, WILLIAM "RED" (born August 10, 1920, in New York City; died November 13, 1998) American basketball player and coach. During the 1960s and 1970s he was highly successful as coach of the New York Knickerbockers of the National Basketball Association. He compiled a better record than any other active coach in pro basketball: up to the 1981–82 season he had 613 victories in regular-season play.

. . .

Holzman, an All-City guard in high school, was an All-American when he played for City College of New York in 1942. After service in the U.S. Navy during World War II, he joined the Rochester Royals of the NBA in 1945. An All-League player, he was part of the Royals' 1950–51 championship team. Red acquired his nickname from the color of his hair—red!

The Milwaukee Hawks hired Holzman as player-coach in 1954. In 1958, he became chief scout for the New York Knicks, a post he held for the next decade. In December 1967, he succeeded Dick McGuire as New York's head coach. When he took over, the club was 15-22 but ended the season with a record of 43-39.

In Holzman's first full season at the helm of the Knicks, the team won 54 games, a club record at the time. A year later, in 1969–70, he skippered the club to its first world title with 60 victories, including 18 straight, then an NBA record. Holzman was chosen NBA coach of the year in 1970.

The 1971–72 Knicks reached the NBA championship finals, and in 1972–73 the team recaptured the world title which it held three years earlier. In that six-year period—known as the Knicks' Golden Era—Holzman's team compiled 320 victories in 492 games, for a winning record of 65 percent. In nine of the 13 seasons that he coached the Knicks, they made the playoffs.

Red retired as the Knick coach upon completion of the 1976–77 campaign, turning the reigns over to Willis Reed, who had been the team's captain. Holzman was named consultant to the team. Reed coached the Knicks in 1977–78 to what was considered a disappointing second-place finish with a 43-39 record. Red was summoned back as Knick coach on November 10, 1978, after the club had played only 14 games of the 1978–79 season.

That year and the next were problematic: the team wound up 31-51 in 1978–79, and 39-43 in 1979–80, neither time qualifying for the NBA playoffs. But the Knicks finished the 1980–81 season with a 50-32 record, enabling the team to make the playoffs. The Knicks, however, lost two games straight to the Chicago Bulls, thus being eliminated early in the playoffs.

Holzman explained in March 1981 how he had managed to survive 28 years of living out of a suitcase. "The answer is so simple, you won't believe it. I'm just one of those people who likes to travel, who likes the movies, and who reads a lot—mostly bestsellers that my married daughter picks out for me. But in the off season, my wife and I never leave our house unless it's to go to the beach."

Bill Bradley, who was elected a United States Senator from New Jersey in November 1980 and who was one of Holzman's stars in the 1960s and early 1970s, wrote of his former coach: "Other men Holzman's age who became coaches in the NBA have difficulty communicating with black players. Holzman never makes racial mistakes. Everyone is subject to the same treatment. It seems natural that he senses the right course, for he grew up in a non-Jewish world where discrimination was a very real part of his own life. He understands the dividing line between paranoia and reality."

In the early 80s his eye was still as sharp as it

was as a youngster. Once, Marvin Webster, the Knicks' center, bet Holzman $10 that he could outshoot him from the top of the free-throw circle. Webster went first, hitting nine out of ten. He was extending his hand to collect his winnings when Holzman scored nine out of ten as well.

Holzman retired as Knick coach in May 1982, following a 33-49 season. In the last few years of his career, his teams had not fared well: the Knicks had made the playoffs only once in the last four seasons before Holzman's retirement.

In 1985 Holzman was elected to the Basketball Hall of Fame, at age 65. Three years later he was elected to the Jewish Sports Hall of Fame, in Israel.

On March 10, 1990 the Knicks held a ceremony at Madison Square Garden in which they retired a jersey with the number 613 on it, representing the number of Holzman's career regular season wins as Knicks coach. Holzman's 613 victories in regular season play was second only to that of Red Auerbach, former coach of the Boston Celtics, in the history of the sport until then.

On September 24, 1991 "Red" was inducted into the New York City Basketball Hall of Fame.

At the start of the 1998–99 NBA season, Holzman was ranked 11th on the list of all-time NBA coaching victories with a record of 696-604.

He died on November 13, 1998 at the age of 78 after suffering from leukemia for some time.

Hirsch Jacobs

The Trainer of More Thoroughbred Winners Than Anyone Else

JACOBS, HIRSCH (born April 8, 1904, in New York City; died February 13, 1970) American race-horse trainer. He saddled more winners (3,569) than anyone else in thoroughbred racing. Between 1946 and 1969, Jacobs bred such winners as Hail to Reason, Affectionately, Straight Deal, and Regal Gleam. By turning unlikely prospects into winners, he earned more than $12 million in purses.

. . .

Unlike the other great horse trainers, Hirsch Jacobs did not come from the South. He was born in New York City, one of 10 children. Soon after Hirsch's birth, his father, an immigrant tailor, moved his family to the East New York section of Brooklyn.

A popular avocation of the residents of his new neighborhood was the raising of pigeons. Young Jacobs loved this activity and by age 12 had learned to identify 100 pigeons by sight. This training of his memory was a great help to him in his future training of horses.

At age 13, Hirsch learned to install and repair steampipes. He got a job as a steamfitter and learned horse racing from Charlie Ferraro, brother of his boss.

In 1924, Charlie bought a horse for $1,500 and asked Hirsch Jacobs to train the animal. Four years later, on December 29, 1929, Jacobs saddled his first winner, a horse named Reveillon, at Pompano, Florida.

Hirsch's unusual ability consisted of taking horses that would not run for anyone else and win-

ning with them. "You just got to use common sense," the short, chunky, red-haired trainer would say. "When a horse feels like running, he'll run. They're like humans. You got to baby them and humor them along; kid them along."

Unlike other great trainers, Hirsch Jacobs bred and trained horses he personally owned. Whereas his rivals tended to concentrate on a few promising horses, grooming them for a handful of highstake races, Jacobs sent his thoroughbreds to the gate in wholesale fashion. As a result, only infrequently would he train a truly famous horse, but he managed to amass a staggering total of purses through the years.

Jacobs was always sensitive to the disappointments in his work. "This business," he said at one point, "is full of heartaches. You get a horse worth $50,000 one morning; by afternoon you can't get $10,000 for him. The biggest menace is sore shins. Anyone can train a horse. But to win, you've got to have a horse that's in shape. That's the only secret there is."

In 1931, Jacobs entered into a life-long partnership with Isidor (Beebee) Bieber.

In 1936, Hirsch had his finest year when he saddled 177 winners. The 84 horses in his stable ran 632 times that year. A $2 bet on each of his horses that started that season would have netted over $142 per horse for the year. That was the year Jacobs started to run horses in the salmon-pink and emerald-green silks which became known as the identifying marks of some of the best thoroughbred race horses.

Stymie, a failure of a race horse Hirsch Jacobs found in 1943, revealed Jacobs' intuition at its best. The two year old had hardly been able to gallop in earlier races, but Jacobs told his partner Bieber, "I've got a feeling about that colt. I like the way he walks." Hirsch bought the horse for $1,500. By the end of his career, Stymie was the world's leading money winner, earning $918,485 in purses.

Jacobs turned another extremely slow horse around in 1955, a filly named Searching. "The walls of Searching's hooves were very thin," Jacobs recalled. "She wouldn't try because she thought her shoes were too tight. So we got her a new pair of shoes, and she started winning." Searching won a total of $327,000.

Jacobs married the former Ethel Dushock in 1933. Her father owned a boarding house near the old Empire City track in Yonkers and it was there that she and Hirsch met. Occasionally, Mrs. Jacobs would try to convert her husband to her own faith, Catholicism. But he always had the same reply: "If they go to the moon and a Catholic greets them, that's the day I'll become a convert." He retained his Jewish faith, but permitted his children to be brought up as Roman Catholics.

Jacobs neither smoked nor drank, but was superstitious. He always wore the same suit for weeks during a winning streak—and he only drove green Cadillacs.

He suffered a stroke in 1966, but remained partially active as a trainer until a month before his death in 1970. He died of a cerebral hemorrhage at the Miami Heart Institute in Miami Beach, Florida.

Hirsch Jacobs is a member of the Jewish Sports Hall of Fame in Israel.

James Jacobs

One of the World's Great Handball Players

JACOBS, JAMES (born February 18, 1931, in St. Louis, Missouri; died March 23, 1988) American handball player. One of the world's greatest. Ranked as one of the top three four-wall handball players of all time. Despite injuries in his prime years, he won 15 national titles. In 1966 *Sports Illustrated* suggested that he might have been the greatest athlete of his time in any sport. By 1972, Jacobs had won the American Handball Association four-wall singles title six times, the four-wall doubles six times, and the three-wall singles three times.

. . .

Jim moved from St. Louis to Los Angeles with his parents when he was five years old. Shortly, thereafter, his parents divorced and he was raised by his mother.

As a boy, Jim Jacobs was in love with comic books. He bought and read hundreds of them. He loved to pretend that he was Dick Grayson, alias Robin, Batman's comic-strip sidekick, and he found that identifying with Robin was a tremendous help to him in sports. He would think of what Robin would do in a stressful situation, and would gain strength by pretending to be this other emotionally unaffected character.

Over the years, Jacobs amassed half a million comic books, said to be the largest collection in the world.

As a teenager, Jacobs played football, baseball, and basketball and was good enough in basketball to be invited for an Olympic tryout. He ran the 100-yard dash in 9.8 seconds; he was also a skeet shot of championship rank.

At Los Angeles High School, Jacobs was rarely eligible for sports due to his poor grades, especially in English. His mother recalled that Jim was happy only at sports. He played halfback in football, shortstop in baseball, and forward in basketball for the George Gershwin chapter of the AZA (American Zionist Association), a branch of the B'nai Brith. Because youngsters of all faiths could play, competition was keen.

With Jacobs on the team, the Gershwin chapter won the AZA title three years in a row. One year it won all three major team championships.

At the Hollywood YMCA, Jacobs often played handball against Art Linkletter, the TV master of ceremonies. Jim Jacobs lost at first. But he began spending time practicing whenever he could. He spent hours in front of a mirror, practicing left-hand returns, although he was right-handed. When he passed the May Company department store, he would halt for five minutes to check his handball form in the reflection of a large window to the surprise of passersby. Within a few months he could whip Linkletter and anyone else in Los Angeles.

Believing that they had a prodigy on their hands, Linkletter and a few others financed Jacobs' trip to the handball Junior Nationals in Bremerton, Washington. There he won the singles title. At that time Jim was also playing American Athletic Union basketball on a team sponsored by a printing company. He was invited to try out for the Olympic team but declined so he could concentrate on handball.

In 1950 Jacobs met Robert Kendler, multimillionaire Chicago home remodeler, who was obsessed with handball and had already taken the dozen or so best players in the country and employed them in his own business. Kendler built the Town Club of Chicago so these players would have a place to practice. Gus Lewis, a former National handball champion, played Jacobs, and then reported to Kendler: "I've just played a kid who doesn't know what he's doing, and for a kid who doesn't know what he's doing, he's a hell of a handball player."

He repeated the feat in 1957, beating Hershkowitz for the third time in the finals. In 1958, Jacobs forfeited the finals due to an injury caused by a collision in a doubles match. He did not play in 1959 because of a heart condition. In 1960 he again took the national singles title, but had to withdraw the following year because of a torn tendon. In 1962 and 1963 he passed up the singles to win the doubles. In 1964 he took the singles title easily.

While engaged in handball, Jacobs was developing a second profession: collecting fight films. While traveling extensively to compete at handball, Jacobs searched for films of important historic boxing matches. By 1961, he had accumulated several thousand prints and become the world's foremost private collector.

"The more I got into athletics myself," he said, "the more I admired boxers. Theirs is the ultimate individual sport, the one where emotional and psychological factors play the largest roles. A fighter has to deal with fear and its counterforce, courage, in a way no other athlete does. It's what makes fighting and fighters so fascinating to me."

Collecting the fight films was not simple. In response to the race riots that had accompanied the victories of Jack Johnson, the first black heavyweight champion, the Federal Government had enacted a law banning the interstate shipment of fight films. The law was in force between 1912 and 1940. Thus, many films had been stored away and were forgotten. Many films deteriorated and later had to be reproduced at considerable cost. The oldest film shows an 1894 James Corbett fight.

In 1961, Jimmy went into partnership with Bill Cayton, producer of the original *Greatest Fight* television series which was aired between 1949 and 1955 after the Friday night fight program. Jacobs' library of fight films was merged with Cayton's collection.

Together with Cayton, Jacobs expanded their collection of fight films into the largest in the world.

Jacobs made his living by splicing these films together in entertaining ways. Of the 1,000 boxing

Kendler hired Jacobs as a home remodeling salesman and invited him to practice at the club during off-hours. This group provided Jacobs with his education. After 18 months there, he was drafted. He served as a rifleman with the First Cavalry Division in Japan and Korea, and after his discharge, Jacobs returned to Los Angeles were he worked as a salesman for a business machine company.

Jacobs worked hard at the Los Angeles Athletic Club, and in 1953, he competed in his first national tournament and finished fifth. In 1954 he was third and in 1955, playing on his home court in Los Angeles, he won the singles, defeating another great handball star, Victor Hershkowitz. Until then, handball had been mostly a power game of "kills," but Jacobs, having mastered the art of ceiling shots, was able to force Hershkowitz to the rear of the court where he could not make his slam-bang kills. Jacobs had thus revolutionized handball. In fairness, Hershkowitz at that time was past his prime.

In 1956, Jacobs again won the national singles.

features he and Cayton produced, three have been nominated for Academy Awards in the documentary film category: *Legendary Champions*, *The Heavyweight Champions*, and *Jack Johnson*.

Jacobs believed that modern fighters are far better than the older ones who appear in his films. "Comparing them with the old-timers," he noted "is like comparing a modern tank to World War I models. Fighters today are faster, stronger, and know more."

Jacobs and Cayton also co-managed three world champion boxers: Wilfred Benitez, Edwin Rosario, and Mike Tyson.

In 1979, Jacobs was inducted into the Jewish Sports Hall of Fame in Israel.

On March 23, 1988, Jacobs died at Mount Sinai Hospital in New York. He was 58 years old. The cause of death was pneumonia, but he "suffered from lymphocytic leukemia for nine years," according to Bill Cayton.

Former heavyweight champion Muhammed Ali was quoted on the day of Jacobs' death as saying that Jacobs had been one of the few people who had stood by him when Ali's title was stripped in the late 1960s.

Irving Jaffee

A Speed Skater Who Won Two Olympic Gold Medals

JAFFEE, IRVING (born September 15, 1906, in New York City; died March 20, 1981) American speed skater. Winner of two Olympic gold medals in the 1932 winter games in the 5,000- and 10,000-meter races. He was stripped of a third gold medal at the St. Moritz Winter Olympics in 1928 through no fault of his own.

• • •

Irving Jaffee was the second of three children of parents who had emigrated from Russia in 1898. His family arrived in New York impoverished, and his father found employment operating a pushcart.

Irving wanted to be a baseball star. The Yorkville section of New York City in which he grew up had spawned Hank Greenberg and Al Schacht, two other baseball heroes. But when Jaffee could not make the baseball team at DeWitt Clinton High School, he was so upset that he quit school.

He took up boxing, hoping to follow in the footsteps of Jewish boxing star Benny Leonard, but in his first fight he was knocked out, ending his career ignominiously.

One evening, some friends asked Irving to go to the Ice Palace in New York City. A schoolmate, Myer Steinglass, recalls that first skating attempt on ice: "He was a grotesque figure that night, somewhat abashed at his gauche posture in his frantic efforts to maintain his balance." From then on, Jaffee always carried a pair of skates under his arm.

Frequently he would skate at the Gay Blades (which later became the Roseland Dance Hall). Admission to the rink was 75 cents, but as Jaffee recalled, "I got in free by getting a job scraping the ice off the rink. I must have scraped tons of it in my lifetime." His sister gave him his first pair of ice skates but they were three sizes too large, and he was forced to wear nine pairs of socks to skate. Even with the extra socks, he often wobbled and fell.

Jaffee was reluctant to enter special skating competitions because he felt that ice skating, a Nordic sport, was not for Jews. But his friends convinced him to compete, sensing that he had great hidden talent and could become a good speed skater.

He began actual skating competition on Monday nights at Iceland in New York. Using the skates his sister had given him, he lost the first nine of ten races he entered. Then, Norval Bapte, one of the great skaters of the time, advised him that his skates were too large. Bapte bought him a pair of secondhand skates for $6 and he took third place in his next race. Jaffee began to develop good endurance and speed, which he credited to a newspaper route which he worked on roller skates on Saturdays and Sundays.

Irving Jaffee's first major competition was the Silver Skates Derby of 1924. He fared poorly that year and again in 1925; but in 1926 he won the Silver Skates two-mile senior championship. Then, the following year he won the five-mile national championship at Saranac Lake, breaking the world record and making him eligible for the 1928 Winter Olympics—or at least so it appeared.

He was not sure he would be going to St. Moritz, Switzerland, site of the 1928 Winter Olympics, until two days before the boat sailed. The authorities felt that he would be no match for the Scandinavian skaters. In the end, the U.S. Olympic Committee decided that he could go, but the boat had to be delayed so he could secure his visa and passport.

His fourth-place finish in the 5,000-meter race at the Olympics that year was the best ever run by an American. In the 10,000-meter race, seven time trials were held, but then the ice began to melt, and

an official of the International Skating Federation called the rest of the race off. Consequently, three skaters did not compete. The Executive Commission of the International Olympic Committee recognized Irving Jaffee, with the fastest time among those who had raced, as the winner. However, the International Skating Federation overturned the Commission's decision, ruling that the race had to be rerun to allow everyone to participate. Since most of the skaters had left St. Moritz by the time of the Federation's decision, the race was canceled. Jaffee's gold medal was, in effect, snatched from him just before he was to receive it as the official winner of the race. Nevertheless, many in the American press, as well as a few of Jaffee's racing colleagues, considered him the winner.

After the 1928 Olympic Games, Jaffee took a job on Wall Street in New York as a broker's clerk. Friends at the office took an interest in his career and sent him to Lake Placid to train. However, his training had to stop when his mother became ill, and he was forced to devote all his time to taking care of her.

As a result, Jaffee had trained too little for the 1932 Winter Olympics, held at Lake Placid, and did not expect to do well. When the Olympic trials were held at Lake Placid, he failed to qualify in the 500- and 1,500-meter races, but still had a chance in the 5,000- and 10,000-meter races.

Irving's teammates at the trials made life unbearable for him, and he suspected there was some anti-Semitism involved. They stole his mattress, started a fistfight with him, and shone a light in his eyes at night so he could not get sufficient sleep. Just before the 5,000-meter race, he slept away from the Olympic Village to be sure that he would get enough rest. He went on to win both the 5,000- and 10,000-meter races. His time in the 5,000 was 9:40.8 and in the 10,000, 19:13.6. Before Jaffee came along the Europeans had dominated the skating races in the Olympics, but with his great performances Irving became an American hero.

With the Depression in full swing, Jaffee needed money more than glory. In 1932, in order to help pay the food bills at home, he sold his Olympic medals plus 400 others to a Harlem pawnshop for $2,000. "They were all gold," he said, "some with diamonds, worth thousands of dollars. Because I didn't redeem them in a year, I never saw them again. I got hundreds of letters from people wanting to buy me some duplicate medals. I refused. It was my doing. I have to pay the consequences." Just prior to the 1976 Olympics in Montreal, the American Broadcasting Company presented a report on Jaffee in an attempt to describe the problems and sacrifices of certain athletes. A nationwide search was made for his medals, but they did not turn up.

In 1940, Jaffee was elected to the United States Skating Hall of Fame. Six years later he was teaching youngsters speed skating at the Newburgh, New York, Recreation Park. He had also been appointed coach of the Delano-Hitch Speed Skating Club.

In the 1950s he became associated with Grossingers, the famous resort in the Catskills, in upstate New York. In 1951, he began the promotion of the world barrel-jumping championships

Four Olympic gold medal winners gather at a dinner in their honor at the 1932 Lake Placid (New York) Winter Olympic Games. (From left) Irving Jaffee, Karl Schaeffer of Germany (men's figure skating gold medal winner), Sonia Henie (women's figure skating gold medal winner), and Jack Shea of Lake Placid (500- and 1500-meter gold medal winner for speed skating).

and it became an annual event. In his later years he assisted in the training of 10 Olympic speed skaters. Though he considered himself on "permanent vacation," as he put it, in the 1970s he was quite busy. He lectured often, and produced an annual show on barrel jumping for ABC television. Golfing was also part of his daily regimen. Irving Jaffee died in a San Diego, California, hospital in 1981.

Jaffee is a member of the Jewish Sports Hall of Fame in Israel.

Martin Jaite

Top South American Tennis Player

JAITE, MARTIN (born October 9, 1964, in Buenos Aires, Argentina–) Argentinian tennis player. He has the distinction of having been a highly-ranked junior tennis player in both Argentina and Spain. A marvelous clay court player, Jaite was ranked 826 in 1982. He climbed steadily, reaching No. 10, his highest rank in 1990. In 1991, he was ranked 46. Jaite won 12 titles and earned $1,873,881 in prize money.

. . .

His name is pronounced mar-TEEN HIGH-te, his friends call him "Marto." It is said that he looks a bit like Paul Newman. "His face blends the same contrasting devilish and beatific expressions through watery blue eyes," wrote one sportswriter.

When Martin was five years old, he won a swimming competition at his club. The organizers forgot to give him his medal. "I was furious," he remembered. He showed his anger by banging a tennis racquet against the locker-room wall. His grandmother encouraged his tennis playing. She gave him a tennis racquet for his birthday—hoping this one would last!

Martin played team handball and soccer at school. He began playing tennis at age six.

In 1975, at age 11, he and his family moved to Barcelona, Spain. Seven years later, in 1982, Martin won the Spanish National championships and the Banana Bowl tournament. He also reached the semifinals of the French Open juniors and the Orange Bowl.

After seven years in Spain, Martin, now 19, returned to Argentina with his mother, Miriam, a psychologist. His father, a psychoanalyst, remained in Barcelona. Jaite gradually moved to the top of the Argentine national rankings. Offered a try-out for the Argentine Davis Cup team, he hesitated. Martin was concerned about offending Spain.

Martin Jaite was known as a great clay court player. He joined the ATP tour in 1983 and won the Spanish satellite circuit soon thereafter. His first good result came in the quarterfinals at Bordeaux in 1983. He rose in the world rankings from 826 at the end of 1982 to 156 by the end of 1983.

Stepping into the shoes of Guillermo Vilas, Jaite began playing for Argentina in the Davis Cup in 1984 when Vilas withdrew because of an injury. He played a match against Jimmy Connors on a synthetic carpet called Supreme, wearing running shoes rather than tennis shoes. "I had never played before on that kind of court and my tennis shoes felt too heavy there." Jaite lost to Connors 3-6, 4-6, 8-10, and the U.S. defeated Argentina 5-0. Jaite finished 1984 ranked No. 54 in the world.

He won several challenger tournaments before posting his first tour victory at Buenos Aires, defeating Diego Perez in 1985. He finished the year 1985 with a world ranking of 20. He had his best Grand Slam showing that year at the French Open where he reached the quarterfinals. He also began to excel in doubles in 1985, teaming with Christian Miniussi at Buenos Aires to take his first doubles title.

Jaite made the finals two straight years at Boston in 1985 and 1986. He also won titles at Bologna and Stuttgart in 1986.

In 1986, Jaite rose to No. 15, showing consistent success on clay. He defeated Boris Becker during an early round of the Tournament of Champions in Forest Hills, New York, before losing in the semifinals. Later in the year, he won tournaments at Bologna, Italy, and Stuttgart, West Germany. For the second year in a row, he reached the U.S. Pro final at Boston. His world ranking at the end of 1986 was 17.

In 1987, he won tournaments in Barcelona and Palermo in consecutive weeks, beating Mats

Paraguay and Andres Gomes from Ecuador) as the only South Americans to rank in the top 10 since the ATP computer rankings began on August 23, 1973.

Jaite achieved greater success on his favorite surface, clay, during the spring of 1990 when he reached the semifinals in his childhood home of Barcelona before falling to the eventual champion Emilio Sanchez. He won his 12th singles title in Nice over Goran Prpic in three sets. He finished in the top 50 in 1991 for the sixth time in the last seven years, with a ranking of 46.

Martin, coached by Daniel Garcia since 1985, was elected to represent the players ranked No. 26-50 on the ATP Tour Player Council for 1991–92. In 1992, Jaite was ranked 100 in the world.

Jaite does not have exceptional power but compensates with spring and leg speed. His clay-court game is especially strong. From the baseline on clay he has learned how to pace the ball accurately and deep to either side. Periodically, upon sensing an opening, he moves quickly to the net. His top-spin backhand, used effectively to return service, is his most formidable shot.

Martin Jaite is the target of great fan adulation in Argentina. "Some of my friends are rather protective of me and noisy while I play," he said. In 1987, the Argentina sports magazine *El Grafico* wrote: "He is No. 1 in Argentina with all the future for himself. . . . Is there any doubt that Jaite is good?"

As of November 2004, Jaite was the holder of 12 titles, placing him 31st among the top 50 all-time tennis singles title leaders. In May 2006, having amassed earnings of $1,873,881, he was 203rd on the list of all time prizewinners.

Since retiring from tennis, Jaite has been tournament director for APT Buenos Aires and director of future events in Argentina. He coached fellow Argentinean David Nalbandian, who ranked 140th in the world as of February 2010.

Wilander in the final of the Spanish event that year. He finished the year ranked 14.

Jaite was a quarterfinalist in the Seoul 1988 Olympics, losing to Brad Gilbert.

In 1988, Jaite failed to win a title and was ranked only 54 at the end of the year. But he bounced back in 1989, winning titles at Stuttgart, Madrid, Sao Paulo, and Itaparica, ending the year with his best rank thus far, 11. He earned a career-high $419,209 that year, surpassing the one million dollar mark in career prize money after winning his sixth career singles title at Stuttgart on July 31, 1989.

In 1990, he won his fourth title in South America at Guaruja defeating Luiz Mattar and later in the year won Gstaad.

Martin Jaite was the latest South American to break into the top ten, accomplishing that feat on July 9, 1990. On that day he reached his highest singles ranking—No. 10. He joined three countrymen (Guillermo Vilas, Jose-Luis Clerc and Al-

Louis "Kid" Kaplan

World Featherweight Champ from 1925 to 1927

KAPLAN, LOUIS "KID" (born December 4, 1902, in Kiev, Russia; died October 26, 1970). American boxer. Ranked by Nat Fleischer as the tenth best featherweight of all time. He was world featherweight champion from 1925 to 1927. His record: 131 bouts of which he won 101 (17 by knockout), drew 10, and lost 13. Seven were no contests.

. . .

Born Gershon Mendeloff, Louis Kaplan came to the United States at the age of five and settled with his parents in Meriden, Connecticut, where his father had set up a junk business. Louis' first job was working as a helper to a fruit peddler. He began fighting as an amateur at age 13, and six years later he turned pro. He fought his first bout under the name of Benny Miller.

When Johnny Dundee vacated the featherweight title in 1925 because he could not make the weight, an elimination tournament was held in which Kid Kaplan took part. On January 2, 1925, Kaplan won the tournament, defeating Danny Kramer in a ninth-round knockout. Kid Kaplan thus became the featherweight champion. Nat Fleischer called the Kaplan-Kramer fight "the tenth best of the first half of the twentieth century."

Kaplan defended his title three times before outgrowing the division. His main adversary at the time was Babe Herman of California, against whom Kaplan fought six times. Before they fought for the title on August 25, 1925, in Waterbury, Connecticut, Herman and Kaplan had fought four times, with Herman winning once and holding Kaplan to a draw the other three times. But when they fought for the title, the match ended in a draw,

The two men fought again on December 18, 1925, in New York's Madison Square Garden and Kaplan won—this time on a decision after 15 rounds.

Kid Kaplan vacated the title in 1927, when he was over the 126-pound weight limit. That year he was approached by racketeers and offered $50,000 to throw the title fight. Although the opportunity to leave the ring a wealthy man was ap-

pealing, Kaplan responded courageously: "I can use the money. But every time I box, my pals bet their hard-earned money on me. I would never be able to face them again, not for a million dollars."

Kaplan was called the "Uncrowned Lightweight Champion," an honor given him after such lightweight fighters of the time as Tony Canzoneri, Al Singer, and Al Mandell would not fight him. They feared his twisting left hook.

Finally, in 1933, Kid Kaplan retired from the ring. In his last fight—against Cocoa Kid in Febru-ary of that year—he had been thrashed solidly. He quit boxing when an eye doctor told him he had lost sight in one eye, and it would not return.

After retiring from the ring, Kaplan acquired a half interest in a Hartford, Connecticut, restaurant, which he retained for the next 15 years. He died in 1970 after suffering paralysis on his left side.

He was inducted into the Jewish Sports Hall of Fame in Israel in 1986 and into the International Boxing Hall of Fame in 2003.

Elias Katz

The Finnish Long-Distance Olympic Star

KATZ, ELIAS (born 1901, in Abo, Finland; died December 25, 1947) Finnish track star. He won a gold medal in the 1924 Olympics as a member of Finland's victorious team in the 3,000-meter team cross-country race. His teammate was the famous Finnish runner, Paavo Nurmi. Katz also won an Olympic silver medal in the 3,000-meter steeplechase in the 1924 Games with a 9:44.0 time.

• • •

At age 19, Elias Katz joined the newly-established Jewish Maccabi Sports Club in Turku, Finland, where he had grown up. That summer, the club sponsored a decathlon event. Katz ran in the 1,500-meter race, his first time on such a long track, and won easily. Friends, sensing that he had special talent for medium-distance races, urged him to continue training. A few weeks later, another Finnish sports club arranged a 1,000 meter race for beginners, and Katz won that one as well.

More races followed, with Katz doing well, coming in second more often than winning. In 1922 he moved to Helsinki, the Finnish capital, where he became a member of the Jewish Athletic Club, Stjarnan (The Star)—later Makkabi.

In 1923, he blossomed into a great track star. He ran the best time for the steeplechase that year, 9:40.9. He also won a 1,500-meter race in 4:14, an excellent time then.

He qualified for the 1924 Paris Olympics. In the 3,000-meter steeplechase, he won his heat easily, setting an Olympic record at 9:43.8, fastest time ever posted until then. But in the finals Katz stumbled and received only the silver medal (his time: 9:44). He won a gold medal in the 3,000-meter cross-country race.

In 1925, Bar Kochba of Berlin, the first Jewish national sports club in Germany and Central Europe (founded in 1898) learned that Katz was Jewish and invited him to come live in Germany and represent the club. Katz responded positively to the situation.

He worked in Berlin as a packer in a department store and as a trainer at Bar Kochba. His presence encouraged many outstanding German Jewish athletes to leave other athletic clubs in favor of Bar Kochba. As a result, the club gained stature in both Jewish and gentile eyes; it grew to 5,000 members and flourished until the Nazis forced it to disband.

Katz participated in all the European Maccabiah Games in the late 1920s, and was quite successful in medium-distance running. On July 12, 1926, he ran the second leg for a Finnish club team which set a world record of 16:26.2 for the 4 x 1,500-meter relay.

In 1927, the Sports Association of Finland appealed to Elias Katz to return to train for the 1928 Olympics. Katz, still a Finnish citizen, returned to Turku. He encountered a horse-drawn cart and decided to challenge the horse to a race. Katz won by a wide margin. Later, that year Elias developed a foot injury which required surgery. He was unable to run anymore and missed the chance to be in the 1928 Olympics in Amsterdam.

Returning to Germany, Katz came upon growing anti-Semitism, and left for Palestine in 1933. There he worked as a common laborer, sometimes as a bricklayer. He married and lived in Rehovot with his wife and a daughter who was born in 1942. He was also a trainer and sports manager for the Maccabi organization in Tel Aviv.

Katz was selected to coach the first Jewish team for the 1948 Olympics in London. But he never got to England.

In December 1947, Katz was employed as a film operator at the Al Mugahzi camp, 15 kilometers south of Gaza. Immediately after the evening film showing, he, the only Jew in the camp, was killed by three Arabs. A Jewish soldier was wounded in the attack. Katz was buried in Ramat Gan, outside Tel Aviv.

Elias Katz is a member of the Jewish Sports Hall of Fame in Israel.

Benny Kauff

A Great Batting Star During World War I

KAUFF, BENJAMIN MICHAEL (born January 5, 1891, in Pomeroy, Ohio; died November 17, 1961) American baseball player. He played between 1912 and 1920 and was best known for his superb hitting. Kauff's career batting average in 859 games in the major leagues was .311, with 961 hits and 454 runs batted in.

. . .

Scouts for the New York Yankees noticed Kauff, a left-handed hitter and outfielder, in 1910, while he was playing with the minor league team in Parkersburg, West Virginia. The Yankees signed Kauff in 1911, but sent him back to the minor leagues where he remained for the next five years.

Kauff did get to play five games for the Yankees in 1912, but he spent the bulk of the season with the minor league team in Hartford, Connecticut, where he had a remarkable .395 batting average. The Yankees came under some fire from baseball enthusiasts for not giving Kauff his chance. In 1914 when the new Federal League came into existence, Benny moved over to that league and became one of its greatest hitting stars.

In 1914, playing for Indianapolis, he led the Federal League in hitting with .370, collecting 211 hits and stealing 75 bases. The following year, playing for the Brooklyn Feds, Kauff again won the batting title, hitting .342; he also stole 55 bases. He was suitably named "the Ty Cobb of the Feds."

Impressed by Benny Kauff's drawing power, John McGraw, the manager of the New York Giants, virtually kidnapped Kauff, hoping thereby to put the Federal League out of business. Until then the Feds had been raiding the player ranks of the National and American leagues.

One day in 1915, McGraw produced Kauff dramatically at New York's Polo Grounds for a game between the Giants and the Phillies. But Phillies' owner William F. Banker refused to let his team take the field as long as Kauff was scheduled to be in the Giant lineup. The game was delayed for more than an hour until National League president John K. Tener was reached by telephone and ordered McGraw to return Kauff to the Brooklyn Feds.

Then, in 1916, the Federal League collapsed and Kauff had his chance after all to play with the Giants. The Giants purchased Kauff for $30,000 from

Harry Sinclair, Brooklyn Feds' owner. Benny demanded a share of the money and when Sinclair rejected his demand, Kauff refused to report to the Giants. Finally, the matter was settled as McGraw and Sinclair agreed to pay Benny $5,000 each.

With that money Benny bought himself some fancy clothes, and when he showed up at Giant spring training in one such outfit, he caused quite a stir. Along with a loud striped shirt, an expensive blue suit, patent-leather shoes, a fur-collared overcoat, and a derby hat, he had on a huge diamond ring and a gold watch encrusted with diamonds. Still, he had come to play baseball, and very soon after arriving, he boasted that he would hit .300 "blindfolded."

He was slightly inaccurate. In 1916, he man-aged to hit only .264 but even so he proved valuable to the Giants. In both 1916 and 1917 (when he hit .308), he helped them win pennants. He hit two home runs in the 1917 World Series, both in one game, against the Chicago White Sox. Chicago, however, won the Series.

During the 1918 season, Benny was drafted into the U.S. Army. He returned to the Giants when the war was over, and played three more seasons, hitting .314 in 1918, .277 in 1919, and .294 in 1920.

In 1920, he was charged with being a member of an automobile theft ring in New York. He was tried and acquitted, but baseball commissioner Kenesaw Landis ordered him barred from baseball for life because the testimony at the trial showed that Kauff had associated with thieves.

Agnes Keleti

The Gymnast Who Won Five Olympic Gold Medals

KELETI, AGNES (born January 9, 1921, in Budapest, Hungary–) Hungarian gymnast. She won five Olympic gold medals and a total of 11 Olympic medals during the 1940s and 1950s.

• • •

At age 15, Agnes developed an interest in gymnastics, joining the famous VAC (Fencing and Athletic) Sports Club, the only Jewish club in Hungary. When the Nazis moved into Hungary in March 1944, however, her gymnastics career came to an abrupt halt.

In 1944, her father and other close relatives were sent to Auschwitz where they died. Only she, her mother, and sister survived. Her mother and sister were saved when the Swedish diplomat Raoul Wallenberg, well-known for having helped many Jews escape the grip of the Nazis in Hungary, obtained refuge for them in a "Swedish house" in Budapest. Agnes eluded the Nazis by buying Christian documents which enabled her to leave Budapest.

After World War II, she returned to gymnastics, winning her first Hungarian title in 1946 in the uneven bars competition. In 1947, she was the star of the Central European Gymnastics Championships. From that year until 1956, she won the all-around Hungarian Championships 10 times. At the same time she continued studying and received the equivalent of a Masters degree in physical education in 1950.

Agnes won many medals in Olympic competition. In London in 1948, she was awarded a silver medal for team-combined competition, although she did not participate because of an injury late in training. (The medal was awarded to Agnes because, though injured during the Olympics, she was still considered a member of the team.) In the 1952 Helsinki Olympics, she won a gold medal in the free-standing exercise, a silver medal in the combined team competition, and two bronze medals in hand apparatus-team and uneven parallel bars.

Keleti became the 1954 world champion in uneven bars and was a team member that year of the squad which won the team exercises with portable apparatus.

In the 1956 Melbourne Olympics, Agnes Keleti won gold medals in the free-standing exercise, beam exercises, parallel bars, and combined exercise-team (portable apparatus). She also won silver medals in the combined exercise and combined exercise-team (nine exercises).

"Hungary," she recalled, "gave me everything. The Communists were very interested in sports for political reasons. It gave them, they thought, much prestige. They could win the population over. It didn't bother them that I was Jewish. There was no discrimination by the regime. I worked so hard so I could see the world. Sport was the best way to achieve that."

It was during the October 1956 Hungarian revolt that Agnes Keleti decided not to return to her native Budapest. Two weeks after the revolt, she and the rest of the Hungarian team left for the Melbourne Olympics. Once there, she defected to the West. A number of her Hungarian colleagues in the Olympic delegation, as well as other Eastern bloc sportsmen in Melbourne, did the same. For some time after the Olympics, Agnes stayed in Australia because her sister lived there. Later their mother joined them. In June 1957, Agnes settled in Israel.

Though she arrived in time for the 1957 Maccabiah Games, she did not compete because at that time gymnastics was not yet a competitive sport in Israel. Instead, she gave two special performances demonstrating her skills. She was then 36 years old which is old for a gymnast.

She then became an instructor in physical education in a Tel Aviv college which later became the Wingate Institute for Sport in Netanya, where she developed a number of national gymnastic teams. She also taught coaches and was instrumental in creating a gymnastics school at Wingate.

In 1959, she married a fellow Hungarian who also taught physical education. They have two sons.

In December 1991, she was invited to Hungary where she was inducted into the Hungarian Sports Hall of Fame.

She coached children in gymnastics in the Israeli town of Ra'anana from 1986 to 1994. After that, she started to work as an instructor in women's gymnastics at the Sharon Hotel in Herzyliya, in which she was still engaged as of the summer of 1998.

Agnes Keleti is a member of the Jewish Sports Hall of Fame in Israel.

Irena Kirszenstein-Szewinska

The Greatest Woman Track and Field Star in the World

KIRSZENSTEIN-SZEWINSKA, IRENA (born May 24, 1946, in Leningrad, Russia–) Polish track and field star. Considered the greatest woman track and field athlete of all time; she won medals in each of the first four Olympics in which she competed—a feat never accomplished before by any runner, male or female. She is recognized as one of Poland's greatest athletes and was named the greatest woman athlete in the world by the Soviets.

• • •

Born to Polish parents who had fled to Russia during World War II, Irena and her parents eventually settled in Warsaw. When Irena's athletic ability became obvious at school, her mother pressed her to join a local sports club, and the youngster became a sprinter and long jumper.

When Irena was 18, she surprised everyone at the 1964 Tokyo Olympics by winning silver medals in the 200-meter run and the long jump and a gold medal in the 400-meter relay. In the long jump she established a national record of 21 feet, 7½ inches and in the 200 meter she set a European record of 23.1 seconds. Irena ran on Poland's winning and world-record breaking 400-meter relay team.

The next year Irena became a favorite of the Poles. She studied economics at Warsaw University and pursued her athletic career. She began the season by tying the world record for 100 meters with an 11.1 time. In a meet in Warsaw against the United States that same year (1965), she defeated two American Olympic champions in the 100- and 200-meter races. She also raced a leg on the winning 400-meter relay team, and took the long jump. In the 200-meter race, she broke the world record with a 22.7 second race.

Her triumphs that year won her recognition as a national heroine in her native Poland. Tens of thousands stood to applaud her. Songs in honor of her achievements were sung. All Poland followed her career. She was stopped on Warsaw streets, stared at in awe, and her autograph was in great demand. Some anti-Semitic Poles found it convenient to forget her Jewish origin.

She was named Poland's Athlete of the Year in 1965. *Tass,* the official Russian news agency, also voted her the outstanding woman athlete in the world. After she won three gold medals (in the 200-meter race, long jump, and 400-meter relay) and a silver medal in the 100-meter race in the European Championships in Budapest in 1966, the British magazine, *World Sport,* chose her as Sportswoman of the Year.

Irena became Mrs. Szewinska in 1967. Her husband Junusz, a photographer who was once a runner and also her coach, is not Jewish. In 1968, in Mexico City, Irena won a gold medal in the 200-meter Olympics race, setting a new world record at 22.5 seconds. She also won a bronze medal in the 100-meter race.

After 1968 she was tired, and was content to spend a year uninvolved in competitive sport. The rest was beneficial both physically and mentally. She felt better, trained better and enjoyed running more. Her son Andrzej was born in February 1970. Irena believed having a child helped her performance in sport. And her performance improved. She devoted all her time outside her family to her passion, track. Because she never tired of the sport she was still able to beat younger rivals.

Between 1971 and 1973 Irena was still an outstanding sprinter, although not number one in the world. She earned two more bronze medals after the baby's birth: in the 200-meter event at the 1971 European Championships and at the 1972 Munich Olympics.

Until 1972 Irena's principal events were the 100-meter and 200-meter sprint, but after Munich she concentrated on the 400-meter race. She followed the advice of her husband and coach, and as a result in 1974 she became the first woman to break 50 seconds at that distance, running it in 49.9 seconds.

She made a great comeback in 1974 after her place at the top had been captured by the younger sprinter, Renate Stecher, of East Germany. In that year Irena chopped a tenth of a second from her 200-meter world mark by running that distance in 22.0 seconds. And she recorded the second fastest time ever for a woman in the 100-meters: a 10.9 second sprint. She set a world record in the 200-meters by running it in 22.21 seconds. Finally, she won the European 100-meter and 200-meter races, beating Olympic champ Stecher in both events. Irena clocked 11.13 in the 100, the third fastest electronic time ever for a woman. She had an undefeated season at each distance. And she even ran a remarkable 48.5 anchor for Poland's team in the 1,600-meter relay at Rome in the European Championships.

For her achievements, United Press International voted her Sportswoman of 1974. *Track and Field News* named her woman athlete of the year. At the 1976 Montreal Olympics, she won the 400-meter race, setting a world record at 49.29, and lowering her own world record by almost half a second. For Irena, it was her most exciting victory. It garnered her a seventh Olympic medal. When asked if her victory was a triumph for the Communist system, she replied: "I know the people from Poland were very happy to see the Polish flag flying highest. But I run because it gives me great pleasure and satisfaction. I run for me."

Her total of seven Olympic (three of them gold) and 10 European (five gold) medals is a record that has no rival in the history of women's track and field. But Irena still maintained that no title gave her as much joy as the birth of her son. Irena con-

tended she kept competing for many years because she enjoyed the training and the competition, especially the important meets like the Olympics. She did not relish easy meets where she knew she would win without difficulty. Her best achievements came in the major competitions where she had to fight to win.

The year 1977 was one of her most successful. She won the 400-meter race in the Düsseldorf World Championships, establishing a new world record of 49.0. In 1978 and 1979, Irena worked toward the goal of trying to be the first person to win eight gold medals in the Olympic Games, bettering the record seven that Mark Spitz won in Munich in 1972. Age finally caught up with her at the 1980 Moscow Games, and she came home without a single medal.

A graduate of Warsaw University, Irena is now an economist, working in the Transportation Research Center in Warsaw.

Visiting the United States on a goodwill tour for the Polish Track Federation in April 1987, Irena was invited to run in a two-mile race in Central Park. As she was 40 years old, Irena was not sure she was up to it. Race officials told her that it was all right if she ran a little, and walked a little. "So I began running. I saw no person walking, so I ran all the way."

Irena's time was 12 minutes, a little more than a minute off the 10:51 posted by the winner. She discouraged the idea that she would begin a new career as a distance runner. "My race was not bad for the first time," she said. "But it was the first and last time."

In the spring of 1998, Kirszenstein-Szewinska observed that she has often been asked whether she wasn't sometimes bored with athletics. "I have always replied 'no.' Sport is my passion. Together with my family, it has brought me all the joys of the world." She is currently serving on the Women's Committee of The International Amateur Athletic Federation. A Federation news release in 1998 suggested that "Irena Szewinska was a model athlete. First and foremost, she should be seen as a highly successful woman."

According to the 1998 *Guinness Book of World Records,* Irena shared the record for the most Olympic medals won in a career by a woman (seven) with two others: Shirley de la Hunty of Australia and Merlene Ottey of Germany.

In 2004, Irena was involved as the head of the Polish Federation of Athletics and as a member of the International Olympic Committee. On August 3, 2005, she was elected to the International Association of Athletics Federations Council in Helsinki, Finland.

Irena Kirszenstein-Szewinska is a member of the Jewish Sports Hall of Fame in Israel.

Sandy Koufax
One of the Best Pitchers of All Time

KOUFAX, SANDY (born December 30, 1935, in Brooklyn, New York–) American baseball player. One of the greatest pitchers of all time. The first pitcher in the major leagues to pitch four no-hit games. He won the Cy Young Award three times in four seasons and in 1972 was the youngest player ever admitted to the Baseball Hall of Fame. He was *The Sporting News'* Pitcher of the Year each year from 1963 to 1966. He struck out 2,396 batters, pitched 40 shutouts and established numerous major league records, including the most seasons (three) with 300 or more strikeouts.

. . .

Sandy (Sanford) was born in the Borough Park section of Brooklyn, the son of Jack and Evelyn (Lichtenstein) Braun. His name at birth was Sanford Braun. At age three, his parents divorced. Sandy and his mother lived with her parents for some time. When Sandy was nine, his mother remarried. Sandy always considered Evelyn's second husband, Irving Koufax, an attorney, his real father.

Sandy Koufax entered Brooklyn's Lafayette High School in the fall of 1949, and played on its basketball and baseball teams. He played first base on the school baseball team. Most of the pitching was done by Fred Wilpon, a future president of the New York Mets.

After high school graduation, Sandy was awarded an athletic scholarship to the University of Cincinnati on the strength of his basketball record. He enrolled in the school in the fall of 1953 and majored in architecture.

Koufax became a member of the baseball team and in the first two games he pitched for the uni-

versity, he struck out 34 batters. A sportswriter named Jimmy Murphy took note of Koufax's performances and informed the Brooklyn Dodgers of Koufax's pitching talents. The Dodgers offered him a $14,000 bonus plus an annual salary of $6,000, a respectable sum at the time. On December 14, 1954, two weeks before his 19th birthday, he signed with the Dodgers.

His first spring training (in 1955) was less than satisfactory. He had come too far, too fast. "I was so nervous and tense," he recalled. "I couldn't throw the ball for 10 days. When I finally started pitching, I felt I should throw as hard as I could. I wound up with an arm so sore that I had to rest for another week." Because he had received the $6,000 bonus, he was required to spend at least two years with the Dodgers, thus forgoing a chance to obtain valuable experience in the minor leagues.

His first start for the Dodgers was on July 6, 1955. He pitched just over four innings, striking out four, and walking eight. In his second start, however, he showed his potential: on August 27th, he shut out the Cincinnati Reds on two hits, striking out 14 batters, the most in one game by any National League pitcher that year. His final two appearances of the season left the Dodgers organization a bit confused, wondering whether Koufax would really be an asset to the team. In one of the two games, he lasted only one inning; in the other he shut out the Pittsburgh Pirates on five hits, striking out six.

That year the Dodgers took seven games to win their first World Series, defeating the New York Yankees. Koufax mostly sat and watched, because Buzzie Bavasi, the Dodger executive, told him, "You have one pitch—high." Koufax acknowledged later that only because he had been signed for a bonus did the Dodgers keep him. "I was a guy trying to find himself," he recalled. "You're on a team that is usually a contender, you have to show control." The Dodgers, he felt, didn't work him enough, so he didn't have an opportunity to improve his control. "If I'd have signed with the Pittsburgh Pirates, they would've been forced to use me. In those days, they were pitching anybody who was alive."

So, for the next six years, Koufax had, as he has said, "good periods, bad periods. Mostly bad." In his first six seasons, he won 36 games and lost 40. He had one day of glory in 1959, and that was the day he struck out 18 batters, tying the major league record set two decades earlier by Cleveland Indian pitcher Bob Feller.

In 1960, with the Dodgers now in Los Angeles, he was 8-13 and ready to throw in the towel. With the season over, he threw all of his baseball equipment away, doubting that he would return. He went into business, but did not like it. "Then," said Sandy, "I decided maybe I hadn't worked hard enough, so the next spring I reported to Vero Beach. Our clubhouse man, Nobe Kawano, handed me the gear and said, 'I took all your stuff out of the garbage.'"

He asked to pitch more frequently to improve his control. He got advice from Joe Becker, the pitching coach, and Norm Sherry, a catcher and Sandy's roommate. "And [Dodger pitcher] Don Newcombe taught me the value of running," recalled Koufax. "He was the hardest worker I ever saw." That season (1961) Koufax was 18-13, striking out 269 batters, breaking a league record held by the legendary Christy Mathewson. From 1961 to 1966, Sandy won 129 games and lost only 47.

In the 1962 season, Koufax was on his way to a great season when an injury forced him to stay out of uniform at the season's midpoint. He was 14-14, with 209 strikeouts, an earned-run average of 2.06, and a no-hitter under his belt, when the index finger of his pitching hand grew numb and he was unable to produce a curve. In mid-July it was determined that be was suffering from a circulatory affliction resulting from a blood clot in the palm. Physicians thought a finger might have to be amputated, ending Koufax's career. But an operation was not required, and the doctors successfully treated the finger with anti-coagulants.

The 1963 season was Koufax's greatest. He was 13-3 by mid-July, including a no-hitter. He wound up the season at 25-5, striking out 306 batters, a figure topped by only three others since 1900. His 11 shutouts was a major league record for a left hander in one season; and his 311 innings pitched were the most by a National League left-hander since 1921. Koufax's earned-run average of 1.88 was the major league's best the second year running. In the World Series against the New York Yankees, his two victories were crucial in helping the Dodgers take the entire event.

Koufax was named Cy Young Award winner unanimously as the best pitcher in the majors that year, as well as the National League's Most Valuable Player.

In 1964, Koufax posted a 19-5 record with an earned-run average of 1.74 before an arm ailment sidelined him at the end of August. On June 4th of that year he pitched his third no-hitter, tying the major league record at that point.

In 1965 he was hampered by arthritis in his elbow, but despite the ailment won 26 games and struck out 382 to break Bob Feller's major league record of 348. On September 9th he pitched a perfect game against the Chicago Cubs, the fourth no-hitter of his career. In 1965, Sandy again won the Cy Young Award.

A host of stories, many of them simply not true, have developed surrounding Sandy Koufax's relationship to his Jewish faith. One which appears true is that the Dodgers took the Jewish High Holy Days into consideration so that Koufax could pitch as much as possible during September or October. Another that Sandy himself denies has it that because of Koufax the Dodger clubhouse was stocked with bagels, lox, and chopped chicken liver, all traditional Jewish foods.

One incident which Koufax confirmed took place in October 1965, when the Dodgers and Minnesota Twins were playing in the World Series. The opening game fell on Yom Kippur, holiest day of the Jewish Year, and Sandy was not at the ball park. Don Drysdale pitched in his place instead and the Dodgers lost 8-2. The following morning, the *St. Paul Pioneer Press* carried a sports column entitled, "An Open Letter to Sandy Koufax." It contained a number of veiled and uncomplimentary references. The column concluded: "The Twins love matza balls on Thursdays." (The Yom Kippur game was played on a Thursday.) Later, Sandy commented, "I couldn't believe it. I thought that kind of thing went out with dialect comics." He pitched the second game later that day and lost 5-1. But he won the seventh and deciding game, and the Dodgers won the World Series. After that, Sandy said, "I clipped the column so that I could send it back to him (the writer of the column) after we defeated the Twins with a friendly little notation that I hoped his words were as easy to eat as my matza balls. I didn't of course [send it]. We were winners."

In 1966, Koufax earned the highest salary ever paid a baseball player at that time: $135,000. That spring, he and fellow Dodger pitcher Don Drysdale had entered into a holdout alliance, threatening to tour Japan and then hinting they would leave baseball and appear in a movie in which Koufax would be an Italian waiter. The Dodgers gave in to Koufax's high demands and he was back in uniform on opening day. His injuries remained problematic, and he made a pact with the Dodger team physician: "Let me know when I run the risk of permanent damage." The doctor, Robert Kerlan, wanted Sandy to quit at the beginning of 1966.

But Sandy persevered. He had an impressive 27-9 record, including winning the game which clinched the pennant for the Dodgers after only two days' rest. He turned in the third lowest earned-run average (1.73) of any major league pitcher ever, and won the Cy Young Award for an unprecedented third time. After the Dodgers lost four straight in the World Series to Baltimore, Koufax hired a hall in the Beverly Hills Hotel and announced his retirement: "I've had it," he declared. "I don't want to wind up with an arm I won't be able to use for the rest of my life."

He tried television, working as a commentator, but disliked it and gave it up. "People started writing that I was living the life of a hermit," he noted, "which wasn't true. All I had done was move to small towns (Ellsworth, Maine, and Templeton, California), but I continued to associate with the human race." He took a job as a manufacturer's representative, selling electrical appliances, but found that "selling wasn't my strong suit." He went back to the Los Angeles Dodgers in January 1979, as a pitching instructor "to make ends meet."

He served in that capacity for 11 years, resigning in 1990.

Sandy remains close to the hearts of his fans years after his retirement from the mound. When Manhattan's Stage Deli took a poll for the all-time Jewish All-Star baseball team in 1989, Koufax received the most votes. (Hank Greenberg was second.)

Sandy is an accomplished do-it-yourself man and among his hobbies are building, painting, and repairing. He is married to actor Richard Widmark's daughter, Anne. Koufax now makes his home in Vero Beach, Florida.

In retirement, Koufax has frequently attended the Los Angeles Dodgers' spring training camp also in Vero Beach, Florida, tutoring the Dodger pitching staff.

One day in March 1998, Koufax, 62 years old, arrived on the scene at the New York Mets' preseason training at Port St. Lucie, Florida. A friend of his—a pitching coach for the Mets—had invited him to drop by.

The Hall-of-Famer took the occasion to talk to the Mets pitchers, giving them advice on how to establish themselves early in the game; how not to be afraid to pitch around an opponent's best hitter; how to pitch away; and how to learn not to be afraid to fail.

He told stories that day to the pitchers of how he pitched around Hank Aaron and how he struck out Mickey Mantle in the 1963 World Series.

Koufax urged the Mets' pitchers to go out and pitch every day with the aim of pitching a perfect game, and if the game was no longer perfect, to aim for a one-hitter and then a two-hitter and a three-hitter. "Fight for every out you can," Koufax told them.

In May 1998, a sports columnist bumped into Koufax at a Westchester golf course and offered him clippings of box scores, pictures, and cartoons of the pitcher that he had collected. Koufax politely declined, saying: "That baseball pitcher people saw many years ago was somebody else. You do that in one part of your life and you go on. I don't look back."

In 2002, Koufax severed ties with the Los Angeles Dodgers over a gossip item that appeared in the *New York Post*, which is owned by the team's parent company, Rupert Murdoch's News Corp. The *Post* contended that a "Hall of Fame baseball hero" had "cooperated with a best-selling biography only because the author promised to keep it secret that he is gay." Koufax is the subject of Jane Leavy's *Sandy Koufax: A Lefty's Legacy*, issued in September 2002. Denying that she had made such a deal with Koufax, Leavy called the item "blatantly unfair, scandalous and contemptible."

During spring training of 2004, the 68-year-old Koufax entertained questions from pitchers for the Florida Marlins. There are three important differences between pitchers of his era and those of the early 2000s, he pointed out. Contemporary pitchers, he added, are bigger and stronger—and some use a split-finger fastball.

In the April 2007 Israel Baseball League draft, Koufax was chosen to pitch for the Modi'in Miracle, but he declined. "If he's rested and ready to take the mound again, we want him on our team," Miracle manager Art Shamsky declared. It was noted that had Koufax accepted, he would have had 14,875 days rest.

Sandy Koufax is a member of the Jewish Sports Hall of Fame in Israel.

Lenny Krayzelburg

Outstanding Jewish Athlete of the 1990s and 2000s

KRAYZELBURG, LENNY (born September 28, 1975, in Odessa, Russia–) American swimmer. While a senior at the University of Southern California in 1998, he was the world's top-ranked backstroker. At the 2000 Sydney Olympics, he won gold medals in the 100-meter backstroke, 200-meter backstroke, and 400-medley relay, breaking two Olympic records. *People Magazine* named him one of the Fifty Most Beautiful People of 2000.

· · ·

When Lenny was a five-year-old in his native Odessa, his father Oleg, a coffee shop owner, wanted him to become a soccer player. Too young for the local soccer teams, Lenny was eager to try some form of organized sports, and with his father's encouragement, he began swimming. Lenny would swim at an army sports club near his home. In early competitions, he would finish second or third, but he never won a national competition. When he was ten years old, Lenny was lifting weights in addition to swimming and running three to four kilometers a day.

Growing up under the Soviet Communists, Lenny was unable to practice being a Jew. He attributes his parents' decision to leave the Soviet Union, at least in part, to anti-Semitism. "They didn't want us to go through something like that," he said in an interview. His family then emigrated from Russia to the United States, where he learned to speak English while swimming with a local team in Santa Monica.

After graduating in the summer of 1993 from Fairfax High, which had no swim team, he swam briefly for Santa Monica (California) College dur-

ing the 1993–94 season and was chosen the 1994 Athlete of the Year and California Junior College Swimmer of the Year.

At the 1994 J.C. State competition, he won the 200-meter backstroke title and is the J.C. national record-holder in that event. He won the 100-meter backstroke (50.71) at the 1995 Summer Nationals Rookie Meet.

Fate hasn't always been kind to Krayzelburg. In 1995, the year he gained American citizenship, he broke his hand in a car accident three days before he was to leave for the U.S. Nationals. The accident left him unable to compete for six weeks. "That was tough," Krayzelburg said. "That was going to be my first Nationals."

Instead of waiting around for his hand to heal, Krayzelburg continued to train, even when it meant just doing kicks in the water. Practice paid off, and he came back to win the 100-meter backstroke at the Summer Nationals Rookie Meet.

Stu Blumkin, then head coach of the swim team at SMCC, realized Krayzelburg's potential—"I knew he'd be very special"—and recommended that he train with Mark Schubert, head swimming coach for the University of Southern California. "I took Lenny to one level," Blumkin said. "But I knew he needed to be with the better swimmers."

He was admitted to USC on a scholarship in January 1996.

In addition to utilizing his natural ability, Lenny was quite happy to adopt the successful swimming techniques of others. "I'm not afraid to learn from someone else, even if I'm better than them." He acknowledged that he tried to imitate swimming rival Neil Walker of Texas. "I've noticed the way he does underwater kicks, and I've tried to implement that in my swimming to get an edge on him."

Krayzelburg burst upon the national scene, winning both backstroke events, at the 1996 Summer Nationals. Despite reaching the finals at the NCAAs and the Olympic Trials, he was still unknown. Most media reports misspelled his name. After the Nationals, they learned how to spell it.

He qualified for the 1996 U.S. Olympic Trials,

where he finished fifth in the 200-meter backstroke (2:00.72) and 13th in the 100-meter backstroke (56.52). But he fell short of qualifying for the 1996 Atlanta Olympic Games. "I knew that wasn't my time to make the Olympics. I told myself, 'This is a great learning experience. Now you gotta start improving.'"

At the NCAAs, he took 26th in the 100-meter backstroke (50.20) and 28th in the 200-meter backstroke (1:48.80).

In August of 1996, Krayzelburg won the 100-meter and 200-meter backstroke at the Long Course Nationals in Florida in 56.11 and 1:59.37, respectively.

At the U.S. Open in December 1997, Krayzelburg won both the 100-meter (55.27) and 200-meter (1:59.20) backstroke events and took 15th in the 50-meter freestyle event. He completed his 1996-1997 junior season by breaking the American record in the 200-meter backstroke twice in August of 1997, first at the U.S. Nationals (1:58.04) and then at the Pan Pacific Championships (1:57.87) in Fukuoka, Japan.

On the difference between swimming the 200-meter race versus the 100 meters, Krayzelburg notes, "I don't have that much front speed. I really get into my rhythm on the second 100." But what really drives him is his competitiveness: "My goal is to win, and then whatever comes with it," he said. "But it's all about winning."

His record efforts in 1997 helped earn him the 1997 Phillips Performance Award for best U.S. swimmer of the year (tied with Neil Walker). In addition to winning the 200-meter backstroke at the Pan Pacs, Krayzelburg also won the 100-meter backstroke in 54.43 (the third-fastest time ever) and took 16th in the 50-meter freestyle (23.67).

At the 1997 U.S. Nationals, Krayzelburg also won the 100-meter backstroke (54.69, a world trials record) and took 24th in the 50-meter freestyle (23.60). In March 1997, Krayzelburg became a five-time All-American at the NCAA Championships and won USC's first NCAA individual title since 1994 when he won the 200-meter backstroke

in 1:41.10. He took second in the 100-meter backstroke in 46.55, a USC record. Krayzelburg also earned All-American honors as part of USC's fifth-place 400-meter medley relay, sixth-place 200-meter medley relay, and eighth-place 200-meter freestyle relay. He won Pac-10 titles in both the 100-meter (46.96) and 200-meter backstroke (1:40.59, a Pac-10 and USC record) and took fifth in the 50-meter freestyle (20.19).

Another setback came during his junior year at USC when Krayzelburg dislocated his shoulder during practice. Once again, instead of moping around, he made use of his time by practicing his kick in the water.

In January 1998, he won two gold medals swimming for the United States at the 1998 World Championships in Perth, Australia, triumphing in both the 100-meter and 200-meter backstroke. He swam the 100 in 55.0 seconds and the 200 in 1:58.84. The American record holder in the 100-meter backstroke, he became the first American swimmer to sweep the specialty at the World Championships.

Krayzelburg has every right to feel confident about his swimming efforts. As of the summer of 1998, this five-time All-American is the world's top-ranked backstroker. "I still don't realize I'm a world champion," Krayzelburg said. "[USC Head Coach] Mark [Schubert] keeps telling me how great of an honor it is."

The defending NCAA champion in the 200-meter backstroke, Krayzelburg took second at the 1998 NCAA Championships in both the 100- and 200-meter backstroke. At the 1998 Pac-10 Championships, he won the 100- and 200-meter backstroke for the second consecutive season.

Krayzelburg's work ethic is one of his strongest qualities, according to his coach: "He might get disappointed, but his reaction to disappointment is to come back and work harder."

Lenny's secret is simple: hard work. "Every time I get into the pool I'm ready to work hard," he said. "I believe there's no point to come into the pool for two hours and just swim. You're pretty much wasting your time. That's why I have to work twice as hard to stay on top. There's always someone there that's trying to beat you. That's something I keep in the back of my mind."

Lenny trained with Brad Bridgewater, the defending Olympic gold medalist in the 200-meter backstroke, before Brad graduated from USC.

A major cause of Krayzelburg's success is his eagerness to compete. "I like training. I like challenges. I'm a very competitive person. I like some kind of competition every day." Not surprisingly, then, Krayzelburg trains five hours a day; he knows that with every race there is pain. He has learned to deal with it and now sees it in a new perspective. "There's a great saying that pain is forever and pride is forever," Krayzelburg said. "I live by that. I just go out there and try to win. Everyone remembers who wins, and no one remembers second place."

In August of 1999, Lenny broke an unprecedented three world records in the 50-, 100- , and 200-meter backstroke events, helping to win three gold medals at the Pan American Pacific Championships. At the Sydney Olympics the following year, he seemingly effortlessly nailed gold medals in the 100-meter backstroke, the 200-meter backstroke, and the 400-medley relay, breaking two Olympic records in the process. "It was amazing to have 18,000 people there watching me swim," he said. "That doesn't happen every day."

After the glory came several setbacks. In the early 2000s, Krayzelberg underwent both shoulder surgery and the repair of a torn ankle ligament. The injuries were costly in that Lenny's training time for the 2004 Athens Olympics was abbreviated. Rather than sweeping the backstroke events as he had at Sydney, in the 2004 competition Lenny had to settle for fourth in the 100-meter backstroke with a time of 54.38 seconds, a mere 2/100ths of a second away from a medal. However, he did win gold when the United States took first place and surpassed the world record in the men's 400-meter medley relay.

Aaron Krickstein

One of America's Great Tennis Players

KRICKSTEIN, AARON (born August 2, 1967 in Ann Arbor, Michigan–) American tennis player. His best career rank was No. 6 in the world on February 26, 1990. As a junior player, he never lost to a younger player. At 16, Krickstein won the U.S. National 18s titles in the Indoor, Clay and National categories. The winner of eight pro singles titles, he is the youngest player to win a professional title. He was ranked eighth in the world in 1989; 20th in 1990 and 34th in 1991. His official career earnings come to $3,710,447.

. . .

When he won his first professional tennis title in October 1983, Aaron Krickstein was still very much a shy, retiring teenager, barely 16 years old. Had he pursued swimming, Aaron might have developed into one of America's great swimming talents. He won the Michigan state swimming titles in freestyle and butterfly at the age of five and six respectively.

But young Aaron, whose father is a doctor and pathologist at Detroit's St. John's Hospital, and whose grandfather was a rabbi, preferred tennis to swimming. He began playing the sport at the age of six. He was influenced by his tennis-playing family: Aaron's three older sisters were all nationally-ranked as juniors. His older sister, Renee, was a member of the women's team at Tulane University. Another older sister, Kathy played tennis at the University of Michigan. From childhood, Aaron's goal was to become a professional tennis player: "I've probably taken more private lessons than any human being alive," he once said jokingly.

A great junior tennis star, Krickstein was ranked at or near the top of every division from the 12 and unders to 18 and unders. He captured the American National Under 16 in Kalamazoo, Michigan in 1982 and followed that with another impressive triumph, taking the National 18s championship, also in Kalamazoo, in 1983.

In 1982, he came under the guidance of tennis coach Nick Bollettieri, attending the Nick Bollettieri Tennis Academy in Bradenton, Florida for the next three years. Bollettieri helped fashion Aaron's hard-hitting tennis style, especially his powerful forehand and strong baseline game.

The teen-aged Krickstein began playing on the pro tennis circuit in early 1983. At first he faltered, failing to get past the initial round in his first five Grand Prix tournaments. However, at the U.S. Open that fall, he proved a sensation, reaching the final 16. In the opening round, he defeated Stefan Edberg in five sets in a tiebreaker.

The youngster filled the grandstands in the third round as he came back from a two-set deficit to defeat Vitas Gerulaitis, the 1979 runner-up. When Aaron won four straight games to win the fifth set 6-4, the ballboys, most of them older than Krickstein, filed by to shake the budding star's hand. That put Aaron in the round of 16, making him the youngest male player to get that far in the U.S. Open. He was one month past 16 when Yannick Noah ended his streak at the U.S. Open.

During that tournament, Aaron's father, Herb, told a reporter: "Look at his body. He's pathetic. But he's fearless on the tennis court." When someone suggested to Dr. Krickstein that his son might become good enough to play on the Israeli Davis Cup team, he thought for a moment, then indicated that his goal was for Aaron to play on the U.S. Davis Cup team.

Aaron turned pro right after the U.S. Open that fall, an awkward step for one so young. "I was kind of afraid to talk to the guys. I felt so young. In the locker rooms I felt out of place. But then I started winning some matches . . . I learned a lot."

His most incredible achievement came in October 1983 when he won the Tel Aviv Grand Prix.

Two months past 16, he was the youngest person ever to win a Grand Prix tournament. With John McEnroe and Jimmy Connors past their primes, Krickstein looked like the next best young American hope. By the end of his first year on the circuit, Krickstein had jumped from 489 to 97 in the world rankings, with cash winnings of $28,763.

But, the next year, 1984, Aaron got off to a slow start. In his first eight tournaments he failed to reach the third round. Bouncing back by May, he began a string of triumphs, reaching the finals of the Italian Open, and winning the

U.S. Pro Championship in Boston. He broke into the top 20 that spring, three months short of his 17th birthday.

Knocking over tennis greats Mats Wilander and Heinrik Sundstrom, Krickstein took two more Grand Prix titles in Tel Aviv and Geneva. He reached top ten status on August 13, surpassing Bjorn Borg as the youngest player to reach the top ten, a record that still stands. He finished the year with a world ranking of 12, despite missing five months due to a stress fracture of the right foot, the first of numerous injuries that have plagued his career.

Krickstein and Michelle Tores, both Americans, were named *Tennis Magazine*-Rolex Watch 1984 Rookies of the Year. Krickstein was the first American male to win the rookie award since Jimmy Arias in 1981.

The following year, 1985, was disappointing for Aaron, though he did rise at one stage to a world rank of seven. His only impressive showing was as runner-up at Hong Kong. He helped the U.S. defeat Japan in the opening round of Davis Cup competition that year, but he suffered a frustrating defeat in Hamburg as the Germans upset the Americans in the quarterfinals of Davis Cup play. A stress fracture of the left foot cost him two months

of tournament play. He finished the year ranked 29 in the world.

In 1986, he was once again runner-up at Hong Kong; a semifinalist at Monte Carlo and at the Tournament of Champions in New York; and a quarterfinalist at LaQuinta and at the World Championship Tennis/Dallas and at the Washington tournaments. He also reached round 16 at the French Open. Earning $138,487 that year, he rose to 26 in the world.

In 1987, Krickstein was a quarterfinalist at Nice, the Tournament of Champions in New York, and in Boston. In July of that year he suffered a stress fracture of the tibia. During his recuperation in October a car side-swiped the New York City cab he was riding in, leaving him with two broken ribs. He was out for seven months, finishing the year at his lowest world rank: 61.

By 1988, Krickstein had made a gradual comeback, getting to the finals in Tel Aviv and Detroit and the quarterfinals at the U.S Open with a second big win over Stefan Edberg. His world ranking jumped to 15 by year's end. On September 7, Krickstein told *The New York Times*: "Over the years I've been hurt so much that I've never gotten my game back. I lost to a lot of players that are good players but who I feel I'm better than when I'm playing my best. It's kind of tough to take that. You just want to get back to where you were, let alone improve your game."

So, when he beat Edberg in five sets to advance to the U.S. Open quarterfinals, Aaron called it the biggest victory of his career. A sportswriter termed the match "perhaps the best Krickstein has ever played and probably the most important." Still a baseliner, he relied on his topspin forehand to overpower Edberg whom he had not opposed on the court since 1983.

Improving even more in 1989, Krickstein earned a career-high $582,6512 and finished No. 8 in the world. It was the first time that Aaron, now age 22, finished in the top ten. He was now coached by tennis star Tim Gullikson. Showing great competitive zeal, Aaron came back to win matches after dropping the first set. Such perseverance earned him the nickname of the "Marathon Man" on the tour. Tennis pro Boris Becker said of Aaron: "He is a tough player. He all the time comes back. He never really gives up and that's his best point."

In January 1989, Krickstein won a tournament in Sydney, Australia, for his first title in four years. In May, he surpassed the one million dollar mark in career prize money. At Los Angeles in September, he won his second tournament of the year. He returned to No.10 in the world on October 16, 1989, the first time since June 10, 1985. That was the longest span of any player between top ten appearances.

His most impressive performance of 1989 came at the Tokyo Indoor where on October 22 he defeated Stefan Edberg and Carl-Uwe Steeb in succession to garner the $100,000 first prize. After defeating Edberg, Krickstein said that his rankings were deceiving. " I feel that my game is better than it was when I was No. 7. It's a great win for me. It should get my confidence going, knowing that I can play with the best." He won 50 of his 70 matches that year.

Though he did not win a title in 1990, Aaron reached the finals in Tokyo, losing to Stefan Edberg. He had wins over Michael Chang and Ivan Lendl (for the first time), and reached the final in Brisbane losing to Brad Gilbert. He played most of 1990 with several nagging injuries. His 1990 prize money was $650,184. He ended the year with a world rank of 20.

He fell to No. 34 in 1991, winning no titles but reaching the runner-up spot at Brisbane. Appearing at the U.S. Open in September, Krickstein borrowed six tennis rackets that belonged to defending Open champion Pete Sampras. Krickstein had complained several months earlier of arm trouble, attributing the problem, at least partially, to his rackets. Krickstein reached the round of 16 for the fourth consecutive year—thanks to the borrowed rackets, it seemed.

In early April, 1992, Krickstein won the $300,000 South African Open. Later, that month, he reached the finals of the Monte Carlo Open. As of July 6, 1992 he was ranked 14th in the world.

Plagued by injuries, he dropped to No. 25 in the world in 1995. He told a reporter: "I have no regrets. I've had a pretty good career so far. Waiting and going on to college first might have been worse for my career. The atmosphere of being on the circuit was good for me."

Of his first Grand Slam appearance, soon after turning pro, when he reached the fourth round of the U.S. Open in New York, he said: "When you're young, you don't even realize what pressure is.

In January 1995, Krickstein recovered from a two-set deficit to upset superstar Stefan Edberg en route to the semifinals of the Australian Open, the ninth time he had come back after being down the first two sets.

Now retired from the ATP tennis tour, Krickstein and his wife, Terri, whom he married on December 26, 1993, live in Palm Beach, Florida.

In May 2006, with earnings of $3,710,447, Krickstein ranked 95th on the list of all-time prizewinners. He continued to serve as tennis director at the St. Andrews Country Club, in Boca Raton, Florida, a position he first assumed in 2004.

Benny Leonard

The Jewish Boxing Champion Who Refused to Fight on a Jewish Holiday

LEONARD, BENNY (born April 7, 1896, in New York City; died April 18, 1947) American Boxer. Considered by some to be the greatest Jewish sports figure of all time and the best Jewish boxer in history. Ranked by Nat Fleischer as the second greatest lightweight fighter ever. From 1917 to 1924, Leonard held the world lightweight title. Career record: 209 bouts, 88 wins (68 by knockout), lost 5, 1 draw, 115 no-decisions.

• • •

Benny Leonard, whose real name was Benjamin Leiner, was the son of Orthodox Jews. He grew up around Eighth Street and Second Avenue in New York City, a Jewish neighborhood, with Italians to the south, Irish to the north. The public baths were near Benny's house: to reach them, one had to walk past where he lived. "You had to fight or stay in the house when the Italian and Irish kids came through on their way to the baths," Benny recalled. When he fought on the street, it was not only with fists, but also with sticks, stones, and bottles. In part because of some of the beatings he took, Benny disliked this kind of fighting intensely.

He fought with gloves for the first time at age 11. His parents had no inkling of what he was doing, but when his mother discovered that Benny was boxing, she asked a relative to give him a job in his printing shop. Benny took the job, but it did not last long. One morning, he came to work with a black eye that he got in a fight. He was given an ultimatum: quit fighting or quit the job. He quit the job. His mother failed to understand the attraction of the ring. "A prizefighter you want to be?"

she asked him weeping. "Is that a life for a respectable man? For a Jew?"

For Benny Leonard it was. His street fights included routing a group of non-Jews who had attacked an elderly Jewish woman and taking on hoodlums who were trying to deface a synagogue. He was the champion of Eighth Street.

Benny was too poor to pay for a seat to see a fight. One night, when he was 16, he sat perched on a skylight atop a small-time neighborhood boxing club, watching the fight in the ring below. Losing his balance, Benny fell onto the ring floor and an angry promoter grabbed him before he could escape. To pay for the broken glass of the skylight that shattered as he fell, Leonard offered to replace a boxer who had failed to appear for his bout that night. Benny won the match, and his career was launched.

He used the name "Benny Leonard" in his early fights so his parents would not know that he was boxing. But the secret could not be kept for long. Leonard was always concerned about his mother's feelings. He called her after every fight, carried her picture around with him, and even earned the nickname, "Mama's boy." To add to her happiness, he would never fight on a Jewish holiday.

Leonard's first big victory occurred in 1915 when he defeated Joe Mandot, a veteran pugilist. The next year he fought the lightweight champion, Freddy Welsh, to two no-decision contests. In their third meeting on May 28, 1917, Leonard knocked him out in the ninth round and became the new lightweight champ.

His most memorable fights were between 1920 and 1923. In a 1920 contest, Charlie White, a hard-hitting left-hander, belted Leonard out of the ring, but Benny still managed to knock White out in the ninth round. Jack Britton, the welterweight champ, beat Leonard on a foul in 1922. The following month, Leonard rebounded from Lew Tendler's hard hitting to win a tough decision. On January 15, 1925 Leonard retired. "My mother was so happy," he recalled. "I was 29, practically a millionaire, and without a scratch."

He might have remained in that happy circumstance had his financial position not taken an eventual plunge. From 1926 to 1931, he bought a hockey team, played in vaudeville, and taught boxing at City College in New York. But the stock market crash of 1929 wiped out all his savings and so in 1931, at age 35, he decided to try a comeback as a welterweight. This decision has been described as the greatest mistake in his boxing career.

Jimmy McLarnin, a hard-hitting fighter of Irish descent, had developed a reputation for stopping Jewish boxers in the ring. Leonard said that a desire "to wipe out McLarnin's successful record against Jewish fighters" was one motive for his comeback. Before he took on McLarnin, Leonard fought some 20 bouts, doing well. But when he met McLarnin on October 7, 1932, the 26-year old Jimmy had little trouble disposing of the ring-worn Leonard.

In World War II, Leonard served as a lieutenant commander in the United States Maritime Service. He was back in boxing as a referee in 1943. In 1947 he was working as a referee at New York's St. Nicholas Arena one evening when, during the seventh bout, he collapsed in the ring and died of a brain hemorrhage.

In his time, Benny Leonard was the most famous Jewish personality in America. He became a legend, due in part to the claim that no one had ever messed his slicked-down hair in over 200 fights. He would enter the ring with his hair in place, and usually leave the same way. Dan Parker, the veteran sports writer, said, "Leonard moved with the grace of a ballet dancer and wore an air of arrogance that belonged to royalty. His profile might have been chiseled by a master sculptor and there wasn't a mark of his trade upon it to mar its classic perfection."

Perhaps the greatest tribute to Benny Leonard came from *Hearst* editor, Arthur Brisbane: "He has done more to conquer anti-Semitism than a thousand textbooks."

In its September 2001 issue, *The Ring* magazine ranked Leonard number 2 on its list of the greatest lightweights of all time.

Benny Leonard is a member of the Jewish Sports Hall of Fame in Israel.

Battling Levinsky

World Light Heavyweight Champ During World War I

LEVINSKY, BATTLING (born June 10, 1891, in Philadelphia, Pennsylvania; died February 12, 1949) World light heavyweight champion from 1916 to 1920. Nat Fleischer ranked Levinsky as the sixth best light heavyweight ever. He fought 272 bouts, winning 66 (25 by knockout), losing 19, with 13 draws and 174 no-decisions.

∎ ∎ ∎

Though his real name was Barney Lebrowitz, Levinsky began his boxing career in 1906 using the name Barney Williams. For the next seven years he fought, but failed to attract much attention in boxing's heartland, New York City.

But, in 1913, when the young Jewish fighter took a new manager, Dumb Dan Morgan, and fought heavyweight Dan "Porky" Flynn, Levinsky moved into the spotlight.

After watching his fighter do well against Flynn in the first round, manager Morgan convinced the ring announcer to announce that Battling Levinsky (Williams' new fight name) was ready to take on any Irishman in the country. Needless to say, Levinsky won the 10-round fight against Flynn that evening.

Battling Levinsky was indeed an appropriate name. In 1914 he battled 35 times, nine times during January of that year (he won twice by knockout that month; the other seven contests were no-decision matches). On January 1st, 1915, he outdid himself when he fought three, 10-round,

no-decision bouts—in Brooklyn, New York, in Waterbury, Connecticut, and in New York City. For his day's work Levinsky collected $400.

Levinsky fought the light heavyweight champion, Jack Dillon, nine times before he managed to capture the title in their tenth meeting. That tenth match was fought on October 24, 1916, in Boston, Massachusetts, when Levinsky finally took the title after a 12-round struggle. The two never met again.

During World War I, Levinsky became a lieutenant in the army and served as a boxing instructor. After the war, he never regained his prewar status. Jack Dempsey, soon to become heavyweight champion, knocked him out on November 6, 1918, in three rounds. That year Levinsky fought only 10 times.

After the loss to Dempsey, Levinsky's reputation suffered. On October 20, 1920, he fought the European light heavyweight champion, Georges Carpentier, in Jersey City, but Carpentier won in a fourth-round knockout. It was suggested that the fight had been fixed, but both fighters denied it.

In a fight against Gene Tunney in New York City, on January 13, 1922, Levinsky defended a new title created by his manager. It was called the American light heavyweight title (the world light heavyweight championship was fought in France). Tunney, on his way to a great career in the ring, beat Levinsky easily in 12 rounds. For the next four years Levinsky did not fight.

In 1929, Otto Van Porat, a Norwegian heavyweight, knocked Levinsky out in five rounds in Grand Rapids, Michigan. Levinsky wanted to give up the ring, but he continued because of financial problems connected with several apartment houses he owned in Philadelphia.

After his retirement from the ring in 1929, Battling Levinsky sold most of his apartment houses and purchased a meat slaughtering house in Chicago. Although he continued to live in Philadelphia, he retained ownership of the Chicago business until two years before his death in 1949.

Battling Levinsky is a member of the Jewish Sports Hall of Fame in Israel.

Marv Levy
Head Coach of the Buffalo Bills

LEVY, MARV (born August 3, 1928, in Chicago, Illinois–) American football coach. Head coach of the National Football League's Kansas City Chiefs from 1978 to 1982, compiling a 31-42 record. Coaching the National Football League Buffalo Bills from 1986 to 1997, he became the only coach to reach, and lose, four straight Super Bowls, from 1991 to 1994. He retired after the 1997 season with an overall record for the Bills of 123-78.

. . .

Marv Levy attended Coe College in Cedar Rapids, Iowa, where he majored in history. In 1950, he graduated with Phi Beta Kappa honors, and the following year earned a Masters degree in English history from Harvard University. Enrolling in Harvard Law School the fall of 1951, Marv decided to drop out to take a job coaching a junior varsity high school team at Country Day School in St. Louis. Levy phoned his father with the news. "The phone went silent for a minute," he said, "then my father just said, 'You better be a good one.'"

While at Coe College, Levy had been an outstanding back on the football team, and from 1953 to 1955 was an assistant football coach at Coe. He joined the University of New Mexico staff in 1956 and for two years served as assistant coach, and received Skyline Conference coach of the year honors both those seasons. He then took over at California in 1960 as head coach, coaching the Golden Bears through the 1963 season, and ending up with a rather dismal 8-29-3 overall record. One of Levy's players at the time was quarterback Craig Morton, who went on to play NFL pro football with the Dallas Cowboys, the New York Giants, and the Denver Broncos.

Next, Levy moved to William and Mary in Williamsburg, Virginia, where he was head football coach for five years. He was named Southern Conference coach of the year in 1964 and 1965.

Levy began his pro coaching career in 1969 with the Philadelphia Eagles with whom he was assistant coach in charge of the kicking teams. In 1970, he joined George Allen's Los Angeles Rams as an assistant coach. The following year, 1971, he moved with Allen to the Washington Redskins, remaining as assistant coach through the 1972 season. Marv Levy coached the special teams for Washington's 1972 National Football Conference championship team. After defeating Dallas 26-3, the Redskins met Miami in Super Bowl VII and lost 14-7. Levy moved to Montreal in 1973 as head coach of the Alouettes.

In Canadian football, three, not four downs are allowed, so mounting an awesome offense is extremely difficult. Hence Levy emphasized defense. This tactic proved successful. His first Alouette squad reached the finals of the Canadian Football League's Eastern Division with a 7-6-1 record, and then went on to win the Grey Cup the following year. Levy's 1974 season record was 9-5-2. The Alouettes won the CFL Grey Cup twice (1974 and 1977) in Levy's five years as coach. His record during those five years was 50-34-4.

Marv Levy was named head coach of the Kansas City Chiefs on December 20, 1977. His strategy was to rebuild Kansas City's defense. "Offense sells tickets," he told a news conference. "Defense wins games and kicking wins championships."

In his first year as coach the Chiefs finished 4-12 as compared with a 7-5-2 record the year before. But the record belied the team's actual strength. Levy used the rather old-fashioned wing-T offense, and despite numerous cynics in the NFL who doubted the Chiefs would move the ball easily, the team was second in the conference in rushing.

In 1979, Levy's second year, he picked up three more victories as against nine losses. He was 8-8 in

1980, and 9-7 in 1981, with a third-place finish in the Western Division of the American Football Conference of the NFL.

After being cut loose by the Chiefs in 1982, he was a television football analyst for the University of California and then, in 1985, coached the Chicago Blitz of the United States Football League. In the fall of 1986, he served as director of football operations for the Montreal Alouettes of the Canadian Football League.

In November of that year, the Buffalo Bills turned to Levy to become head coach, their third head coach in 14 months and their tenth in 27 seasons. The franchise had earned a reputation as the worst-managed team in the NFL over the previous 20 years. An eager Levy itched to return to the sidelines.

Although he was only 2-5 for the remainder of the 1986 season, Levy performed magic in Buffalo, taking the Bills to four AFC East titles in five and a half years, three AFC title games, two AFC championships, and two Super Bowl appearances.

By 1987, Levy began turning the Bills around, with a 7-8 record. The year 1988 produced the great leap forward as the Bills turned in a 12-4 record, winning the divisional playoff against Houston, 17-10. But they lost the conference championship to Cincinnati, 21-10.

The Bills had another good year in 1989, ending up at 9-7, but losing the divisional playoff to Cleveland, 34-30.

Levy's coaching reached its pinnacle in the early 1990s. He had a great year in 1990 with a 13-3 record. The Bills won the divisional playoff against Miami, 44-34, and the conference championship against the Los Angeles Raiders, 51-3. They lost, however, to the New York Giants in the Super Bowl in January 1991, 20-19.

In 1991 the Bills under Levy were 13-3, winning the divisional playoff against Kansas City, 37-14, and the conference championship against Denver, 10-7, but losing the Super Bowl in January 1992 to the Washington Redskins, 37-24.

Levy is known to be obsessive about planning

for a game. He sometimes stays up till 4 A.M. mapping out game plans. He loves to have his team run the ball, and dislikes the fancy offensive schemes. When he coached the Kansas City Chiefs from 1977 to 1982, he employed the winged-T formation which, according to one sportswriter, was the "equivalent of driving a Model T in the Indianapolis 500." During the week of the 1991 Super Bowl in which Buffalo played against the New York Giants, Levy said: "You should try and stick to the basics as much as possible. And I think you could say that it has worked so far."

In 1992, Levy's Bills were 11-5 for the season, but the Bills got trounced in the 1993 Super Bowl, losing to the Dallas Cowboys 52-17. In 1993, the Bills had a 12-4 season record and again reached the Super Bowl. Leading the Dallas Cowboys 13-6 in the first half of the 1994 Super Bowl, the Bills raised everyone's hopes, only to end the game down 17 points.

The 1994 season was less successful for the Bills, as they were only 7-9 in season play, but in 1995 and 1996 they bounced back with successive 10-6 records.

In the summer of 1995, Marv was diagnosed with prostate cancer. He kept the news secret, hoping to get through the season and then have surgery; but by October, Marv decided to have the surgery right away. Doctors said he'd have to stop coaching for six to ten weeks; he returned in three weeks, after doctors told him the cancer was gone.

In 1997, the Bills were still competing for the playoffs until late in the season, but for only the second time in the previous ten years, the Bills failed to qualify for the playoffs, finishing the year 6-10. Marv Levy retired after the 1997 season with an overall record of 123-78.

The Harvard-trained Levy has been known to use words that confound his players. Steve Tasker, a Buffalo guard, once devoted part of his play notebook to Levy tongue-twisters such as: extrapolate, inculcate, clandestine, debacle, salient and slovenly. "As you can see," Tasker said later, "some of them are used to describe how we play." Levy once called a referee "an over-officious jerk."

A student of history, Levy frequently lectured the Bills on the past, telling them war stories, often from the Civil War or World War II. Safety Leonard Smith recollected: "He gives you the whole scenario so you can see the stages of what it took to get to that point. He equates that to football, showing us that it takes several steps to reach our goals. In the end, everybody gets the message."

He tried to disabuse those who believed he was too much of an intellectual, though. "I'm a coach, I always felt good around coaches. I'm one of them. I'm not a professor."

For the 1999 season Levy joined Fox Sports, analyzing NFL games. On August 4, 2001, he was elected to the Pro Football Hall of Fame, joining Sid Gillman, Sid Luckman, Ronald Mix, and Al Davis as one of only five Jews to be so honored.

In 2004, in a weekly column that appeared on NFL.com, the National Football League's Website, Levy expressed his thoughts about NFL players, coaches, and games.

From 1999 until his appointment as general manager and vice-president of the Bills in January 2006, Marv Levy did local broadcasts for the Bills' pre-season games. Denying a rumor that Marv might once again be asked to assume coaching duties, team owner Ralph C. Wilson, Jr., bluntly remarked: "To say it very, very succinctly, Marv Levy is our general manager. He will never be the coach."

After the Bills' last game of the 2007 season, Levy stepped down as general manager and returned to live in his native Chicago. According to Actionheroreviews.com, at the time of his retirement Marv Levy was ranked 15th of all-time winning NFL coaches. His book *Game Changers: 50 Greatest Plays in Buffalo Bills Football History*, coauthored with Jeff Miller, was published in 2009.

Ted "Kid" Lewis

First Boxer with a Mouthpiece

LEWIS, TED "KID" (born October 24, 1894, in St. George's-in-the-East, London, England; died October 14, 1970) British boxer. He was world welterweight champion in 1915 and again from 1917 to 1919. In 260 bouts, he lost only 24. Lewis was the only British fighter to win a world title in the United States. He became Britain's youngest champion when he won the featherweight title shortly after his 17th birthday.

. . .

At the age of 14, he won his first professional fight, earning for himself a cup of tea and sixpence. Upon winning his next bout, the reward was greater. He received a silver cup, only to find it melted down after being left on the mantelpiece overnight. As time went on, the purses became larger and the rewards of victory more worthwhile.

Lewis won the British and European featherweight titles in 1913 and 1914. In the 1913 bout, he became the first boxer to wear a mouthpiece. In 1914, Lewis whose real name was Gershon Mendeloff, went to Australia with his family and from there to the United States. Within a year, he had established himself as a contending welterweight. Lewis was the first Englishman to box successfully in the U.S. He was considered speedy, shrewd, and a brutal puncher.

Between 1915 and 1921, Lewis engaged Jack Britton in a series of 20-round bouts that extended over six years. These grudge matches were to decide the world welter-

weight title. Of the 20 fights, 12 were no-decisions, one was a draw, three went to Britton, and four were victories for Lewis. The first Lewis triumph was in 1915 in Dayton, Ohio, and with it "Kid" Lewis won the welterweight championship for the first time. He lost the title to Britton for the last time in March 1919.

Ted Lewis returned to Britain in 1921 and within a few months won the Empire and European welterweight titles and the British and European middleweight championships. In June 1922, he added the Empire middleweight title. In that same year he fought his most famous fight when he

took on Georges Carpentier for the European heavyweight championship. During the first round, the referee stopped the action to speak to Lewis. Lewis dropped his guard and turned to the official to complain of a beltline smash from Carpentier. Meanwhile, the Frenchman drilled home a right to Lewis' unguarded jaw and the English boxer sagged to the canvas. The referee counted him out.

From 1925 to 1929, Lewis fought well, record-ing seven straight wins by knockout in 1927. In a decade of boxing, Lewis had won three division titles. In his 20 years as a boxer, he had fought in six divisions. He retired from the ring in 1929 and settled in Vienna.

The Jewish Sports Hall of Fame in Israel induct-ed Lewis in 1983. In his authoritative 1984 book, *The 100 Greatest Boxers of All Time*, Bert Randolph Sugar ranked Lewis number 33.

Mortimer Lindsey
The Champion Newark-born Bowler

LINDSEY, MORTIMER JOEL (born December 20, 1888, in Newark, New Jersey; died May 16, 1959) American bowler. One of the top American bowlers in the early twentieth century. One of the first 11 men originally chosen for membership in the American Bowling Congress Hall of Fame in 1941. He held three American Bowling Congress titles.

• • •

As a child, Mort Lindsey was an all-around athlete; a catcher for amateur baseball teams in the Bronx; a tennis and basketball player in YMHA and YMCA leagues. He even skated for a medal in a six-day roller skating competition in a rink at 116th Street and Lenox Avenue in New York City. Mort tried boxing too at the 86th Street YMHA in New York, won a few fights, but made no further progress.

He began bowling at age 14, finishing second in his first tournament, a juvenile competition in which wooden balls were used. The locale was the 92nd Street YMHA in New York. The following year he won the event and felt confident enough to stride into wrestler George Bothner's bowling alleys at 84th Street and Third Avenue to challenge all comers. He was hardly dressed for the role of the tough guy: he wore knee-britches and ribbed stockings. George eyed him coldly. "Beat it kid," the wrestler ordered.

"But I came here to bowl," protested Mort.

"So what," retorted Bothner eyeing his short pants. "You're a kid. Get out."

Then noticing Mort's disappointment, the wrestler relented ever so slightly: "Well, maybe I could see you roll a ball."

Mort rolled a ball, and Bothner, surprised, admitted, "That's not so bad, kid. Come back when you're in long pants." That was all Mort wanted to hear.

Getting George Bothner's approval was Mort's first major victory of his bowling career. He rushed home, badgered his parents to get him a pair of long pants, and returned to 84th Street for some pointers, and with that his bowling career was launched. Encouraged by Bothner, he entered a juvenile tournament at Bergman's alleys and beat many of the name stars by taking first prize.

Mort's mother, Minnie, tried desperately to keep her son away from those nefarious bowling alleys. "She never wanted me to be a bowler," Mort recalled somewhat sadly. "Mom thought I should grow up to be a doctor or lawyer. In her book you couldn't become great as a bowler." Even when Mort won the 86th Street YMCA championship at age 14, he could not convince her that there was a career to be carved out of rolling a ball down a narrow alley.

It took his mother quite some time—until Mort was 27, in fact—before she appeared reconciled to Mort Lindsey the bowling champ. While bowling in the American Bowling Congress tournament in St. Paul, Minnesota, in 1915, Mort was handed a package containing a pair of tiny, gilded, five button shoes. The accompanying card read: "I am sending you these shoes for the ABC tournament because they are the first shoes you struck out in. Mom." Minnie Lindsey was signaling her approval of her son's favorite pastime by showing she could recall the first time Mort had knocked down all the pins with a single ball—in bowling jargon, a strike!

As soon as Mort graduated from public school, he began working for an insurance broker. At 17 he was thought good enough to write policies of any amount for the firm, the New Hampshire Fire Insurance Company. For the next seven years, he continued working, eventually changing employers and moving to Johnson and Higgins of Wall

ponents to select their favorite pair of bowling alleys for each match. "Sure it took guts," he said later, "but you'd be surprised at the psychological effect. The other fellow immediately suspected some trickery and began to sweat. Then you knew you had him."

Mort started competing seriously in bowling in 1912 when he joined a team known as the Brunswick All-Stars of New York. They won the ABC title with a 2,904 total at Chicago, Mort contributing a 557 score. In 1914 the team was barred from competing in the same tournament because Mort lived in New Haven. So, he organized his own team of local bowlers into the New Havens. They won the title in Buffalo, New York, with a 2,994 total, including a 624 score by Mort.

In 1915 Lindsey came to Ohio with the Gergman Stars of New York City and captured the Ohio crown with a 2,990 score (Lindsey: 603). That same year he married Esther D. Dugan.

From 1915 to 1925, Mort Lindsey led the ABC bowlers with an average of 201 and 47/90 (the 200 class in those days was select and small).

Once, during World War I, Lindsey was nearly arrested as a German saboteur. Traveling from Detroit, Michigan, to Windsor, Ontario, he carried a 16-pound bowling ball in a case. Police surrounded Mort suddenly when the Canadian customs believed the object to be a bomb. It took Mort some time to convince the police that the ball was only to be used in an exhibition tour.

He remained in Bridgeport until 1918, when he was inducted into the U.S. Navy. While still in his naval uniform, Mort won the All-Events ABC crown in Toledo, Ohio, in 1919, with a 215 average and a 1,933 total (664-579-690). He was honorably discharged as a second-class seaman late in 1919. He then opened an auto and tire accessory store in Stamford, Connecticut.

Street. In 1911, he decided to make bowling his full-time occupation.

That year, in partnership with Morris Herman, Mort Lindsey opened a five-lane, ten-pin alley behind a bar in New Haven, Connecticut, on Church Street near Crown. Lindsey was always having fun with bowling. That year he and another bowler, George Kelsey, rolled a 12-hour marathon in bathing suits in New Haven; Mort spotted his opponent 550 pins and won by 5!

In 1912, Lindsey moved to Bridgeport, Connecticut, where, again with Morris Herman, he opened a combination bowling and billiard parlor above Reedy's Bar on Congress Street. The parlor had 13 billiard tables and six bowling alleys.

This was the time when Mort began touring the country, betting large amounts on himself and practically never losing. He even permitted his op-

For five years, Mort Lindsey worked at the store, but in 1924 opened his own eight-lane bowling alley which also had five pool and billiard tables. He managed the bowling alley until 1943, but was forced to close it when it became impossible to get enough pinboys to work. He could have kept the place going by hiring underage youngsters, but he refused.

In the years following World War I, Lindsey won several tournament victories: the New York City doubles tournament, in 1926; the New York State doubles, in 1928; the Dwyer Classic, in New York, in 1931; and the Petersen tournament, in Chicago, in 1934. He won the New York state singles and doubles title three times, and bowled 17 perfect 300 games in his career, his last in Stamford, Connecticut, in 1941. Mort also gave bowling exhibitions in the United States and Canada and made bowling films that were nationally distributed.

As late as 1952, when he was 64, Mort Lindsey came from behind to win the Bowlers Journal Tournament. Mort Lindsey participated in 46 of the 55 ABC tournaments up to 1959, missing his 47th due to the illness that shortly preceded his death that year.

Harry Litwack

A Modest Basketball Coach Who Left a Mark

LITWACK, HARRY "CHIEF" (born September 20, 1907, in Galicia, Austria; died August 7, 1999) American basketball coach. He coached Temple University, Philadelphia, Pennsylvania, from 1953 to 1973, with a career record of 373-193, still the most wins of any Temple coach.

. . .

Harry Litwack, who arrived in the United States with his father as a youngster of five, became a star basketball player at South Philadelphia High School from 1922 to 1925. Upon graduation he entered Temple University where he not only made the team, but was captain for two years. Harry was one of only a handful of men in Temple basketball history to have been named captain for two seasons. For seven years he played for the Philadelphia SPHAs (the all-Jewish basketball team from the South Philadelphia Hebrew Association) in the Eastern and American leagues.

Harry began his coaching career at Gratz High School in Philadelphia, where he ended the season with a remarkable 15-2 record. From 1931 to 1951 he served as freshman basketball coach at Temple University without ever having a losing season. His overall record was 181-32. From 1949 to 1951 he also held down the job of assistant coach of the Philadelphia Warriors under coach-owner Eddie Gottlieb.

As Temple coach, Harry led the Owls to 13 post-season tournaments, including the 1969 National Invitation Tournament championship. His team wound up in third place at the NCAA playoffs in 1956 and 1958. In 1958 Litwack was named the New York Basketball Writers Association Coach of the Year.

Among the achievements Harry cherished the most were four All-Americans he produced during his career at Temple: Guy Rodgers, Hal Lear, Bill Kennedy, and John Baum.

Litwack had the reputation of being a quiet, nondescript figure who rarely made good copy for sportswriters. Litwack noted that "in 43 years of coaching and playing, I had only one technical foul called against me."

One sportswriter described him this way just after his 1969 NIT victory: "His hair is white but he still steps crisply in those Italian suits he wears, and those expensive ties he is never without, and those never-out-of-sight cigars he either has between his lips or fingers."

Litwack has only a vague recollection of how he obtained the nickname "Chief." He explained that All American Temple basketball star Guy Rodgers pinned it on him "when we were in a huddle at a timeout and I explained something. He said 'OK, chief' and it stuck to me."

In addition to winning the 1969 NIT championship, Litwack's team that year had a 27-3 record

and racked up 25 straight wins for the longest streak in the nation that season.

In 1972, Harry Litwack retired. In that year his team had a 17-10 record for its 14th consecutive winning season. Harry was named to the Basketball Hall of Fame in 1975 and to the Jewish Sports Hall of Fame in Israel in July 1981. He and his wife, Estelle, have two daughters, both of whom are Temple graduates.

Since 1959, Litwack was associated with Bill Foster, the head coach of South Carolina University, in operating the Pocono Mountain Basketball Camp, considered one of the finest instruction camps in the nation. Six months of the year Harry was busy with the camp, and the other six months he spent in Miami Beach, Florida, where he watched basketball on TV, played golf, and relaxed.

Litwack died at his home in Huntingdon Valley, Pennsylvania at the age of 91 on August 7, 1999.

Sid Luckman

A Great Leader and Football Brain

LUCKMAN, SIDNEY (born November 21, 1916, in Brooklyn, New York; died July 5, 1998) American football player. The first modern T-formation quarterback, Luckman was considered the greatest long-range passer of his time in pro football. A genius at football strategy, he led the Chicago Bears, for whom he played from 1939 to 1947, to five Western Conference titles and four National Football League championships. In 12 years with the National Football League, he attempted 1,744 passes, had 904 completions for 14,686 yards, and passed for 139 touchdowns.

. . .

Sid Luckman's father sparked his son's interest in football when he gave the eight-year-old child a football. Sid attended Erasmus High School in New York City. Despite offers of college scholarships from 40 universities, Sid planned to attend the U.S. Naval Academy in Annapolis, Maryland. But when Navy played Columbia at Baker Field in New York during Sid's senior year of high school, the Navy athletic director Rip Miller took Sid into both teams' locker rooms. "As soon as I met [Columbia Coach] Lou Little," recalled Luckman, "I was impressed—the way he dressed, the way he spoke, I knew I wanted to play for him."

And that was that—almost. Sid chose Columbia, and Columbia chose Sid, but the university had no athletic scholarship program. So the new college student had to work his way through college, painting walls, and washing dishes in fraternity houses to pay for his room and board. His college football years (1936-38) produced a disap-

pointing 10-14-1 record but Sid was hardly to blame. In his final year, 1938, he was named All-American, the team finished at 3-6.

Luckman became one of the best triple-threat men in college football, starring at tailback. In 1937 he returned a kickoff 82 yards against Army, boomed a 72-yard punt against Syracuse, and threw a 60-yard pass against Pennsylvania. He also connected on a 65-yard pass against Brown University in 1938. His college passing record was 180 completions (20 of which went for touchdowns) in 376 attempts for 2,413 yards, a 47.9 percentage. Said Coach Lou Little: "We would have had a very ordinary team, or less than that, without him." In truth few people realized just how good Sid Luckman was until he turned pro. Only then did he play for teams which brought out his full ability.

At certain moments in 1939 it appeared unlikely that Sid Luckman would ever become a pro football player. A routine form sent by the Chicago Bears in January of that year notified Sid that he had been selected by the club in the draft. He was asked in the letter if he was interested in playing professional football. The diffident football star wrote back: "I have no intention of playing professional football. In fact, I have been advised against it. My plans are to enter the trucking business with my brothers."

Bears owner George Halas did not give up. He wrote Sid a lengthy letter, pleading with him to change his mind. Sid, letter in hand, went off to talk with Columbia's Lou Little to ask whether he thought this "guy Halas was on the up-and-up." Little said he thought Halas was serious and so Sid Luckman wrote back asking for an interview.

Halas had to negotiate with the Pittsburgh Steelers for Luckman. The Steelers had a draft choice before Chicago, and Halas had arranged that Pittsburgh send Sid to the Bears in exchange for another player. Though they later regretted it, the Steelers agreed. Sid became a Bear officially on July 24, 1939.

George Halas was developing a new T-forma-

tion and he thought that Luckman was the best man to run it, even though Sid had been a tailback in high school and college. Said the Bear owner, "Sid made himself a great quarterback. No one else did it for him. He worked hard, stayed up nights studying and really learning the T. Sid wasn't built for quarterback. He was stocky (5 feet, 11½ inches, 190 pounds), not fast and not a great passer in the old tradition. But he was smart and he was dedicated." Halas once observed that Sid Luckman never called a wrong play in his career. He used to spend hours practicing pivots, feints, handoffs, and ball-handling in the dressing room, at home, in hotels on road trips, and even between seasons.

In 1940 Sid gave the T-formation permanence and credibility. In that year's title game against the Washington Redskins, the underdog Bears destroyed their opponent, 73-0. Luckman, who played only the first half because the game was so one-sided at halftime, scored one touchdown and passed for another. The day after the game, *The New York Times* said of Luckman: "No field general

ever called plays more artistically or engineered a touchdown parade in more letter-perfect fashion."

That 1940 title was the first of four the Bears would win with Luckman as quarterback (they captured the championship in 1941, 1943, and 1946). Between 1940 and 1943, the Bears won four Western Division titles. From 1941 to 1944 and again in 1947, Luckman was All-Pro.

The year 1943 was Sid's greatest. On November 14, 1943, playing at the Polo Grounds in New York, he gave the greatest performance of his life. He passed for a record seven touchdowns against the New York Giants and thus surpassed the old record of six, set by Sammy Baugh. "Strictly luck," Sid said afterward. "All I could think of when that seventh touchdown went in was the day I saw Lou Gehrig (the great New York Yankee baseball star) hit four home runs in Yankee Stadium." That year Sid guided the Bears to an 8-1-1 record. The 28 touchdowns he tossed in 10 games in 1943 remained a record until the Baltimore Colts' Johnny Unitas broke it in 1959 with 32 in 12 games. In 1943, Sid also passed for five touchdowns in the NFL title game when the Bears defeated the Washington Redskins 41-21. Not surprisingly, he was named the NFL Most Valuable Player that year.

On January 4,1944, Sid Luckman entered the U.S. Navy as an ensign in the Merchant Marine stationed at Sheepshead Bay, New York. He was assigned to an oil tanker plying the Atlantic, and served for eight months of hazardous sea duty. At times he got shore leave to play for the Bears. In 1944, the Bears finished second and then dropped to fourth in 1945, the only season that Luckman played that they had not finished second or higher.

Despite the Bears' weak 1945 season, Sid shared the passing title with Sammy Baugh and led the league in touchdown passes (14) and yardage gained (1,725). In 1946, when the Bears won the title, Sid threw 17 touchdown passes. In 1947, his final year, he threw 24 touchdown passes, his second highest annual total.

In 1949, two years after he had retired, Ed Fitzgerald of *Sport Magazine* asked Luckman whether he was religious. "Well, yes," was the reply. "I go to the temple regularly and I observe the High Holidays and I never go to bed without saying a little prayer." After his retirement he became an executive with a Chicago cellophane company. At the same time he helped tutor Chicago Bear quarterbacks. For his help, he was voted a share of the Bears' playoff money in 1956.

When Luckman was selected to join the Pro Football Hall of Fame in 1965, Lou Little his former coach, said of Sid: "He was a great passer, of course, and a great football brain, but people forget he was a great leader. That was some gang he had to handle, those Bears. But they responded to his leadership."

In 1988, Luckman received the Walter Camp Distinguished American of the Year award. Sid Luckman is a member of the Jewish Sports Hall of Fame in Israel.

Luckman died on July 5, 1998 at the age of 81 in a hospital in North Miami Beach, Florida. He had once said that he wanted three sentences on his tombstone: "He had it all. He did it all. He loved it all."

Amos Mansdorf
Greatest Israeli Tennis Star

MANSDORF, AMOS (born October 20, 1965 in Tel Aviv, Israel–) Israeli tennis player. He replaced Shlomo Glickstein, who dominated Israeli tennis from 1976 to 1986, as Israel's best tennis player in the late 1980s and early 1990s. Mansdorf's best career rank was 18, on November 16, 1987. He also won five singles titles. His career earnings total $2,412,691.

• • •

Amos Mansdorf remembers how at age six he would watch his parents play tennis on the lone court at the Herzyliya Country Club. Eager to play, he was told to wait until he was ten. "I was not allowed even to walk on the court." Still, the game fascinated him. "When Amos was missing, we knew where to find him," recalled his father, Jacob, an engineer and expert on water desalinization. "He always had his nose to the fence of the courts."

Three years later, Amos, age nine, responded to the Tel Aviv University tennis club newspaper ad seeking talented young tennis players. Competing against more veteran players, he was not accepted into the youth program.

In 1976, when Amos was 10 years old, tourists and diplomats, using the courts at beachside hotels, were still virtually the only tennis players in Israel. But that year tennis enthusiasts from South Africa, England and the U.S. financed the Israel Tennis Center, a hard-court facility on an old strawberry patch in Ramat Hasharon, near Tel Aviv.

Amos' mother, Era, a school principal, encouraged him to try out for the children's program at the Center. Recalling his earlier rebuff, Amos was at first reluctant. "Then, like a Jewish mother, she said I should go, that the guy at the University Club was an idiot and didn't know what he was talking about."

Amos tried out and from the moment the Center's coaches first laid eyes on him they sensed his potential. He was one of the first entrants in the Center's fledgling youth program.

A few months later, his parents planned to take Amos on a vacation to Greece. "I think I'll skip it," he told them. "I would rather stay home with Grandma and play tennis." Upon their return from Greece, the elder Mansdorfs heard Amos proclaim at the dinner table: "I'm worried. When I play at Wimbledon, how will I adjust to grass?"

He eventually got to Wimbledon—11 years later.

At age ten, he was a latecomer to the sport: "Ten is not early anymore for children to play tennis," he said. "Some of the others were better than me at first. But after a year, I was better than everybody in my age group. I never had a doubt that I would be a professional tennis player."

Amos' performance as a teen-ager reinforced his career choice. In 1983, during his senior year of high school, he won the Asian Junior Championship in Hong Kong. He also reached two finals in Challenge Tournaments in Ashkelon, Israel, and Helsinki, Finland.

Mansdorf wished that he had spent more of his teen-age years at one of the high-profile tennis camps in the U.S. where, he believes, he would have benefited from the high-level coaching. "I received good coaching in Israel, but everybody here was learning. They know a lot more now than they did then. The crucial years are from 15 to 21. It's very, very hard to learn things after that time."

When he turned 18, Amos faced a different kind of camp—a military camp.

The Israeli Army, requiring much time and energy of its soldiers, tends to retard the career of the nation's star athletes, though the IDF (Israeli Defense Force) does permit those stars to continue in their sport when possible.

Amos feared his tennis career would be severely harmed when, in early 1984, he began his three-year military stint. "I realized that I wasn't going to get the right training. I was very, very frustrated because I knew that I couldn't expect to do well against people in the U.S. and Europe who were playing twice a day." Indeed, the first three months of basic training proved so fatiguing for Amos that he played no tennis at all.

He was determined, however, not to give up on his tennis. Following basic training, Mansdorf was stationed close to Tel Aviv, enabling him to play frequently whenever he was on guard duty. "When I did guard duty, I was so tired I couldn't practice the next day, but I'm not complaining."

Mansdorf felt that other players on the tennis tour had no comprehension of what he had gone through in the IDF. "Some of them (in other countries) just have to show their faces once, and sign some papers, but they don't have to actually take part in military training. So they don't understand that in Israel you really have to do basic training and play soldier." The soldier-tennis player clearly made an impact: he was sometimes referred to in the press as "Sergeant Mansdorf."

His goal was a world ranking within the top 200 by the time he completed his military service in February 1987. Amos went much further. A semifinalist at the Tel Aviv Grand Prix in 1984, he reached the quarterfinals of the U.S. Open that year as well. He also represented Israel at the Summer Olympics for the first time in 1984.

In 1985, he was a runner-up at Tel Aviv; a semifinalist at Madrid; and a quarterfinalist at Adelaide, Jerusalem, and Parioli. He played in his first Wimbledon tournament in 1986, reaching the third round before losing to Ivan Lendl.

That same year, he was the winner of the Jerusalem Challenger, a semifinalist at Tel Aviv, and a quarterfinalist at Milan and Cologne. Deciding to play in the South African Open in November 1986, Amos stood accused by the Israeli press of aiding apartheid. He was urged to withdraw. Mansdorf refused. "Considering all the trade that goes on between Israel and South Africa," he said, "it would be hypocritical for me not to go there. I

would never do anything to promote apartheid." He won the tournament, his first Grand Prix triumph, climbing into the top 50 for the first time. Incredibly, when he was ready to step out of army uniform in February 1987, he was ranked No. 36.

As an IDF reservist, Mansdorf could be called up in case of war. "But if I'm in the semis at Wimbledon," he said. "I don't think they'd call me back. My being there would be good for national pride."

Though hardly a John McEnroe, Amos has a well-known temper on the courts. He has broken rackets, whined about line calls, and stomped off the court. Once, he was suspended for a month for jumping over the net and shoving his opponent whom he thought was cheating. Dismissing the incident, Amos said "It wasn't a hard push, just a Mediterranean macho one."

Mansdorf and McEnroe "squared off" against one another in February 1987 in the semifinals of the U.S. Pro Indoor Championships in Philadelphia. Amos took the first set 7-5. While changing over for the second set McEnroe cursed his opponent. Amos swore back—but in Hebrew. "I'm not stupid," he recalled. "I didn't want to get fined." McEnroe's continuing verbal abuse of his opponent brought him a $1,000 fine. John, however, bested Amos in the next two sets, 6-2, 6-3.

Pleased that he had not lost his temper, Amos noted that "If I had, McEnroe would be in the hospital. When somebody hits me, I hit back harder. If he ever does that to me again, I'll smash his face." In March 1992, Mansdorf reported that he and McEnroe had "become friends." Amos also noted that "I'm not known as bad-tempered. On the contrary, I have the reputation on tour of being in control and a good fighter."

The year 1987 was a great one for Mansdorf. He was a runner-up at Vienna; a semifinalist at Philadelphia and Johannesburg; and a quarterfinalist at Adelaide, Rotterdam, the Paris Indoor, and Wembley. *World Tennis* magazine named him 1987's most improved player on the men's tour.

His two singles victories, one over sixth-ranked

Miloslav Mecir, helped Israel to upset Czechoslovakia in Davis Cup competition that March, a feat regarded as one of the country's outstanding achievements in sports. Mansdorf remembers the victory as the "best moment" of his tennis career. The following July, India eliminated Israel in New Delhi. On November 16, Amos reached his highest world ranking of 18. He finished 1987 with a world ranking of 27.

In 1988, he was a semifinalist at Tel Aviv; a quarterfinalist at Memphis, Indian Wells, Orlando, Basle, and Wembley; and he reached the round of 16 at Key Biscayne-Lipton. He won singles tournaments in Auckland and the Paris Indoor. In the first round in Paris, he defeated Mats Wilander and defeated Brad Gilbert in the finals for the $262,000 first prize—the biggest paycheck of his career.

In 1989, he won no singles tournaments but was runner-up at Auckland and Singapore. He was a semifinalist at Scottsdale and Tel Aviv; he reached the round of 16 at the Australian Open and Wimbledon; and he reached the doubles quarterfinals at Memphis (with Mikael Pernfors) and the Queen's (with Ivan Lendl). Mansdorf finished 1989 with a world ranking of 39.

In 1990, he won a singles title at Rosmalen, his first win on grass. He was also runner-up at Tel Aviv, losing to Andrei Chesnakov, and a semifinalist at Auckland and Toulouse. He reached the round of 16 at the U.S. Open in 1990 as well. He finished that year with a world ranking of 33.

In January 1991, as the Persian Gulf war began, Mansdorf was just starting his second-round match against Aaron Krickstein in the Australian Open. Mansdorf lost and returned to Israel at once. "This is Israeli reality and I'm part of it," he said simply. "My mind's not on tennis. But I'm a professional, and it shouldn't really affect my game." When he was asked if he would play again soon, he retorted angrily: "How will it look to the public if I go (play tennis) and Israelis are sitting in their gas masks?" During the war Mansdorf and fellow Israeli pro Gilad Bloom played an exhibition match at Kfar Hamaccabiah for children

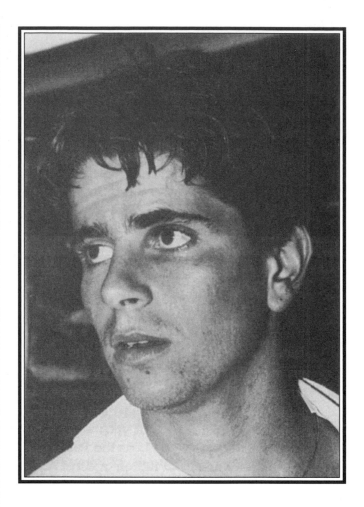

whose homes were destroyed by Iraqi Scud missiles. Mansdorf completed 1991 with a world ranking of 62.

Thanks to a string of 12 wins in three tournaments, he approached a top 20 ranking in 1992.

In February, he reached the semifinals at the $780,000 Federal Express International tennis tournament in Memphis and was defeated by 26th-ranked South African Wayne Ferreira, 6-2, 6-3. He reached the finals of the $1 million U.S. Pro Indoor championships in Philadelphia, but lost to Pete Sampras.

Mansdorf won $76,000 in the Philadelphia tournament. To reach the finals, Mansdorf beat the world No. 3 and Wimbledon champion Michael Stich. His previous best effort against a top-ten player had been his 1988 defeat of then fourth-ranked Boris Becker in Orlando, Florida.

Mansdorf's return to form in 1992 came a few months after he took on his long-time friend

Yarom Baron, a former Israeli tennis player, as his new coach.

In late April, 1992, on the eve of Israel's Davis Cup match against Hungary in Tel Aviv, Mansdorf was dropped from the Israel Davis Cup Team for refusing to practice with a younger member of the team. Team captain Shlomo Glickstein, who cut Amos from the team, would only say that his decision was due to a difference of opinion between him and Mansdorf over training methods. Despite Mansdorf's absence from the team, Israel easily defeated Hungary, 5-0.

Mansdorf went out in the second round of the 1992 Wimbledon tournament in late June, 1992, losing to the previous Wimbledon champion, Michael Stich, in four sets. Amos was ranked 29th in the world on July 6, 1992.

Mansdorf does not consider himself religious but he does feel a certain responsibility to the Jewish community wherever he plays. "I try to show people an Israeli can be a normal guy. Tennis can improve our relations with the rest of the world."

Amos was married on March 13, 1991 in Tel Aviv. His wife, Ifat, works in the Diamond Exchange in Ramat Gan. They have two children.

In the fall of 1993, Mansdorf was ranked 28th. He ended his career in November 1994 when doctors told him that he could continue to play, but would never play at his best, as he was suffering from chronic fatigue syndrome. He told reporters: "I'm not happy, but it's time to stop. You just have

no energy, you can't train hard enough to stay in the top 50, and for me, if you can't stay in the top 50, then it's not worth it."

He had won six ATP tournaments during his 11-year career. His highest career ranking was 18th in 1988.

As for his future, Mansdorf said: "The worst thing is to sit around and do nothing. I'm not going to look back at my tennis career either." He joined his father-in-law and grandfather in the diamond business.

In early 1996, Mansdorf got into a tiff with local tennis circles when he accused the Israel Tennis Association of mismanagement, suggesting that it was run in "an amateur fashion," a charge that was vehemently denied by ITA officials. He also lashed out at ex-tennis star Shlomo Glickstein's handling of the Israel Tennis Academy, arguing that he was responsible for the dearth of top Israeli players.

Mansdorf continues to sell diamonds in the Israeli city of Ramat Aviv. Remaining active in the Israeli tennis program, from 2001 to October 2004 he served as captain of the Israel Davis Cup team and from 2003 to October 2004 as chairman of the professional committee of the Israel Tennis Federation. In November 2004 Amos was serving as an adviser to the Israel Tennis Federation.

On May 8, 2006, Mansdorf was ranked 167th on the list of the largest ATP prize money leaders, with earnings of $2,412,691. In 2006, he undertook the coaching of rising Israeli tennis star Shahar Pe'er.

MARTIN, SYLVIA WENE (born 1928, in Philadelphia, Pennsylvania–) American bowler. Considered one of the greatest women bowlers. She was America's Woman Bowler of the Year in 1955 and 1960; Pennsylvania's Sportswoman of the Year in 1961; and Philadelphia's outstanding athlete in 1963. She has bowled three perfect (300) games in her career, a world record which stood for 15 years.

• • •

Sylvia first visited a bowling center when she was 12, but not to play, only to accompany her brother and sister. Her brother had rather patronizingly informed her that she was not big enough to bowl. The next night, petite (4 feet, 11 inches, 112 pounds) Sylvia went to the bowling center and bowled a 96 in her first game.

After a week she was able to knock down 100 pins; after a month she bowled her first 200 game; less than 10 years later she bowled her first perfect game. The date: March 28, 1951. The place: Philadelphia. It was the first time a woman had bowled a perfect score on the east coast of the United States.

For the next four years Sylvia ran the family grocery store during the day and practiced her bowling at night. Sylvia had a 206 league average in both 1952–53 and 1953–54, then the world record league average—which stood for the next 12 years. She also bowled fourteen 700 series (six in the 1954–55 season alone, a record), another world record which stood for five years. She won 31 city and state bowling titles in her home state of Pennsylvania.

In March 1955, Sylvia joined the American Ma-

chine and Foundry (AMF) Company's bowling promotion staff and for the next 15 years gave exhibitions and instruction throughout the United States.

She won the Bowling Proprietors Association of America (BPAA) All-Star Individual Match Game title in 1955 in Chicago and again in 1960 in Omaha. In both those years, she was named Woman Bowler of the Year by the Bowling Writers Association of America.

In 1959 Sylvia won the Women's International Bowling Congress (WIBC) doubles, with Adele Isphording, with a 1,263 total score (each bowler bowled three games). In August of that year, Sylvia's book, *The Women's Bowling Guide,* was published.

Sylvia Wene Martin scored her second perfect game on December 11, 1959, in the finals of the World's Invitational Match Game Tournament. That marked the first time a woman had bowled a perfect 300 game in any national competition. Just 28 days later, on January 8, 1960, in Omaha, she did it again—her third perfect game. This time it

came in the qualifying rounds of the BPAA All-Star tournament which she went on to win.

Using an orthodox four-step approach, she became the first woman in the world to bowl more than one 300 game and the first woman to bowl two in the same season.

After her 1955 All-Star victory she left her family's grocery store and decided to devote herself exclusively to bowling. She continued to bowl for AMF into the middle 1960s, and in 1965 was second in the Bowling Proprietors Association of America National Doubles tournament. Her partner was Jeanette Robinson.

In 1964 Sylvia bowled against Dick Weber, the great American bowling star. The unusual match was held on a regulation-size bowling lane constructed in the tail section of an American Airlines Astro-Jet flying from New York to Dallas at an altitude of 25,000 feet, and going 600 miles per hour. The stunt was designed to demonstrate the size of this new cargo plane. Weber won the match, described as "somewhat bumpy." This $6 million promotion by AMF company and American Airlines made the *Guiness Book of Records* for the "highest" game (25,000 ft. up) ever bowled.

Sylvia retired from bowling in 1965 because of a painful sciatic nerve back condition. She was able to devote more time to hobbies such as roller-skating, accordion-playing, and sketching. In 1966, Sylvia was elected to the Women's International Bowling Hall of Fame (in the "Superior performance" category).

She married Samuel Martin and they lived in Philadelphia for four years, then moved to Florida. They purchased a motor home and traveled throughout the country, living in different areas of the U.S. for six months to a year, including Arizona, California, Colorado, Utah, and Texas. In 1982 they decided to make their home in Las Vegas, Nevada. Sylvia's husband died in 1984 and Sylvia remained in Las Vegas. Sylvia's hobbies now include sewing and organ-playing.

In a 1974 list of the greatest women bowlers in history, Sylvia Wene Martin ranked fifth. In 1979 Sylvia was elected to the Jewish Sports Hall of Fame in Israel.

Daniel Mendoza
Father of Modern Boxing

MENDOZA, DANIEL (born July 5, 1764, in London, England; died September 3, 1836) English boxer. The most celebrated Jewish sportsman of his time, he was England's 16th heavyweight champion (and thus world champion). Mendoza revolutionized boxing in England, introducing the "Mendoza School" (or the "Jewish School"), with its science of footwork, sparring, new punches, and strategy, replacing the brutal slugging that had passed for sport until then.

. . .

Mendoza is considered the father of modern, scientific boxing because of the defensive moves he devised that enabled him to fight much heavier opponents. He became the first boxer to receive royal patronage, and his acceptance by royalty helped elevate the position of the Jew in English society. After defeating the best fighters around, he was recognized as world champion and reigned as such from 1791 to 1795.

In 1812, Pierce Egan, the author of *Boxiana,* a study of boxing in that period, noted that although Daniel Mendoza was not "the Jew that Shakespeare drew, yet he was that Jew." And then he goes on to say, "In spite of his prejudice, he [the Christian] was compelled to exclaim—Mendoza was a pugilist of no ordinary merit."

Born to Jewish parents in Whitechapel (a section of London), and the recipient of a Jewish education, Mendoza spent his life defending Judaism—often with his bare fists. After his Bar Mitzvah, he wanted to become a glazier, but he whipped the glazier's son in a fight and lost his job. Then, he worked in a fruit and vegetable shop. His next job was in a tea shop where, while defending the owner from a disgruntled client who appeared ready to spring at the owner, Mendoza attracted a crowd. The famous boxer Richard Humphreys, known as the "Gentleman Boxer," witnessed the scene and offered himself as Mendoza's second in the fight. Word spread about the young man's talents, and the following Saturday Mendoza was matched against a professional fighter. Mendoza, who soon became known as "The Star of Israel," won the fight for which he was paid five guineas.

Mendoza became a salesman for a tobacconist, but he was forever getting into fights. Always believing he was the injured party, he was ready to battle against brutality and injustice of any kind. In 1790 he won his first professional fight, a match which eventually won him the patronage of the Prince of Wales. Mendoza was the first boxer to earn this honor. He was proud of this honor and of his heritage, for he proudly billed himself as "Mendoza the Jew."

Promising his wife that he would give up the ring, Mendoza stipulated only one condition: a fight with Richard Humphreys—by now his archrival. He had received bodily punishment in previous fights and therefore had worked out a new style of defense, one using sidestepping, a straight left and special guarding techniques. Some

had complained that Mendoza, rather than standing up in true British bulldog style and hammering away at an opponent until he dropped, had adopted the cowardly manner of retreating and running away from his opponent.

Mendoza got his chance to fight Humphreys and to test his style. The fight was set for January 9, 1788, at Odiham in Hampshire, and the Jews of England, eager for a champion and a hero, bet much money on the contest. Humphreys won in 15 minutes (many fights at this time were recorded this way), and the Jews despaired.

Humphreys' patron, Mr. Bradyl, received this message from the victor: "Sir, I have DONE the Jew, and am in good health." Signed, Richard Humphreys.

A second fight between the two rivals was held on May 6, 1789, at Stilton. Mendoza's training quarters were at the Essex home of Sir Thomas A. Price. Mendoza won this second fight, which was attended by nearly 3,000 spectators, and England had a new hero. Daniel Mendoza's name was

added to the scripts of numerous plays, songs were written about him, and he could fill a theater for appearances earning 50 pounds. In time, Mendoza would appear three times a week. The two men fought a third time at Doncaster on September 29, 1790, and Mendoza won easily.

In the early 1790s, fighting was so highly regarded that Mendoza was induced to open a small theater at the Lyceum in the Strand, in London, for the purpose of public exhibitions of sparring and teaching interested dandies of London's society.

By defeating Bill Warr on Bexley Common on November 12, 1794, Mendoza became English heavyweight champion. He held the title until his defeat by John Johnson on April 15, 1795. The latter won by grabbing Mendoza's shoulder-length hair and battering him senseless in the ninth round.

Mendoza continued to fight. On March 21, 1806, he took on Harry Lee at Grimsted-Green in Kent. In the 53rd round, Mendoza was declared the winner. On July 4, 1820, Mendoza met

Tom Owen at Barnstead Downs: the 56-year-old Mendoza lost when the younger man was declared the winner in the 12th round; an anonymous poet (signed only W.W.) lamented his fading glory in the pages of a magazine in Edinburgh on October 8, 1820: "Is this Mendoza?—this the Jew of whom my fancy cherished so beautiful a waking dream, a vision which has perished?..."

Mendoza was only 5 feet, 7 inches tall, weighing 160 pounds, but he had an enormous chest. He always fought larger men. He commented on his new technique to combat those larger fighters in an 1820 address: "I think I have a right to call myself the father of the science, for it is well known that prize fighting lay dormant for several years. It was myself and Humphreys who revived it in our three contests for supremacy, and the science of pugilism has been patronized ever since."

Daniel Mendoza became a wealthy man, but his generosity landed him in debt. After his boxing career ended, he ended up in a debtors' prison. He wrote *The Art of Boxing* in 1789 and *The Memoirs of Daniel Mendoza* in 1816. He did some teaching, theatrical touring, became a recruiting sergeant, caterer, process server, and pubkeeper. Just before his death he had been running an inn. He died in poverty, leaving his wife and 11 children.

In 1965, he was one of the inaugural group chosen for the Boxing Hall of Fame in the United States. *The Punishing Blow*, a play about Mendoza written by Randy Cohen, debuted in New York in 2009.

Daniel Mendoza is a member of the Jewish Sports Hall of Fame in Israel.

Walter Miller

The Jockey Who Loved Baseball

MILLER, WALTER "MARVELOUS" (born 1890, in New York City; died 1959) Considered the greatest jockey of the early twentieth century. During a four-year period he rode 1,094 winners. His best season record of 388 winners, achieved when he was only 16 years old, stood for 46 years.

■ ■ ■

Walter Miller came from an Orthodox Jewish family. One day in 1904, Walter's father, a wealthy butcher, took the youngster to the racetrack. Fascinated by what he saw, the 14-year-old frequently skipped school to see the races. When Walter's father realized that the boy had been smitten by horses, the older Miller consented to his son's becoming an apprentice to a trainer.

The 98-pound Walter rode his first race in 1904 on a filly named May J. The horse's odds were 3,000-to-1 and Miller was forgiven for not winning. A few days later though, he won for the first time, riding a 60-to-1 shot to victory.

At the time Miller loved baseball almost as much as riding. He once captained a racetrack baseball team scheduled to play a semipro outfit on a field near Sheepshead Bay. While teammates and opponents waited impatiently for him, Miller finally drove up to the field in a flashy runabout drawn by a high-stepping horse. He and his valet alighted, and the valet helped him don his spanking new uniform; the valet would also minister to Walter between pitches. Viewing himself as a great moundsman, Miller was in fact quite the opposite. He once even tried out for John McGraw's New York Giants, but McGraw thought Miller too small.

Baseball's loss was horse racing's gain. In the fall of 1904 Walter went to California to ride for Sunny Jim Fitzsimmons. Sunny Jim recalled that Miller liked baseball as much as riding at the time: "I used to have to go across the street from the track to take him out of a baseball game so he could ride his horses."

While his baseball playing was nondescript, his riding was spectacular. In Walter's four years of riding, he came home first 1,094 times in an era when most jockeys failed to go to the post 500 times in a year. Once, in a span of two days, he rode eight straight winners. In 1906 he won five straight races, and he once went five for six.

In 1905 Walter had 178 firsts in 888 mounts. He scored his greatest successes under the colors of the James R. Keene stable.

Just two years after learning to ride, in 1906, he made track history, becoming the first jockey ever to ride more than 300 winners in one year. That same year Miller also raced 300 seconds and showed 199 times in a total of 1,384 races. His 388 victories remained the most wins in one year until 1952 when Willie Shoemaker rode 485 firsts.

Riding 1,384 times meant that Miller rode about five races every day of the racing season from March 1, 1906, to the year's end. His most prestigious victories that year were in the Brooklyn Handicap, Dwyer, Alabama, Preakness, Toboggan, Belmont, Futurity, Saratoga Cup, and the Travers races.

In 1907 he won the national riding title for the second straight year, with 334 victories in 1,194 races. At that time he was earning more than $50,000 a year. In 1908 Walter had a total of 870 mounts, with 194 winners. Over half the horses Miller rode throughout his career finished in the money. Miller is a member of the Jockey Hall of Fame (inducted in 1957).

Eventually his problem was that of size, the plague of many jockeys. Walter grew too large, attaining a height of 5 feet, 8 inches, and weighing 160 pounds. To ride at the increased weight, he went to Europe. But by 1912, Miller had returned to the U.S., stopped riding entirely, and was playing semipro baseball in Emeryville, California.

Miller's greatest fan was his mother. For two years, she accompanied him to the track, and backed each of his mounts with a $10 bet. In 1908, she told a confidant that she had lost $8,200 gambling—obviously by betting on horses ridden by jockeys other than her son.

Charlie Miller, a racing expert who was no relation of Walter, analyzed Miller's winning technique: "It was Walter's wonderful knack of making his horse break instantly from the tape which enabled him to secure an unbeatable advantage. With a quick eye, he never lost sight of the starter, sat bolt upright in the saddle, giving his horse an almost free reign, and seemed to sense the start an instant before it happened. For a few seconds, Miller rode like a demon. Then, having secured the rail position, he took his mount up for a breathing spell, but always remained in front."

Later in his life, Miller pursued a business career. He operated a florist's shop, became a jockey's agent, and was proprietor of a bar called "The Jockey" on the Boulevard Montparnasse in Paris. He also owned a men's haberdashery. In 1945 he became seriously ill and required surgery. A few months later, he suffered a mental breakdown from which he never recovered.

MIX, RONALD (born March 10, 1938, in Los Angeles, California–) American football player. An offensive lineman for the San Diego Chargers, he was unanimously chosen to the all-time AFL team by the Pro Football Hall of Fame. In 1979, he became the second AFL player to be admitted to the Pro Football Hall of Fame.

. . .

Ron Mix grew up in the suburb of Hawthorne, California. He was raised by his mother after his father deserted the family when Ron was a small child. Ron wanted to be a baseball player, but a coach advised him that he did not have the potential to be a good one.

Early in his high school career Ron, who weighed 115 pounds, was described as "skinny and not very fast" but by his senior year his weight was up to 180 pounds, and he had earned an athletic scholarship to the University of Southern California.

Mix played on losing teams in his first two seasons at USC. Because of a vision problem, he was given contact lenses and moved to tackle. His football career took a sudden leap forward in 1959 when the USC Trojans, which Ron co-captained, were 8-2 and he won All-America and All-Pacific honors. Ron was also voted USC's outstanding lineman of that year.

In 1960, the National Football League's prestigious Baltimore Colts and the Los Angeles Chargers of the newly-formed American Football League vied for Ron Mix's signature. Had Carroll Rosen-

bloom, the Jewish owner of the Colts, known that Mix was Jewish, presumably he might have offered the California lineman enough money to sign on.

Rosenbloom and the Colts offered Mix $8,500 while the Los Angeles Chargers came through with a $12,000 proposition and so, as Mix noted, "It was one of my easier decisions. It was not sentiment, but economics that dictated matters. Baltimore has a large Jewish population. But scouting reports rarely include a man's religion." Mix, the first quality player to be signed by the American Football League, planned to play for two years and then become a teacher. The gridiron soon won out over the classroom.

In Mix's second year with the Chargers, the team moved to San Diego, where it became one of the powers of the new league under coach Sid Gillman. San Diego won the Western Division title five times in the league's first six years. In 1963, the "skinny kid" weighed 250 pounds. He made the All-AFL team as tackle and guard, and the Chargers won the league title with a crushing 51-10 victory over the Boston Patriots.

Ron was an aggressive and highly-skilled lineman. "When you're running behind Mix," observed Paul Lowe, the San Diego Charger running star who had been a collegiate opponent of Ron's at Oregon State, " it's like you're a little kid and your big brother is protecting you from the wolves." "Big brother's" skill as an offensive lineman was proven by the record: In his entire pro career Ron was assessed only two holding penalties. During that career, Mix played in seven All-Star games.

Meanwhile, Ron studied law at night and wrote articles on football for several publications. Partly because of those law studies, and his rugged style of play on the football field, he was known as the "intellectual assassin."

Despite his strong reservations about his sports career, he was proud of being a Jewish sports hero. "I only *disliked* pro ball," he noted after retiring from the pros. "I *hated* football in college." "To some people I guess I represent a kind of racial

hero," Ron once declared to a sportswriter. "Sure, it would be best if people would say, 'That's Ron Mix, a human being who made good.' But until that time in history comes around, I'm proud when they say 'There's Ron Mix, a Jewish football player who made good.'"

Sport Magazine wrote in 1967 that "his technique, desire, strength, and balance still impress. He's known as a 'pop-out' blocker, the kind who gets his man with a quick initial thrust. He can get to the outside linebacker or defensive end in a hurry. At times he could deal with three men in one play; he could also block the corner man, stay on his feet, and get the safety as well."

In 1970, Ron Mix retired and announced that he planned to finish law school and run for public office. The Chargers, in a fitting tribute, retired his jersey number 74. Ron completed his law studies and passed the California Bar that year, but did not enter politics. The Oakland Raiders succeeded in luring him back to the gridiron and he played for them in 1971.

In 1973, he rejoined the Chargers as executive counsel. A year and a half later, he became the general manager of the Portland team in the short-lived World Football League.

In 1979, Mix was inducted into the Pro Football Hall of Fame, only the sixth offensive lineman to be so honored. Ron observed that "as an offensive lineman it's nice to get some attention…All that running and lifting weights—it was a lot of hard work. This makes it all worth it."

Asked if any other Jew had been admitted to the Pro Football Hall of Fame, Mix commented, "I don't know, but I think we own the ground and lease to the place."

In 1990, Sid Gillman, the great coach of the 50s and 60s, called Mix "the best offensive lineman I've ever seen, there was nothing he couldn't do." Informed of Gillman's praise, Ron Mix said with a smile, "Who am I to argue with a Hall of Fame coach?"

As of 2010, six Jews have been elected to the Pro Football Hall of Fame: Al Davis, Benny Friedman, Sid Gillman, Marv Levy, Sid Luckman, and Ron Mix.

Mix is a member of the Jewish Sports Hall of Fame in Israel. He has been a practicing attorney in San Diego in recent years. Part of his practice has been representing retired players in workmen's compensation claims for athletics-related injuries.

Charles Myer
The Indian Who Refused to Play in Dallas

MYER, CHARLES SOLOMON "BUDDY" (born March 16, 1904, in Ellisville, Mississippi; died October 31, 1974) American baseball player. Considered one of the greatest Jewish second basemen in American baseball. Won the American League batting title in 1935. Hit .300 or better for nine seasons. In a 17-year major-league career, he had 2,131 hits, 850 runs batted in, and a batting average of .303.

. . .

While playing college baseball at Mississippi A & M, Myer had an offer to join the Cleveland Indians organization. He accepted and was ordered to report to Dallas, Cleveland's minor league team in the Texas League. Myer was determined to play in the major leagues, and refused to play for Dallas. Although the Indians were upset by his attitude, they brought him up to the majors briefly. Very shortly thereafter they released him as a free agent. Buddy Myer then signed with New Orleans, a minor league team in the Southern League. That year (1925) he hit .336 and drove in 44 runs, sparking the interest of several major league clubs.

One day two scouts, Joe Engel of the Washington Senators and Jack Doyle of the Chicago Cubs, observed Myer playing for New Orleans. Spotting Engel, Doyle asked the Senators' man what he was doing there. "Not a thing," lied Engel, who had his eye on Myer. Engel excused himself for a moment to buy a drink, and managed to get Myer's signature on a Senator contract in the interim. The two scouts then watched as Myer did some smart hitting and fielding; then Doyle decided that he wanted a "drink." He returned angry and called Engel a double-crosser, "Nothing here worth looking at?" roared the Cubs' scout to the happy Engel.

Myer went on to play with the Senators for 15 seasons. In 1926, the Senators were convinced that Myer was a weak shortstop and sold him to the Boston Red Sox where he played during the 1927 and 1928 seasons. Myer did so well with Boston (in 1927, he hit .288; in 1928, .313) that Senator owner Clark Griffith reacquired him in 1929 in a trade for five players. Instead of shortstop, Myer was shifted and became the second baseman for the Senators beginning in 1929. Washington won the American League pennant twice (1925, 1933) while Myer was playing for them.

Buddy Myer's best year was 1935 when he hit .349 to win the league batting title. He was second in total hits with 215. Clark Griffith said he would not sell Myer for less than half a million dollars, an astronomical figure at the time. Myer came in fourth for the Most Valuable Player award in the American League; Hank Greenberg took the prize that year.

A persistent stomach ailment cut short Myer's career, and he eventually retired in 1941. He established a new career for himself, becoming a banker in New Orleans.

He was inducted into the Jewish Sports Hall of Fame in Israel in 1992.

Laurence E. Myers

The First Amateur Runner to Break 50 Seconds... With One Shoe On

MYERS, LAURENCE E. "LON" (born February 16, 1858, in Richmond, Virginia; died February 15, 1899) American track star. Considered the greatest short-distance runner of the 19th century, he was the first to run the quarter mile in less than 50 seconds. From 1880 to 1888, Myers held the world record for the 100-yard, 440-yard, and 880-yard dashes. His best event was the quarter mile; he lowered the world record from 50.4 to 48.8 seconds. At one time or another over a 21-year period, Myers held all the American records for races 50 yards to one mile.

. . .

During Lon Myers' teenage years, he moved from Richmond, Virginia to New York where doctors advised him to exercise to improve his health. A weakling type, Lon had disproportionately long legs. But the 5 foot, 7¾ inch frame bearing his 112-pound weight was well-suited to running. He began to run seriously in November 1878, at age 20.

In September 1879, Myers set the first of his many world records, breaking the quarter-mile record with a time of 49.2. He thus became the first amateur to break 50 seconds, accomplishing this while running the last 90 yards of the 440-yard race without wearing one of his shoes. In that same year Myers also won the AAU titles in the 220-yard, 440-yard, and 880-yard events.

In 1881 he was one of the best amateur runners. He won a series of AAU titles, and lowered his quarter-mile record to 48.6 seconds. He set a new record in the half-mile as well with a 1:56 time.

When Myers toured England, the *London Globe* said: "His mode of progression is elegant in the extreme, his action being perfectly free, his stride long, and full of power." He was so warmly received that he wrote a New York newspaper: "I am quite sure I could be Lord Mayor of London, if I was large enough, when the next elections take place."

In November 1882, Myers ran in a series of three races with the great middle- and long-distance English runner, W. G. George, to determine who was the world's greatest runner. The tremendous amount of publicity surrounding the contests produced huge crowds. The first race was held at the Polo Grounds in New York in cold weather. Myers won the 880-yard race. But the Englishman took the second contest, the mile, and the third, the three-quarters of a mile. In 1884 Myers journeyed to England to challenge George to a rematch, but the Englishman refused. Myers remained determined to defeat his rival.

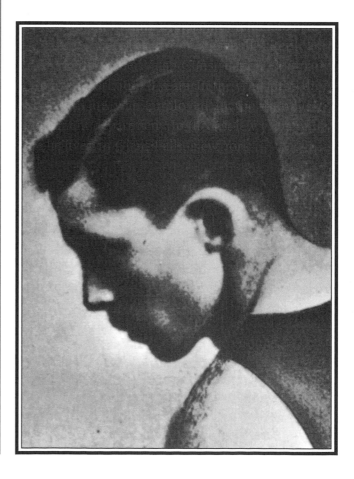

In 1885, Myers became a professional. The following year he and George ran in a three-race exhibition: 880 yards, one-half mile, and one mile. This time Myers won all three races. In Australia, a year later, the two staged another exhibition, and again Myers swept the entire program. If W. G. George was the undisputed middle and long-distance champion of the 19th century, Lon Myers had proven he was the best at short distances.

Myers remained a bachelor all his life. From the cash gifts he received upon retiring as an amateur in 1885, he went into the bookmaking profession, which was then legal. He died of pneumonia when he was only 41 years old.

Lon Myers is a member of the Jewish Sports Hall of Fame in Israel.

Harry Newman

Outstanding College Football Player of 1932

NEWMAN, HARRY (born September 5, 1909, in Detroit, Michigan; died May 2, 2000) American football player. He played for Michigan from 1930 to 1932 as quarterback. In 1932, he was first-team All-America and winner of the Douglas Fairbanks Trophy as outstanding collegiate player of the year. Between 1933 and 1935, he played pro ball with the New York Giants.

• • •

Newman's father died when he was 19 years old, so his mother had to finance his college education on her own. Newman enrolled at the University of Michigan in 1929.

In 1930, Michigan's coach suggested that Harry take instruction from Benny Friedman, the former Michigan quarterback, at a summer camp. The results were rewarding. Newman's quarterbacking that year helped Michigan achieve a 5-3-1 season. They shared the Big Ten Conference title with Northwestern University. In 1931, Newman, as a sophomore, helped Michigan share (with Northwestern and Purdue) in the winning of the Big Ten Conference title with an 8-0-1 record. In 1932, Michigan's Wolverines won the conference title on their own with an 8-1-1 record. Newman was outstanding, scoring 57 of the 83 points Michigan racked up against Big Ten opponents. In Michigan's last three games, he scored all the points. Of a possible 480 minutes of play, Newman was in on all but 43 minutes! Grantland Rice, picking Harry Newman for his 1932 All-American team, called him "one of the most effective, triple-threat backs the season has produced." Added Rice: "He made Michigan's run of eight successive victories possible with his forward passing, his broken field running, and his place kicking."

In 1933, his rookie season with the New York Giants, Harry led the team to an 11-3 record. The inaugural NFL championship game was played that year, and Newman's 29-yard touchdown pass to Red Badgro, providing the Giants with a 7-6 halftime lead, earned him the distinction of completing the first touchdown pass in an NFL championship game. Newman's success notwithstanding, the Giants were defeated by the Chicago Bears 23-21. However, with Newman's help, the Giants captured the NFL title the following year.

In 1934, in a midseason game against the Green Bay Packers, Newman carried the ball 39 times for 114 yards as the Giants won 17-3. But Newman's career was prematurely shortened by an injury he sustained during a game against the

Chicago Bears. A Bear end, Bill Hewitt, tackled Harry so hard that he was knocked out cold, and two bones in his back were broken. Newman missed the rest of the season. That year, the Giants were 8-5-0. They defeated the Bears in the title game by a score of 30-13, without Harry Newman playing. Newman decided to retire.

The Giants asked Newman to return midway through the 1935 season, and though Harry played, because of his injury, he had lost much of his ability. The Giants were 9-3 that season. They won the East Conference title, but lost to the Detroit Lions 26-7 in the NFL title game.

After retiring from football, Newman operated an automobile agency in Detroit. He was inducted into the Jewish Sports Hall of Fame in Israel in 1992.

Harry Newman died on May 2, 2000, at the age of 90. In 2005, he was selected as one of the 100 greatest Michigan football players of all time, ranking 12th on the all-time team.

Tom Okker
An Agile Dutch Tennis Player

OKKER, TOM (born February 22, 1944, in Amsterdam, Holland–) Dutch tennis player. He is Holland's greatest tennis player and one of the best Jewish tennis players of all time. Okker was ranked third in the world in 1974, his highest world ranking.

• • •

Tom Okker began playing tennis at the age of 10. His mother was not Jewish, but his father was. Tom started to take the game seriously after winning a few junior championships. He began to travel to tournaments around the world and found that his game improved considerably after playing in Australia. There, he recalled, he had the best training possible, as did other young tennis hopefuls.

When Tom came to play in the seventh Maccabiah Games in Israel in 1965, he was totally unknown. He won both the singles and mixed doubles easily. In that same year he won the Wimbledon Plate. In 1966, he was runner-up in the British Hard Court singles tournament.

In 1968, the year he turned pro, Tom made his big breakthrough in tennis. He was Italian singles champion that year as well as doubles champ (with Marty Riessen). Tom took the German doubles championships and the South African singles title as well as South African doubles title. He was also United States indoor doubles champion. Entering the U.S. Open for the first time in 1968, he reached the finals and fought a titanic battle against Arthur Ashe. Ashe eventually won 14-12, 5-7, 6-3, 3-6, 6-3.

At 5 feet, 10 inches and 140 pounds, Okker has never displayed raw power. Okker thought that the secret of the game was to reach the ball in time to make the shot. He knew that power was impor-

tant but not the only element in this game. Aware that he didn't have a big serve, he knew he had to develop other facets of his game to compensate.

In early 1973, he won or did well in very few tournaments but, by the summer, he became the hottest player around, winning the Dutch and Canadian Open tournaments along with tournaments in Washington (beating Arthur Ashe in the final), Seattle, Chicago (beating John Newcombe), Madrid, and London (beating Ilie Nastase). That year he won $173,550 in prize money.

For five straight years in the early 1970s, he was in the top ten. Okker's quickness and agility earned him the nickname of "The Flying Dutchman;" his nervous manner and inability to sit still won him the title of "Tom the Twitch."

His finest achievement was in winning the U.S. Open doubles with Marty Riessen in 1976. In

1977, he was ranked No. 1 in men's doubles. He teamed with John Newcombe twice to win doubles titles at the Italian Open (1973) and the French Open (1973). He reached the semifinals of Wimbledon in singles in 1978 and the quarterfinals in 1979. He won the first two Grand Prix events played in Tel Aviv, in 1978 and 1979.

In 1980 Okker had an excellent year playing doubles. He won the International Championships of the Netherlands in Hilversum, Holland, playing with Balazs Taroczy; the Egyptian Open, teamed with Egypt's Ismail El Shafei; and the Birmingham International Indoor, in Birmingham, Alabama, with partner Wojtek Fibak. He was also a finalist (with Fibak) in the Grand Prix Masters in New York and the Braniff World Doubles Championship in London. In singles that year he was a semifinalist at the Grand Prix in Basel; and a quarterfinalist in the Tel Aviv Grand Prix.

In 1981, Tom reached the semifinals of the doubles tournament at Wimbledon (teaming with Dick Stockton). He also helped to organize the Masters program (over 35 years of age) as well as playing in its tournaments. In the 1970s he had been living in Engleberg, Switzerland, but moved back to Holland in 1978. He keeps a home in Switzerland. Tom is married and has two daughters: Nathalie, born in 1971, and Esther, born in 1976; and a son Stephan, born in 1981. He left the tennis tour in 1983.

Okker continues to play in senior tennis tournaments, and he owns an art gallery in Hazerswoude-Dorp, the Netherlands.

As of November 2004, as the holder of 31 titles, Okker ranked 16th among the top 50 all-time singles open era title leaders. On May 8, 2006, having accumulated winnings of $1,257,000, Okker placed 299th on the list of all-time prize money leaders.

Barney Pelty

Noted American League Pitcher at the Turn of the Century

17-12. Against the Chicago White Sox that season, he permitted only one run in 32 innings.

Retiring from baseball, he returned to his hometown of Farmington, Missouri, and opened a notions store. He also managed semipro teams, and became involved in politics. He pitched his last game in 1937—an exhibition game against Hall-of-Famer Grover Cleveland Alexander, who beat him.

PELTY, BARNEY "THE YIDDISH CURVER" (born September 10, 1880, in Farmington, Missouri; died May 24, 1939) American baseball player. Considered one of the best American League pitchers of his day. A right-hander, he played for the St. Louis Browns from 1903 to 1912, and for the Washington Senators in 1912. He played in 281 games and had a 92-118 record.

. . .

St. Louis bought Pelty from the Cedar Rapids, Michigan minor league team for a sum of $850. His first major league start came on August 22, 1903, against Boston. He won 2-1 on an eight-hitter. Because of this victory, the team considered him good luck, since he won without knowing the signals too well. When he did not pitch, he served the team in the coaching box.

Pelty pitched 22 major league shutouts, but was shutout 32 times himself. He was beaten 1-0 nine times during his career. The St. Louis Browns were such a weak team in 1905 that Pelty led the club with a 13-14 pitching record; three other pitchers on the team lost 20 games each that season.

Pelty's best season came in 1906 when he was

Lipman Pike

Baseball's First Professional Player

PIKE, LIPMAN E. (born May 25, 1845, in New York City; died October 10, 1893) American baseball pioneer and the earliest known Jewish track champion. He became baseball's first professional when, in 1866, the Philadelphia Athletics paid him a regular salary. His career batting average in the National League: .304.

• • •

Lip Pike's parents were born in Holland; they raised their five children in Brooklyn. Lip's first appearance in a baseball game was one week after his Bar Mitzvah; he played first base for the Nationals with his brother at shortstop.

Pike played on numerous teams between 1858 and 1864. In 1865, he joined the strongest club in Brooklyn, the Atlantics, where he was used mainly as a substitute. In 1866, the Athletics noticed him and offered him the sum of $20 a week, a large amount at the time, to play third base. By accepting, Pike became baseball's first professional player. The first all-professional team was established in Cincinnati three years later.

Lip stayed with the Athletics for only one year. But he still managed to become the game's first home-run star, belting six homers in one game on July 16, 1866. The next year Pike became player-manager of the Irvington, New Jersey, team and in midseason began playing for the New York Mutuals. He was their star until the end of 1868 when he returned to the Brooklyn Atlantics.

In 1871, Pike became player-manager of the Troy, New York, team of the National Association, baseball's first professional league. His career (1871-75) batting average in that league was .321.

In 1872 he played outfield for the Lord Baltimores, another National Association team.

Pike's athletic career was not confined to baseball. He had remarkable speed and ran competitively. On August 4, 1873, he won the Maryland State 100-yard championship for a $100 purse. Later that month, Pike raced against a famous trotting horse named "Clarence" and won, earning $250. For both races, his time was 10 seconds flat, better than the then-existing record.

In 1874, Lip was player-manager in Hartford, Connecticut, and the following two years played with the St. Louis Brown Stockings (in 1875, St. Louis was part of the National Association; in 1876, of the National League).

Pike moved to Cincinnati in 1877 as player-manager at the start of the season. Yielding the managership, he stayed on as an outfielder, and became the National League's second home run champion, hitting four homers that year. In those years, the ball was so dead that it barely reached the outfield when hit hard. By 1878 Pike played for the Providence (Rhode Island) Grays of the National League.

The following year Lip continued to move around. He was player-manager for Springfield, Massachusetts (of the National Association), and for part of the 1880 season he played for Albany, New York (also with the Association). That season he had his best batting average: .356. In 1881, he became co-manager of the Brooklyn Atlantics, then an independent team; but he ended the season with Worcester, Massachusetts, of the National League.

There he ran into difficulties. Worcester was having a poor season and the team's manager suspected that Lip was not playing his best. The manager made Pike the scapegoat and refused to let him play. A year later, however, Lip was allowed back.

In the meanwhile, he had announced his retirement and had entered the haberdashery business in Brooklyn. Pike tried to make a comeback with the original New York Mets at age 42, but he played only one game for that American Association team—and retired again. He died suddenly, in 1893, at the age of 42, a victim of heart disease.

After his death, the editor of *Sporting Life* chose him as one of the all-star outfielders for the 1870-80 era. In its obituary *The Sporting News* wrote:

"[Pike] was one of the baseball players of those days who were always gentlemanly on and off the field—a species which is becoming rarer as the game grows older."

In 1985, he became a member of the Jewish Sports Hall of Fame in Israel.

Jacob Pincus

The Jockey Who Never Discussed His Horses' Chances

PINCUS, JACOB "JACOB THE SILENT" (born September 13, 1838, in Baltimore, Maryland; died January 23, 1918) American jockey and trainer. A jockey who was considered the foremost American rider of his day during the 10 years prior to the American Civil War. He was the first trainer to develop and saddle an American winner of the English Derby.

• • •

At age 12, Jacob Pincus worked as an exercise boy in Charleston, South Carolina. Two years later, in New Orleans, he rode his first thoroughbred, a mare named Ida, but present-day records do not suggest how well Pincus did. From there he headed for Saratoga, New York, where he became the greatest jockey in America before weight and age forced him to give up riding.

He worked as a trainer in the South for a while, but during the Civil War he moved to New Jersey. There, he trained horses for August Belmont Sr., and Pierre Lorillard, two well-know owners and figures in New York society. In 1869, he saddled Mr. Belmont's only Belmont Stakes winner, Fenian.

Pincus haltered Lorillard's Iroquois who won the English Derby of 1881, and it was not until 1954 that another American-bred horse won the famous British race. He remained in Britain in 1882 and then returned to the U.S. where he worked for a brief time as a race starter.

From 1885 to 1887 Pincus worked for the Belmont Stables. But, England was so close to his heart that he returned there and lived in Newmarket until 1906, working as a trainer of a small stable during that time.

Pincus earned the nickname "Jacob the Silent" because he would never discuss his horses' chances. After his retirement, he would often visit the New York racetracks. August Belmont Sr. provided Pincus with a pension for life.

Maurice Podoloff

First President of the National Basketball Association

PODOLOFF, MAURICE (born August 18, 1890, in Elizabethgrad, Russia; died November 24, 1985) American basketball administrator. First president of the National Basketball Association. He helped bring the NBA to national recognition by livening up the game and getting its games televised nationally, starting in 1954.

• • •

Maurice Podoloff came to the United States at the age of six. Raised in New Haven, Connecticut, he finished New Haven's Hillhouse Hill School in 1909 and completed his undergraduate work at Yale University in 1913. Two years later he graduated from Yale Law School.

The Podoloff family owned the New Haven Ice Skating arena. Maurice, after becoming a lawyer, became president of the American Hockey League.

In 1946, when he was president of that league, the owners of the teams being organized into the new Basketball Association of America (later the NBA) approached Maurice to become the first president of their 11-team venture. He knew most of the owners through his position as a hockey league president. Al Sutphin, then owner of Cleveland's American Hockey League team, had suggested Maurice as president of the new BAA.

Podoloff was appointed first commissioner of the BAA on June 6, 1946, at $9,000 a year. "I never cared for basketball. I never cared for hockey," he said. "I was hired to do a job." He was made president because they assumed he was honest and that he would devote himself to the financial aspects of

the league. "If I had been a sportsman," he said shortly before his death, "I probably would have loused it up."

Three years later, in August 1949, Podoloff presided over the merger of the BAA and the NBA.

In those days the NBA was a far cry from the popular league it was to become. The owners of the new league were often at odds with one another. Teams played in high school gyms and roller rinks. Referees, underpaid and undertrained, had difficulty handling games. Franchises, chronically short of cash, had trouble surviving. "There was always a crisis," said Boston Celtic President Red Auerbach, "but Podoloff kept the league going—just like a juggler."

He also figured how to liven up the game. At the time the NBA was a big bore. The worst example

came on November 22, 1950, when the Detroit Pistons beat the Minneapolis Lakers by the score of 19-18. Recalled Podoloff: "We had fouling, stalling, people were leaving the arenas in the last few minutes until that little guy [Danny Biasone, then owner of the Syracuse Nats] came up with his brainchild in 1954: the 24-second clock." Podoloff contends that had it not been for Biasone, the NBA would not have lasted another five years.

Until then, a team could hold on to the ball indefinitely, slowing up the game, and losing crowd interest. A special owners meeting was called in Syracuse. Biasone split the Nats into two teams for a practice game using a stopwatch, and permitting the players only 24 seconds to shoot.

The owners liked the idea and instructed Podoloff to have a 24-second clock made. Walter Brown, owner of the Boston Celtics, volunteered to get his own clock made, but Podoloff decided he would try to get one of his own. Said Podoloff: "My brother Nate knew a clock man, Bob Rosten in New York, and he got a clock made up for $300, and it worked perfectly. I ordered enough clocks for everybody in the league. Walter Brown paid $1,200 for his clock, and it wouldn't even start."

After the introduction of the 24-second clock, Podoloff was able to convince television to carry the NBA games nationally on a regular basis. "If it wasn't for the 24-second clock," he says. "we never would have had TV; the games would have dragged too long with no excitement at the end." NBA games were shown for the first time on national TV in 1954.

Podoloff, who was elected in 1973 to the Basketball Hall of Fame, tried personally to get Danny Biasone, the father of the 24-second rule, into the Hall of Fame, "but," says Maurice, "he missed by two votes."

After 17 years on the job, Podoloff retired as NBA president following the 1963 season. He then lived in the Sound View Specialized Care Center, a nursing home in West Haven, Connecticut. The home overlooks downtown New Haven, where Maurice grew up.

He told Dave Anderson of *The New York Times* in May 1977 that he had entered the nursing home "with a nervous breakdown but I got all over that." He said that he did not watch basketball games on TV. "I don't like the game," he said frankly. " I never liked the game."

Podoloff died in New Haven, Connecticut, at the age of 95 on November 24, 1985. A year later he was inducted into the Jewish Sports Hall of Fame in Israel.

Edward Reulbach

The Only Man to Ever Pitch Two Shutouts in a Doubleheader

REULBACH, EDWARD MARVIN "BIG ED" (born December 1, 1882, in Detroit, Michigan; died July 17, 1961) American baseball player. One of the National League's best pitchers in his day. He pitched 13 years in the major leagues and was the only man ever to pitch two shutouts in a doubleheader. His career pitching record was 181-105.

• • •

Reulbach, a right-hander, played for the Chicago Cubs from 1905 to 1913 and during that time the Cubs won the National League pennant three times (in 1906, 1907, and 1908), and the World Series in 1907 and 1908.

Achieving the mark of a great pitcher more than once, Ed Reulbach won 20 or more games in 1906 (20-4); 1908 (24-7); and in 1915 (21-10) pitching for Newark of the Federal League. The year 1907 was another good one: he won 17 and lost 4, playing for the Chicago Cubs.

In 1908, Ed Reulbach pitched a double shutout in a doubleheader against Brooklyn (he had pitched two full games in a single day without yielding a run). Those two games were part of a string of four straight shutouts he pitched, equaling a National League record. Reulbach pitched 42 shutouts

in his major league career. In World Series play, he was 2-1, with one victory in each of the 1906 and 1907 Series.

He played on the same Cub teams as the famous pitcher Mordecai (Three Finger) Brown and the legendary double-play combination of Joe Tinker, Johnny Evers, and Frank Chance.

After retiring from baseball, Reulbach worked for the Walsh Construction Company of New York for 20 years. In the years preceding his death he was employed in the company's equipment department. In the last few years of his life he lived in Glens Falls, New York.

Al Rosen

He Wanted to Be a Jew of Whom All Could Be Proud

ROSEN, AL "FLIP" (born March 1, 1925, in Spartanburg, South Carolina–) American baseball player. Picked by Arch Ward, originator of the All-Star Game, as his all-time All-Star third baseman. The first unanimous selection as Most Valuable Player when he won the award in 1953. He played with the Cleveland Indians from 1947 to 1956. In 1950, he hit 37 home runs to lead the American League. Between 1950 and 1954, he knocked in over 100 runs in each season. He led the league in runs batted in both in 1952 and 1953. He had a career batting average of .285 in 1,044 games.

• • •

Al's mother encouraged him to indulge in sports. When the boy suffered from violent asthma attacks, his mother, following doctor's advice, encouraged him to play outside as much as possible. "When he was little," Al's mother recalled, "I'd watch him playing with the other boys, gasping as if each breath would be his last." The asthma, which he had until age 16, eventually cured itself.

The Rosen family settled in Miami, Florida. At age 14, Al went to a baseball school, earned some money playing semipro softball, and was All-City third baseman at Miami High School. He won a scholarship to Florida Military Academy where he played football, basketball, and baseball and even boxed. He won the middleweight title in the Florida high school tournament, but baseball was his great love. "People would let you know you were a minority," he said. "You could accept it or reject it. My tolerance level was low. I took my share of whippings. But I learned to take care of myself."

In 1941, at age 16, Al Rosen won a tryout with the Cleveland Indians' Class A farm team at Wilkes-Barre, Pennsylvania. Showing a weak bat, he was offered $75 a month to play Class D ball with Thomasville in the North Carolina State League. Shocked at how little money he had been offered, he chose instead to enter first the University of Florida, and then the University of Miami. Between baseball seasons he earned his degree. While at the University of Miami, he played end on the football team and won the Florida intercollegiate boxing title. He obtained his lifetime nickname of "Flip," as a softball pitcher, because of the way he "flipped" the ball to the batter.

In 1942 Rosen joined the Boston Red Sox system, and left soon thereafter for military service in World War II. Serving in the U.S. Navy, he spent time on Okinawa. In 1946, he was discharged as a lieutenant.

Between 1946 and 1949, he had a great batting record in the minors, playing with several teams in the Cleveland chain. In 1947 he hit .349 with Oklahoma in the Texas League; at one point he hit seven doubles in a row, and was named best player in the league.

In 1948, he accomplished something few others have done: he hit five straight homers for Kansas City. He won a brief trial in the majors with the Indians that year, but was shipped back to Kansas City, where he hit .327, 26 homers and was voted Rookie of the Year. He had one more chance with Cleveland that year and was again disappointed. His march up the ladder was slow, in part because his fielding was weak.

In Al's third attempt at the majors—in 1950—he succeeded. In his first month up, he hit eight homers and by July 4th had 25. That year he hit .287; slugged 37 homers, knocked in 116 runs, and won Rookie of the Year honors. In 1951, he drove in more than 100 runs, but his batting average dropped to .265, and his home run total to 24. In 1952, Rosen returned to the groove, with 28 homers and 105 RBIs.

"As far as I'm concerned," observed Marty Marion, a former major league shortstop, "I have yet to see a better clutch hitter." Rosen's manager, Al Lopez, noted: "After a pitcher gets him out, he'll come back to the bench and say, 'I'll get him next time.' And by golly, he does."

In 1953, Ed Sullivan, the *New York Daily News* columnist and TV star, wrote that Al Rosen was of Jewish parentage, but a practicing Catholic: "At the plate, you'll notice he makes the sign of the cross with his bat." Denying the story, Rosen said that he made a superstitious "x" on the plate before coming to bat since he was a youngster, insisting that he was a proud Jew.

Indeed, Rosen wanted his name to be even more Jewish than it was—Rosenthal or Rosenstein. He wanted no mistake about what he was. "And," said the third base star, "when I was up there in the majors, I always knew how I wanted it to be about me. I wanted it to be, 'Here comes one Jewish kid that every Jew in the world can be proud of.'" Rosen refused to play baseball on the Jewish high holy days.

In 1953, he might have won the batting title had he played on those days and gotten a few hits. His .336 batting average that year fell just short of the top mark. He lost the batting title on the last day of the season, missing out by just .001. He did win the home run crown with 43 homers and the RBI title with 145. And he was the unanimous choice for Most Valuable Player in the American League in 1953.

From 1952 to 1955, Rosen played in the All-Star games. In the 1954 All-Star game, he tied two All-Star records: two homers and five RBIs. (The American League won that year 11-9.) That same year he was switched from third to first base, and his batting average fell to .300, due in part to an injured index finger. Rosen was injury-prone throughout his career: he broke his nose 13 times (often from ground balls, and once in a college boxing match).

Between 1954 and 1956 he was hampered often by injuries. Feeling unable to play at the level he wished, he retired and devoted full time to his off-season career with the brokerage firm of Bache and Company with whom he worked for almost 20 years.

by George M. Steinbrenner which purchased the New York Yankees from CBS in 1973. Rosen was named executive vice president of the Yankees in December 1977. He served in that capacity until March 27, 1978, when he was appointed president and chief operating officer of the ballclub. In 1978, the Yankees won their second straight World Series, defeating the Los Angeles Dodgers.

On July 19, 1979 Rosen resigned his post with the Yankees and became executive vice president of Bally Park Place, a hotel and casino in Atlantic City, New Jersey. He remained at Bally until he joined the Houston Astros in October, 1980, at first, as executive vice president, then president and general manager. On January 5, 1981, Rosen underwent successful open-heart surgery in Houston. He served with Houston until 1985 at which time he became the president and general manager of the San Francisco Giants.

During Rosen's tenure, the Giants won one National League pennant and two division championships, had five winning seasons, and achieved franchise home and road attendance records.

In 1987, Rosen was voted Major League Executive of the Year by *The Sporting News*, *United Press International* and *Baseball America* after the Giants won their first National League West championship in 16 years.

At the end of the 1992 season, Rosen retired as president and general manager of the Giants. Rosen is now a private investor and plays golf "every chance I get."

Early in 2003, Major League Baseball Commissioner Bud Selig appointed Rosen to a new marketing task force called "Baseball in the 21st Century," the specified aim of which was to consider all aspects of the game, including such issues as whether to expand the playoffs.

Rosen is featured in *Jews and Baseball: An American Love Story*, a 2010 film narrated by Dustin Hoffman that celebrates the contributions of Jewish major league players and explores the special meaning that baseball has had to American Jews.

Al Rosen is a member of the New York Jewish Sports Hall of Fame and the Jewish Sports Hall of Fame in Israel.

ROSENBERG, AARON "ROSY" (born August 26, 1912, in Brooklyn, New York; died September 1, 1979) American football player. He played guard for the University of Southern California in the early 1930s and at the time was considered the greatest guard in football. In 1932 and 1933 he made a number of All-American teams.

• • •

Aaron Rosenberg's father was a tailor in Brooklyn. When Aaron was seven, he was hit by an auto, and his family moved to Los Angeles to help Aaron recuperate. Aaron played football for his high school team and for four consecutive years made the All-Los Angeles city high school team.

Rosenberg enrolled at the University of Southern California (USC) in 1930, a time when the school was a major football power. While Aaron was a sophomore, USC pulled off a great upset, defeating Notre Dame at South Bend, Indiana, 16-14, thus ending a string of 26 straight wins for the Irish. USC had a 9-1-0 record that year, and scored a 21-12 triumph over Tulane in the Rose Bowl. The next year the USC Trojans were 9-0-0, trouncing Pittsburgh 35-0 in the Rose Bowl.

By 1933 the USC team, with Aaron Rosenberg now playing guard, had won 27 straight games before Stanford defeated it 13-7. For that Stanford game Rosenberg had to wear a mask to protect his broken cheekbone. USC ended the season (Rosenberg's senior year) at 10-1-1.

Rosenberg was large (6 feet, 200 pounds), and possessed great speed. He often blocked two or three men on a single play.

Grantland Rice, the sportswriter, picked Rosenberg for All-America in 1933. Wrote Rice: "Howard Jones [the USC coach] calls him the best guard he ever coached. He [Rosenberg] undoubtedly was the best running guard in football and because of his great defensive skill Jones gave him a roving assignment behind Southern California's six-man line. Playing in line with two inexperienced tackles this year [1933], he still held the Southern California defense together. He was the spearhead of the Southern California running game and his effective blocking was responsible for much of [quarterback Cotton] Warburton's success as a ball carrier."

After football, Rosenberg became one of the movie industry's top producers. He got his start during his summers in college when he worked on the production side in Hollywood. He became an assistant director after college, continuing in that job from the mid-1930s until World War II when he did service as a naval officer.

Aaron Rosenberg returned to Hollywood after the war as an associate producer. He became full producer for Universal Studios late in the 1940s.

Among the 30 films he produced between 1949 and 1973 are: *Johnny Stool Pigeon*, his first in 1949: *The Iron Man*, 1951; *The Glenn Miller Story*, 1954; *The Benny Goodman Story*, 1956; *Mutiny on the Bounty*, 1962; *Tony Rome* and *Caprice*, 1967; *The Detective* and *Lady in Cement*, 1968; and *The Boy Who Cried Werewolf*, 1973.

Rosenberg died of a massive stroke at age 67 while playing golf in Torrance, California.

Maxie Rosenbloom

The Boxer Who Slapped His Way to Fame

ROSENBLOOM, MAXIE "SLAPSIE MAXIE" (born November 1, 1907, in New York City; died March 6, 1976) Light heavyweight boxing champion from 1930 to 1934. Overall record: 206 victories (18 by knockout), 35 losses, 35 draws, 20 no-decisions, 2 no-contests. In 16 years of fighting he was knocked out only twice.

• • •

Maxie Rosenbloom, who never went beyond the fifth grade and spent part of his childhood in a reformatory, began boxing in the Union Settlement House in New York. He had his first pro fight at age 19, when he scored a third-round knockout.

At first Maxie would slug it out with opponents, then he switched to a hit-and-run style. It was because the boxer would often slap his opponents with open gloves that sportswriter Damon Runyon nicknamed him "Slapsie Maxie." When asked why he fought that way, Rosenbloom said, "I always hated to hit hard."

Maxie earned undisputed claim to the light heavyweight crown on June 25, 1930, when he defeated James Slattery in Slattery's home town of Buffalo, New York, in 15 rounds. He beat Slattery a second time in Brooklyn, New York, on August 5, 1931, also in 15 rounds.

During his four and one-half years as champion, Rosenbloom fought 106 times, an average of once every 15 days. In eight bouts his title was on the line.

Although Maxie was considered a clever boxer, he was an especially weak hitter. His hit-and-run tactics were not universally appreciated. To "Love in Bloom," a popular song of the day, sportswriter Dan Parker wrote a parody based on Maxie's movements in the ring. It went in part: "Can it be the cheese that fills the breeze with rare and magic perfume? Oh, no, it isn't the cheese, it's Rosenbloom."

John Kieran, a former sports columnist for *The New York Times*, once wrote that "anyone who gets into the ring with Rosenbloom is slapped with great frequency and a moderate amount of vigor. Whether or not this furious slapping is to be regarded as a high form of pugilistic artistry is another question."

Rosenbloom's 15-round, 1933 decision over Adolph Heuser, Germany's light heavyweight champ, at Madison Square Garden in New York, was considered an important factor in Germany's decision to prohibit its athletes from competing with Jewish athletes. The Germans were unwilling to take a chance that their claim of Nazi superiority over "non-Aryans" might be called into question by a German competitor losing to a Jewish athlete.

Maxie lost his title to Bob Olin on November 16, 1934, in a lackluster decision that was booed by the fans who came to Madison Square Garden. The fight was held under the rules of the New York State Athletic Commission which had restricted hitting with an open hand. Hence, no slaps for Maxie.

After Rosenbloom's fight career ended in 1939, he opened a nightclub in California, but the club did not fare well. Rosenbloom then pursued an acting career. His first role was in a Carole Lombard picture, and over the years he appeared —most often as a gangster or a punch-drunk fighter—in about 100 films, including *The Kid Comes Back*, in 1938; *Each Dawn I Die*, in 1939; *The Boogie Man Will Get You*, in 1942; and *Irish Eyes Are Smiling*, in 1944.

Rosenbloom once explained that he landed his first acting role because Carole Lombard wanted him to teach her to box "to help her in fights with Clark Gable [her husband]."

Maxie earned a fortune during his career, but money seemed to have little value to him. "I don't think he was ever inside a bank," said a close friend. Frank Brachman, who managed Rosenbloom, said the most frequent messages he had from his fighter were telegrams which read, "Send more dough."

In 1937 Rosenbloom married the former Muriel Fader, but the partnership ended in divorce eight years later, and from that time on, Rosenbloom's reputation became that of a playboy. He neither drank nor smoked, but he was an avowed womanizer.

As an entertainer, Maxie was quite successful. His broken syntax, and his sharp wit made him particularly appealing. He once joked that he had quit the ring because "Joe Louis wouldn't fight me. I guess he was afraid of me—afraid he'd kill me." Rosenbloom was elected to the Boxing Hall of Fame in 1972, just a few years after his mental and physical health began to deteriorate. The doctors attributed the decline to his having taken too many punches to the head during his career. This, they believed, resulted in brain damage.

In 1984, Rosenbloom was inducted into the International Jewish Sports Hall of Fame. A year later he became a member of the World Boxing Hall of Fame, and in 1993 he joined the International Boxing Hall of Fame.

Fanny Rosenfeld

A Canadian Track and Field Star Who Would Not Intermarry

ROSENFELD, FANNY "BOBBIE" (born December 28, 1903, in Katrinaslov, Russia; died in December, 1969) Canadian track and field star. In 1950 she was chosen Canada's female athlete of the half-century by the sportswriters of Canada. In the 1928 Amsterdam Olympics, she won a gold medal for Canada on the lead-off leg of the 400-meter relay team that set a world record of 48.4. She also captured a silver medal in the 100-meter sprint.

. . .

Soon after she was born in Russia, Fanny and her family emigrated to Canada. During the difficult journey, Fanny contracted smallpox. Her family settled in Barrie, Ontario, where her father went into the junk business. Fanny learned how to play softball and hockey on corner lots with the boys.

She showed exceptional athletic talent while in her teens. When she was 16, a track meet was held in Barrie to celebrate the end of World War I. Groans went up from the other girls entered in the same sprints as Fanny because they knew the results were a foregone conclusion. So Fanny gave them a three-yard head start—and still she managed to win.

Fanny received her nickname "Bobbie" after she arrived home one day with her long hair cut off or "bobbed" so that it would not bother her in sports—a change of hair style which caused only anguish to her mother.

Once, while at an informal track meet held during a picnic, a friend persuaded Bobbie to enter the 100-yard dash. She did. Despite her bulky, unsuitable bloomers, she outran the reigning Canadian champion. In 1920, Constance Hennessey, a founder of the Toronto Ladies Athletic Club, described Bobbie as someone who "didn't look powerful but was wiry and quick. Above all she was aggressive, very aggressive physically."

In 1922, the Rosenfelds moved to Toronto. There Bobbie took courses in stenography and eventually worked as a stenographer for a local chocolate factory, Patterson's. She played on the factory's women's teams and became an outstanding athlete in softball and ice hockey.

At the same time, Bobbie, then 19, took up track and field. By the mid-1920s, she had won Canadian titles and set national records. In September 1925, she tied the world record of 11.0 for the 100-yard dash. That same year she was Patterson's Athletic Club's only entrant in the Ontario Ladies Track and Field Championships. At that meet she won the discus, 220-yard dash, low hurdles, and long jump, and placed second in the 100-yard dash and javelin.

She held a variety of Canadian national records in the standing long jump, the running long jump, the eight-pound shot, the discus, and the javelin. Still she also participated in other sports. In 1924 she won the Toronto Ladies Grass Court Tennis Title.

In 1928, women's track and field appeared on the Olympic program for the first time. Bobbie was chosen to represent Canada in three events. She won a gold medal in the 400-meter relay. A controversy arose whether Bobbie had won the 100-meter dash; the American runner, Elizabeth Robinson, was awarded first place though the Canadian fans were convinced that Bobbie had won. Bobbie took a silver medal. Unfortunately, photo finishes were not in use at the time. At the Games, Rosenfeld took a fifth in the 800-meter race.

After the 1928 Olympics, Bobbie returned to softball and hockey for a while. In the winter of 1929, Rosenfeld got her revenge, beating Elizabeth Robinson in the 100-meter race at the Milrose Games in New York. She called this the most satisfying victory in her career. But, catastrophe struck that year; arthritis forced her into bed and onto crutches for the ensuing 18 months. At one stage, the doctors even considered amputating one foot at the ankle, but a family doctor resisted and the foot was saved. However, Bobbie's track career was over. Rosenfeld returned to playing softball and hockey, but another bout with arthritis in 1933 ended her active participation in sports.

Though she never married, she did have one love affair which was doomed by religion. For a long time, she dated a young man from a Christian family, but eventually they parted, since neither his family nor hers would approve their marriage.

In the spring of 1937, Bobbie began writing for the *Toronto Globe and Mail*. Her column, "Feminine Sports Reel," focused on women in sports in Toronto, but also commented on Canadian sports in general.

Rosenfeld retained a refreshing sense of humor about herself and her misfortunes. "If I had stayed in Russia," she once said, "my running prowess might have won me the distinction of having invented the human foot." When she was asked if the arthritic problems that plagued her in her final years were due to her intensive sports activity, she commented, "It is probably the result of reaching for another bottle of beer or something." While watching a baseball game, she yelled at a player who was hesitating in a tight play, "Play the bag, play the bag, any old bag but me."

Bobbie Rosenfeld did not hesitate to attack the sports establishment in her columns. She severely criticized the female selections for the British Empire track and field teams in 1937, complaining that certain topflight athletes had not been chosen because they were not personal friends of the nominating committee members.

She stopped writing about sports in 1957 and switched to the *Globe and Mail* promotion department. She was public relations manager when she retired in 1966. Soon thereafter, her health deteriorated quickly and she died three years later. In 1974, an article in *Canada's Sporting Heroes* warmly remembered Bobbie: "From her first emergence as an athletic marvel, she was described in the press as 'refreshing and irreverent.' From the start, Bobbie Rosenfeld balanced intense competitive fire with an instinctive comic sense; she lived out her pain-wracked life with the same flair she had when she burst upon the sporting scene."

Fanny Rosenfeld is a member of the Jewish Sports Hall of Fame in Israel.

Barney Ross

First To Hold Lightweight and Welterweight Crowns Simultaneously

ROSS, BARNEY (born December 23, 1909, on the lower East Side of New York City; died January 17, 1967) The world lightweight and junior welterweight champion from 1933 to 1935, world welterweight champion from 1934 to 1938, and the first boxer to hold the lightweight and welterweight crowns simultaneously. In 82 professional fights, he won 74 (24 were by knockout), lost 4 (none by knockout), drew 3 and had 1 no-decision.

■ ■ ■

He was born Barnet David Rosofsky, on Rivington Street, on the Lower East Side of New York City. His parents had been Russian immigrants who had come to the United States in 1903. At the age of two he moved with his family (he was the third oldest of five children) to the Jefferson Street Jewish section in Chicago. His father Isadore, a Talmudic scholar, made sure the Rosofskys' two and a half room home had an Orthodox atmosphere. He opened a grocery store across the street where he tragically met his death on December 13, 1924, when two holdup men broke into the store and killed him. Barney was just a boy of 14 at the time.

The death of his father placed a terrible burden on his mother who now had to care for four sons and a daughter. Unable to provide for their support, Barney's mother suffered a nervous breakdown. His two younger brothers and sisters were placed in an orphanage, Barney and an older brother were taken in by a cousin.

Prior to the holdup, Barney had forsaken sports in school in order to concentrate on religious stud-

ies. But he lost all interest in religion as a result of the tragedy in his family. He had hoped to become a Hebrew teacher, but he abandoned that hope. Instead, he began to search for a way to make quick money. He wanted to bring the family together again. "Everything that happened to me afterward," he wrote, "happened because of that senseless, stupid murder."

He took on odd jobs, but consistently got into trouble with the law. (He was caught running illegal crap games, for example.) Somehow he managed to finish two years at Medill High School in Chicago, but the need for cash led him into the life of a minor racketeer. He became a messenger for the notorious Al Capone. In a rare moment of goodness, Capone gave Barney $20 and advised him to go straight, certain that that's what Barney's father would have wanted for his son.

Sensing that he had some talent for the ring, Barney took up the fight game. He didn't want his mother to know what he was up to so he changed his name to Barney Ross.

His tremendous talent began to show when as an amateur, in 1926, he walked away with the featherweight title in the New York-Chicago Golden Gloves tournament. The Chicago ghetto had given him the necessary toughness, and by the time he was 18 he had fought 250 fights as an amateur. On his 18th birthday, encouraged by another Jewish boxing champ, Jackie Fields, Barney Ross turned pro.

Now Ross learned the real techniques of the ring: how to feint, how to bob, to shift, and to move in the ring. With 50 bouts under his belt, he was ready to take a crack at Tony Canzoneri, the lightweight champion. Even more satisfying, just before that fight, he had managed to reunite his family. The bout was held in Chicago on June 23, 1933, and though the critics insisted that Tony deserved to win, Ross triumphed in a ten-round decision. The new champion missed the post-fight celebration: he had to walk his mother, now a great enthusiast of her son's fight career, home from the stadium. It was Friday night, the Jewish Sabbath, and, being a religious woman, Mrs. Rosofsky would not ride.

Ross gave Tony Canzoneri a rematch in September of 1933. This bout was held in New York City's Polo Grounds. While training for the fight in Wisconsin, Barney renewed his interest in Judaism: "Before I took off for my roadwork," he recalled, "I dug out the bag of *tefilin* (phylacteries) which I hadn't touched for a couple of years, fastened the little boxes around my arm and my head, and said my morning prayers." Barney won the rematch.

Soon after, in a Chicago synagogue, the rabbi advised Barney that, "You cannot behave badly. You cannot let bad things be written about you." Hitler, said the rabbi, was mistreating Jews in Europe. "You must set an example of decency and goodness so that the world will know what horrible lies Hitler is telling."

In the next year and a half, Ross defended his title five times. But, older and heavier, he eyed the welterweight division, confident that he could lick the reigning champ, Jimmy "Baby Face" McLarnin. McLarnin was the nemesis of Jewish pugilists: he had already knocked out a half dozen of them. A fight was arranged for May 30, 1934, at the Long Island Bowl. Interest was high. It was only the third time that a lightweight had fought a welterweight champion with the latter's title at stake. The bout went fifteen rounds and Ross took the split decision. His victory, said the *Chicago Tribune,* was "clean-cut, brilliant, methodical. The defending champion was outfought, outboxed, and outmaneuvered." Ross's manager, Sam Plan, noted after the fight, "The real secret of his success is his ability to come back after being hit and press the fighting." Writing of that first Ross-McLarnin fight, James P. Dawson of *The New York Times* described Barney as a "cagey boxer, a smashing body puncher, the possessor of an effective left hook, and with the physical equipment to withstand assault and keep coming in; he is no fluke champion."

Chicago welcomed Barney Ross home with a parade to City Hall. He was now a ring immortal,

BARNEY ROSS

having become the first man to win both lightweight and welterweight crowns.

Ross gave McLarnin a rematch on September 17, 1934, a match that was postponed four times in 11 days, once because of the Jewish New Year, Rosh Hashana. In a bitterly-debated decision, McLarnin regained his title, although of the 28

boxing reporters on hand, 22 thought Ross should have won. Barney resigned his lightweight title shortly thereafter because of weight problems.

He and McLarnin fought for a third time, on May 28, 1935, at the Polo Grounds in New York City. This time Barney won in a fifteen-round unanimous decision. In the third round, Ross broke the thumb of his left hand and endured terrible pain through the rest of the fight.

On September 23, 1937, Barney fought a title defense against the Filipino, Ceferino Garcia, famous for his bolo punch. Three days before the fight, Ross broke his left hand on a sparring partner's skull. Having become a heavy gambler, and having lost much of his $500,000 in boxing earnings at the track, Barney had little choice but

to appear in the ring against Garcia. He fought mostly with his right hand, and won easily. The hand, however, never healed properly.

On May 31, 1938, Ross took on Henry Armstrong, and for five rounds did well. Then, after the eleventh round, the referee wanted to stop the fight and award it to Armstrong. "Let me finish," Barney Ross pleaded to the referee, "It's the last favor I'll ever ask of you. I'll never fight again." He was still on his feet at the last bell, though he lost the fight. "A champion," he said, "has the right to choose how he goes out." Barney's career was over. He had fought 329 times and had never been knocked out.

Just before his last fight, Ross married a Jewish woman, Pearl Spiegel, whose father had a clothing store in New York City. Entering into partnership with his father-in-law, Barney soon discovered that he had no business sense. The marriage did not last long and Barney left the clothing business and tried acting. This didn't work and soon thereafter he opened a cocktail lounge in Chicago. Barney then fell in love with a non-Jewish showgirl, Cathy Howlett.

When the Japanese attacked Pearl Harbor Barney was assigned to teach boxing. But he didn't feel right doing this type of service. He wanted to serve overseas.

In April 1942, at age 32, Barney Ross joined the Marines. By November he was on Guadalcanal with the Second Marine Division. The Americans were engaged in a bloody battle with the Japanese for control of this strategic Pacific Island. On the night of November 19, 1942, Ross and four other Marines found themselves cut off from the main body of American soldiers. All except Ross were killed or wounded in the opening salvo, and Ross alone kept the enemy at bay with rifle fire and grenades, taking time out to pray in Hebrew. After a 13-hour battle, Ross and his buddies were relieved: 22 Japanese lay dead around Ross' defensive position. He was promoted to corporal on the spot. Other awards, including the Silver Star, would follow.

When Barney Ross came home from the war in February 1943, he was suffering from malaria, and his hair was white, having turned that way overnight. For a while he went on speaking tours, but soon the effects of malaria forced him to retire from public life. To ease his pain, he was given morphine, to which he soon became addicted. He squandered a fortune on drugs and before long his personal life was in ruins. Cathy divorced him. In 1946, Ross turned himself over to the Public Health Service narcotics rehabilitation center at Lexington, Kentucky, where after four months he was pronounced cured. This was an unusual feat for a morphine addict. In 1947 he remarried Cathy and spent the rest of his days trying to help others in similar straits. He fought dope racketeers, testified before Congress, and aided victims of drug addiction. A movie, *Monkey On My Back,* with Cameron Mitchell, told the story of his life.

He died after a battle with throat cancer. Rabbi William Gold said in his eulogy, "Barney Ross was his own worst enemy. He was so generous to others that the only person he neglected was himself. He left no funds, no estates named after himself. All he left to be remembered by is a world full of friends."

Ross is a member of the Jewish Sports Hall of Fame in Israel.

Esther Roth

First Israeli to Reach the Olympic Finals

ROTH, ESTHER (born April 16, 1952, in Tel Aviv–) Israeli track and field star. At age 18, she was one of the best women sprinters in the world. She held the world record (7.1) for the 60-meter indoor hurdles for one day. She broke Israeli records in numerous track and field events, including the 100- and 200-meter races, long jump and pentathlon. In 1976, she became the first Israeli to reach the finals of an Olympic event.

. . .

Esther, a sabra (native-born Israeli), was born to parents who emigrated to Palestine in 1940 from Moscow. She ran under her maiden name, Shachamorov, until she married Peter Roth in 1973.

At the Eighth Maccabiah Games in 1969, Esther won the 100-meter, 200-meter, and long jump. At the 1970 Asian Games in Bangkok, she won gold medals in the hurdles and pentathlon and a silver medal in the long jump. By age 18 she was considered a top contender for the 1972 Olympics in Munich. "It was everything I had lived for," she recalled. Yet when the time came, disaster struck her fellow-Israeli athletes, and she narrowly missed being a part of those tragic events.

Palestinian Arab terrorists struck at the Munich Olympic village, taking Israeli athletes hostage. In the end, 11 Israelis were killed in the attack. Esther Roth and the rest of the women's team escaped because their quarters were in a separate building, 200 meters away from their male teammates. "It might have been easier if we had been attacked, too," she observed later. "As it was, we did not know any more about what was happening than anyone else. There was no accurate news. The loudspeakers kept making routine announcements about sporting events. They kept playing music."

She lost her coach, Amitzur Shapira, who had worked with her for seven years. After the attack she said, "The dream was over." She had reached the 100-meter semifinal but, because of the raid, had to bow out. She was ready to hang up her track shoes: "Munich took something out of me," she remembered. "I didn't want to compete any longer."

But, in time she did return to competition. She ran in the Ninth Maccabiah Games in 1973, and again she won the 100-meter, 200-meter, and long jump. At the time she was three months pregnant. "I didn't know, and the doctors didn't know. But I won the gold medals anyway. I had a feeling I might have been, but wasn't absolutely sure. Anyway, my son, Yaron, had a gold medal even before he was born."

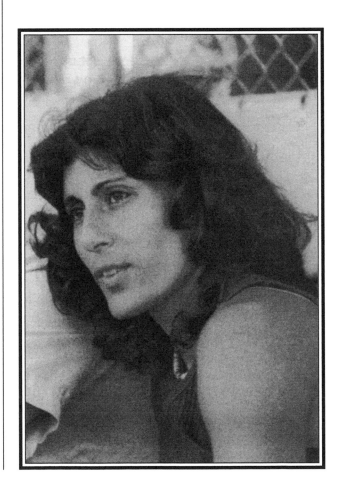

The 1974 Asian Games were scheduled for September of that year, but Esther Roth had a problem getting ready for the big event. She and husband Peter (her coach) had just become the parents of their first child in February, and Esther's training had to be limited because she had undergone a Caesarean delivery. "I only trained for three months after waiting three months from the time of the birth," she recalled. The results: she dominated the Games, winning three gold medals in the 200-meter dash, the 100-meter hurdles, and the 100-meter sprint.

At the 1976 Olympics in Montreal, Esther became the first Israeli to reach the finals of an Olympic event—she did so in the 100-meter hurdles. She had cruised through her preliminary heat and in the semifinals won fourth place in a photo finish. In the finals, she managed a sixth. Despite not taking one of the top medals, she did manage to set a new Israeli record of 13.04 for the event. She bettered that just two months later (12.93) in Berlin. The Montreal Olympics were the last major inter-

national competition for her. Israel's expulsion from the Asian Federation and the Israeli boycott of the 1980 Moscow Olympics kept her from engaging in major meets.

In 1977, she competed in the World Cup Games in Dusseldorf and in the Tenth Maccabiah Games. In the Maccabiah, she set records in the 100-meter hurdles, the 200-meters, and the 4 x 100-meter hurdles.

She was named Sportswoman of the Year three times by the Israeli newspaper *Ma'ariv*, and once by the newspaper *Yediot Aharonot*. The 1976 Olympics showed that she was the greatest woman hurdler outside of Eastern Europe. Of those days, she recalled: "Most other athletes were training two or three times as hard as I was. It's unhealthy. They pushed themselves too hard and used dangerous artificial stimulants. I enjoy my sport. I remember in Montreal how all the other athletes were tense and nervous. They couldn't understand how I was always able to laugh and joke around."

She announced her retirement from competitive

athletics in September 1979, but a month later she was persuaded to reverse her decision to compete in the Moscow Olympics the following summer. She, of course, did not participate in those Games because Israel, along with other countries, boycotted them. Her last competition was in the United States just before the Moscow Olympics.

Currently, Roth teaches physical education at a junior high school in Ra'anana, near Tel Aviv. She and her husband have two children, Yaron and Michal.

In an interview with *The Jerusalem Post* in July 1997, she acknowledged that she had been heavily disturbed by the decision taken by Olympic officials at Munich in 1972 to continue the Games despite the terrorist attack on her fellow Israeli athletes. However, when a similar decision was made at the 1996 Atlanta Olympic Games to carry on the competition despite the bombing (which killed one and injured 100), she changed her mind.

She told a reporter: "I came to the conclusion that when terror strikes or accidents occur at a sporting event of national and international significance perhaps there is no other choice than to carry on. The Olympics and the Maccabiah Games demand years of effort and sacrifice from those taking part. Should all this be thrown away? In spite of the pain of the wounded and their loved ones, do we have any alternative but to carry on? After all, there is always the possibility that something will happen. We will never be able to protect ourselves from the unexpected."

The recipient of the Israel Prize for Sports in 1999, Esther Roth was again honored on April 26, 2004, when she one of sixteen Israeli sports figures who participated in Israel's fifty-sixth Independence Day torchlighting ceremony. She is still considered Israel's greatest woman track star, her 11.45-second 100-meter run in 1972 remaining Israel's fastest mark.

He won three tournaments in 1976, and finished second three times, becoming the second highest money winner on the pro-bowlers tour. In 1977, he was the best bowler on the pro tour, first winning the Showboat Invitational, and then coming up with a startling triple: first in succession in the PBA Doubles Classic (with Marshal Holman), the Fresno Open, and the Southern California Open. He led the tour in earnings that year with $105,583. His bowling average was 218.174.

In 1978 Mark won eight tournaments with a record 219.834 average for 1,047 games. He accumulated $134,500 in prize money and established a bowling record by earning money in each of the 25 tournaments in which he competed. He was named *Sporting News'* PBA Player of the Year.

In 1979 Roth again dominated the PBA tour, walking off with the most money and highest average. He had a record high average of 221.662, and led the tour in tournament victories, winning six, to give him a career total of 22 since 1975. Mark was named to Pro Bowling's 1979 All-America team.

Roth's critics argue that he just rears back and throws, with no real style. Other commentators have called Roth's style theatrical and swashbuckling. Roth throws the ball unusually fast, with a fury and power rarely seen in a bowling alley. These qualities have made him a distinctive bowler, which he seems to enjoy. At one time, his tight grip used to tear the skin off his right thumb, but he has since learned to protect the thumb, without losing any of the fire of his shot.

When asked to advise young pros, Roth urges them to take four or five smooth steps, to refrain from hooking the ball too much, and to keep arms straight and close to the body. After that, Roth advises youngsters to develop their own styles.

To prepare for a day at the lanes, Mark goes through a routine in his hotel room that is not to be believed. It's all designed to release emotional tension. Mark does not necessarily go through it all the time, only when he feels uptight. First,

Mark Roth

Four-Time Bowler
of the Year

ROTH, MARK (born April 10, 1951, in Brooklyn, New York–) American bowler. One of the giants of the sport. He won 34 Professional Bowlers Association titles and was PBA Player of the Year in 1977, 1978, 1979, and 1984. Between 1976 and 1990, over 8,000 matches, he delivered a 215-plus average—the best long term output in PBA history. He was elected to the PBA Hall of Fame in his first year of eligibility, 1987.

. . .

Mark turned to bowling because he was too small for other sports. He bowled mostly at the Rainbow Lanes in Sheepshead Bay, not far from his Crown Heights home in Brooklyn, and would often spend the summer Saturday nights in the alleys alone. His mother, disturbed at his staying at the lanes until 2 A.M., tried to convince him that the sport was worthless. But Mark told her that the lanes were better than the street corner.

Roth, however, did not seem to have the potential to become a great bowler. To compensate for his size, he threw the ball as hard as he could. And since he had difficulty making spares, he began hooking the ball a great deal.

Roth would soak the ball to make it hook even more. Eventually, he learned to control the hook, but he had other problems. He took more steps than most bowlers, and his backswing was high. He did not take enough time before releasing the ball like other bowlers. He simply stood up and threw the ball.

Roth was on the bowling tour for four years before winning his first event: the King Louis, in

Mark emits a primitive shriek, then some guttural burbling, followed by an occasional "wahoo" and "eeiii" or two. Then he sends roundhouse punches flying in the air. For the next 30 seconds, he'll stare out the window and repeat the words, "firp, firp, firp, firp." Then he hurtles through the air, plops on the bed, and shouts, "Let's go," into the pillow. Finally, Roth slams the pillow against the wall, feathers fluttering, walks past a maid outside the door, wishes her "Good morning!" and goes off to bowl.

In 1980, Roth played in 28 tournaments and won the PBA event in Rochester, New York. His 216.928 average was second highest on the PBA tour. The following year, 1981, Roth won three PBA tournaments: Las Vegas, Lansing, and Cleveland. His 216.699 was the leading PBA average that year. He won four PBA events in 1983 and had earnings that year of $158, 712. In 1984, he won four PBA Championship titles and was voted the 1984 *Sporting News* PBA Player of the Year for the fourth time, the first since 1979.

In 1986, Roth told a sportswriter: "I'll never win the PBA's sportsmanship award. You have to be too nice. Bowlers who are nice don't have enough killer instinct. I'd rather win than be nice."

In 1987, he won the Greater Buffalo Open in Buffalo, New York. His earnings that year reached $93,245.

From 1988 to 1991, Roth fared less well, earning $81,375 in 1988, but only $11,190 in 1991. He had been plagued with injuries, including tendonitis in his right wrist and a painful nerve in his right foot that required surgery. The years 1992 ($9,260), 1993 ($6,797), and 1994 ($10,191) were not particularly impressive. But in 1995 he won a PBA tournament in Markham, Ontario, Canada, earning $57,270 that year. He did not take part in PBA competition in 1996, but returned in 1997 and earned $12,123.

As of the spring of 1998, Mark Roth had 34 ca-

reer titles and career earnings totaling $1,498,271. In the early 2000s, Roth was bowling in senior pro tournaments, capturing his first senior pro title in Seattle in June 2001.

In 2004, Roth was manager of Florida Lanes in Tampa, Florida. Only two other bowlers, Earl Anthony and Walter Ray Williams Jr., have won more titles than he. When asked in 2004 who was the best bowler in history, Roth rather frankly replied that he was.

In October 2006, Mark Roth won the first Generations Senior Bowling Tour event, averaging 241 over the three-game final. On June 4, 2009, he suffered a stroke, which left him partially paralyzed on the left side. On March 6, 2011, during the Mark Roth Plastic Ball Championship, Roth rolled a ball for television, downing seven pins.

Angelica Rozeanu
World's Greatest Woman Table Tennis Player

ROZEANU, ANGELICA ADELSTEIN (born October 15, 1921, in Bucharest, Romania; died February 21, 2006) Romanian table tennis player. Considered the world's greatest woman table tennis player in history. She captured 17 world titles, including six straight singles titles from 1950 to 1955. She also led Romania to five Corbillon Cup victories. Angelica was the first Romanian woman to win a world title in any sport. She also won the women's doubles crown twice and the mixed doubles crown three times.

● ● ●

At age nine Angelica Adelstein learned how to play table tennis at home in Bucharest on her dining room table. She and her brother Gaston put up a net on the table and he taught her how to play.

Two years later, a YMCA club opened near her house, and there she began to play table tennis with strong male players. By age 15, Angelica was competent enough to win her first important event, the Romanian National Women's Championship in Chernovitz, Romania. She won that title every year thereafter until 1957 (except for the war years 1940 to 1945 when she did not compete).

The year she won her first title, 1936, she met the great Hungarian table tennis star Victor Barna, and decided to copy his backhand drive. Much later, Barna commented to a journalist that he was proud that Angelica's backhand was similar to his, but he was sure she hadn't copied it from him.

Young Angelica was an eager devotee of all sports, including tennis, cycling, and swimming. But, she came to regard table tennis as her favorite, perhaps because she excelled at it.

In 1938, she won her first major international victory, the Hungarian Open in Czegled, Hungary. But the Romanian Government, apparently for anti-Semitic reasons, refused to give her a passport that would have permitted her to participate in the world championships in London that year.

Then, in March 1938, she traveled to the world championships in Cairo. There, she reached the quarterfinals before losing to world champion Vlasta Risova, a Czech. By the time Angelica had returned to Romania, the Nazis had taken control of the country and one of their new anti-Jewish measures was to ban Jews from entering sports centers, effectively preventing Angelica from playing table tennis. She was unable to play throughout the war.

After the war she again began to train, playing with male players to strengthen herself. In 1944, she married fellow Romanian Lou Rozeanu.

In 1948, she played a grueling match at the World Championships in Wembley against Giselle Farkas. Angelica followed a defensive strategy and lost by a shade. Thereafter, she decided to change her tactics from defensive to offensive play and started to practice a surprise attack from both sides. Her strong forehand drive was now complemented by an excellent backhand.

Rozeanu reached her peak comparatively late. In 1950, in Budapest, Hungary, when she won the first of her six straight world singles titles, she was 29 years old. She also helped the Romanian team to victory in the Corbillon Cup (named after Marcel Corbillon, a past president of the French Table Tennis Federation), given to the world's best women's table tennis team.

In 1951, in Vienna, she played even better, repeating her performance and adding the mixed doubles title. In 1952, she won the world singles title in Bombay, India. That year she became Romania's national table tennis coach and held the post until 1958. In 1953 in Bucharest, she won the women's world singles title and helped Romania win another Corbillon Cup.

In 1953, on her first visit to Russia, she helped to popularize table tennis there. She returned in 1955 and 1960.

By this time, Rozeanu could play any match with confidence. Still she was nearly always nervous at the beginning of a match. But, by just playing and concentrating on the game, she became quite calm as the match progressed.

Between 1948 and 1950, Angelica was a sports reporter on the Romanian newspaper *Romania Libera*. She was also president of the Romanian Table Tennis Commission from 1950 to 1960. She was given the highest sports distinction in Romania—the coveted title of "Merited Master of Sport"—in 1954. In addition she has received four "Order of Work" honors from the government. In

1955, she was appointed a deputy of the Bucharest Municipality.

In 1956 Rozeanu played in the women's World Championships in Tokyo, where she was aiming to win an unprecedented seventh straight world title. In a tense and close match which some have called the best in the history of table tennis, Angelica lost to an unknown Japanese player, Kiyoko Tasaka. The score was 21-19, 22-20, and 32-30.

In addition to the 12,000 spectators crowded into the Tokyo Gymnasium, players and umpires who had been engaged in other matches stopped to watch the Rozeanu-Tasaka match. When the score went above 30 in the last game, the count indicator could no longer be used.

Rozeanu, calling the defeat the worst of her career, impressed the Japanese with her performance. One Japanese writer for the *Table Tennis Report Monthly Magazine* noticed the "gorgeous coat and diamond ring she wore with her manicured nails."

In 1958, the post of chairman of the National Table Tennis Federation in Romania was held by a Nazi-oriented Communist. A purge of Jewish table tennis players began. Angelica was banned from playing in international matches. She was accused of engaging in the "cult of personality." When the chairman himself was purged, Angelica returned to favor. In March 1960, she traveled to Russia and won three titles there, in singles, doubles, and mixed doubles.

Rozeanu divorced her husband, Lou, in 1959. In February 1960, he immigrated to Israel, hoping that Angelica and their daughter, Michaela, then 14, would follow. In August of 1960, Angelica and Michaela went to Vienna as tourists, then went directly to Israel. The Romanian government promptly recalled all the honors bestowed on Angelica. Upon arriving in Israel, she moved in with her former husband, who is presently a professor of thermodynamics at the Haifa Technion. Although they were legally divorced, Angelica considered herself and Lou to be husband and wife. They did not feel it necessary to remarry formally, and they lived together until they separated for good in 1969.

In 1961 Angelica won the Maccabiah Games table tennis championship. She continued to win singles and doubles titles in Europe, but it became too expensive for Israel to send her abroad. In 1962 the sports authorities explained the country's difficult economic situation to her, and angry and disappointed, Angelica decided to give up the game. By that time she had won some 100 international titles.

She became a coach for a Tel Aviv sports club, Mercaz Hapoel, but became disillusioned when, rather than serve in the top echelon of table tennis as she had in Romania (she had been a national coach in the 1950s), she was asked to give exhibitions with youngsters in different parts of the country.

In 1964, she was invited to coach the national team but the players made her uncomfortable because she was a woman.

In February 1969, Angelica married Dr. Eliezer Lopacki, a Polish-born psychiatrist who came to Israel in 1950. He died in June 1979. Her daughter, Michaela became an engineer at Elbit computers in Haifa, where Angelica began working in 1969. In 1980, Angelica was chosen as one of the firm's "excellent workers."

In April 1983, she retired from the firm. Since then, she has attended world championships in table tennis in Sweden, Germany and Japan.

In 1995, she became a member of the Table Tennis Hall of Fame.

Throughout her years in retirement, Angelica has attended various world championships in table tennis, the latest being those held in Bratislava, Slovakia, in 1996 and Manchester, England, in 1997.

In 1998, she appeared in the *Guiness Book of World Records*, as she had for many years, for having the greatest number of women's singles world championship victories (six) in table tennis, a feat she accomplished from 1950 to 1955.

A member of the Jewish Sports Hall of Fame in Israel, Angelica Rozeanu died in Haifa on February 21, 2006, following a brief illness. In tribute, Beatrice Romanescu, marketing director for the Romanian Table Tennis Federation, observed: "She was a living legend. I don't know whether Romania will ever have a table tennis player like her."

RUBENSTEIN, LOUIS (born September 23, 1861, in Montreal, Canada; died January 3, 1931) Canadian skater. North America's first famous figure skater. World figure skating champion in 1890; Canadian champion from 1883 to 1889; and American champion in 1888, 1889, and 1891. He was also North American champion in 1885.

. . .

Louis Rubenstein was the son of Polish immigrants to Canada. He won his first figure skating title, the Montreal Championship, in 1878. The following year, in the same competition, he came in third. Realizing that he had such hard training before him if he were going to win more skating titles, he devoted the next four years to rigorous effort on the ice.

In 1883, he won his first Canadian championship. Then, in 1884, and again in 1885, he made a successful tour of the Canadian Maritime Provinces. Rubenstein gave numerous exhibitions of his skating, and when local skaters challenged him to a contest, he won every time.

Rubenstein won his fame at the unofficial world figure skating championship, held in St. Petersburg, Russia, on February 1, 1890. (The first official world championship was not held until 1896.) A sum of $400 was raised to send him to that skating event in Russia.

Arriving in Russia, Louis went from problem to problem. Beginning immediately, a 6-foot Russian policeman followed Louis around wherever he went. (One afternoon, Rubenstein managed to break free of the man by taking a brisk five-mile walk, forcing his ominous shadow, who could not stand the pace, to return to the hotel early to await Louis' return.)

Upon arrival at his hotel that first day, Rubenstein handed in his passport (as was required of all visitors) and heard nothing for a few days. Then he was summoned to the police station where an officer asked if he were Jewish. Rubenstein replied in the affirmative, and was told he would soon get his passport back. But he did not.

Two days later, while practicing, he was again summoned to the police station. When he asked for his passport, he was taken to another police office. There he was instructed to leave St. Petersburg within 24 hours. "You are a Jew," the officer declared, "and there is no necessity to further discuss the matter. We cannot permit Jews to stay in St. Petersburg."

Rubenstein, aghast at the Russian's behavior, appealed to the British ambassador, Sir R. Morier, who expressed sympathy for Rubenstein and anger at the Russians. Morier assured Rubenstein he would be able to participate in the championships if the ambassador had anything to say about it.

The following morning, roused out of bed, Rubenstein had to appear before a prefect of police. He was informed that, due to the British ambassador's intervention, he would be allowed to stay until the championship was over, but he would have to leave immediately after that. When his passport was returned, he noticed that the words "British subject" had been crossed out and in their place was "L. Rubenstein, Jew; must leave St. Petersburg by the 10th February." The British envoy told Rubenstein that "foreign Hebrews" were not popular in Russia and he doubted that Louis would have a fair chance in the championship.

Rubenstein was a master at figure skating: he could repeat a routine on the ice three or four times without blurring the original outline of the pattern. His figures were considered elegant and graceful.

The competition consisted of three events: the execution of nine compulsory figures, five figures selected by the skater, and a 10-minute freestyle performance. Only two of the nine judges were familiar with figure skating: after watching him at practice, they would offer advice to the local skaters based on what they had learned from the Canadian. Though the judges may have been partial to their own native skaters, they clearly had admiration for Louis' skills—even before he began the competition.

Rubenstein went on to defeat his competitors in St. Petersburg. The judges would have liked nothing better than to deny him first prize because he was Jewish. But, since he dominated the field, they had little choice. Louis' conviction that he was, as he put it, "the only dangerous person in St. Petersburg," was eased somewhat after the competition, because he knew that he would soon leave Russia. Although the Canadian skater's treatment in St. Petersburg actually came up for discussion in the Canadian Parliament shortly thereafter, nothing concrete was done about the matter. Never again would Rubenstein experience the slightest anti-Semitism; the Russian instance was unique in his career.

After tying for first place in the American championships in 1891, Rubenstein retired from competitive skating.

Louis Rubenstein continued to be involved in sports in a variety of ways. At one time or another, he was president of different Canadian organizations involved with bowling, skating, tobogganing, bicycling, and curling. He was a great bowler, averaging 173.4 in 129 bowling games between 1892 and 1900. *The Montreal Star*, in an article on

February 6, 1895, wrote of his presidency of the Canadian Bowling Association and called him the "Father of Bowling in Canada."

It was the family business—Rubenstein Brothers Silver, Gold and Nickel Platers and Manufacturers—which made it possible, because of its success, for Louis to spend so much time in sports. The fact that Louis was a bachelor was another reason why he had so much free time. He was elected Montreal City Alderman in 1914 and held that post until his death in 1931. Louis was elected to the Canadian Hall of Fame and the Jewish Sports Hall of Fame in Israel.

Abraham "Abe" Saperstein

Founder, Coach, and Owner of the Harlem Globetrotters

SAPERSTEIN, ABRAHAM M. (born July 4, 1903, in London, England; died March 15, 1966) Founder, coach, and owner of the world-famous Harlem Globetrotters, a famous comedy basketball group. The Globetrotters developed a new, zany style of playing the game, becoming the busiest, funniest, and most remarkable basketball team in the world. Saperstein made basketball truly international through them.

. . .

At the age of five, Saperstein came to the United States from England with his nine brothers and sisters. He grew up in a rough Irish neighborhood in Chicago, graduating from Lakeview High School in 1919. After playing semi-professional baseball for a while, he drifted into pro basketball, although he was only 5 feet, 5 inches tall. He earned $5 per game.

In 1927, Saperstein took over an all-Negro American Legion basketball team called the Savoy Big Five, named for Chicago's Savoy Ballroom. He changed the team's name to the Harlem Globetrotters. Then, piling his five players into a battered Model-T Ford bought from a funeral director, he took the team on the road. They played their first game on January 7, 1927, in Hinckley, Illinois, and earned the impressive sum of $75.

Saperstein was once asked how he came to use the name Harlem Globetrotters. "We chose Harlem," he said, "because, well, because Harlem was to the fellows what Jerusalem is to us. And Globetrotters? Well, we had dreams. We hoped to

travel. We made it, all right. We made it all the way to Israel, as a matter of fact."

Saperstein not only owned the team, but was its coach, chauffeur, trainer and physician. At times he was its only substitute player. He was often described as a roly-poly dynamo and was nicknamed "Little Caesar."

Unmatched as a coach, he was also unmatched as an impresario. As a result of his guidance, the Globetrotters became a team that performed basketball magic on the court. Every game in which they participated was like a circus. The five players were talented clowns whose handling of the ball was sheer magic. They gave the audience much to marvel at and laugh about at the same time.

"Laugh standards are the same all over the world," Saperstein once declared, "and that is our playing area. Wars, depressions, chaos, and one crisis after another are common place all around the world. Our fans, and there are millions of them, are looking for an escape from worry and tension when they come out to see us play and we never want to fail them."

The Globetrotters' first tour, in 1927, was a huge

success. They wound up with a 101-6 record. The following year, their record was 145-13, and two years later it was 151-13. So good were the Globetrotters that finding opponents became a problem. It was then that Saperstein introduced the fancy, razzle-dazzle type of play which livened up the show, and for which the team became known.

It was only in 1940, 13 years after they began playing, that the Globetrotters started making money. "We never missed a meal," recalled Saperstein, "but we sure postponed a lot of them." The team traveled through blizzards and tornadoes, on dog sled, in jalopies, and in horse-drawn wagons. By 1950, the Globetrotters were so famous the world over, that Saperstein had to split them into two touring squads. During the winter of 1958-59, the teams posted a startling 411-0 record.

When critics began saying that the Globetrotters were capable only of clowning, Saperstein organized a series of games against college all-stars.

The Globetrotters won the series 11-7.

The team traveled to 87 countries. The players—including such famous ones as Reece (Goose) Tatum and Marques Haynes—always gave the impression that they were not too serious about the game. But they really were. They were there to entertain and they did that well. Pope Pius XII said after an exhibition: "These young men are certainly very clever."

Go, Man, Go, a movie about Saperstein and the Globetrotters, was released in 1954, with Dane Clark playing the Globetrotters' founder. From 1927 to 1967 the Globetrotters played before five million fans, including 75,000 on one occasion in Berlin in 1951. The team won the world title in 1940 and the International Cup in 1943-44.

In the years before his death, Abe Saperstein took on new business ventures, but with little success. He sought franchises in Los Angeles and San Francisco to be part of the National Basketball Association, but was refused. So, in 1961, he formed his own loop, the American Basketball League.

Saperstein not only owned the Chicago team in the league, but served as league commissioner as well. The league, however, folded after only 18 months, with Saperstein and other club owners suffering major financial losses.

Saperstein died of a heart attack while in Weiss Memorial Hospital, in Chicago, Illinois. He had hoped to live to see the 50th anniversary of the Harlem Globetrotters, but he died 11 years too soon.

Abraham Saperstein is a member of the Jewish Sports Hall of Fame in Israel.

Richard "Dick" Savitt

The Only Jew Ever to Win the Wimbledon Singles Event

SAVITT, RICHARD (born March 4, 1927, in Bayonne, New Jersey–) American tennis player. The first Jewish tennis player of impressive stature. He warranted a *Time* magazine cover story (on August 27, 1951). He was ranked in the top 10 between 1950 and 1952 and No. 3 in 1957. He was Wimbledon singles champion in 1951, the only Jew ever to win the Wimbledon Singles Event.

. . .

Savitt was an only child in a middle-class family, whose father was the owner of a food brokerage firm. As a boy, Dick was interested in football, baseball, basketball—but not tennis. At age 13 he began playing and ball-boying at the Berkeley Tennis club in Orange, New Jersey, where he watched some of the tennis greats like Bobby Riggs and Jack Kramer.

Dick began playing the game seriously at age 13, and in the summer of 1941, he won a local junior tournament in Maplewood, New Jersey. In 1944, his family moved to El Paso, Texas because of his mother's poor health.

At El Paso High School Dick was a forward on the basketball team in his senior year. He was also Texas State tennis champion and No. 4 in the national under-18 (junior) group. He was on the second-team, All-State basketball team as well.

After graduating from high school in 1945, he served for one year in the U.S. Navy and was stationed at the Naval Air station in Memphis, Tennessee. He played on the third-ranking armed forces basketball team in the winter of 1945-46.

In 1946, Savitt enrolled at Cornell, but an injured knee in his first year forced him to concentrate on tennis, rather than basketball. Savitt played tennis in an old armory in Ithaca, New York, with ROTC tanks roaring in the background. In 1947 and 1948, Dick was ranked twenty-sixth in the country in tennis.

In 1949 he won the Eastern Intercollegiate Tennis Tournament held in Syracuse, New York. He was ranked 16th nationally that year. In 1950, Savitt won several tournaments in the U.S., was ranked sixth in the country, and reached the semifinals of the U.S. Nationals at Forest Hills.

In 1951 Savitt monopolized the headlines of the tennis world. His play was described as "aggressive, nervous, often impatient, and always overpowering." He defeated Australia's great Frank Sedgman in five sets and Ken MacGregor in four sets on successive days to win the Australian championship in January. Savitt was the first foreigner to win the Australia championship since

Don Budge of the United States scored his grand slam in 1938.

In July 1951, Savitt won the men's singles at Wimbledon, defeating Herb Flam in the semifinals and Ken MacGregor in the finals. *The New York Times* called Savitt the "world's number one amateur player." He did not turn pro because at that time the pro circuit was limited to a few barnstormers.

Standing 6 foot 3 and weighing 185 pounds (and slightly round-shouldered), Savitt was considered then the greatest backcourt player in the world. It was his simple, overpowering attack, smashing serve, and deep, hard-hit ground strokes that kept his opponents scrambling in the backcourt, always on the defensive. His deep-set eyes were unsmiling and intent as he concentrated on his opponents.

Had it not been for a leg infection in September 1951, he might well have added the U.S. National title at Forest Hills to his collection of victories. He lost to Vic Seixas in the semifinals.

Savitt was chosen as a member of the Davis Cup team in 1951, but after winning in the early rounds of the competition, he was bypassed and did not play in the challenge round in December. The Australians took the Davis Cup that year, and many felt that the U.S. would have won had Savitt played. Some believed that anti-Semitism was the main reason for Savitt's not playing, but he himself doubted this. Actually, when Savitt and Herb Flam made the Davis Cup squad in 1951, it marked the first time that Jewish players had accomplished this.

In February, 1952, Savitt won the National Indoor Singles title. In October of that year he announced his retirement from big-time competitive tennis in order, as he put it then, "to go to work." Some thought that Savitt had retired because he was snubbed in the Davis Cup competition of 1951. But Savitt's explanation seemed more realistic. After all, tennis in the early 1950s had few of the rewards of later years when top players made large sums of money, and it was reasonable that a

young man like Savitt would decide to devote his time to the business world where money could be made. After October 1952, Savitt never returned to full-time tennis.

Dick Savitt's first full-time job was with an oil company, Texfel Petroleum of Dallas, Texas. Instead of accepting an executive job at the top, for the first two years he roamed the oil fields of Louisiana and Texas, working on an oil rig. After that, he took an administrative job, handling leasing arrangements for oil exploration. Then, in 1957, he was appointed office manager of Texfel Petroleum in New York.

Savitt continued to play tennis, but in a much more limited way. In 1957 he won the Eastern Grass Tournament in Orange, New Jersey. In 1958 he won the Men's Indoor singles title, defeating Budge Patty in the final, and losing his only set of the tournament in that final match. Savitt won other tournaments that year in Atlanta, River

Oaks, and Tulsa. He was called the "mightiest hitter in amateur tennis" (in the official U.S. Lawn Tennis Association Yearbook). In 1961 he traveled to Israel where he won the Maccabiah singles and doubles.

Savitt started playing father-son doubles tournaments in 1976 with his son Robert. In 1981, when Dick was asked about his greatest moment in tennis, he replied: "Winning the National Father and Son Championships this summer [1981] was number one. Number two was winning Wimbledon."

Savitt is a stockbroker in New York. He spent many years helping to organize the tennis program at the Israel Tennis Centers where he taught coaches and youngsters. He continues to visit Israel twice a year in support of the country's tennis program for youngsters.

Richard Savitt is a member of the Jewish Sports Hall of Fame in Israel.

Adolph Schayes
The First Modern Basketball Forward

SCHAYES, ADOLPH "DOLPH" (born May 19, 1928, in New York City, New York–) American basketball player. Schayes played for the Syracuse Nationals from 1949 to 1963. When he retired, he had scored more points (19,249) than any player in the game. He was voted to the All-National Basketball Association team 12 times.

. . .

Dolph Schayes inherited both his love for sports and his height (6 feet, 8 inches) from his father, a Romanian Jew, who was an avid sports fan and 6 feet, 4 inches tall. Dolph played basketball throughout junior high school, high school, and college in his native Bronx. At age 16, he entered New York University.

Schayes became known as a good, hard-working college player, but his coach doubted he had the physique to make it as a pro. When he graduated in 1948, he had collected All-American honors and the Haggerty award as the best player in the New York metropolitan area.

The New York Knicks nearly succeeded in signing Schayes, but Knick president Ned Irish offered him $1,000 less than Syracuse and so, in 1948, Dolph decided to sign with the Syracuse Nationals. The Nats moved all 6 feet, 8 inches and 220 pounds of him from center to forward. He became the first modern basketball forward: big, fast, mobile. His long-range, two-handed set shots and driving lay-ups were almost impossible to stop

without fouling. His foul-shooting was as excellent as was his rebounding. And he was often his team's assist leader.

Schayes was named Rookie of the Year in 1949. He personified the spirit of the Nats; each time he scored a basket he would run to the opposite end of the court, fist clenched triumphantly above his head.

From February 17, 1952 until December 27, 1961, he played in 764 straight games, including playoffs. In 1957 he broke Minneapolis Laker George Mikan's career point total of 11,764. Schayes scored his 19,000th point in 1963. He won the rebounding title in 1951 and wound up in fourth place on the all-time rebounding list at his retirement. His record for the most free throws made (6,979) stood until 1972.

Schayes would not budge from the lineup even when injured. In 1952 he broke his right wrist, and a cast was put on, but he could not be kept off the court. "The cast made me work on my left-handed shots, which soon improved." Dolph was one of the few people who look upon a fracture as a blessing in disguise.

The Nats won only one world championship with Schayes (in 1955), but they were always in the playoffs. In 1964, the Nats left Syracuse to become the Philadelphia 76ers, and that same year Dolph became their head coach. In his first two seasons, the team was in third place in the Eastern Division. But it won the title for the 1965-66 season. Schayes was named NBA Coach of the Year for leading the 76ers to that title, but he was fired the next year after his team failed to retain the title. (Boston defeated the 76ers in the playoff semifinals.)

From 1966 to 1970, Dolph served as supervisor of NBA referees. In 1970, he was back coaching a new NBA franchise, the Buffalo Braves. But after the opening game of the second season (1971-72), he was dismissed, primarily for not disciplining his players enough.

Schayes felt that being Jewish had little or no effect on his basketball career. "There never was any hint of anti-Semitism in pro basketball," he wrote. "Since many of the fans in the large metropolitan area were Jewish in the early days of the NBA, I was fairly well received."

In 1977, Schayes became head coach of the U.S. Maccabiah Games basketball team. With the help of his 6 foot, 11 inch son, Dan, the U.S. team upset the Israelis, 92-91, in the championship game.

He lives in Syracuse, New York and is in the apartment management business.

He was involved in the World Maccabi Games in 1989 as a co-director of the masters (35 years and over) basketball team. In 1991, he coached a masters team in Montevideo, Uruguay, during the Pan Am Maccabi Games.

Dolph Schayes was voted by the NBA one of its top 50 players during its first 50 years; David Stern, NBA Commissioner, made the announcement on October 30, 1996.

Dolph Schayes is a member of the Basketball Hall of Fame and the Jewish Sports Hall of Fame in Israel.

Dan Schayes

Great NBA Star of the '80s and '90s

SCHAYES, DAN (born May 10, 1959, in Syracuse, New York–) American basketball player. He played for Syracuse University from 1978-81, averaging 14.6 points per game in his senior year. In his first ten NBA seasons (1981 to 1991), he averaged 9.5 points per game. He is the son of former NBA star Dolph Schayes.

• • •

Danny Schayes was four years old when his father Dolph, an early superstar of the NBA, retired from basketball. The son recalls nothing of his Dad's remarkable career. Though Dolph did not insist that his son take up the game, Danny "grew" into it: 6 feet, 11 inches, and 235 pounds, the youngster was a natural for the court. He had the added advantage of learning fundamentals at home—from Dolph Schayes! "It was hard not to enjoy the game," recalled Danny.

He became a star basketball player at Jamesville-DeWitt High School near Syracuse, New York. But when the time came to decide on a college, father and son disagreed. Dolph wanted Danny to avoid nearby Syracuse University which already had an impressive starting center, Roosevelt Boule, then only a sophomore. Dolph was concerned that Danny would not get to play much. Danny, however, liked Syracuse, and decided to enroll there. In the summer of 1977, at age 18, Danny played on the victorious American team at the Maccabiah Games in Israel. He admitted that "It helped that my dad was the coach." (He played again on the 1981 team.)

Danny entered Syracuse in the fall of 1977. During his first three years at Syracuse, Dolph's fear proved all too true: While Roosevelt Boule grabbed the headlines, Danny spent most of the time on the bench as a backup center and forward. He averaged six points and four rebounds a game.

It was no wonder he gave little thought to a pro basketball career. Graduate school in chemistry or medical school were his preferences. Dolph, however, had faith that Danny could reach the NBA. "When Danny plays with four other players, the four others get better," said Dolph. "He has the ability to pass and be at the right place at the right time."

With Boule no longer at Syracuse after the spring of 1980, Danny Schayes came into his own. In the 1980-81 season, his senior year, he averaged 14.6 points per game, with a college-high 284 rebounds. Even with his star status, Danny found it difficult to slip out from under the shadow of his famous father. And not without reason. When Syracuse lost to Villanova in Philadelphia 88-78 on February 17, 1981, Dolph, sitting in the stands, was incensed by a series of questionable calls, including a key goaltending ruling against Danny. He marched down to the court after the final buzzer to protest the officiating.

"Older people think of me as Dolph Jr.," said a perplexed Danny Schayes on January 30, 1981. "But they're the people who aren't fans of what I do or fans of the team. It's getting to the point where I'm a college senior in a national program, and it's what *I* do that counts."

Danny's senior year at college turned him into NBA material. He was drafted in the first round by the Utah Jazz. Playing in 82 games during his rookie 1981–82 season, Danny averaged 7.9 points per game. Known for the accuracy of his jump shot, he scored 544 points and captured 427 rebounds.

Two years into his NBA career, Danny was traded to Denver for veteran center Rich Kelley. At Denver in 1985, he became a starting center, replacing Nugget hero Dan Issel. In time, he gained a reputation as a respected center.

Both Dolph and Danny Schayes take pride in their Jewish identities. Dolph had several Jewish contemporaries in the NBA. But since 1986, when former Knick Ernie Grunfeld stopped playing in the league, Danny has been the only Jew on an NBA roster. Asked why that was the case, Danny replied that it was probably due to so many Jews being too short for professional basketball. Dolph speaks of Danny as a good Jew. "The fans know he's Jewish," says Dolph, "and Danny tries to play well so they will be proud of him."

Does he feel under pressure, being the only Jewish NBA player?

"There's no pressure on me," Danny noted. "I just try to play the game and have fun. I don't think anyone is expecting me to do something I'm not capable of. I like the letters I get from fans across the country. Every game, there's people cheering for me, and I appreciate that. Believe me, I see the people waving *yarmulkes* at me from the stand all the time, and I smile, and understand."

As of the 1987–88 season, Danny had been playing eight years in the NBA. That season he reached his career high in points per game (13.9), rebounds per game (8.2) and shooting percentage per game (.540). He averaged 16.4 points per game in the playoffs.

That led to his signing a six-year $8.7 million contract—an impressive accomplishment given the fact that he had averaged 8.9 points per game for his career up to that time. The following season (1988–89), he averaged 12.8 points and a 6.6 rebound per game.

Known as a good jumper, he drills 20-footers in with ease. Cutting to the basket on fast breaks, he often gets fouled.

In 53 games for the Nuggets in the 1989-90 season Danny Schayes averaged 10.4 points and 6.4 rebounds per game, making 49 percent of his field-goal attempts and 85 percent of his free throws.

He was traded for the second time in 1990, this time going to the Milwaukee Bucks. Milwaukee Bucks head coach Del Harris said of Schayes: "Dan Schayes has been a major part of our team, and without him, we probably wouldn't have made the playoffs. I plan to have him as our center in the years ahead." More praise came from Philadelphia 76ers head coach Jim Lyman: "He's a hard-nosed player who can score inside and outside, a real team player."

In his first 10 years in the NBA—from 1981 to 1991—Dan Schayes averaged 9.5 points per game.

He played for the Milwaukee Bucks until 1993, spent a brief time with the Los Angeles Lakers, and then signed with the Phoenix Suns for the 1994-95 season, averaging 4.4 points and 3 rebounds for the Suns. In December 1995, he signed with the Miami Heat, providing injury relief and backup support for the Heat's star Alonzo Mourning. He averaged 3.2 points and 2.8 rebounds in 32 games.

In the late 1990s, Dan Schayes played with the Orlando Magic and the Minnesota Timberwolves. When he signed to play with the Timberwolves in October 1999, he was one of only six players to have spent at least 18 seasons in the NBA, all-time leader Robert Parish having played 21 years.

Schayes was inducted into the New York Jewish Sports Hall of Fame in March 1998. In December 2001, he became a special consultant to the Continental League's Brevard Blue Ducks.

Jody Scheckter
World Racing-Car Champion

SCHECKTER, JODY (born January 29, 1950, in East London, South Africa–) World driving champion. The first South African to win the world championship, Scheckter has been called one of South Africa's greatest sports figures.

. . .

Scheckter's paternal grandfather moved the family from Russia to South Africa. Jody began racing go-carts at age 10. Jody's father owned a garage which Jody worked in, in East London, South Africa, which introduced the youngster to the taste of the auto world. Jody raced stock cars between 1968 and 1970 with great success on the local tracks.

South African stock-car racing had its wild side with no holds barred. Drivers did not hesitate to bump into each other and at times pushed their colleagues off the track.

After defeating all his opponents in South Africa, he won a "driver to Europe" grant. He raced in Europe from 1970 to 1972, progressing to Formula Ford and Formula Two racing. His aggressive driving style, in which he would continuously hog the road, irritated other drivers.

One of his best years was 1972. He was named Motoring Sportsman of the Year in South Africa and awarded his nation's highest sports honor, the Springbok colors. One year later he was voted the Jewish South African Sportsman of the Year and also won the American Formula 5000 championship.

Scheckter's flamboyant style was most distinctive. He seemed to be driving sideways almost as much as he drove forward. Scheckter felt that his background in stock-car racing contributed to this impression since the stock or saloon cars do move more sideways. The flag stewards tended to retreat when Scheckter came through a corner and, coming out of the turn, Jody seemed to regain control of the car only at the last split second.

Scheckter, according to *The New York Times*, does not steer a car into a corner, rather he flings it at a target. Having no experience with accidents, he is considered fearless. Being hungry and ambitious, he drives at "ten-tenths of effort."

Scheckter enjoyed racing but found the commercialism troubling. By 1974 his flamboyant driving style was slightly tamed as he joined the Formula One circuit, winning the British and Swedish Grand Prix. The British Guild of Motoring writers named him Driver of the Year, and that year he placed third in the world championship.

The following year was less successful, though Scheckter did win the South African Grand Prix as 100,000 fans cheered him on. A year later he won the Swedish Grand Prix again and came in third in the world championship.

In 1977, Scheckter recorded triumphs in Argentina, Monaco, and Canada, and was runner-up in the world championship. Once again he was chosen South African Jewish Sportsman of the Year. The year 1978 was not terribly successful for Jody, but in 1979 he won in Belgium, Monaco, and Italy, and became the first South African to win the world title.

Scheckter increasingly felt the pressures and dangers of motor-car racing and in 1980, at the age of 30, he quit. He admitted that if he had been a tennis star, he would have continued for another year to earn the additional money. "But," he noted, "motor racing is not like that. You can't go out there with all the dangers and do the job just for the money." He moved to the United States where he became a very successful businessman. He was admitted into the Jewish Sports Hall of Fame in the spring of 1983.

In 1999, then living in London, Scheckter devoted himself to overseeing the racing career of his two sons. He since became interested in organic farming, a passion he pursues today at his Laverstoke Park farm, located forty miles west of London.

Mathieu Schneider
National Hockey League Star

SCHNEIDER, MATHIEU (born June 12, 1969, in New York City–) American ice hockey player. He was drafted by the Montreal Canadiens in June 1987. One of only five Jewish players in the National Hockey League, he played his first full season for the Montreal Canadiens in 1989-90 and has developed into one of the finest defensive players in the NHL.

• • •

Mathieu grew up in Toms River, New Jersey. Because his mother had a French Canadian background, the boy's father Sam thought it appropriate that his son take up hockey. So he bought Mathieu his first pair of skates and took him to the Rockefeller Center ice skating rink. The boy was only three years old!

"My Dad liked hockey," Mathieu recalled, "because size was never a factor. If didn't matter if you were 5 foot 10, but for football you had to be 6 feet or taller, and weigh over 200 pounds." Serving as his coach while Mathieu was growing up, Sam was not satisfied with the hockey instruction available in New Jersey, where the family lived in the late 70s. So the father began his own hockey school. Another pupil was Mathieu's brother Jean Alain. Mathieu set his goals high: "It became my dream to become a pro hockey player." Both he and Jean Alain succeeded. Mathieu's brother is a forward for the Cornwall Royals of the Ontario Junior Hockey League.

When Mathieu was 12 the Schneiders moved to Rhode Island where he attended a Catholic school, Mount Saint-Charles Academy. Mathieu's French Canadian mother Aline converted to Judaism from Catholicism when she married. "I am a proud Jew and I will bring up my kids to be proud Jews," Mathieu Schneider said emphatically.

Mathieu played defense even as a youngster. "My father thought you could learn the game better from defense. It's more of a thinking position than playing wing. You get to see a whole play develop in front of you. You're more of a quarterback playing defense. You start the play, breaking out of your end. The main thing, of course, in playing defense is to keep the other team from scoring."

Schneider left the Academy after 11th grade and, at age 17, began playing for Cornwall, scoring 36 points in 63 games. He had just completed his first season at Cornwall when he received a big boost to his career. Less than 24 hours after Schneider turned 18 he showed up at the Joe Louis Arena in Detroit on June 13, 1987 and heard the Montreal Canadiens announce his name. He was Montreal's fourth choice in the 1987 draft. "Being drafted by an organization like the Canadiens was a dream come true for me," said Mathieu.

After a four-game tryout with the Canadiens, Mathieu returned to his junior club. His continued steady play gained him a spot on the first all-star team. When the Cornwall Royals season ended, Schneider joined the Sherbrooke Canadiens (the Montreal affiliate in the American Hockey League) for the playoffs. After a strong 1989 season with Sherbrooke, he was called up to play for the Canadiens in the National Hockey League where, as an NHL rookie, he exhibited solid offensive and defensive skills.

The Canadiens had large expectations for Mathieu on the backline. During the summer of 1990 they traded away an all-star defenseman, Chris Chelios, in return for forward Dennis Savard, "Following the trade, a lot of people expected me to step into Chris's skates right away," Mathieu said. "I kept saying all summer that the reason they traded Chris was because we had done well as a unit, not because I was there." Mathieu did not want to be judged as a replacement for Chelios, but rather as someone who had contributed to the team.

Mathieu Schneider is one of five Jews on the roster of the National Hockey League's 26 teams.

The others are Ron Stern (Calgary Flames), David Nemirovsky (Florida Panthers), Steve Dubinsky (Chicago Blackhawks) and Doug Friedman (Edmonton Oilers).

In the spring of 1991, during a game between the Canadiens and Buffalo Sabres, one of the Sabres uttered some abusive words at Schneider. The word "Jew" was among them. "That was the first time I heard any of that stuff," said Mathieu. "I made a mental note that the next time I had a chance, I would run the guy into the sideboards. And I did. What he said to me you wouldn't say to anyone. I still take whacks at him." No wonder that Schneider, a tough defenseman, spends a lot of time in the penalty box.

That incident intensified Schneider's Jewish consciousness as well as his assertiveness. It was reported by the *Montreal Gazette,* the local daily, and picked up by other American and Canadian newspapers. "I'm sure a lot of people realized I'm Jewish through that, " said Schneider. He felt the press exaggerated the incident. "Prejudice is a part of life," Mathieu philosophized. "It is just something we have to deal with in our own way. Since that incident no one has said anything to me."

Schneider shrugs off the verbal give and take of the game: "If somebody can get you to take a penalty by calling you names on the ice, he's doing his job. I think it's just something that goes with the sport. People say things sometimes during the heat of a game and you have to take it with a grain of salt."

A bit small for hockey, Schneider tries to compensate by being aggressive. "Aggressive is being physical, getting good hits, finishing checks," he explains. "There's no way I'm gonna beat up guys out there. I'm not gonna push guys around. I have to finish my checks and be

strong in front of the net and in the corners. If I go out and I don't get a good hit early in the game, I can pull through a period and get by. But along comes the second period and all of a sudden . . . Bing! Bang! . . . there's a couple of goals. You have to be awake and aware all the time and be physical."

Schneider turned into Montreal's best defenseman and starred when the team won the National Hockey League Championship Stanley Cup in 1993. In 1994, he led Montreal's defense in scoring

and set career highs in goals scored, assists, and total points. He scored five goals in the strike-shortened season.

On April 6, 1995, Matt was traded to the New York Islanders. A year later he was chosen to play in the NHL's All-Star game. That same year he was traded to the Toronto Maple Leafs, and was a star on the U.S. team that won the World Cup.

In February 1998, the United States, for the first time, sent its best professional ice hockey players to the Winter Olympics, played this time in Nagano, Japan. Matt was named to the team of NHL stars representing the United States. The U.S. team, however, was eliminated by the Czechs in the quarterfinals.

Matt was earning, as of the spring of 1998, $2.5 million a year. Mike Murphy, Matt's Maple Leafs coach, called him the best player on the team.

After playing for several NHL teams in the late 1990s and early 2000s, in March 2003 Matt was acquired by the Detroit Red Wings. During the 2003–2004 season, he scored four game-winning goals, a career best, and played in all twelve of Detroit's 2004 playoff games. He played three more seasons with the Red Wings, scoring a career-high 21 goals and 59 points in 2005–2006. He then signed with the Anaheim Ducks, with whom he tallied 39 points in 65 games.

On September 26, 2008, the Ducks traded Schneider to the Atlanta Thrashers, and in February 2009 he was traded back to the Montreal Canadiens. In August 2009, the Vancouver Canucks signed Schneider to a one-year $1.5 million contract.

On March 3, 2010, Schneider was traded from the Vancouver Canucks to the Phoenix Coyotes. At the end of 2010, Schneider decided to hang up his skates and enjoy retirement.

Barney Sedran

The Best "Little Man" to Play Basketball

SEDRAN, BARNEY (born January 28, 1891, in New York City; died January 14, 1969) American basketball player. One of the best of the early pro basketball players. He and Max Friedman were known as the "Heavenly Twins." Nat Holman called Barney the best "little man" to play the game.

. . .

Barney was born on the East Side of New York to Russian immigrant parents who changed their name from Sedransky to Sedran. Since there were few baseball diamonds on the East Side, Barney, like other youngsters of the neighborhood, turned to basketball. He usually played with his four brothers.

Barney attended DeWitt Clinton High School but, at 5 foot 4 inches and 118 pounds, he was not even given a tryout for the basketball team. He went on to City College, leading the basketball team there in scoring for three years, but it was only when he became a professional that his talent for the game really was noticed.

Barney Sedran was the smallest man in pro basketball, but he learned to move quickly and used the technique of feinting to avoid larger players. He often played every night of the week in three different leagues, a common practice at the time. In those years there were no backboards in basketball. Nonetheless, during the 1913–14 season, when Sedran was playing for Utica, New York, against Cohoes, New York, he managed to score 17 fields goals from the 25-30-foot range, an all-time record.

Sedran helped to form the New York Whirlwinds in 1920, considered one of the best basketball teams of all time. Nat Holman and Max "Marty" Friedman were on the same team.

A major basketball event of those years was a scheduled three-game series between the Whirlwinds and the original Celtics in New York. The first game of the series was played on April 11, 1921, and Sedran's Whirlwinds won 40-24. The five goals Barney scored made him

the game's high-scorer. Three days later, the Celtics won 26-24. The third game was not played because two Whirlwind players, Nat Holman and Chris Leonard, bolted to the Celtics, which in effect marked the end of the Whirlwinds as a team. (Pro basketball, in those days was much more fluid than today.) Barney played on 10 championship teams in 15 seasons as a pro player. He then coached such teams as Kate Smith's Celtics, and the Brooklyn Jewels.

When Barney's playing days were over he went into the garage business with Max Friedman.

Barney Sedran was elected to the Basketball Hall of Fame in 1962 and to the Jewish Sports Hall of Fame in Israel in 1989.

Al Singer

The 1930 World Lightweight Champion

SINGER, AL "The Bronx Beauty" (born September 6, 1907, in New York City; died April 20, 1961) American boxer. He was world lightweight champion in 1930. His career record: 70 fights of which he won 60 (24 by knockout), lost 8, and had 2 draws.

. . .

Al was born on Broome Street in the heart of New York's Lower East Side. His family was Orthodox and middle class. His parents moved to the Bronx when he was quite young.

As a child Al was apprenticed to a diamond cutter. Despite the opposition of his parents, he took up boxing and had a successful career as an amateur before turning pro at age 19.

Singer went from total obscurity in the boxing world in 1927 to lightweight champion just three years later. For his first pro fight in 1927 he received $75.

In 1928 Al fought the former featherweight champion Tony Canzoneri and held him to a draw. It was Al's 35th pro fight. Jimmy Dawson of *The New York Times* called Singer the new Benny Leonard. A handsome man, Singer was nicknamed "The Bronx Beauty."

On July 17, 1930, more than 35,000 fans crowded into Yankee Stadium in the Bronx to watch the lightweight title fight between Singer and Sammy Mandell. Singer was 21 and had only three years of professional fights behind him. Still, he had lost only five of the 56 bouts he had fought. Mandell was 26, had been a pro for 10 years, and had the crown four years earlier from "Rocky" Kansas. The scheduled 15-round match was only 1:46 into the first round when Singer drove a hard left hook into Mandell's jaw that sent him to the canvas. Mandell was knocked out and Singer won the title.

Singer's reign as titleholder was the shortest in history to that date. He lost the title to Tony Canzoneri when the two fought on November 14, 1930, just three months and 28 days after the Mandell bout. Canzoneri scored a 66-second knockout in the first round.

Al Singer fought very little after that, retiring in 1931. He then went into the women's wear business. In 1935 he tried to make a comeback. However, by the end of that year he put down his boxing gloves for good. He had what is known in boxing as a "glass jaw," a problem that afflicts some boxers. A solid blow to the jaw affects their nervous system and results in a knockout.

During World War II, Al served in the army. Later, he owned several nightclubs, worked in New York's garment district, and sold mutual funds. For a time he was a judge for the New York State Athletic Commission.

Al Singer was inducted into the International Jewish Sports Hall of Fame in 2006.

Harold Solomon

Greatest Jewish Tennis Player of the 1970s and 1980s

SOLOMON, HAROLD (born September 17, 1952, in Washington, D.C.–) American tennis player. Ranked No. 15 in 1974, he rose to No. 5 in 1980. In 1981, he slipped to 22nd. Solomon was the greatest Jewish tennis player of the 1970s and early 1980s. Known as the "human backboard" due to his patient baseline game and unmatched ability to keep the ball in play.

. . .

Harold grew up in Silver Spring, Maryland. He comes from a tennis-conscious family, and has played the game since the age of five. Harold's father, businessman Leonard Solomon, built a tennis court in the backyard of the family home. For Harold, tennis provided a way of establishing a personal identity. "When I was a young kid," he once said, "I used to lie awake at night thinking about dying without anyone ever knowing I existed. I think now maybe people would know I lived."

It was in college that people started noticing Harold Solomon. He enrolled at Rice University in Houston, Texas, during the fall of 1970 and became a political science major. (By 1975, he had completed three years of college, but decided to discontinue his studies in favor of becoming a full-time professional tennis player.) In 1970 Harold won the Interscholastic Singles title as well as the Clay Court singles championship. In 1971, he was the top-rated player on a Rice team which won the Southwest Conference tennis title. Solomon made the All American tennis teams in 1971 and 1973.

The year 1971 was a good one for Solomon. He played in 18 tournaments, winning seven of them.

Out of a total of 60 matches, he lost only 11. He won the U.S. Amateur Clay Court singles but for the most part did not play in major tournaments. Unranked until 1971, he rose to No. 10 in the American amateur rankings that year, a rise more dramatic than any other player's.

In the spring of 1972, at the end of his sophomore year in college, Solomon turned pro. He achieved a rank of sixth in the American rankings that year. In July 1974, he won his first big pro tournament beating Guillermo Vilas in the finals of the Washington Star International tournament. In the 1974 French Open he was a semifinalist.

Two of Solomon's greatest successes came in 1975 and 1976 when he won the South African Open. Through most of the 1970s Harold played for the American Davis Cup squad (from 1972 to 1975 and from 1976 to 1978). He won the Tournament of Champions in 1977.

Solomon's slow, methodical style of play has left opponents frustrated, and, at times, angry. Ilie Nastase, the great tennis star of the 1970s, noted that Solomon hits so many balls "you are tired in [the] head, tired in [the] legs . . . tired." And Dick Stockton, another tennis player, once shouted to Solomon from the other side of the court, "Hit the ball like a man, Solly."

Others found playing Solomon no easier. "When you played Harold," observed Erik Van Dillen, another tennis pro, "you'd better bring your lunch and dinner—you might be out there all day." His adversaries on the court called him "The Mole" because he's so small and he just keeps digging.

Solomon spent so much time on the tennis court with American tennis star Eddie Dibbs that the two were dubbed the "Bagel Twins." They practiced together, traveled together, played doubles together. Some believed they were so named because both are Jewish, but this impression is erroneous, Dibbs is not a Jew. Still, Dibbs takes credit for the nickname, explaining it in this way: losing a set 6-0 is called "the Bagel," because a Bagel has a hole in it, and the hole looks like a zero. Because he often lost sets by a

score of 6-0, Dibbs referred to himself as the Bagel Kid. When Solomon and Dibbs became partners, "Bagel Twins" seemed to be a fitting nickname.

In 1979, Solomon won three Grand Prix titles (North Conway, Baltimore, and Paris-Crocodile). He was runner-up in three others. But 1980 was his best year, a year in which he played in 23 tournaments, winning 64 matches and losing only 23. That year, he reached the finals at the Las Vegas tournament, beating John McEnroe in the quar-

ters; winning the German Championships at Hamburg; and then reaching the semifinals in the French Open. 1980 was also the year in which he won the ATP (Association of Tennis Professionals) Championships in Cincinnati, Ohio, and tournaments in Baltimore and Tel Aviv. At one stage during 1980 Harold was among the top five players on the ATP computer.

In July, 1980 Harold Solomon was elected to a one-year term as president of the ATP and in July

1981 was reelected for one more year. Although he was chosen by *Playgirl* magazine as one of the ten sexiest men of 1980, he is a serious person and a concerned citizen. He and his wife Jan have worked hard since 1977 for the Hunger Project, an association based in San Francisco that was determined to eliminate death by starvation in the world by the turn of the century.

In 1981, Solomon had a disappointing year on the tennis tour. He reached the semifinals in the German Open in May, but suffered first-round losses in the next 11 tournaments. As a result, his computer ranking slipped into the 20s. He still managed to earn $111,541 that year, making him the 28th highest money winner for the year. In 1982, though semiretired, Solomon ranked 45th in the world rankings.

In 1985, he was runner-up in two ATP tournaments. He played only six tournaments that year. His career total prize money came to $1.8 million.

Solomon was president of the ATP from 1980 to 1983. He served on the Men's International Professional Tennis Council from 1985 to 1987 as one of three player representatives. He was a member of the ATP board of directors from 1979 to 1983 and again from 1985 to 1987.

In 1987, he said that "If I have any regrets, they would be that my style of play was not as appreci-ated in this country as it was in others...I guess it's not as exciting to see eight million balls being hit back and forth, but I wonder, is it any more exciting to see Boris Becker and Ivan Lendl each hitting 40 aces?"

Solomon has coached touring pro Justin Gimmelstob. In June 1996 he was selected to the ATP Tour Board. He works with the Hunger Project in the Miami, Florida, area. He and Jan have a daughter, Rachel, and a son, Jesse.

In 1993, he won the worldwide senior circuit singles title in Cincinnati, Ohio, and repeated the feat in 1996 at Ponte Vedra Beach, Florida.

Since the late 1990s, Harold Solomon has coached Anna Kournikova and Jennifer Capriati. As of November 2004, with 22 titles, he was ranked 21st among the top 50 all-time singles open era title leaders.

Harold Solomon was inducted into Israel's Jewish Sports Hall of Fame in 2004. As of May 8, 2006, with earnings of $1,802,769, he placed 211th in the ranking of all-time prizewinners.

Along with partner Andy Brandi, Harold now runs The Harold Solomon Tennis Institute, located in Fort Lauderdale, Florida. Founded in January 2006, the institute's mission is "to provide unparalleled personal attention to a small group of students who are committed to excellence and who aspire to college or professional careers."

Mark Spitz
Greatest Jewish Swimmer of All Time

SPITZ, MARK (born February 10, 1950, in Modesto, California–) American swimmer. He has been called the greatest Jewish athlete of all time and the greatest Jewish swimmer in the history of that sport. His reputation was acquired largely from his remarkable feat in the 1972 Munich Olympics, where he won seven gold medals, setting a new world record in each event. He tried in vain to make a comeback at the age of 40, seeking but failing to earn a place on the 1992 American Olympic swimming team.

• • •

Overall, between 1965 and 1972 when he retired from competitive swimming, Spitz won nine Olympic gold medals, one silver, and one bronze; five Pan-American gold medals; ten Maccabiah gold medals; 31 national AAU titles, and eight NCAA championships. During those years, he set 33 world records. He was "World Swimmer of the Year" in 1967, 1971, and 1972.

Mark learned to swim at age six. By age eight he was practicing swimming 75 minutes a day.

In recalling those days, Mark said, "I had no idea where I was going when I started swimming. It was more or less like a social activity with my friends, and I had goals to be somebody like (pro football star quarterback) Johnny Unitas."

To make it possible for Mark to attend coach George Haines' successful Santa Clara (California) Swim Club, the Spitz family moved to Santa Clara from Sacramento. Arnold Spitz wanted his son to be a winner. "Swimming isn't everything," he often said, "winning is." Coach Haines believed in Mark. He knew he had promise.

In his first year at Santa Clara (1964), Mark

qualified for the national long course championships in the 400- and 1,500-meter freestyle events. The next year, at age 15, he won four gold medals and set four new records at the Maccabiah Games in Israel. "Coming here," Spitz said, "was how it all began." He had finished only fifth in the 1,500 meters at the American nationals, but in Israel "getting all those firsts did something for me. Any kid of 15 has to benefit." In 1966, as a high school sophomore, Mark became the third man in history to better 17 minutes in the 1,500 freestyle, and won his first national title, the 100-meter butterfly.

Mark's first really outstanding year came in 1967. His achievements included: two short-course and two-long course national titles, five American and seven world records in the 100- and 200-meter butterfly races, and the 400-meter freestyle. He also won five gold medals at the Pan-American Games in Winnipeg, Canada. *Swimming World* magazine named him World Swimmer of the Year.

At the Colorado Springs trials for the 1968 Olympics that were to be held in Mexico City, Spitz experienced much anti-Semitism from his teammates. His coach, Sherm Chavoor, said, "They tried to run him right off the team. It was 'Jew boy' this and 'Jew boy' that. It wasn't a kidding type of thing either. He didn't know how to handle it." Spitz confidently predicted that he would outswim everyone at Mexico City.

His predictions did not come true. While he won two gold-medals in the relays, a silver in the 100-meter butterfly, and a bronze in the 100-meter freestyle, he finished last in the final of the 200-meter butterfly. Although Spitz was actually not well during the meet, suffering from tonsillitis and diarrhea, he nevertheless felt enormously disappointed and embarrassed. He had tried three times for a gold medal in an individual event, and three times he had failed. The only gold he came home with was earned by swimming on the Americans' unbeatable relay team.

In 1969, Spitz entered Indiana University,

studying to become a dentist. His three triumphs in his freshman year helped the school retain the NCAA title. In fact, during each of Spitz's four years there, Indiana won the NCAA title.

In 1969 Mark was back in Israel participating in the summer Maccabiah Games. He won six swimming gold medals and was named the outstanding athlete of the games. In 1971, after another great year of collecting AAU and NCAA titles and world records, Spitz became the first Jewish recipient of the AAU's James E. Sullivan Award, given to the amateur athlete of the year.

In 1977, he told a reporter for an Israeli magazine: "I feel that being a Jewish athlete has helped our cause. We have shown that we are as good as the next guy. In mentality we have always been at the top of every field. I think the Jewish people have a more realistic way of looking at life. They make the most of what's happening at the present while preparing for the future."

Spitz carried his 170 pounds on a tightly compact 6 foot, 1 inch frame. He has the ability to flex his lower legs slightly forward at the knees, which has allowed him to kick six to 12 inches deeper in the water than his opponents. His moustache, he said, kept water out of his mouth.

At Indiana, Spitz and coach James (Doc) Counsilman had a daily routine they found humorous and relaxing: Mark would put his toes in the water and say it was too cold. Counsilman, spotting his star swimmer getting out of the water, would take a leather belt and chase him around the pool into the stands, and finally back into the water.

At Munich, where the 1972 Olympics were held, Spitz gave the greatest swimming exhibition ever witnessed. In eight days at the Swimhall, he won four individual (the 100- and 200 meter freestyle and the 100- and 200 meter butterfly), and three relay gold medals, all in world record time. In trying to explain his Munich performance, Mark said, "Day in and day out, swimming is 90 percent physical. You've got to do the physical work in training, and don't need much mental. But in a big meet like this, it's 90 percent mental and 10 percent physical. Your body is ready, and now it becomes mind versus matter." Coach Sherm Chavoor, remembering that some expected Spitz to repeat his poor performance in Mexico City at Munich, said after Mark had won his seventh gold medal: "He did a pretty good job for a guy who was supposed to choke."

When 11 Israeli athletes were killed at Munich by Palestinian terrorists, Spitz was put under special security guard and then whisked away. It was felt that he might be next on the terrorists' list.

After the 1972 Olympics, Spitz retired, and there was talk of his becoming a film star, another Johnny Weismuller perhaps, but nothing developed. Upon his return from Munich, he received $5 million in endorsement contracts; he was the first athlete to capitalize on his athletic career. He appeared on television specials along with entertainers Sonny and Cher, Bob Hope, and Bill Cosby. A poster showing him posing in a red-white-and-blue swimsuit along with his seven gold medals became the hottest-selling poster of a sports figure. "I'm a commodity, an endorser," Spitz said at the time, somewhat in self-mockery.

In 1973 he married and began doing some sports broadcasting. He bought a Los Angeles home with a large swimming pool—and then invested in real estate in California and Hawaii and became a real estate developer in Los Angeles and Honolulu. In October 1981, his wife, Susie, gave birth to their first son.

Partially out of boredom, partially entranced with the challenge, he decided in the summer of 1989 to try to make a comeback as a swimmer. He was 39 years old and his goal was winning another gold medal, this time at the 1992 Olympics in Barcelona. He chose to concentrate on his best event, the 100-meter butterfly, the one men's event in which he felt confident of succeeding. Pablo Morales holds the record of 52.84 seconds. Spitz's 1972 time of 54.27 seconds would have given him seventh place at the 1988 Olympics.

Because so few athletes continue to compete into their 40s and because Spitz granted frequent interviews, his comeback garnered a great deal of publicity. Many were skeptical. Spitz himself seemed to vacillate between robust self-confidence and curiosity. "I think we're going to redefine what 40 year-olds can do," he opined, acknowledging that the odds seemed against him. "The safe thing to say is I won't make it. That's more logical." Yet he brimmed over with optimism. "I personally wouldn't want to swim against Mark Spitz in the Olympics."

During training sessions with the UCLA varsity swimming team, Spitz found himself showered with questions from the team. Eventually, he came to believe he was being overly generous in giving out pointers. "I finally woke up one morning and said. 'One of these dudes is going to beat me because of one of these little comments I'm making. I'd better cool it.'" And he did.

When a *Time* magazine reporter asked Spitz in May 1990 why he wanted to make a comeback, he replied: "In everyday life there is always *mañana*. There is no urgency. One of the most difficult things for people who have been successful in sports is to adapt to the daily world where you can't get an answer from someone until 5 o'clock tomorrow. There is always an excuse. Living 40 or 50 years like that doesn't get too exciting after a while."

Practicing first two hours a day, then four, he added weight lifting to his regimen this go-round.

Some suggested that Mark Spitz's comeback was merely a marketing maneuver to add financial value to his name. He dismissed such talk, suggesting that it would be foolish to engage in such arduous training just for the financial rewards.

Spitz ultimately found the competition too tough. Shorn of his moustache, four pounds heavier than he was 20 years ago, Spitz was beaten badly in two exhibition 50-meter butterfly races in the spring of 1991—first by world record holder Tom Jager, 26, then by Matt Biondi, 25, the five-time gold-medal winner at the 1988 Olympics. He finished 1.78 seconds (a body length-and-a half) behind and a full two seconds behind Bi-

ondi. Noting that he had trouble getting into the water quickly, Spitz said that the current crop of swimmers gets into the water faster than those of a generation ago. "A lot of it has to do with the spring. They kind of go up a little higher and out a little further, obviously from doing weight training with their legs."

When he failed to qualify for the U.S. Olympic swimming trials in early March 1992, Spitz announced that he was giving up on his comeback attempt. "I'm fighting something unavoidable and not exclusive to me. It's called old age."

After he failed to qualify for the 1992 Olympics, Spitz stopped swimming for three months, but he now works out with the UCLA masters swim team. "I squeak, rattle, and roll," he jokes. But he's relaxed and enjoying himself. "I have a whole different mission now," comments Spitz. "I enjoy the camaraderie."

He lives in Los Angeles with his wife and their two sons, Matthew and Justin. He invests in real estate and serves as a spokesperson for SmarTalk Teleservices, a phone card company. The waterproof Mark Spitz model Swatch watch became the best-seller of the firm's recent Centennial Olympic line.

Spitz's remarkable 1972 seven-gold-medal achievement was challenged at the 2004 Athens Olympics by swimmer Michael Phelps. Phelps fell one title short, winning six golds and two bronzes.

In July 2005, Spitz led the eight-hundred-member United States delegation to the Maccabiah Games. In an interview, he recalled that he had won his first gold medal at the Maccabiah Games forty years earlier.

Richard J. Foster's biography of Spitz, *The Extraordinary Life of an Olympic Champion*, was published in July 2008. In August of that year, at the Beijing Olympic Games, American swimmer Michael Phelps won eight gold medals, thereby shattering Spitz's long-held record.

Mark Spitz is a member of the Jewish Sports Hall of Fame in Israel.

David Stern

The Man Who Resurrected the NBA

STERN, DAVID (born September 22, 1942, in New York, New York–) American commissioner of the National Basketball Association. Blessed with a shrewd business and marketing mind, he has turned the NBA around, rescuing it from severe financial distress in the early 1980s and turning it into a highly successful sports business in the early 1990s. David Stern has been consistently ranked by *The Sporting News* as one of the most powerful people in sports.

• • •

David Stern grew up in New York City. His parents ran a delicatessen located on Eighth avenue in the Chelsea district of Manhattan. As a youngster, Stern recalls going with his father to New York Knicks Basketball games at Madison Square Garden. "Even though the Knicks didn't have a good record, they were *my* Knicks," he said.

Stern graduated from Rutgers University in 1963 and Columbia Law School with honors in 1966. The closest he came to big-time basketball was playing for his law firm's team in the New York Lawyers League. Stern was forced to quit after injuring his knee.

He began handling legal business for the National Basketball Association in 1967 as an attorney with the law firm of Proskauer Rose Goetz and Mendelsohn, which represented the league. In 1974, only 32 years old, he became a partner in the firm.

In 1975, when Larry O'Brien became NBA Commissioner, Stern's role in handling major NBA legal issues increased though Stern remained behind-the-scenes. The key problem was over how much to pay the players. A year later, relying heavily upon David Stern, O'Brien reached an out-of-court settlement with the Players Association that granted free agency to the players and had the effect of sending salaries relentlessly skyward.

Persuaded in 1978 by O'Brien to take charge of the NBA's legal affairs, Stern left his law firm to become the league's general counsel. Two years later, O'Brien created the position of "Executive Vice President, Business and Legal Affairs," and gave Stern the job. Stern's mandate was to productively utilize marketing, television and public relations to boost the stature of the NBA.

In truth, Stern had become the de facto commissioner even before he was formally appointed. He had supplanted O'Brien, doing most of the hiring for the NBA's front office, overseeing the growth of the league's marketing division, and negotiating with the television networks and the players' union.

When O'Brien was ready to retire toward the end of 1983, he urged the NBA's 23-member Board of Governors not to look outside for a successor. The Board unanimously chose Stern as the NBA's fourth commissioner. Stern was only 42 years old when he took over February 1, 1984.

Stern's appointment occurred as the league was going through its darkest financial period. Seventeen of its 23 teams had been losing money and the league considered shutting down four of the weakest teams. Free agency, skyrocketing player salaries, and quarreling owners had contributed to the NBA's poor image as had the public perception that the league was drug-ridden. Fewer and fewer fans came to games, television ratings fell, and corporate sponsors fled.

In 1980, the stature of the NBA reached a low. Attendance for regular-season games dropped by one million from the year before. Gross revenues were just over $100 million. On average, 10,021 fans came to the games, only 58 percent of capacity. In the sixth (and as it turned out final) game between the Lakers and the 76ers for the 1980 Championship, CBS aired the game tape-delayed.

Yet David Stern recognized that the NBA, despite its financial woes, had a wonderful product to sell, if it could only be marketed properly.

Once he took over the reins in early 1984, Stern began to turn the league around. In April 1983, prior to his appointment as NBA Commissioner, Stern had fashioned a revolutionary agreement between owners and players that was designed to stop the owners from squabbling with one another and to give the players greater financial incentives. And, most important, it was meant to keep several teams from folding. The accord gave 53 percent of the year's gross revenues to players, the balance to owners. In effect, this capped salaries at 53 percent of NBA sales. In exchange, the players reversed their previous opposition to a salary cap. As a result, former adversaries—the owners and players—became partners. Stern's arrangement produced continuing labor peace for the NBA and enduring prosperity for owners and players. The salary cap grew from $3 million per team in 1983, its first year, to $14 million for the 1992-93 season,

In addition, Stern labored hard to curb the NBA's widespread drug problem. The policy he laid down as commissioner has been called the most progressive one in all sports. The NBA and Players Association agreed that a player who used drugs could come forward voluntarily without fear of punishment. The NBA would quietly aid him in treating the problem. The league retained the right to administer drug tests to players if reasonable cause existed. Those who failed the test were tossed out of the NBA, and only allowed to apply for reinstatement after two years. Random drug tests for rookies began in 1988. As a result of Stern's efforts, the NBA's drug-infested image largely disappeared.

Stern's genius has been in marketing the NBA. To him, the ideal model was Walt Disney and his theme parks, "They have theme parks and we have theme parks. Only we call them arenas. They have characters: Mickey Mouse, Goofy. Our characters are named Magic (Johnson) and Michael (Jordan). Disney sells apparel; we sell apparel. They make home videos; we make home videos." As Stern puts it: "I'm the chief executive officer of an entertainment company, and so you have to sell and sell and sell."

Under Stern, the NBA stepped up the business of selling the NBA. Stern created Team Services, the NBA division that disseminates marketing information among clubs, thereby overcoming the "us-against-them" attitude. In his first six years as Commissioner, NBA team gross revenues more than tripled.

Stern made sure that television enhanced the league's image rather than hurt it. He would call CBS, which televised NBA games from 1973 to 1990, on Monday mornings to critique the weekend's telecast. Once he complained to CBS for completing a 1983 telecast of a New York Knicks-Philadelphia 76ers game by panning its camera across a large expanse of empty seats at Madison Square Garden. "David's what we call a shaker and a mover," said Magic Johnson. "He gets it done."

So successful was Stern as NBA Commissioner that the NFL sought to lure him away to replace

Pete Rozell in the summer of 1989. Stern said no. Six months later, the NBA team owners presented him with a new contract worth a reported $17.5 million for five years, plus a $10 million signing bonus, the highest-paying contract for any sports commissioner. Stern's salary before had been $1 million a year.

Thanks to Stern, the value of the NBA franchises grew faster than in any major-league sport. A team that wanted to join the league in the early 1980s had to pay only $16 million; by the early 1990s, the figure had grown to $125 million.

League attendance climbed rapidly, with average arena attendance reaching 90 percent of capacity by the early 1990s; many of the NBA's 29 teams sell out every game. Since the 1983-84 season, the NBA's gross revenues from television fees and gate receipts have risen from $160 million to $1.7 billion, and gross retail sales of NBA-licensed merchandise have climbed from $44 million to $3 billion. The NBA has also gone into publishing, photo licensing, and trading cards.

In 1997, the NBA more than doubled its national television revenues, reaching a $2.6 billion contract with NBC and two cable stations, TNT and TBS, over four years. Sales of such retail merchandise as warm-up suits and hats licensed by the NBA Properties subsidiary were reaching $3 billion at retail that year, as compared with only $107 million in 1986. "David Stern can sell an anvil to a drowning man. He can sell a pogo stick to a kangaroo," said Pat Williams, general manager of the Orlando Magic.

Since Stern has made a conscious effort to protect his family's privacy, little is known about his private life other than the fact that he lives in Scarsdale, New York, with his wife, Dianne Bock Stern. They have two sons, Eric and Andrew.

Team owners point to his guts as the main reason Stern has succeeded. Golden State Warriors former owner Jim Fitzgerald said: "He'll do something that will raise the hackles of three or four owners. But he will just shake his head and say, 'I'm sorry. But we'll all be better because of it in a few years.'"

In February 1997, the NBA celebrated its 50th anniversary with a special All-Star Game weekend that included the naming of the 50 greatest NBA players of all time. That summer the NBA launched a new professional women's basketball league, the WNBA (Women's National Basketball Association), with 10 teams in 1998, expanding to 12 in 1999. By the spring of 1998, the NBA had offices in 11 countries.

One of David Stern's most interesting challenges in the late 1990s was to ensure that the NBA would remain popular. Superstars such as Magic Johnson, Larry Bird, and Michael Jordan helped to provide that popularity. But, with their departures, attendance began to sag and Stern was hoping for new superstars to rekindle the public's enthusiasm for the league.

In May 2002, a *Business Week* reporter asked Stern for his reaction to Michael Jordan's comeback season with the Washington Wizards. "It was the best of all worlds for us," said Stern. "We were in the post-Jordan era, and we had Michael Jordan."

In the summer of 2003, Stern was working hard to maintain the NBA's reputation following legal entanglements on the part of several league stars, most notably the Los Angeles Lakers' Kobe Bryant.

Stern's most difficult moment as NBA chief came in November 2004, when the worst brawl in the league's history broke out in a game between the hometown Detroit Pistons and the visiting Indiana Pacers. Fans hurled items at the players, who responded by charging into the stands and attacking the fans. Stern suspended the Pacers' Ron Artest for the balance of the season and meted out lesser punishments to other players.

By 2006, great strides had been made in addressing the problems of the NBA, and David Stern set out to give the league more appeal internationally. By March of that year, the NBA featured eighty-two international players from thirty-eight countries and territories on official rosters (active and inactive). The number of European players in the league had doubled, and Stern began to entertain the idea of establishing a European division.

George Stone

The 1906 American League Batting Champion

STONE, GEORGE ROBERT "SILENT GEORGE" (born September 3, 1876, in Lost Nation, Nebraska; died January 6, 1945) American baseball player. He was the 1906 American League batting champion, hitting .358 for the St. Louis Browns. Played in the major leagues for seven years, and had a career batting average of .301.

. . .

While working as a clerk in Coleridge, Nebraska, in 1902, Stone had been playing baseball for fun on a local team. In a game with a team which included pro players from Omaha of the Western League, Stone had five hits, including three home runs. Word spread about the man with the good bat and Stone began to take baseball seriously. Soon thereafter, he played in his first professional game.

That year, George played with minor league teams in Omaha and Peoria, hitting .346 in 138 games, and leading the league with 198 hits and 34 stolen bases. He was brought up to the major leagues to play for the Boston Red Sox for a brief period in 1903, and then sent back down to the minors to play for Milwaukee. In 1904, playing for Milwaukee, he led the American Association in batting with .406 and hits (254). The Red Sox traded him to the St. Louis Browns and he played for them from 1905 to 1910.

The year 1905 was Stone's real rookie season and he did well. The left-handed outfielder led the American League in hitting for much of the season, finishing with a .296 average. He managed to lead the league in hits with 187, and total bases with 260.

Stone had an awkward batting style. Though lefthanded, he usually placed the ball between second and third base, but rarely pulled the ball. "If he stood up," noted a commentator in a baseball magazine in 1909, "and pulled the ball to right field once in a while, I think that he would be the most wonderful batter that baseball ever saw."

Still, he did not fare badly. Stone's best season was 1906, when he won the American League batting title. That year, he hit 20 triples and was runner-up in hits with 208.

The next year he had a poor start, but still finished with a .320 batting average, third best in the American League. In 1908 Stone contracted malaria and managed to play in only 148 games. In 1909 he hurt his ankle badly, sliding into first base. The ankle never healed and he finished his playing career with Milwaukee in 1911.

After retiring from baseball, Stone divided his time between his new career as a banker and an old hobby for which he now had more time: playing the violin. In 1916, he became part owner of the Lincoln (Nebraska) baseball team, but he sold his interest the following year, severing all ties with baseball.

Steve Stone

The 1980 Cy Young Award Winner

STONE, STEVE (born July 14, 1947, in Cleveland, Ohio–) American baseball player. Won the Cy Young award as the best pitcher in the American League during the 1980 season. That year he won 25 games and lost seven. Prior to that, from 1971 to 1979, he had a mediocre 78-79 record pitching for the San Francisco Giants, Chicago White Sox, and the Chicago Cubs. His career record as of the end of the 1981 season was 108-93, with an earned-run average of 3.96, and 1,065 strikeouts.

▪ ▪ ▪

An only son, Steve grew up in South Euclid, Ohio. His father fixed jukeboxes, his mother was a waitress. An all-around athlete as a youngster, Steve shot a hole in one at golf at age 11, and won the Cleveland junior tennis title at age 13. Sandy Koufax, the Dodger pitching superstar, was his idol. At Bush High School in Cleveland, where he graduated in 1965, Steve won All-Star honors in baseball as a junior and captained the team as a senior. In 1965, when Steve was 18, he was the winning pitcher in a state high school All-Star game.

He graduated from Kent State in Kent, Ohio, in 1969 with a degree in history and government, and a distinguished baseball record. During his senior year Steve signed with the San Francisco Giants.

When Stone played in the minors between 1969 and 1971, he averaged virtually one strikeout per inning (399 strikeouts in 400 innings). The first year he pitched for the Fresno, California, minor league team he won 12 and lost 13 games. Once that year he struck out 17 batters in one nine-in-ning game. The following year Stone was 14-8, pitching for Amarillo (Texas) and Phoenix (Arizona). In 1971 Steve was 6-3 when the Giants brought him up in midseason to the majors. He finished that season, his first in the major leagues, at 5-9.

Stone married a woman he had known since high school in 1970, but they were divorced two years later.

In 1972, after a 6-8 season with the Giants, he was traded to the Chicago White Sox. Pitching for the White Sox in 1973, Stone was 6-11. After the season ended, he was traded to the Chicago Cubs for whom he pitched in 1974 (8-6), 1975 (12-8), and 1976 (3-6). Because of a sore shoulder he could pitch in only 17 games (75 innings) in 1976. He was on the disabled list from April 25 to July 2. His condition almost forced him to leave baseball.

After playing out his option with the Cubs, Stone signed with the Chicago White Sox on November 24, 1976. In the next two seasons he had

He was 2-3 with a 4.74 earned run average through May 5. But then he went on to win 23 of the next 27 games with a 3.06 earned-run average and nine complete games. This included 14 straight wins in 17 starts from May 9 to July 26. That was the longest winning streak in the American League since 1974. In the All-Star Game that year, Stone retired the first nine batters in order.

Steve's 25 wins led the majors in the 1980 season. He was the second straight Baltimore pitcher to win the Cy Young Award (Mike Flanagan won it in 1979). Steve also topped the league in winning percentage (.781) and was seventh in earned-run average (3.23). He was named American League Pitcher of the Year by *The Sporting News* (based on a vote of fellow-players) and was selected as the top right-hander on American League All-Star teams selected by the Associated Press and United Press International.

What was responsible for Stone's vast improvement? He attributed it to the fact that he had stopped thinking of himself as a mediocre pitcher. He revised his thought processes so that negative images of himself were eliminated. He credits Oriole pitching coach Ray Miller with two worthwhile suggestions: quickening his pace so the fielders would stay alert between pitches, and finding his best pitch—usually his curve—in the early innings and then sticking with it.

He had his own style of preparing for a pitching assignment, part of which involved superstition. Each time Steve pitched at home, he had breakfast at a local pancake house with Baltimore sportswriter Peter Pascarelli. In the afternoon before he pitched, he visualized how he would get each batter out, and then he left for the park. He would always stop at the same drive-in for a chocolate milkshake and would always listen to the same soft rock on his car stereo going from his suburban Towson home to Baltimore's Memorial Stadium.

When informed that only one American League Cy Young winner in the 1970s had improved his

15-12 and 12-12 records, respectively. His 15 wins in 1977 was a career high until then. He played out his option with the White Sox in 1978 and signed a four-year contract with the Baltimore Orioles on November 29, 1978.

Stone was 11-7 with Baltimore in 1979, getting off to a slow start. (By July 10, he was only 6-7.) After July 10, he was 5-0.

Steve had a bonus provision in his contract whereby he would receive an extra $100,000 in any season that he won the Cy Young Award. He did not think it was a serious proposal, but rather something his agent had just added. Stone thought a bonus for a winning season would have been more sensible. "It was," Stone said, "like an insurance salesman telling you, 'We'll give you $50,000 if an elephant falls on you.' He knows darn well an elephant isn't going to fall on you."

An elephant fell on Steve Stone that 1980 season.

won-lost percentage the year following the award, Stone suggested, "Put me down for 30 wins and a no-hitter."

A gourmet cook for six years, Steve was a partner in Lettuce Entertain You, a chain of nine restaurants in Chicago. He sold his share because he planned to open a moderately priced but high-class eatery called Steven, in Scottsdale, Arizona. He jokingly remarked that he hoped to trim the bill for a gourmet meal from $75 to $72 or $73. The restaurant opened in January 1981.

He developed a pain in his pitching elbow in spring training before the 1981 season began. The injury was diagnosed as tendonitis, and Stone was told to rest. He pitched only 34 innings at the start of 1981, and was 2-3 before going on the disabled list in mid-May with the sore elbow. He was still disabled in June when the baseball strike brought the whole season to a halt. While recuperating, Stone worked at his Scottsdale restaurant.

By the spring of 1982, there was no real improvement in his pitching arm. He ruled out surgery though he was told that after 18 months of rest, his arm might be completely healed. In early June 1982, Steve Stone announced at a news conference in Baltimore that he was retiring from baseball. After leaving the mound, Stone fulfilled a long-time ambition, becoming a sports broadcaster in 1983, doing television play by play over TV station WGN for the Chicago Cubs. When in August of 1991 Cincinnati Reds pitcher Jose Rijo made his first appearance since fracturing his right ankle a few months earlier, Stone said over the air: "He broke it in two places. I, of course, told him to stay out of those places." Stone resigned as a Cubs broadcaster in October 2004, when the team voiced displeasure with his critical commentary. In 2009, Stone signed on as color commentator for the Chicago White Sox television broadcasts.

Stone has also written free-form poetry and published articles in *Sports Illustrated* and the *National Jewish Monthly*. "I've always been proud of being Jewish," he said. "If you're a good enough pitcher, they don't care if you're a Martian."

Steve Stone was inducted into Israel's Jewish Sports Hall of Fame in 2004.

Kerri Strug
The Olympic Gymnast Who Won the Hearts of Millions

STRUG, KERRI (born November 19, 1977, in Tuscon, Arizona—) American gymnast. Few knew her name prior to Atlanta, although Kerri Strug had been competing at the highest levels of gymnastics competition for five years. She had even helped her American teammates win a bronze medal in the 1992 Olympics in Barcelona. But it was at Atlanta that the name Kerri Strug became equated with courage and glory and her tale of how she overcame pain and injury to help the American gymnastics team win gold touched millions of people in America.

• • •

She was born in Tucson, Arizona, on November 19, 1977. She came from a family of gymnasts, and so no one was surprised that she took up the sport as a child. As a toddler, she attended gymnastics meets where her older brother Kevin and her older sister Lisa performed. Kerri's mother Melanie insisted that she take ballet lessons, but the child's heart was in the gym.

Her parents called her a little daredevil. She retained all sorts of scars from falls she took even before she became a gymnast. Once, she sped her tricycle through the house and crashed into a dresser, requiring stitches in her head. She roller-skated (and gashed her head); in kindergarten, she jumped off a swing (and cut her chin); she used the backyard swings (and cut her knee). The burgeoning gymnast thought sitting while going down a slide too boring; she ran down the slide on her feet!

For a while she had her own private gym, an empty room where she walked on her hands and performed other gymnastic tricks. One day, her parents decided to put furniture in the room, and Kerri cried at her loss of space. Still, she continued to tumble on the carpet, she learned a back walkover from sister Lisa, and eventually became advanced enough to take private lessons from the University of Arizona's coach, Jim Gault.

She was short—only 4 feet, 9½ inches—and she had a high-pitched voice. Schoolmates teased her about both. Knowing that she could run circles around those kids inside the gym helped her overcome the teasing.

At age eight, she won nearly every gymnastic event she entered. She came in third place in her first international competition when she was 12 years old; that same year she won the Junior B National Championship. Reluctantly, her parents let her train at the summer camp of Bela Karolyi in Houston. He had coached Nadia Comaneci and

AP / WIDE WORLD PHOTOS

Mary Lou Retton, two superstar gymnasts. Kerri promised her parents that she would keep up with school while in Houston. She began each day at 7:30 A.M. with three hours of training followed by school from 11 A.M. to 3:30 P.M.; the day ended with another three-and-a-half-hour training period, from 5:00 P.M. to 8:30 P.M.

At age 13, the training paid off: She became the youngest female to win an event title, taking first in the vault at the 1991 U.S.A. Gymnastics Championships. A year later she became the youngest member, at 14, to make the 1992 Olympic gymnastics team, which earned a bronze medal. Kerri hoped to make the All-Around Finals (only the top three gymnasts from each team advance) but missed by .014 of a point. She felt great disappointment at not making the Finals, motivating her to remain in the sport until the Atlanta Olympics four years later.

At times she thought of quitting, sometimes feeling homesick, sometimes bothered by her coaches' criticism of her performance. "By the next day," she wrote (1996, *Heart of Gold*), "I would have calmed down and found the courage to continue."

Kerri suffered stomach pains in early 1993. Her idol Mary Lou Retton urged her to resist the advice of her coaches who had insisted that she continue to train, but Kerri kept training and ripped some stomach muscles at a European competition. She missed training for six months, remaining at home in Tucson while finishing high school. She completed high school a year early with straight A's. She trained on her own. Feeling better about herself, she suffered another injury in the summer of 1994, falling from the uneven bars, resulting in a badly sprained back. With the Team World Championships two months away, she began physical therapy in earnest. She felt a renewed self-confidence. "In a strange way," she wrote, "the fall helped me rise to a new level. Surviving that setback taught me how to manage my fears." She helped the American team capture second place at the 1994 Team World Championships.

By the end of 1995, Kerri returned to train with Karolyi in Houston. As a result, she won the America's Cup All-Around title, which was her first International All-Around title since joining the senior elite grouping. She was buoyant about herself and her Olympic prospects now. She finished in second place in the all-around and first in the floor and vault at the U.S. trials.

Kerri's behavior at home suggested why she was so good in gymnastics. "You open Kerri's closet and all the short-sleeved shirts are with the short-sleeved shirts, and the long-sleeved shirts are with the long-sleeved shirts," her mother notes. "Her room is always neat; the bed is always made." Kerri notes: "My drive comes from being a perfectionist. I got that from my dad. We put everything into whatever we do."

Arriving in Atlanta, she was dubbed the "stepsister to the stars," since other American female gymnasts like Shannon Miller and Dominque Dawes were well-known veterans and Dominique Moceanu was an up-and-coming hopeful. Kerri and one other teammate, Amy Chow, were the only two of the seven members of the 1996 American gymnastics team to hold amateur status. Kerri had a good reason to refuse money: she wanted to compete as a college gymnast at UCLA, and only amateurs could do that.

She carried a heavy burden into Atlanta. Her critics complained that she became nervous under pressure, that she lacked a certain mental toughness, and did not perform at her best. Even her coach Bela Karolyi teased her, calling her on occasion "the baby."

Then came the event that changed her life. As millions watched her on television that evening of July 23, 1996, and 32,620 more watched her live at the Georgia Dome, Team U.S.A. was entering its final team event with a decent lead. The only event that lay ahead for Kerri and her teammates was the vault, a springboard leap over a padded metal horse. Never before had an American women's gymnastics team taken home gold in team gymnastics.

By the end of the first evening of competition, Kerri's American team was just behind the Russian team in points. Two nights later, with 32,000 looking on in the Georgia Dome, at a certain stage, the American team forged ahead narrowly and improved the margin after the floor exercise. But when Dominique Moceanu's turn came, she fell twice on her vault. The America team's chances for gold appeared to be ebbing. Moceanu's low scores put huge pressure on Kerri, who was anchoring the team in her best event.

Kerri was the last to vault. "I wasn't aware of the exact score." "Still, I could feel the gold slipping away. . . . Everyone believed victory rested on my shoulders."

She was confident. But on her first vault, she landed short and fell backward, landing on her seat. "The moment my feet hit the floor I heard a pop. As I scrambled to stand, a fiery pain shot up my left leg." She traced the popping noise to her left ankle. She tried to walk. The ankle felt like it would fall off. She limped down the runway.

She was now faced with the most difficult choice an athlete must face—whether to continue to compete though seriously injured, or retire at once from the competition. In Kerri's case, with seconds to make that decision, she had to choose between jumping again, an effort that, if she succeeded, could help her team win the gold (or so everyone thought); or quit then and there, saving herself for the individual competition a few days off. In fact, Kerri's score of 9.162 was enough to guarantee an American victory, making Kerri's second vault unnecessary. But no one on the team realized that. "We had no idea what the score was," said co-head coach Mary Lee Tracy. "What we saw was a kid who was shaking her leg but who saluted and ran down the runway."

Bela Karolyi yelled, "You can do it." Kerri looked back at him, feeling as if she might burst into tears. She had no way of knowing if she could perform up to her high standards. She knew something was wrong. But she was determined.

She decided to give it a try. "I did what my heart told me was right," she wrote. Reaching the end of the runway, she felt the adrenaline pumping through her body. She told herself encouragingly, "You can do this! You've done it a million times. You're ready." Then she prayed, "Please, God, help me out here." Suddenly, she realized the pain was gone. She raced to the springboard, landed on both feet and heard another snapping noise. She lifted her injured ankle and balanced on one foot— then collapsed to her knees. The judges gave her vault a 9.71 score. The gold medal belonged to the American team. Kerri Strug had performed a miracle— under the worst possible physical limitations.

She was carried off to doctors, who put her on a stretcher, wrapping her ankle up. The doctors wanted to take her to the hospital right away. She begged to be allowed to stay for the awards ceremony. Agreeing, Bela lifted her off the stretcher, carrying her in his arms to the stand where the medal presentation was about to begin. "I felt a mixture of emotions," Kerri wrote. "I worried about my ankle, but mostly I felt overwhelming pride for our team and country." (She discovered later that the team would have won the gold without her second, painful vault, but "it didn't matter to me.") The injury kept her from competing in the All-Around.

Suddenly America had a new sports heroine. As *Time* magazine noted: "...it was fitting that Strug's moment of Olympic glory was the storybook climax to one of the most brilliantly managed team efforts in U.S. Olympics history. She played through pain, convinced that she had to for the team, risking a worse injury and jeopardizing her own chances for more medals. Maybe she shouldn't have done it; later it became apparent that she needn't have done it. But she did, and America got another electrifying moment to put into its collective sports memory bank."

In 2000, Strug was inducted into the Jewish Sports Hall of Fame in Israel. After earning an undergraduate degree in communications from Stanford University in 2001, Kerri remained at the university to obtain a Master's in sociology the following year. Following graduation, she first worked as a second-grade teacher in San José, California, and then as a White House intern. In 2004, Strug was working full-time as a student correspondence official at the White House. In August of that year she appeared on *Strong Medicine*, cast as a gymnast whose estranged sister needs a liver transplant after surviving a drive-by shooting.

In March 2005, Kerri joined the U.S. Justice Department's Office of Juvenile Justice and Delinquency Prevention staff as a presidential appointee. She also works with the March of Dimes and gives motivational speeches.

On April 25, 2010, in a ceremony in Tucson, Arizona, Kerri Strug wed Robert Fischer.

Eva Szekely

Hungarian Olympic Swimming Star

SZEKELY, EVA (born April 3, 1927, in Hungary–) Hungarian swimming star. She won a gold medal at the 1952 Olympics, a silver one at the 1956 Games, and set 10 world and five Olympic records. She also established 101 Hungarian records and held 68 Hungarian national swimming titles.

• • •

From as early as Eva could remember, she felt like a stranger in her native Hungary. When she was 11 and studying at a German school in Budapest, Eva had many Jewish classmates. But she had trouble identifying with her co-religionists: she disliked them for showing their fear of anti-Semitism.

Eva belonged to a local swimming team just before World War II broke out, and was happy that it was her talent that counted, and not her religion. But, in 1941, at age 14, she was expelled from the team as "undesirable." For the next four years, during the war, she dreamed of becoming an Olympic swimming champion.

From 1944 to 1945 the Szekely family lived in a Swiss-run "safe house" in Budapest. Forty people lived in two rooms in an apartment house that was considered "protected" from German intrusion. For exercise each morning Eva would climb over others asleep on the ground floor and run up and down five flights of stairs 100 times. "I realized," she wrote much later, "that there is one thing that cannot be taken away from anybody: one's inner security, which consists of faith, discipline, will-power, knowledge, humanity, and never accepting the finality of evil."

Eva never lost faith. Although some knew that she was Jewish, and held it against her, she pursued her career in swimming, confident that she would one day reach the Olympics.

After the war, Eva began participating in international meets. In 1947, in Paris, she met Dezso Gyarmati, a Hungarian water polo star, whom she married four years later. Then her career began to turn around. The 1948 Olympics in London was her first, and she came in fourth in the 200-meter breaststroke.

In the years between Olympics, Eva was performing miracles in the swimming pool. On May 9, 1951, she set a world record of 1:16.9 for the 100-meter breaststroke.

At the 1952 Helsinki Olympics, both she and Dezso won gold medals. He, for water polo play; she, for the 200-meter breaststroke which she swam in 2:51.7, setting an Olympic record. The following year, on April 10, 1953, she set a world record of 5:50.4 for the 400-meter individual medley.

Eva and Dezso's daughter, Andrea was born in May 1954. Two years later, leaving her behind, they went to the 1956 Melbourne Olympics just a few days after the Hungarian revolt had started. En route they spent a night in Pakistan, and at the Karachi airport Eva had second thoughts about leaving her daughter behind. She tried to convince an American fighter pilot to take her back to Europe. He agreed to be at the airport at midnight. But, when she arrived, there was no trace of him. Standing on the middle of the runway, Eva broke into tears, and had no choice but to continue on to Melbourne.

Once in Australia, the only news that she and Dezso had was that Budapest had been devastated, that people had been shot en masse, and those still alive were starving. Despite the trauma, Dezso won a gold medal as captain of the winning water polo team and Eva took a silver medal in swimming. She did not sleep for a week and lost 12 pounds. Finally, she and Dezso received a phone call from her father in Hungary who reported that everyone in the family was fine.

Eva did not return with the Hungarian Olympic team to Hungary. Instead, she and Dezso went to Austria. Shortly thereafter the two returned to

Budapest to try to bring out Andrea and Dezso's mother. It was not easy.

The new Russian puppet government in Hungary had apparently learned that Eva and her family wanted to defect. On February 20, 1957, four men dragged Dezso into a vacant Budapest building and tore at his body with a cat-o-nine-tails and razor blades, leaving him for dead. But with a forged passport in hand, he, Eva, their daughter, and Dezso's mother reached the Austrian border shortly after daylight the next day. The Hungarian police stamped the passport and then suggested that this called for a drink. Fearing the police would turn them in, Dezso had no choice but to join them at a local bar. Fortunately for him, the policemen drank more than him, and so the water polo star, driving fuzzily, finally crossed the border into Austria.

Eva and Dezso came to the United States in early 1957. They lived for some time with Eva's cousin in New Jersey. In all, they were in America for one year before moving on to Naples, Italy, where Dezso found a coaching job. But difficulties with his work forced them to return to Budapest in 1958. Upon reaching Hungary, Eva retired from competition but Dezso continued to play water polo.

After retiring from active swimming in 1958, Eva trained youngsters to swim in local competition with an eye toward the Olympics. She also spent considerable time coaching her daughter Andrea.

In 1964 Eva and Dezso were divorced and she spent even more time on raising Andrea and on building her into a great swimmer. Andrea, by then age 18, reached the high point of her career when at the 1972 Munich Olympics she came in first in the semifinals in the 100-meter butterfly, establishing a world record. She finished third in the butterfly finals, winning a bronze medal. She then went ahead to win a silver medal in the 100-meter backstroke.

In June 1980, the retina of Eva's right eye was damaged. She underwent four operations in the next two months, with only local anesthetics. Though Hungarian physicians tried a variety of treatments, including the use of laser beams, they concluded that nothing could help. She went to Cologne, West Germany, where another operation was performed. This time the operation succeeded.

Eva is a retired physician in Budapest. Her former husband, Deszo Gyarmati, was a member of the Hungarian Parliament.

She is a member of the International Swimming Hall of Fame and of the Jewish Sports Hall of Fame in Israel.

Brian Teacher
World Class Tennis Star

TEACHER, BRIAN (born December 23, 1954, in San Diego, California–) American tennis player. Won the Australian Open in January 1981. In 1981, he climbed from No. 59 to No. 7 in the world. In 1982, Teacher was 18th in the world rankings.

• • •

Brian graduated from Crawford High School in San Diego, California, in the spring of 1972, and entered the University of California at Los Angeles in the fall of that year. He followed in the footsteps of two other UCLA graduates— Arthur Ashe ('65) and Jimmy Connors ('71). Brian joined the pro tour in June 1976.

In 1977 Brian Teacher managed to reach the finals in two Australian Events, the South Australian and New South Wales Opens. He created an even bigger stir at the 1978 Seiko World Super Tennis tournament in Tokyo. There, he beat both Connors and Ashe at a time when few others could. He reached the finals only to lose to Bjorn Borg.

Teacher went on to claim his first Grand Prix title later in 1978, capturing the Cathay Trust Open in Taipei, Taiwan. The following year, 1979, Brian's game was disappointing, despite a win at Newport, Rhode Island, over Stan Smith at the Miller Hall of Fame Championships.

In 1980 he fared better, reaching five finals— Los Angeles, Hong Kong, Taipei, Bangkok, and New South Wales—and collecting the runner-up check at each event. Teacher made it to the final round of 16 of the U.S. Open that year, losing to Roscoe Tanner in four sets.

Brian played well in doubles in 1980, teaming with American tennis player Bruce Manson. The pair won five titles out of eight appearances in final

rounds. At the end of the year, he and Manson won titles in Toronto, Cincinnati, and Palm Springs, and a fourth several weeks later in Taipei. He also teamed with Butch Walts, winning several tournaments in Frankfurt.

In 1981, Teacher reached the semifinals at Las Vegas and at Queen's Club (England), and the quarters at Frankfurt and Los Angeles; he also had a great win over Vitas Gerulaitis in Las Vegas and won the doubles title at the Association of Tennis Professionals Championship in Palm Springs (with Manson). Teacher earned $50,000 for winning the Australian Open in January 1981, the largest paycheck of his career until then. He

was 15th highest in yearly earnings on the pro tennis tour, winning $163,646 in 1981.

In 1982, Teacher finished well, winning a World Championship Tennis event in Dortmund, reaching the quarter-finals at the Australian Open and San Francisco, and the final at Maui. In 1983, he won the Columbus and Munich World Championship Tennis crowns. His 1983 ATP ranking was No. 29.

He was less successful in 1984 when he was runner-up at Bristol and Gstaad but won no tournament. He fell to an ATP ranking of 66 in 1985 and 104 in 1986.

Tall and lean at 6 feet, 3 inches and 175 pounds, Teacher preferred fast surfaces where he could best utilize his blistering serve-and-volley game. A modest fellow, he once said of himself: "I'm not one of the more well-known players, but outside of a very few guys—Borg, McEnroe, Connors, and a couple of others—who is? I don't expect it, I don't really know if I would want the kind of attention they get. But I know it doesn't bother me that I don't have it now."

In 2001, Brian Teacher was inducted into the Intercollege Tennis Association Men's Hall of Fame, in Princeton, New Jersey. A resident of Los Angeles, Brian Teacher's career earnings total $1,426,514, ranking him 265th on the list of all-time prize money leaders.

Following his playing career, Teacher coached Andre Agassi and Greg Rusedski, as well as #1 doubles players Jim Grabb, Richey Renenberg, Daniel Nestor, and Max Mirnyi. He runs the Brian Teacher Tennis Academy, which operates in various locales in southern California.

Eliot Teltscher

Outstanding Tennis Player of the Early 1980s

TELTSCHER, ELIOT (born March 15, 1959, in Palos Verdes, California–) American tennis player. One of the outstanding Jewish tennis players of the early 80s. In July, 1982, he was ranked seventh in the world. At the end of 1981, Teltscher was ninth best. In the four previous years he had made phenomenal progress, going from 99th place in 1977, to 48th in 1978, to 27th in 1979, to tenth in 1980. In 1981 he earned $157,630, making him the 18th highest money winner of the pro tour. His highest career ATP rank was No. 6 in 1982.

. . .

Eliot's mother was born in Israel and his father came there during the Holocaust, joining the British Army in order to avoid being arrested. Eventually, they made their way to the United States where Eliot's father became an outstanding table tennis player and a soccer judge.

Teltscher took up tennis at the age of nine when he and his older sister, Judy, accompanied their parents to the Jack Kramer Tennis Club near their home in Palos Verdes. A sibling rivalry developed as Eliot and Judy competed against one another. He learned tennis, he later claimed, to demonstrate to Judy that he was better than she. Judy stopped playing, and Eliot went on.

Playing in his first tournament at the age of 10, he lost in an early round, which was a humbling experience. But in his second tournament he reached the finals. Eliot went to Israel at the age of 13 to celebrate his Bar Mitzvah at the Western Wall in Jerusalem. During the visit, his Israeli relatives arranged for him to play against another up-and-coming young tennis player at the Tel Aviv Coun-

try Club, a local boy named Shlomo Glickstein. Glickstein could not handle Teltscher any better and Eliot won easily.

In 1978, Teltscher attended UCLA on a full athletic scholarship, working out on the court at least four hours a day. He became an All-American, and turned pro after one year of college play. He is known for his speed, deceptive strength, and competitiveness. His UCLA coach Glen Bassett, said: "Eliot believes in himself. He's very tough out there on the court."

In 1977, when he received a ranking of 99 in the world, he was runner-up at the Wimbledon Junior and the U.S. Open Junior competitions. His first big-time triumph came at Hong Kong in 1978. By that time he was ranked 48th in the world. Ilie Nastasie called Teltscher at that time "the best player I've played in the United States this year."

In 1979, when he climbed to No. 27 in the world, Teltscher won a title in Atlanta and reached the semifinals five times. In the process, he recorded victories over Jose-Luis Clerc, John McEnroe, and Jose Higueras.

In 1980, Teltscher won tournaments in Atlanta and Miami and was runner-up five other times. In New Orleans in 1980, he won the doubles with Terry Moor and was runner-up at the Japan Open.

Early in 1981 Eliot and Tim Gullikson lost the San Juan (Puerto Rico) final to the Mayotte brothers after Teltscher had routed Gullikson for the singles crown. In the spring of 1981 Eliot and Terry Moor reached the French Open doubles final. That summer, Eliot reached the semifinals of Boston's U.S. pro tournament.

Teltscher ranked among the top 15 from 1980 to 1984. He earned a career high $267,630 in 1981. Eliot won the French Open Mixed Doubles (with Barbara Jordan) in 1983, the Japan Open in 1983, and the South African Open in 1984.

He dropped in the world rankings from 9 to 24 in 1985 because of an injury. By the late summer of 1985 pain from recurring nerve problems in his serving arm forced him to forego the U.S. Open. His world ranking dropped to 53 in 1986.

Teltscher returned to excellent form in 1987. At age 28, he beat Jimmy Connors for the first time in his career, defeating the American No. 1, 6-3, 6-1, in Chicago to reach the semifinals. Teltscher reached the finals in two events; he was a runner-up in Scottsdale and the champion in Hong Kong. He ended that year ranked No. 20.

In the early 1990s Teltscher was a tennis coach at Pepperdine University in Malibu, California. In the spring of 1998, he was working for the United States Tennis Association as a national coach—coaching junior players. He is married with one daughter, McKenna.

In May 2003, Eliot Teltscher was named coach of the U.S. tennis team that competed at the 2003 Pan American Games. As of November 2004, his 10 career titles earned Eliot the bottom spot on the list of the top 50 all-time open era singles title leaders. As of May 2006, with accumulated earnings of $1,653,997, he was ranked 224th on the list of all-time list of prizewinners.

Otto Wahle

First Austrian Olympic Swimmer to Place in a Distance Event

WAHLE, OTTO (born 1880, in Austria; died August 11, 1965) Austrian swimming champion. He emigrated to the United Sates and became the first American swimmer to win a place in a distance event in the Olympics.

. . .

Wahle was frequently the Austrian national swimming champion. He came to the U.S. at the turn of the twentieth century and lived in New York City until his death. Even after he settled in the U.S., he continued to represent Austria in Olympic competition, but wore the colors of the New York Athletic Club in American competition.

In the 1900 Paris Olympics he finished second to John Jarvis of Great Britain in the 1,000 meter race. He also took a silver medal in the 200-meter obstacle race. In 1904 he captured third place in the 400-meter race.

In 1912 Wahle coached the American Olympic swimmers who went to the Stockholm Olympics. Among his swimmers was General George S. Patton Jr. who competed in the swimming event in the modern pentathlon.

A swimmer and water polo player for the New York Athletic Club, Wahle became coach of the club at the same time that he was a member of the Amateur Athletic Union Records Committee. He served as Olympic swimming coach for the American squad in 1920 as well.

Wahle played an important part in the growth of swimming as a competitive sport in the United States, contributing many of the rules first listed in early AAU manuals. They were modeled on those of the Amateur Swimming Association of England.

Wahle's profession was accounting. He worked as an accountant with the law firm of Guggenheimer and Untermyer in New York until five years before his death in 1965.

Kevin Youkilis

Boston Red Sox
Gold Glove Winner

YOUKILIS, KEVIN (born March 15, 1979, in Cincinnati, Ohio–) American baseball player. Known for both his ability to get on base and his sensational fielding, Youkilis is a Gold Glove first baseman who holds the all-time record for consecutive errorless games in that position. A member of the Boston Red Sox World Series championship teams in 2004 and 2007, he is an intense, scrappy, gritty player famous for his dirt-stained jersey and home-plate collisions.

• • •

Although variously described as "roly-poly" (in high school), "pudgy" (in college), "thicker-bodied" (by the Boston Red Sox scout who recruited him), and "husky" (by his mother, Carolyn), 6–foot 1–inch, 220–pound Kevin Youkilis has long excelled on the playing field. "He does not look like an MVP candidate; more a refrigerator repairman, a butcher, the man selling hammers behind the counter at the True Value hardware store," remarked *Boston Globe* columnist Jackie MacMullan.

At age 16, Kevin's great-great-great grandfather fled Romania for Greece to avoid conscription by the anti-Semitic Cossacks. Returning to Romania after a year, still fearing conscription, he abandoned the surname "Weiner" and adopted the Greek name "Youkilis."

Kevin's great-uncle Paul immigrated to America in the 1930s, when Prohibition was still in force. To raise sufficient funds to bring his 10 siblings from Romania, he became a rum-runner, and in time the entire Youkilis family arrived in the U.S., settling in Cincinnati.

A jewelry wholesaler by trade, Kevin's father, Mike Youkilis, dreamed that one day his son would run the family business. But at the early age of four, Kevin got his first taste of ball-playing when he was invited to join a neighborhood T-ball team. Seven years later, as a pitcher, he was tossed from a game after disputing the umpire's calls. "Kevin was right," Mike remarked. "The guy was calling a lousy game."

Continuing to dispute bad calls in high school, Kevin was often right and the umpires wrong. The reason: Kevin's 20/11 vision. The young man had the unusual talent of being able to identify pitches and where they were headed earlier than most hitters.

Although Kevin's mother was a Christian by birth, his father was born Jewish, and Kevin was raised in a Conservative Jewish household. He always identified himself as a Jew, and mom Carolyn later converted to Judaism. Mr. and Mrs. Youkilis made sure that Kevin attended Hebrew School and had a Bar Mitzvah. After reaching that milestone, he was allowed to decide what kind of a Jew he wanted to be. Today, Kevin credits Judaism with having instilled in him an appreciation for the importance of discipline both on the field and off.

A star on Sycamore High School's 1994 AAU championship baseball team, Kevin played third, shortstop, first, and outfield. By graduation, he had set school records for career home runs, walks, and slugging percentage. At the University of Cincinnati, he played ball from 1998 to 2001. Although second-team All-American as a college junior and senior, Kevin clearly had a great eye, rarely striking out looking. Nonetheless, the young man received no Major League draft offers.

"He was kind of a square-shaped body, a guy [who] in a uniform didn't look all that athletic," his high school coach, Brian Cleary, said. "He looked chubby in a uniform. . . . I think the body did scare some people away." Kevin's reaction: "Big fellas can hit, too. I've always felt like I've had to prove myself. The chip on my shoulder has been there for years."

Following Kevin's college graduation, Mike Youkilis unsuccessfully tried to entice his son into the family jewelry business. Eventually drafted by the Boston Red Sox, Kevin received a $12,000 signing bonus. "Kevin," said Mike, "would have played for a six-pack of beer."

Playing in the minor leagues from 2001 to 2004, Kevin debuted as a third baseman with the Lowell Spinners, for whom he hit .317. He was named Red Sox Minor League Player of the Year in 2002. Receiving national recognition for the first time in 2003, Youkilis was mentioned in the 2003 Michael Lewis best-seller *Moneyball: The Art of Winning an Unfair Game*. Lewis referred to him as "Euclis, the Greek God of Walks," a moniker that stuck because of Youkilis's numerous walks.

On May 15, 2004, Kevin was called up to the major leagues. So excited was he that he got only four hours of bedrest the night before. Sleep deprivation notwithstanding, he homered in his second at-bat. That was the greatest day of his life, Youkilis said, in part because his parents were seated behind the Boston dugout. During that inaugural year in the majors, he played in 74 games, hit .260 and 7 home runs. On September 24, 2004, Yom Kippur, Youkilis appeared in the Red Sox dugout and suited up but declined to play.

During spring training of 2005, Kevin broke his toe, but after a few says maintained that he was ready to resume action. He was sent to play minor league ball for Boston's Triple A franchise, the Pawtucket Red Sox; and after 43 games was called up to the Red Sox permanently. In 2006, Youkilis's first full season in the major leagues, he became the first-string Red Sox first baseman, playing in 127 games. Scoring 100 runs, he had a .279 batting average.

In 2007, Kevin had a career-high 23-game hitting streak, leading the league with a perfect 1.000 fielding percentage and setting an American League record of 1,079 errorless chances at first

base. He won the 2007 Gold Glove award for first basemen. That distinction notwithstanding, his earnings that year were $424,500, the fourth lowest on the club.

Having signed a one-year contract for $3 million for 2008, Kevin Youkilis established a new major league record for first basemen on the 27th of April, when he fielded his 1,701st consecutive chance without an error. That streak was broken at 2,002 fielding attempts on the June 7th that followed.

Youkilis was the American League's starting first baseman on the 2008 All Star team. That year he led the league in at bats per RBI (4.7). Moreover, he was third in slugging percentage (.569) and sixth in batting average (.312), and was deservedly named winner of the American League Hank Aaron Award for best offensive performance of the 2008 season.

In November 2008, in Cabo San Lucas, Mexico, Kevin married Enza Sambataro, CEO of his charity, Hits for Kids. An ardent philanthropist, Youkilis attributes that pursuit to his faith: "In the Jewish religion, one of the biggest things that is taught is giving a *mitzvah*."

On January 15, 2009, Youkilis signed a four-year $41.25 million contract with the Red Sox. Later that year, *Sporting News* named him number 36 on its list of the 50 greatest active baseball players. During the 2009 season, he hit .305, with 27 homers and 94 RBIs. "Statistically, if you consider 2008 and 2009, you could make the case [that] there has been no better player in the league [dur-ing that time period]," said Red Sox Executive Vice President Theo Epstein.

During the 2010 season, he hit .307, with 19 home runs and 62 RBIs. But having suffered a muscle tear, his season was limited to 102 games. Midway through the 2011 season, Kevin's career major league batting average was .292, with a total of 123 home runs and 527 RBIs.

As for his degree of Jewish ritual observance, Kevin Youkilis does not keep the kosher dietary laws, and he attends synagogue only on the high holidays. "We keep the faith," he says. "We believe in what we believe."

Thumbnail Sketches

ALBERT, MARV (born June 12, 1943, in Brooklyn, New York-) American sports announcer. One of America's most popular broadcasters. He graduated from New York University in 1964, majoring in journalism. He started his broadcasting career in 1963, assisting Marty Glickman on Rangers and Knicks radio broadcasts. From 1969 to 1997, Marv was the voice of pro hockey's New York Rangers and from 1967 to 1997 the voice of the NBA's New York Knicks. He has also done play-by-play for the NFL's New York Giants. A former ball-boy with the New York Knicks, Albert achieved prominence in 1969, when at the age of 26, he did radio broadcasts of the New York Knicks' drive to the NBA championship. His distinctive trademark shout of "Yes-s-s!" following an especially important basket was also the title of his 1981 book on sports broadcasting. He was an NBC-TV network broadcaster from 1977 to 1997. He appeared on *The Late Show with David Letterman* over 100 times, easily the most frequent guest on that show. Albert's career came to a halt in May 1997 when he was indicted on sodomy and assault charges in a Washington, D.C., suburb. The divorced Albert was accused of physically abusing a 42-year-old woman in his room at the Ritz Carlton Hotel in Arlington, Virginia. The charges carried a maximum penalty of life in prison. Albert reached a settlement during trial, pleading guilty to a misdemeanor assault-and-battery charge. Spared a prison term, Albert resumed his NBA play-by-play broadcasting activities in the early 2000s. But in November 2004, James Dolan, chairman of Madison Square Garden and president of Cablevision, relieved Albert of his duties as voice of the Knicks, berating him for being too critical of the team. In June 2011, Albert joined CBS Sports to call play-by-play for *The NFL on CBS*.

■ ■ ■

ALEXANDER, JOE (born April 1, 1898, in Syracuse, New York; died 1975) American football player. Playing for Syracuse University, he was an All-American guard in 1918 and 1919, and an All-American center in 1920. He played pro football with a number of teams from 1921 to 1927, especially the New York Giants. In 1925 he was on the National Football League All-Star team. In 1934 he served as assistant to coach Benny Friedman of CCNY. He was head coach of CCNY in the early 1940s before retiring to devote more time to his medical practice. He became a world-famous lung specialist.

■ ■ ■

ARNOVICH, MORRIS "MORRIE" (born November 16, 1910, in Superior, Wisconsin; died July 20, 1959) American baseball player. He played for the Philadelphia Phillies from 1936 to 1940; the Cincinnati Reds in 1940; and the New York Giants in 1941 and 1946. In 590 games, he had a career batting average of .287.

■ ■ ■

BACHER, ARON "ALI" (born May 24, 1942 in South Africa-) South African cricket player. He played international cricket in the 1960s and in the early 1970s as a member of the South African national cricket team, retiring in 1974. He was appointed captain of the team for the 1970 test matches against England, the first Jew to reach that position. Bacher was an outstanding proponent of multiracial cricket and, as a physician, devoted his early years in medicine to nonwhites. When violent opposition in England arose in the early 1970s to South African apartheid in sport, South Africa ceased to participate in international cricket competition, thus cutting short Bacher's career. During the 1980s, Bacher promoted cricket in South Africa, organizing what became known as "rebel tours" of English, West Indian, Sri Lankan, and Australian teams to South Africa. These tours, which defied the international sporting boycott of South Africa, kept cricket alive in South Africa. In 1986, Bacher began a program to introduce cricket to the majority black population in South Africa's townships. In early 1992, Bacher was managing director of the new non-racial United Cricket Board of South Africa. Bacher's pledge in 1994 that his country would have its first black test cricketer before the turn of the century was realized three years early when Mkhaya Nitni became the first black man to represent South Africa when he played in the Australian tour opener in

Perth, Australia, in November 1997. "His selection will give a huge impetus to South African cricket development," said Bacher, thrilled at the turn of events. "It will ensure that kids in the townships know it's possible to play for South Africa." He stepped down as managing director of the UCBSA in the early 2000s.

• • •

BARTON, HARRIS (born April 19, 1964 in Atlanta, Georgia–) American football player. A star lineman for the San Francisco 49ers of the National Football League since 1987, he began his pro career as a guard and then became one of the league's better tackles. During his first pro year in 1987, he was named to the All-rookie teams of UPI, *Pro Football Weekly* and Pro Football Writers of America. He is 6 feet, 4 inches tall and weighs 280 pounds. Barton played center and left tackle while at North Carolina in the early 1980s and was chosen for many All-American teams. He was named the Atlantic Coast Conference Outstanding Offensive Lineman in 1986. When Barton and kicker Lee Gliarmis began playing football at North Carolina in 1981, they put *Sports Illustrated* covers on their walls each week of the school year. The magazine paid tribute to their project by putting Barton and Gliarmis on its cover. Barton continued to play for the 49ers through the 1996 season, but he missed the 1997 season due to an injury. After retiring in 1998, Barton co-founded Champion Ventures, an investment firm that encourages high-tech startups.

• • •

BAUTISTA, JOSE (born July 26, 1964 in Bani, Dominican Republic–) Baseball pitcher. He played in the major leagues from 1988 to 1997; his best year in the majors came in 1993, when he went 10-3 with two saves and a 2.82 earned-run average in 58 appearances for the Chicago Cubs. During his major league career, he played for four other teams as well: the Baltimore Orioles, San Francisco Giants, Detroit Tigers, and St. Louis Cardinals. Jose Bautista grew up in the predominantly-Catholic Dominican Republic. His mother, Rachel Cohen, was the daughter of Russian Jews. His father was a

Catholic. In 1981, at age 17, he was signed by the New York Mets as a non-drafted free agent. The righthanded pitcher spent eight seasons in the minor leagues before beginning his major league career with the Orioles. In 1988, he was 6-15 with a 4.30 earned-run average in 33 games. He began his career as a starter, then became a reliever. In 1989, his pitching record was 3-4; 1990, 1-0; and 1991, 0-1. He did not play in the majors in 1992, had that great year in 1993, but was 4-5 during the strike-shortened 1994 season. On April 7, 1995, Bautista signed a contract with the San Francisco Giants. He finished the season at 3-8 with a 6.44 earned run average in 52 games. He pitched in more than 50 games for the third straight season. In the 1996 season, he served primarily as a middle reliever for the Giants after being called up from the Triple-A League Phoenix club on May 4. He made 37 appearances for San Francisco, compiling a 3-4 record. In 1997, he was 2-2 pitching 21 games for the Detroit Tigers and 0-0 pitching in 11 games for the St. Louis Cardinals. His career total was 32 wins and 42 losses in 312 games for an earned run average of 4.62. Raised as a Jew, Jose celebrated both Chanukah and Christmas as a child. He married Lee Robichek, a Jewish woman from Venezuela. Jose is fifth all-time in career games pitched (312) among Jewish major league baseball players. In 2011, he was managing the Great Falls Voyagers, a Chicago White Sox farm team.

• • •

BERGER, JAY (born November 26, 1966, in Fort Dix, New Jersey–) American tennis player. Ranked 250 at the end of 1985, he won his first two titles in Buenos Aires in 1986 and Sao Paulo in 1988. He climbed to a world rank of 82 in 1986; 47 in 1987; and 34 in 1988. He won a third title in 1989 at Charleston. His trademarks: an ability to fight out long points, a no-wind-up serve and a habit of breaking his racquet strings frequently. In 1989, he reached the quarterfinals of the U.S. Open. He ended that year with a world rank of 10. On April 16, 1990, he enjoyed a career-high ranking of 7. That year he also reached the finals in Toronto, losing to Michael Chang, reached two semi-finals, and earned a career-high of $349,354. His world ranking at the end of 1990 was 18. To psych himself up for a match, he often writes notes to himself during the changeover. Knee problems limited him to only three tournaments in 1991. As of May 8, 2006, with earnings of $992,136, Jay Berger placed 361st in the ranking of top prize money leaders.

■ ■ ■

BERGMANN, RICHARD "THE OLD LION" (born 1919, in Vienna, Austria; died 1970) Table tennis player. Regarded as the greatest defensive player in table tennis history. In 1937 Bergmann became the youngest player to capture the world singles title. He won seven world titles in all, including four singles championships. Small and stocky, he was famous for the nearly impossible shots he was able to make in table tennis. When the Nazis invaded Austria in 1938, he fled to Great Britain, and later moved to the United States. He is a member of Israel's Jewish Sports Hall of Fame.

■ ■ ■

BLUM, WALTER "MOUSY" (born September 28, 1934, in Brooklyn, New York–) American jockey. Considered one of the best jockeys of the late 1950s and early 1960s. He was American riding champion in 1963-64. Blum rode his first mount, Ricey, on May 4, 1953, and had his first victory 13 rides later. His first $100,000 stakes victory came on Royal Beacon in the 1957 Atlantic City Handicap. On June 19, 1961, he rode six horses to victory on an eight-race card at Monmouth Park. In 1963, his 1,704 mounts were the second highest ever ridden in a season. He rode the winners of more than $26 million of purses and was national riding champion in 1963 and 1964. He rode 4,383 winners in a 22-year riding career, and retired after the 1975 season. When he rode his 4,000th winner in 1974, he was only the sixth U.S. jockey to do so. Blum was elected to racing's Hall of Fame in Saratoga, New York, in 1987. In

Richard Bergmann

March 2002, he was inducted into the Jewish Sports Hall of Fame, in Commack, New York.

■ ■ ■

BREGMAN, JAMES STEVEN (born November 17, 1941, in Arlington, Virginia–) American judo champion. He won a bronze medal in the 1964 Tokyo Olympics in the middleweight division. (Judo was introduced as an Olympic sport in 1964.) Bregman won the U.S. National middleweight title on his way to capturing the Tokyo medal. On August 19, 2009, the U.S. Judo Association promoted Bregman to the rank of Kudan.

■ ■ ■

BREWS, SIDNEY (born May 29, 1899, in Blackheath, England; died 1972) South African golfer. Starting in 1925, he won 30 Open championships in six countries. During the 1920s and 1930s he won six South African Opens and six professional titles. A convert to Judaism, he won the Belgian Open in 1929 and the Dutch and French Opens in

1934 and 1935. He was the runner-up in the 1934 British Open and won the Philadelphia Open in 1935.

• • •

BRODY, GYORGY (born July 2, 1908, in Hungary; died August 5, 1967) Hungarian water polo player. Considered one of the best water polo goalkeepers of all time. Brody appeared for the Hungarian national team 74 times. He received gold medals at the 1932 and 1936 Olympics as a goalie for Hungary. He was on the 1928 Hungarian national championship squad and the 1934 European championship team. After the 1956 revolution in Hungary had failed, Brody emigrated to South Africa. He died there 11 years later. Brody is a member of the Jewish Sports Hall of Fame in Israel.

• • •

COHEN, ROBERT (born November 15, 1930, in Bone, Algeria–) Boxing champion. Cohen is an Orthodox Jew who had studied to become a cantor. He began pro boxing in 1951 and was world bantamweight champion from 1954 to 1956. In 42 bouts he had 36 wins (14 by knockout), three losses, and three draws. He left the ring in 1959. He became a member of the Jewish Sports Hall of Fame in Israel in 1988.

• • •

DANILOWITZ, ABRAHAM PHINEAS "PINKY" (born August 1, 1908, in Krugersdorp Transvaal, in South Africa; died July 25, 1995) South African bowls champion. He began bowls in 1948 at age 40. His best year was 1957-58 when he won the South African singles championship. The next year, 1958, he became world champion. In that year, he broke the world record of 27 straight singles games winning 84 straight, a record which still stands. He later won the Western Transvaal bowls title twice and was runner-up in the South African singles in 1964. Pinky has been forced to quit playing bowls for health reasons.

• • •

Pinky Danilowitz

Robert Cohen

DARMON, PIERRE (born January 14, 1934, in Tunis, Tunisia–) French tennis player. France's best player in the late 1960s. He had great success at Wimbledon in 1963 when he and Jean Claude Barclay reached the men's doubles final, which they lost to Rafael Osuna and Antonio Palafox of Mexico. He played 69 Davis Cup matches for France from 1956 to 1967 and won 47 of them. In 1957 he won the singles and doubles of the French national championships. From 1990 to 1996, he was executive vice president for Europe of the Association of Tennis Professionals (ATP) Tour, headquartered in Monte Carlo. In 2002, he was awarded the Davis Cup Award of Excellence by the International Tennis Hall of Fame.

■ ■ ■

EPSTEIN, MICHAEL (born April 4, 1943, in the Bronx, New York–) American baseball player. Played nine years in the major leagues: with the Baltimore Orioles in 1966 and 1967; the Washington Senators from 1967 to 1971; the Oakland A's in 1971 and 1972; the Texas Rangers in 1973; and the California Angels in 1973 and 1974. In 907 games he had a career batting average of .244, hit 130 home runs, and had 380 runs batted in. In 1971 he tied a major league record with four home runs in four straight times at bat. In 1969 he hit 30 home runs and in 1972, 26.

■ ■ ■

FIEDLER, JAY (born December 29, 1971, in Oceanside, New York–) American NFL quarterback. In the NFL since the mid-1990s, Fiedler reached the pinnacle of his success as the starting quarterback for the Miami Dolphins in the early 2000s. A distant relative of the late Boston Pops Orchestra conductor Arthur Fiedler (Jay's grandfather was Fiedler's second cousin), Jay has been 28-13 as a starting NFL quarterback. A 1994 Dartmouth graduate, in 2000 Fiedler became the first Ivy Leaguer since 1974 to start at quarterback in an NFL season-opener. In 2001, he became only the second Miami Dolphins quarterback (the other was Dan Marino) to throw for 3,000 yards in one season, and the third team quarterback to throw 20 or more touchdowns (the other two: Marino and Bob Griese). In 2002, notwithstanding the fact that he broke his thumb midway through the season, Jay threw 179 passes for 2,024 yards, or 61.3 percent completed. In his entire career, he threw 720 passes for 8,413 yards, or 60 percent completed. In 2003, he led the Dolphins to a 7-4 record in his 11 starts. Plagued with injuries, Fiedler played briefly but retired in 2007. ESPN broadcaster Chris Berman alluded to Jay's faith by calling him *Fiedler on the Roof* and singing "If I Were a Rich Man" when Fiedler played particularly well.

■ ■ ■

GLASER, PAMELA (born August 17, 1957, in Boston, Massachusetts–) American karate champion. In 1982, she was the top-ranked American female athlete in amateur karate, holding a Second-degree Black Belt and competing in the kata form of the sport, which involves a prearranged series of movements, blocking and striking an imaginary opponent. In November of that year, she made headlines when a federal judge ordered that she be included on the USA AAU National Karate Team despite the fact that she had missed tryouts, which had fallen on Rosh Hashanah. That ruling notwithstanding, when Pam reached Taiwan to compete in the World Union of Karate Organizations International Championships, the American coaches denied her participation, arguing that she was not in adequate shape. When Pam married Moshe Ernstoff in 1986, she began using her Hebrew name, Sara-Rivka, and her husband's surname, Ernstoff. Ten years later, she moved to Israel. In May 2005, she took a silver medal in the Miyagi Chajun World Championships, in Niagara Falls, Canada, competing against women half her age. That year she also became a Fourth-degree Black Belt. Sara-Rivka was divorced from her husband in 2006. In November 2008, a single mother with five children and one grandchild, she was teaching karate and self-defense to children and adults in Jerusalem.

■ ■ ■

GOMELSKY, ALEXANDER "SASCHA" (born January 18, 1926 in Kronstadt, former USSR; died August 16, 2005) Basketball coach. Considered the father of modern basketball in the former Soviet Union. After a mediocre playing career with an army team in Leningrad between 1947 and 1952, Gomelsky started to coach basketball in the Latvian Republic. After his successes there, he moved to the Z.S.K.A. team in Moscow and to the position of national coach. His first achievement was winning the silver medal in the Tokyo Olympics in 1964. On several occasions, when Soviet teams failed to win major championships, Gomelsky was relieved of his duties as coach, but was always recalled and was quite popular in Russia. He was the coach of the USSR basketball team that won the controversial gold medal over the U.S. during the 1972 Munich Olympics, the first time the U.S. had been denied the Olympic gold medal in basketball. The team won bronze medals at both the 1976 and 1980 Olympics, and sat out the 1984 Olympics due to the Soviet boycott of the games. He coached the Soviets to a gold medal in Seoul at the 1988 Olympics. Gomelsky was president of the Soviet National Basketball Federation from 1988 to 1991. In September 1991, he told a reporter: "I know United States basketball is the best in the world. Not only in the NBA. College basketball is very nice too. But sometimes, I win." In 1991, Louisiana State coach Dale Brown called him "the best foreign coach I've ever seen. He has coached some of the best big men in the world." On his 70th birthday, Gomelsky received a congratulatory message from Russian President Boris Yeltsin. In the message, Yeltsin called Gomelsky "a symbol of Russian basketball and a man whose name is associated with the triumph and outstanding victories of Russian basketballers." Gomelsky is a member of the Jewish Sports Hall of Fame in Israel.

▪ ▪ ▪

GUBNER, GARY (born December 1, 1942, in New York City, New York–) American shot-put champion and weightlifter. In 1962 he set an indoor world record of 64 feet 11¾ inches (19.805 meters) in the shot. That same year he set four junior world records in the heavyweight lifting class.

Alexander Gomelsky

Then, in 1965, he set an American national press record of 412 pounds on his way to lifting 1,180 pounds, the fourth highest total in history.

▪ ▪ ▪

GUREVITSCH, BORIS MENDELOVITSCH (born March 23, 1931, in the former Soviet Union–) Wrestler. He represented the former Soviet Union when it first participated in the Olympic Games in Helsinki in 1952. He became the first Jewish athlete from the former Soviet Union to win an Olympic gold medal when he won the flyweight division (52 kilograms) in Greco-Roman wrestling. One year later, Gurevitsch won the first of his two world championship titles. He was named Merited Master of Sports in the former Soviet Union and retired from sports at the end of the 1950s. He is a member of the Jewish Sports Hall of Fame in Israel.

▪ ▪ ▪

GUTTMANN, BELA (born March 13, 1900, in Budapest, Hungary; died August 28, 1981) Soccer player and coach. One of the best soccer players of the 1920s, Guttmann played for the famous Hakoah Vienna soccer team from 1922 to 1933, except for two years when he was on a Jewish soccer team in New York. He was on the Hakoah team that won the Austrian championship in 1924. After Guttmann's retirement from active play in 1933, he coached for the next 30 years in different countries, including the Hungarian, Portuguese, and Austrian national teams. His teams won two European cups, 10 national championships, and seven national cups. Guttmann is considered one of the greatest Jewish players and coaches of all time. He is a member of the Jewish Sports Hall of Fame in Israel.

· · ·

GYARMATI, ANDREA (born May 15, 1954, in Hungary–) Hungarian swimmer. Her mother is Eva Szekely, the great swimmer, and her father, Dezso Gyarmati, the water polo champion. Andrea became a successful swimmer in her own right. At 14, she came in fifth in the 100-meter backstroke and butterfly in the 1968 Mexico City Olympics. She swam the world's fastest 100-meter butterfly in 1969 and was Europe's second best in the 100-meter and 200-meter backstroke and third best in the 100-meter freestyle. She won an Olympic silver medal in the women's 100-meter backstroke and a bronze medal in the 100-meter butterfly event in the 1972 Munich Olympics. She was Hungary's top sportswoman between 1970 and 1972. She lives in Budapest and works there as a pediatrician.

· · ·

HUGHES, SARAH (born May 2, 1985, in Great Neck, New York–) American figure skater. Sarah made history by coming from far behind in the 2002 figure skating competition at the Salt Lake City Winter Olympics to take the gold medal. When the 16-year-old high school junior came in fourth in the short program, she was seemingly out of gold medal contention. But two days later, on February 21, 2002, she gave the best skating performance of her life in the long program. Her unprecedented combinations helped her surpass favorites Michelle Kwan and Irina Slutskaya to

become the first skater to win gold after finishing fourth in the short program. With that performance, Sarah became the first woman to land two triple-triple jump combinations—the triple Salchow-triple loop and the triple toe-triple loop—in one program. A Long Island native, Sarah began skating when she was three, chasing after her older hockey-playing brothers David and Matt onto the skating rink that their father, John, an attorney, had built in the backyard. Sarah also has three sisters: Rebecca, Emily, and Taylor. Sarah's mother, Amy, who is Jewish, drove her daughter to daily practice. Amy was diagnosed with breast cancer in 1997, but following extensive treatment she was declared cancer-free in 1999. Since earning the gold, Sarah's life has been hectic. Returning from Salt Lake City, she was the star attraction at a victory parade attended by 60,000 fans in Great Neck. She was a presenter at the Grammy Awards, and her picture appeared on the front of the Wheaties cereal box and on the cover of numerous American magazines. In March 2003, she won the Sullivan Award, the prestigious honor given to the outstanding amateur American athlete for the previous year. On May 25, 2009, Sarah graduated from Yale University with a B.A. in American Studies. She plans to attend law school in the near future. In 2011 she was dating Andrew Giuliani, son of former New York City mayor Rudy Giuliani.

· · ·

KLOSS, ILANA (born March 26, 1956, in Johannesburg, South Africa–) South African tennis player. She won the Wimbledon junior singles title in 1973, but has excelled at doubles. She was the South African doubles champion in 1974 and 1976; she won the French doubles and U.S. Open doubles in 1976; the British hardcourt championships in 1976; and the 1977 U.S. clay court championship. Her usual partner was Linky Boshoff. Kloss won the German and Canadian championships in 1977. She has served since February 2001 as the CEO and commissioner of World Team Tennis, overseeing the ten-team WTT Pro League and the nationwide grassroots Recreational League programs.

· · ·

KRAMER, BARRY (born November 10, 1942, in Schenectady, New York–) American basketball player. He was All-American in 1963 and 1964, first team, playing for New York University. Kramer won the Haggerty Award as the outstanding player in the New York metropolitan area. He was the country's second best scorer in 1963, averaging 29.3 points per game. During his college career, he averaged 22.5 points per game, scoring 1,667 points in 74 games. In 1964-65, he played in the NBA for the San Francisco Warriors and the New York Knicks, averaging 3.6 points in 52 games. In the 1969–70 season, he played in the ABA for the New York Nets, averaging 3.9 points per game. After retiring from professional basketball, Kramer obtained a degree from Albany Law School and become a surrogate Court Judge in Schenectady.

■ ■ ■

KRAMER, JOEL (born November 30, 1955, in San Diego, California–) American basketball player. He played basketball in the late 1970s at San Diego State University, where he was All-Pacific Coast Athletic Association (PCAA) First Team in his last two college seasons and PCAA Player of the Year as a senior. He played with the Phoenix Suns for five years from 1978 to 1983 where he made his mark as a formidable rebounder. Since 1984, Kramer has worked as a CPA for Miller Wagner.

■ ■ ■

KRONBERGER, LILY (born November 12, 1890, in Budapest, Hungary; died May 21, 1974) Hungarian figure skater. Kronberger was the first skater to try an entire free skating program with musical accompaniment. In 1906, she was third in the first figure skating world championships. She came in third the following year as well. In 1908, she became world champion and repeated that feat for the next three years. She is a member of the Jewish Sports Hall of Fame in Israel.

■ ■ ■

Henry Laskau

LASKAU, HENRY HELMUT (born September 12, 1916, in Berlin, Germany; died May 7, 2000) American track star. He won 42 American national titles, a feat matched by only a few others. A middle-distance runner in Germany, he came to the U.S in 1940 and returned to running after the war. He took up walking and became a national champion in 1947, remaining undefeated in the sport in the U.S. until 1956. In 1950 he set a world indoor mile record of 6:19.2. In 1957 Laskau won the Maccabiah 3,000-meter walk. He later became a walking official and coach. In 1983, he was named to the USA/Mobil All-Time Track and Field team. He has been a volunteer official at meets throughout the U.S. Laskau officiated both walking events at the 1984 Olympic Games in Los Angeles.

■ ■ ■

Gyula Mandy

LEAND, ANDREA (born January 18, 1964, in Baltimore, Maryland–) American tennis player. One of the surprise amateur sensations of the 1981 tennis season. In addition to making the semifinals of the Junior Wimbledon tournament that year, she was also ranked in the top ten in the International Tennis Federation's Junior Ranking circuit. During the summer of 1981, Andrea, then 17, won the Maccabiah singles title and the Maccabiah mixed doubles. Two months later, at the U.S. Open in New York, she reached the final 16 and then defeated Andrea Jaeger, rated second in the world at the time. Leand was the number one ranked junior in the U.S. in 1981. She entered Princeton University in the fall of 1981, but left after her freshman year to join the pro tennis circuit. During the next three years, she climbed as high as No. 13 in the world in May 1983 but sank later to No. 49. She was ranked 46 in 1983 and 35 in 1984. She returned to Princeton University in 1985, won her degree in psychology three years later, and was back on tour in 1989. Since returning to the tour, she ranked 150 in 1989, 142 in 1990 and 181 in 1991. Since the early 1990s, Andrea has been writing for publications that include *USA Today*, *The Baltimore Sun*, and *Tennis Week Magazine*. She has also been a television commentator for the ESPN/STAR network. In 2006, she was considered the foremost authority on women's tennis.

■ ■ ■

MANDEL, GYULA (born in July 1899, in Budapest, Hungary; died 1969) Hungarian soccer player. Born Julius Mandel, he played soccer despite a serious injury that shortened one of his legs. Mandel played on the Hungarian national team 32 times as fullback. After his playing career ended, he became one of Europe's best coaches; he coached the Hungarian national team in its heyday at the beginning of the 1950s. In 1956, Mandel was called to coach in Brazil; when he returned to Hungary, he accepted an invitation to coach the Israeli national team. In the four years he managed the team (1959-63), he created an Israeli team that was competitive with the Europeans. In 1963, Mandel returned to Hungary and acted as adviser and talent scout for the national soccer federation. He is a member of the Jewish Sports Hall of Fame in Israel.

■ ■ ■

MASSU, NICOLAS (born October 10, 1979, in Vina Del Mar, Chile–) Chilean tennis player. In 2000, Massu's first full year on the ATP tour, he was a finalist in a tournament in Orlando, Florida. A year later he won his first singles title, and in 2003 he became a top 20 player. On August 15, 2004, Massu was ranked 14th in the world, making him the top male Jewish tennis player. At the 2004 Athens Olympics, he won gold in both the singles and doubles event, becoming the first Chilean to win an Olympic gold medal. "Now I can die happy," Nicolas exclaimed. In 2007, he was ranked 80th in singles, then rose to 75th in 2007. Massu was ranked 112th on December 28, 2009.

■ ■ ■

MEISL, HUGO (born November 16, 1881, in Maleschau, Bohemia (Czech Republic); died February 17, 1937) Czech soccer administrator. Meisl was connected with soccer from his early childhood as a player, referee, journalist, and official. He became general secretary of the Austrian Soccer Federation during the 1920s and 1930s. He managed Austria's national team which he turned into the "Wunderteam" (miracle team) in the 1930s. He was instructor and founder of the first international club competition, the Metropa

Hugo Meisl

Cup. Austria and many other European governments honored him for his achievements. He is considered one of the greatest soccer experts of all time. Meisl is a member of the Jewish Sports Hall of Fame in Israel.

. . .

MELNIK, FAINA (born June 9, 1945, in Bakota, Ukraine, former Soviet Union–) Russian discus thrower and shot-putter. Considered one of the world's greatest female discus throwers ever. In her international debut at the 1971 European Championships, she set a world record with a throw of 64.22 meters; then a few weeks later, she improved it to 64.88 meters. In 1972 she extended the world record three times. Melnik won a gold medal at the Munich Olympics in 1972. She bettered the world record several more times. Her longest throw was 70.50 meters in 1976. In 1984, Melnik was inducted into the Jewish Sports Hall of Fame in Israel.

. . .

MIDLER, MARK (born September 24, 1931, in Moscow, former Soviet Union–) Russian fencer. Midler

began fencing in 1943 and became a Merited Master of Sports. A Moscow school teacher, he first became a member of the Soviet national fencing team in 1954. In 1960, as captain of the Soviet Olympic fencing team, he won a gold medal in team foil competition. In 1964 he again won a gold medal at the Olympics in team foil, and that year he was captain of the National foil team. He is a member of the Jewish Sports Hall of Fame in Israel.

. . .

OBERLANDER, FRED (born May 23, 1911, in Vienna, Austria; died 1996) Austrian wrestler. Former European wrestling champion in 1935; runner-up in 1932. He was Austrian champion in 1930; French champion eight times; and eight times British heavyweight champion (from 1939-45 and 1948). He was also Canadian heavyweight champion in 1951. Oberlander served as chairman of the Canadian Wrestling Association for some time. In 1974, he was named to the Canadian Amateur Sports Hall of Fame.

. . .

PINTUSSEVICH, ZHANNA (July 6, 1972, in Nezem, Ukraine–) Ukrainian sprinter. One of the world's top sprinters in the late 1990s, she clocked the fastest time in the women's 100 meters second round on August 2, 1997, in Athens at the sixth World Athletics Championships. The little-known sprinter hit the tape first in her group with a brilliant time of 10.90 seconds, the second fastest that year after the 10.89 set by Gail Devers of the United States. Zhanna went on to win the silver medal in the 100 meters final. The next day (August 8, 1997) at that same event, she won the women's 200 meters gold medal. Her winning time was 22.32 seconds. Zhanna began running when she was 13 years old, training seriously for the first time when she began boarding school the next year near Kiev. She first came to prominence at age 15 when she won sprinting events at the Soviet Union Youth championships in Belize, Georgia. At age 16, she was a member of the Soviet relay team that came in third at the Junior World Championships in Toronto in 1988. At age 19, in 1981, she won the 100- and 200-meter sprints and was second in the 400-meter relay event at the European Championships in Athens, Greece. She graduated from a physical education institute in Kiev at age 18. In 1992, she competed in the indoor European Championships in Genoa, Italy. A year later, in 1993, she came in third in the 60-meter sprint in the indoor World Championships in Toronto. Coming in only fifth in the Soviet Championships, she did not earn a place on the Ukrainian track team that participated in the 1992 Olympics in Barcelona. In 1995, she was fifth in the 100-meter race in the World Championships in Gotebord, Sweden. At the 1996 Atlanta Olympics, she came in eighth place in that event. In August 2001, she became the fastest woman in the world by defeating American Marion Jones in the finals of the 100-meter race held at the World Athletics Championships, in Edmonton, Canada. Pintussevich's time was 10.82 seconds. Competing in the 100-meter race at the Athens Olympics in August 2004, she failed to advance past the semifinals.

• • •

PRINSTEIN, MYER (born December 22, 1878, in Szczuczyn, Poland; died March 10, 1925) American track star. In the early twentieth century, he won four Olympic medals and twice held the world's record for the broad jump. At the 1900 Paris Olympics, Prinstein won a gold medal in the hop, step, and jump (now the triple jump). In the 1904 St. Louis Olympics, he repeated the feat and added the running broad jump to his list of gold medals. At the 1908 Athens Olympics, he again won the broad jump. Prinstein became a lawyer after retiring from track and field in 1910. He is a member of the Jewish Sports Hall of Fame in Israel.

• • •

ROSENBLUTH, LEONARD (born January 22, 1933, in New York City, New York–) American basketball player. All-American basketball player for the University of North Carolina between 1955 and 1957. In 1957, his senior year, Rosenbluth averaged 27.9 points per game and led his team to the national title. He then played for the NBA's Philadelphia Warriors during the 1958-59 season. Rosenbluth teaches American history at

Myer Prinstein

Coral Gables High School in Florida while coaching a basketball team at Deerborne, a nearby private school.

• • •

ROTTMAN, LEON (born July 22, 1934, in Romania–) Romanian canoeing champion. The most successful canoeist in the sport's history. In the 1956 Olympics, Rottman won two gold Olympic medals for Romania, the first in the 1,000-meter Canadian singles with a time of 5:05.3 and the second in the 10,000-meter Canadian singles with a time of 56:41.0. In the 1960 Games, he won a bronze in the 1,000-meter Canadian singles with a time of 4:35.87. He was elected as a member of the Jewish Sports Hall of Fame in 1981.

Leon Rottman

• • •

SCHACHT, AL (born November 11, 1892 in New York City, New York; died July 14, 1984) American baseball player and entertainer. Known as the "Clown Prince of Baseball," he had a brief career as a major league pitcher, but became famous afterward as a pantomime entertainer at baseball games. Schacht's first appearance as a baseball clown came in 1914. As the announcer called out the starting pitcher and catcher, Schacht, then playing for the Newark, New Jersey, team in the minor leagues, took his place on a horse led by a black attendant. He performed during the 1930s and 1940s.

• • •

SHAMSKY, ART (born October 14, 1941, in St. Louis, Missouri–) American baseball player. He played in the major leagues from 1965 to 1972, first for the Cincinnati Reds until 1968, and then for the New York Mets from 1968 to 1972. In eight years he played in 665 games and had a career batting average of .253, with 68 home runs and 233 runs batted in. He played the outfield and first base. In August 1966, he hit home runs in four

straight times at bat to tie a major league record. He became a consultant with the real estate investment firm of First Realty Reserve in New York and a sports broadcaster for WNYW Television, Channel 5. He also owns a restaurant, Legends, near New York's City Hall. Shamsky managed the Modi'in Miracle to a third-place finish (22–19) in the Israel Baseball League's 2007 inaugural season. They lost to the Bet Shemesh Blue Sox 3–0 in the championship game.

■ ■ ■

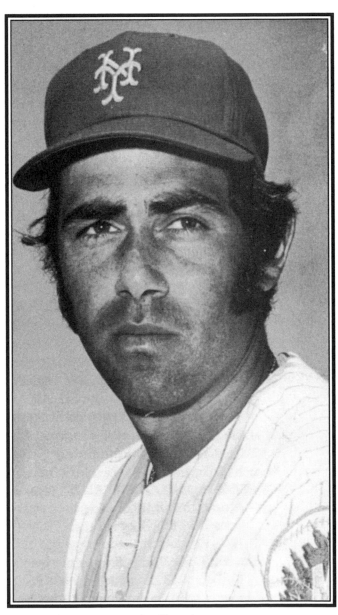

Art Shamsky

SHERMAN, ALEXANDER "ALLIE" (born February 10, 1923, in Brooklyn, New York–) American football player and coach. He quarterbacked Brooklyn College from 1939 to 1942 and then played pro football, mostly for Philadelphia until 1947. He became coach of the New York Giants in 1961 where he remained until 1968. Under Sherman, the Giants won the Eastern Division title from 1961 to 1963. He was twice NFL-Coach-of-the-Year, 1961 and 1962. From 1977 to 1994, Sherman worked for Warner Communications in the sports program. In 1983, he was in charge of the Home Sports Entertainment pay television sports channel for the Pittsburgh-Houston-Dallas-Houston cable franchise. In the late 1980s, he was a television commentator for National Football League telecasts. Since 1994, he has served as president of New York City's Off-Track Betting Corporation.

• • •

SHERRY, LAWRENCE (born July 25, 1935, in Los Angeles, California; died December 17, 2006) American baseball player. He was a relief pitcher in the major leagues for 11 years. His career won-lost record was 53-44 with a 3.67 earned-run average. In relief he was 47-37 with 82 saves and a 3.56 earned-run average. He was with the Los Angeles Dodgers from 1958 to 1963, the Detroit Tigers from 1964 to 1967, and the Houston Astros and California Angels in 1968.

• • •

SPELLMAN, FRANK (born September 17, 1922, in Paoli, Pennsylvania–) American weightlifter. In the 1948 Olympics, Spellman, a professional photographer, won a gold medal, establishing an Olympic record of 860 pounds (390 kilograms) in the middleweight division. He is a member of the Jewish Sports Hall of Fame in Israel.

• • •

SPERO, DONALD (born August 9, 1938, in Glencoe, Illinois–) American rowing champion. National single and double sculls champion in 1963. National single scull and quadruples champion in 1964. Spero has been called the best sculler ever produced in the U.S. In 1966 he won the world single sculls title. After getting his doctorate from Columbia University in physics in 1968, he became president and co-founder of the Fusions Systems Corporation in Rockville, Maryland.

• • •

TENDLER, LEW (born September 28, 1898, in Philadelphia, Pennsylvania; died November 15, 1970) American boxer. Nat Fleischer has ranked him as the ninth best lightweight of all time. Others have called him the best left-handed boxer ever to fight in the ring. His fights with Benny Leonard, then lightweight champion, on July 27, 1922 and July 23, 1923, were major ring events, but Tendler was unable to snare the title from Leonard. He also lost a fight for the welterweight title on June 2, 1924, when Mickey Walker defeated him in a 10-round decision. Experts agree that Tendler might have been lightweight champion in any era but Leonard's. Tendler's record was 59 wins (37 by knockout), 11 losses, two draws, 94 no decision fights, and one no contest, in 167 bouts. Tendler went into the hotel and restaurant business in Philadelphia and Atlantic City after leaving the ring. In 1992 he was inducted into the Jewish Sports Hall of Fame in Israel.

• • •

VAN DAMM, SHEILA (born January 17, 1922, in Paddington, England; died August 23, 1987) British racing driver. European woman driving champion in 1954 and 1955. The first woman to drive for a British manufacturer. Van Damm won the Monte Carlo Rally in 1955. That was the first time a British woman had won in 23 years. In the early 1960s she ran the well-known Windmill Theatre in the Soho District of London.

• • •

WALK, NEAL (born July 29, 1948, in Cleveland, Ohio–) American basketball player. In his third year at the University of Florida, he was the outstanding rebounder in the nation with just under 20 rebounds per game. The next year, as a senior, he was the only major college player in the nation to rank among the top 10 in both scoring and rebounding. Walk was an All-American choice as well. In 1969, he was drafted by the Phoenix Suns where he played from 1969 to 1974. He will always be remembered as the center the Phoenix Suns received when in 1969 they lost a coin flip that gave UCLA's Lew Alcindor, who became Kareem Abdul-Jabbar, to the Milwaukee Bucks. Walk's best season was 1972–73 when he averaged 20.2 points per game. He averaged 16.8 points per game in 1973–74, and 15.7 points per game in 1971–72. Walk joined the New York Knicks in February 1975 and played for them for the next two seasons (until 1975–76). In 1975–76 he averaged 7.4 points per game. For two years, beginning in September 1979, Walk played in Israel for Ramat Gan Hapoel. He then returned to the United States. A benign tumor, probably present from birth, grew slowly until it stretched and damaged his spinal cord, affecting his ability to walk. Two operations in the late 1980s to remove the tumor from his spine left him a paraplegic, confining him to a wheelchair. In 1989, he became a member of the Samaritan Wheelchair Suns in the Southern California league of the National Wheelchair Basketball Association. Doctors hope he will one day walk again. Walk has been working for the Phoenix Suns in its Community Affairs Department.

■ ■ ■

WITTENBERG, HENRY B. (born September 18, 1918, in Jersey City, New Jersey; died March 9, 2010) American wrestler. Considered one of the world's greats, between 1938 and 1952 he won 400 consecutive matches. He won a gold medal in the light heavyweight division in the 1948 London Olympics and a silver medal in the 1952 Helsinki Games. Wittenberg is a member of the National Wrestling Hall of Fame, the Helms Hall of Fame, and the Jewish Sports Hall of Fame in Israel.

■ ■ ■

WOLF, WARNER (born November 11, 1937, in Washington, D.C.–) American sports broadcaster. One of the most prominent sports personalities on local New York TV. He began on radio in 1961 as a country and western disc jockey and then worked on call-in sports shows. He became the top sports announcer in his native Washington, D.C., in the 1970s. Moving over to ABC Sports in March 1976, he remained in New York for the next 16 years. He has appeared on Monday Night Football, Wide World of Sports, and NCAA College Football Scoreboard. In 1980, WCBS hired Wolf and he worked for the New York City CBS affiliate for the next 12 years. In 1992, Wolf went to Washington, D.C., where he was a sports commentator for WUSA-TV. He was dismissed in August 1995 following a dispute over his refusal to change the format of his sportscasts. He returned to the local CBS television station in New York in February 1997. "This is one great trip back to the future," Bill Casey, Channel 2's news director, said of Wolf's return. Wolf is best known for such snappy phrases as "boo of the week" or "OK, let's go to the video tape," which was also the title of his book published in the spring of 2000. In May 2004, WCBS-TV abruptly fired Wolf at the age of 66. Shortly thereafter he assumed sportscasting duties for *Imus in the Morning*, a radio and television program emanating from New York. He also hosts a Saturday sports talk show on ESPN radio.

■ ■ ■

ZASLOFSKY, MAX (born December 7, 1925 in Brooklyn, New York; died October 15, 1985) American basketball player. He was considered one of the finest two-handed shooters in the early days of pro basketball. In 1948, he led the NBA in scoring with a 21-point average. Zaslofsky played first for St. John's and then in the NBA from 1946 to 1956, with the Chicago Stags and the New York Knicks. When he retired in 1956, he was the National Basketball Association's third highest all-time scorer with 7,990 points. Zaslofsky coached in the American Basketball Association in the late 1960s: he had a 36-42 record with the New Jersey Americans in 1967-68, the team which eventually became the NBA New Jersey Nets. Zaslofsky is a member of the Jewish Sports Hall of Fame in Israel.

Israeli Sports Figures

AMIR, ELDAD. See **SELA, YOEL**

. . .

AVERBUKH, ALEX (born October 1, 1974, in Siberia, Russia–) Pole vaulter. Following his emigration from Russia to Israel in 1999, Alex competed at the 2000 Sydney Olympics, finishing 10th in the pole vault final. Earlier that year, he became the No. 1 European pole vaulter by taking gold at the European Indoor Championships in Belgium. At the Israel Athletics Championships in July 2000, Averbukh broke the Israeli pole vault record again, with a jump of 5.85 meters. In 1999 at Seville, with a jump of 5.80 meters, he became the first Israeli medal-winner at the World Athletics Championships. In 2002 he was European champion, and in April 2004 he was honored as one of sixteen Israeli sports figures chosen to participate in his country's fifty-sixth Independence Day torchlighting ceremony. Alex was Europe's pole vault champion in 2006. He retired after the 2009 Maccabiah Games.

. . .

BERKOWITZ, MICKEY (born February 17, 1954, in Kfar Saba, Israel–) Basketball player. A pillar on Maccabi Tel Aviv's teams that won the European Cup in 1977 and 1981. Mickey first joined the Maccabi Tel Aviv youth club at age 11 and subsequently became a major Maccabi Tel Aviv basketball star. He also played on the Israeli national team that won a gold medal at the 1974 Teheran Asian Games and a silver medal at the 1979 European championships in Torino, Italy. His highest scoring game in an international contest occurred in the 1975 European championships in Belgrade, Yugoslavia, when he scored 44 points against Turkey. He was named Israel's Sportsman of the Year in 1975. In 1986, Berkowitz was named Best Basketball Player of the Year. After that season, he left Maccabi Tel Aviv to play for Maccabi Rishon LeZion. In 1996, Berkowitz, considered the greatest player in Israeli basketball history, retired from basketball. In 2008, he was named one of the 50 Greatest Euroleague Contributors.

. . .

BROCKMAN, SHIMSHON (born September 21, 1958, in Tel Aviv, Israel–) and **FRIEDLANDER, EITAN** (born September 16, 1957, in Kibbutz Rosh Hanikra, Israel–) Israeli sailors. Both Brockman and Friedlander come from sailing families. In June 1977, they took third place in the European Championships in Rust, near Vienna, Austria. The next year, they won the World Championship

Mickey Berkowitz

in the 420 non-Olympic class at Hyere, France. In July 1979, the two won the European Championships at Dania, Spain. In 1980, they won the World Sailing Championships in the 420 non-Olympic class in Quiberon, France. Because Israel boycotted the 1980 Olympics, in protest against the Soviet invasion of Afghanistan, they did not participate at the Moscow Games. In September 1982, they were runners-up at the European Championships at Lake Balton, Hungary. In November 1982, they were named Israeli Sportsmen of the Year by the Israeli newspaper *Yediot Aharanot*. At the 1984 Los Angeles Olympics, they finished eighth. They failed to qualify for the 1988 Seoul Olympics. Friedlander retired from competitive sailing in 1988, Brockman in 1991. Brockman is an aeronautical engineer for the Israel Electric Company in Haifa. Friedlander is general manager of Yamit, a Tel Aviv water-sports retailer.

■ ■ ■

BRUCK, YOAV (Born March 6, 1972, in Israel–) Swimmer. In 1997, he shared Israel's Sportsman of the Year honors with swimmer Eytan Ohrbach. Bruck represented Israel in the Barcelona Olympics in 1992 and in the Atlanta Olympic Games in 1996. He finished eighth in the 50-meter freestyle event in the Rome championships. He was a member of the team that reached the finals at Atlanta in the 4 x 100-meters mixed relays (eighth place). At the 2000 Sydney Olympics, his medley relay team came in eighth. Bruck holds the Israeli record for the 50-meter freestyle: 22.79 seconds. In 2001, Bruck was inducted into Auburn University's Wall of Fame.

■ ■ ■

CARMEL, ZEFANIA (born December 21, 1940, in Baghdad, Iraq; died September 22, 1980) and **LAZAROVE, LYDIA** (born January 16, 1946, in Sofia, Bulgaria–) Israeli sailors. In August 1967, they were members of the world championship Israeli sailing team that won the team racing competition on the Hudson River in New York City. Carmel won the world championship in individual sailing in Sandham, Sweden, in 1969. That same year Carmel and Lazarove also won the world

championship in the 420 non-Olympic sailing class in Sandham, making them Israel's first world champions in any sport. Carmel drowned in September, 1980, off Bat Yam, Israel, while training on a windsurfing boat. He was 39. Both Carmel and Lazarove are members of the Jewish Sports Hall of Fame in Israel. The two were honored in May 1998 as two of Israel's top 50 athletes in its history.

■ ■ ■

CHAIT, GALIT (born January 29, 1975, in Kfar Saba, Israel–) and **SAKHNOVSKI, SERGEI** (born May 15, 1975, in Moscow, Russia–). Israeli ice dancers. In 2002, in Nagano, Japan, they became the first Israelis to win a medal at the World Figure Skating Championships, taking home the bronze in ice dancing. In 1998, they became the first Israeli ice dancers to compete at an Olympics, finishing 14th. Chait was also the first Israeli ice dancer to participate in a World Championships, competing in 1994. Holding dual Israeli-American citizenship, she began skating at age eight at New York's Rockefeller Center. She was first paired with Russian Maxim Sevostianov; they fin-

Galit Chait and Sergei Sakhnovski

ished sixth in the U. S. Nationals in 1994. Chait paired with Sakhnovski in 1995. Chait and Sakhnovski captured the silver medal at the Cup of China in November 2004.

■ ■ ■

CHODOROV, YA'ACOV (born June 16, 1927, in Rishon LeZion, Palestine; died December 30, 2006) Soccer player. Considered the best goalkeeper in Israel's soccer history and a goalie who would meet international standards. He played more than 30 times on Israel's national soccer team from 1947 to 1967 and, in 1949, was named Israel's Sportsman of the Year. In 1951, the great English soccer team Arsenal offered Chodorov a contract but, since he was unwilling to leave Israel, he refused. He has been a tour guide for the United Jewish Appeal in Israel for 34 years. Chodorov was awarded the Israel Prize in May 2006, but he was unable to attend the ceremonies due to a stroke.

■ ■ ■

COHEN-MINTZ, TANHUM (born October 8, 1939, in Riga, Latvia–) Basketball player. Considered one of the best basketball players Israel has produced and one of the best pivots ever in European basketball. A six-foot, eight-inch center, Cohen-Mintz played for Israel's national basketball team 89 times from 1958 to 1971 and scored 1,076 points. In 1961, he was selected Israel's Sportsman of the Year. In 1964, he was named to the starting five of the European All-Stars, the first Israeli to receive that honor. He retired as a senior officer in the Israel Defense Forces and then worked as an engineer for an Israeli chocolate manufacturer. In 1998, he was named by the Israeli newspaper *Ma'ariv* as one of Israel's five best basketball players in the nation's history.

■ ■ ■

ERLICH, JONATHAN "YONI" (born April 5, 1977, in Buenos Aires, Argentina–) and **RAM, ANDY** (born April 10, 1980, in Montevideo, Uruguay–) Israeli tennis players. Playing as partners, in July 2008 Erlich and Ram attained their highest world doubles ranking, 5th. The duo took a major step forward by winning the Men's Doubles Champi-

onship at the 2008 Australian Open in straight sets over Arnaud Clement and Michael Llodra 7–5, 7–6, the Israelis' first Grand Slam win after capturing numerous ATP titles. But Erlich and Ram's breakthrough achievement was at Wimbledon in 2003, when they became the first Israelis to advance to the semifinals of a Grand Slam event. In 2006, partnering with Vera Zvonareva, Ram became the first Israeli tennis player to win a Grand Slam event, the Wimbledon mixed doubles title. In 2007, with partner Nathalie Dechy, he won the mixed doubles event at the French Open. While Erlich was recovering from right elbow surgery from September 2008 to May 2009, Ram continued to partner with others. Ehrlich and Ram reunited in May 2009, losing in the final round of the Israel Open ATP Challenger. In 2011 they continued to play doubles together.

■ ■ ■

FRIEDMAN, GAL (born September 16, 1975, in Hadera, Israel–) Windsurfer. In September 1995, he won a silver medal at the European Championships held on the Isle of Wight, England. He won a silver medal in the World Championships held in Haifa in March 1996 and a few months later, still a soldier in the Israel Defense Forces,

Ya'acov Chodorov

won a bronze medal at the Atlanta Olympics. In recognition of his feats that year, he was named Israel's Sportsman of the Year in 1996. In November 2002, he took first place at the World Championships in Thailand, helping him to move from sixth to second in the world rankings for the end of 2002. Friedman's greatest feat was winning gold in the August 2004 men's mistral sailing event. It was Israel's first ever gold medal, and Israel's Olympic committee rewarded him with 285,000 Israeli shekels ($65,000). "I feel like I'm in a dream," he said later. "An entire country was pushing me." The race was carried live on Israeli television and radio. Friedman retired from windsurfing in 2008 and as of 2011 was coaching.

• • •

FRIEDLANDER, EITAN. See **BROCKMAN, SHIMSHON**

• • •

GELFAND, BORIS (born June 24, 1968, in Minsk, Belarus–) Israeli chess player. In December 2009, Gelfand won the Chess World Cup in Siberia, earning $100,000. In January 2010, he was ranked sixth best chess player in the world. At his peak in the 1990s, he was ranked third in the world after Gary Kasparov and Anatoly Karpov. Junior Champion of the Soviet Union at age 17 and European Junior Champion at 19, he tied for first place in the World Junior Championship at age 20, in 1988. Since immigrating to Israel from Belarus in 1998, he has spent half of each year abroad, mostly in front of a chessboard or computer. When Boris was but five years old, his father gave him a book about chess and taught him the rules. Of chess, he says, "I just love this game more than ever. I enjoy every moment of it, even though it's such exhausting work."

• • •

GERSHON, PINHAS "PINI" (born November 13, 1951, in Tel Aviv, Israel–) Basketball coach. Pinhas began coaching Israel's most successful basketball team, Maccabi Tel Aviv, in 1999. Since then, he has won three European Championships (2001, 2004, 2005). Gershon retired following the 2001 season, but he returned

Eran Groumi

for 2003–2004, trouncing Skipper Bologna in the Euroleague final 118–74. Named Euroleague Coach of the Year in 2004–2005, Gershon became a national hero and one of the most sought-after coaches in Europe. In 2006, he led Maccabi Tel Aviv to the Euroleague Final Four. Coaching the Greek Olympiacos in 2007, Gershon led the team to the national finals. In November 2008, two months after leading the National Team of Bulgaria to EuroBasket 2009, he signed as Maccabi Tel Aviv coach. During 2010 Gershon left Maccabi Tel Aviv after losing in the national finals to Hapoel Gilboa Galil. In July 2011 he signed on to run the operations of the Israeli basketball team Hapoel Holon, which he coached in the 1970s.

• • •

GROUMI, ERAN (born June 5, 1970 in Jerusalem, Israel–) Israeli swimmer. His potential was spotted during participation in a swimming program at Jerusalem's YMCA at age eight. At the 1989 Maccabiah Games, he broke the Israeli record in the 200-meter butterfly for men with a time of 2:04.80. At the Israeli Winter Championships in Haifa in February 1992, he won four events, including the 100-meter backstroke in 57.39 seconds. In early May 1992, at an international tournament in Vienna, he won the gold medal in the 200-meter backstroke, equaling his national record of 57:39; it was the third straight race that year in which Groumi had completed the distance in less than the qualifying time of 57:92 for the Barcelona Olympics. Then he failed to qualify for the 1996 Atlanta Olympics; however, in August 1997 at the European Championship in Seville, Spain, he set the Israeli record for the 50-meter and 100-meter butterfly (25.13 seconds for the 50-meter event and 54.48 seconds for the 100-meter race). In 2006, a resident of Tel Aviv, Eran was active on the boards of several swimming organizations.

■ ■ ■

HATUEL, LYDIA (born August 15, 1963, in Casablanca, Morocco–) Fencer. As a youngster she watched in frustration as her two older brothers, Haim and Yitzhak, practiced fencing at home. She begged them to let her try the sport. Telling her that she was too small, they said she would have to wait until she reached the second grade. Once she took sword in hand, she reached the heights. In 1979, at age 16, she became Israeli women's fencing champion, a title she held for many years. *The Guiness Book of Records* listed her after she had won the title six straight times. She reached the semifinals at the Los Angeles Olympics in 1984, but did not participate in the Seoul Olympics because her event fell on Yom Kippur. In June 1991, she came in eighth in the World Championships in Budapest, Hungary. Haim Hatuel is her coach. She took 22nd place, out of 40 competitors, at the 1992 Barcelona Olympics. She came in eighth place in the World Cup in Moscow in 1995 and 13th at the Atlanta Olympics in July 1996. She teaches physical education in Kiryat Haim, near Acre.

■ ■ ■

HERSCOVICI, HENRY (born February 12, 1927, in Bucharest, Romania–) Shooter. He was a distinguished shooter for the Romanian team before immigrating to Israel in 1965. During the first Asian Shooting Championship in Tokyo in 1967,

Lydia Hatuel

Herscovici won gold and silver medals which helped him to be selected Israel's top athlete that year. He was not successful in the 1968 Mexico City Olympic Games, but four years later in Munich he came in 23rd. Two years earlier (1970) he won two gold, one silver, and one bronze medal in the Bangkok Asian Games. From 1965 to 1982, he held five Israeli records. Herscovici has been a watchmaker for years and at present owns a store in Tel Aviv.

■ ■ ■

INBAR, AMIT (born August 9, 1972, in Hadera, Israel–) Windsurfer. He took up windsurfing because his older brother Eran, a world-class windsurfer, needed some competition during practice. Amit became world No. 1 in 1991, after placing first and second in European competitions. On August 2, 1991, Inbar finished second in the board windsurfing World Championship. It was held on the same Barcelona off-shore course where the Olympic competition was held. In mid-May 1992, Inbar won a silver medal at the World Windsurfing Championships in Cadiz, Spain. In early June 1992, he was ranked No. 1 in the world after winning the international pre-Olympic tournament in Holland. Though heralded as a possible

Amit Inbar

Championships in 1997, Katash played for the national team in 40 games, scoring 537 points. A premium shooter, he averaged 22 points a game during his career. In July 1998, after almost becoming the first Israeli to play in the NBA, Katash signed on with the Greek team Panathinaikos. He helped the team win the European championship in 2002, defeating Tel Aviv Maccabi. Katash retired after that season due to a knee injury. In 2004, he was coaching Hapoel Galil Elyon in Israel. He has since been coaching basketball in Europe and more recently in Israel.

• • •

KORSITZ, LEE (born in 1984, in Michmoret, Israel–) Israeli sailing champion. In 2003, at age 19, Korsitz burst onto the sailing scene, winning the Olympic Sailing World Championships in Cadiz, Spain. In 2004 she was serving in the Israel Defense Forces, where she was selected as an "outstanding athlete," allowing her to continue her training. Lee was one of sixteen Israeli sports figures chosen to participate in Israel's fifty-sixth Independence Day torchlighting ceremony, held on April 26, 2004.

• • •

KRASNOV, DANNY (born May 27, 1970, in Moscow, former Soviet Union–) Pole vaulter. Krasnov is the biggest success story among the many Russian athletes who arrived in Israel in the early 1990s. A former Russian youth champion who vaulted to the impressive height of 5.61 meters in the Moscow Open Championships in Moscow in 1991, later that year he immigrated to Israel (June 12th). He first came to notice in Israel when he reached the finals at the 1992 Barcelona Olympics, only the second Israeli athlete (Esther Roth was the first in 1976) to accomplish that feat; he finished eighth. In August 1994, he reached the finals of the European Championships in Helsinki, Finland, placing sixth with a leap of 5.70 meters. Later that same month, he lifted his national pole-vaulting record another five centimeters to 5.75 meters at the Brussels Grand Prix, finishing second behind the then world record holder Ukranian Sergei Bubka, who cleared 5.95. This result placed

medal-winner at the Barcelona Olympics in 1992, he finished in eighth place. In July 1993, he won the European Championships held in Belgium. In September 1994, Inbar was fifth in the World Championships held in Canada, and in September 1995 he came in fourth in the European Championships in England. He finished second in the 1997 World Championships, won the 1998 European Championships, and two years later came in second in that same competition. Inbar placed fourth in the 2003 World Championships.

• • •

KATASH, ODED (born October 10, 1974, in Israel–) Basketball player. From 1996 to 1998, he played for Maccabi Tel Aviv, Israeli champions all three years and winner of the State Cup in 1998. Prior to playing for the Tel Aviv team, he played one season for Maccabi Ramat Gan and one season for Hapoel Upper Galilee. He helped Hapoel reach the playoff finals in 1995. A star of Israel's national team at the Barcelona European

Krasnov among the world's top ten pole vaulters. Hopes were high for him to win a medal in Atlanta in 1996, but he came in 11th to 12th place only, reaching 5.60 meters. In August 1997 in Athens, Greece, he came in ninth in the World Championships. Krasnov lives in Jerusalem.

▪ ▪ ▪

LADANY, SHAUL (born April 2, 1936, in Belgrade, Yugoslavia–) Israeli walking champion. He still holds the world record in the 50-mile walk in Ocean Township, New Jersey: seven hours, 23 minutes, and 50 seconds. He won the 100-kilometer world championship in Lugano, Switzerland, in October 1972, in nine hours and 31 minutes. Ladany won the national walking championship in Israel 28 times (from 1963 until 1988); in the U.S. seven times (from 1973 to 1981); in Belgium twice (1971 and 1972); in Switzerland once (1972); and in South Africa once (1975). He won the London-to-Brighton walking competition in England in 1970, 1971 and 1973, a race of nearly 53 miles. In 1976, he was the first athlete ever to win both the American Open and Masters (40 years and over) 75 kilometer walking championship, held in New Jersey. He repeated that achievement in 1977 and in 1981 (by which time the event had become a 100-kilometer race). In 2006, clocking in at 21 hours, 45 minutes, 34 seconds in a race held in Ashtabula, Ohio, Ladany became the first septuagenarian to walk 100 miles within 24 hours. He is professor of Industrial Engineering and Management at Ben-Gurion University, Beersheba, Israel.

▪ ▪ ▪

LAZAROVE, LYDIA. See CARMEL, ZEFANIA

▪ ▪ ▪

LEIBOVITCH, KAREN (born July 25, 1973, in Hod Hasharon, Israel–) Disabled Israeli swimming champion. Leibovitch won three gold medals in swimming competitions at the 2000 Paralympics

Shaul Ladany

in Sydney, Australia. She holds four world records in swimming. After being wounded during army service, Leibovitch turned to sports as part of her recovery and became one of the world's best disabled athletes. A motivational speaker, she recounts her story to numerous audiences. Karen was one of sixteen Israeli sports figures chosen to participate in the country's fifty-sixth Independence Day torchlighting ceremony, held on April 26, 2004.

▪ ▪ ▪

MARCUS, DEBRA TURNER (born May 16, 1941, in Reading, England–) Israeli track star. She contracted a mild case of polio in July 1959, at age 18, and only two weeks after she got out of bed she entered the European Maccabi Championships in Copenhagen, Denmark, where she won the 100-meter race. Although her illness took its toll, Marcus managed to win the 100-meter race in the 1961 Maccabiah Games as well as taking a second in the 200-meter race. When she settled in Israel in 1964, she decided to retire from track. Marcus taught high school physical education in Tel Aviv for a while but then returned to running. In 1966 she won the European trials for the Asian Games in the 100- and 200-meter races. Then, at the 1966 Bangkok Asian Games, Marcus won a gold medal in the 200-meter sprint and a bronze in the 100-meters. She was named Israel's Athlete of the Year in 1966. She ran a sports program in a disadvantaged Jerusalem neighborhood from 1976-81, then, from 1981 to 1985, taught track and field at Jerusalem's Hebrew University. From 1992 to 1993, she was coordinator for the International Program of the Hebrew University-Hadassah. From 1993 to 1997, she lived in England, working with retirees; she returned to Israel in 1997 and is engaged in research on the elderly and leisure at Hebrew University.

Debra Turner Marcus

• • •

MATUSSEVICH, KONSTANTIN (born February 25, 1971 in Cherkass, the Ukraine–) High jumper. He reached the height of his career after immigrating to Israel on May 22, 1995, from the former Soviet Union. His greatest achievement prior to early 2000 was a high jump of 2.35 meters at an international competition in Norway on July 13, 1997, setting an Israeli high-jump record. At the World Championships in Athens, Greece, in 1997, he placed seventh with a jump of 2.29 meters. He represented Israel in the Atlanta Olympics in 1996 but failed to reach the finals. He came in fourth place in the indoor European Championships in Stockholm, Sweden, in 1996 with a jump of 2.31 meters. In 1995, he competed in the World Championships in Goteborg, Sweden, and was 17th with a jump of 2.24 meters. He was Israeli high-jumping champion three times— in 1994, 1995, and 1996. Prior to moving to Israel, he came in third place in the national championship in the former Soviet Union in 1992 with a jump of 2.28 meters. On February 5, 2000 he set a national indoor record of 2:36 meters at a track event in Perth, Australia. He came in fifth in the 2000 Sydney Olympics, and two years later, in 2002, he was the Israeli national champion.

• • •

MELAMED, AVRAHAM (born November 6, 1944, in Palestine–) Swimmer. He participated in the 1964 Tokyo Olympics. His greatest achievement came at the Mexico City Olympic Games in 1968 when he reached the semifinals in the 100-meter butterfly. In 1966 he won a silver medal at the Asian Games in Bangkok. His best achievements in the butterfly style were 59.1 for the 100 meters and 2:12.8 for the 200 meters. He was Israel's Sportsman of the Year in 1963. He was selected as one of Israel's top 50 athletes in its history, honored at a ceremony at Tel Aviv University in May 1998.

■ ■ ■

MELNIK, YONA (born May 27, 1949, in Kassel, West Germany–) Judoist. Between 1968 and 1980, he was Israel's national champion in the welterweight (below 70 kilograms) division 12 times, and in the open division twice. He took up judo at age 12 at the Maccabi Sports Club near Tel Aviv. He won the Scandinavian Open in 1975 and 1977. He took third place in the British Open in 1975 and 1980. Melnik won gold medals at the Maccabiah Games in 1973 and 1977. He retired in 1980 and was Israel's national judo coach for the next five years. From 1977 to the early 1990s, the club he coached, Hapoel Petach Tikvah, dominated the sport in Israel. His students have won over 350 medals in Israeli championships. He manages several judo clubs and coaches judo to all ages.

■ ■ ■

MERON, RAMI (born January 17, 1957, in Baku, former Soviet Union–) Wrestling. In June, 1975, Meron came in sixth in the World Youth Championships in Bulgaria; then, two months later he settled in Israel. From August 1975 until 1979, he was Israel's outstanding wrestler. In September 1975, he represented Israel at the World Championships in Minsk in the former Soviet Union; he came in seventh in the 68 kilogram class. The following year at the 1976 Montreal Olympics, Meron came in seventh. Then, in 1977, he came in fourth in the World Championships in Las Vegas. He owns a felafel restaurant in Tel Aviv.

■ ■ ■

NAHUM, ROGEL (born May 21, 1967, in Petach Tikvah, Israel–) Track and field star. Not since Esther Roth's heroics in the 1970s has Israel possessed a track and field star of Rogel's caliber. While he has not performed well at the international level, in July 1991, he smashed his own national triple-jump record, propelling himself over 17 meters for the first time. His jump of 17.17 meters at the National Track and Field Championships in Tel Aviv was the 13th best in the world. (The world record was 17.95.) He cleared 17.31 meters at the same contest but that jump was not recognized because of a high trailing wind. Nahum qualified for the Barcelona Olympics when he cleared 17.20 meters at the Expo '92 contest at Seville, Spain, in early June 1992. He failed to make the finals of the triple-jump, managing only 16.23 meters. At the Atlanta Olympics in 1996, he came in 17th. A year later, at the indoor World Championships in Paris, he was sixth. In February 1998, he placed fourth in the World Championships in Seville, Spain.

Rogel Nahum

Paulina Peled

■ ■ ■

OHANA, ELI (born February 1, 1964, in Israel–)
Soccer player. He was Israel's Sportsman of the
Year in 1993. He played for the Betar Jerusalem
team, national soccer champions in 1998. He excelled playing for the national team and appeared
in 52 games, scoring 18 goals. In 1988, he led the
Belgian team Mechlin to the European Cup Hold-
ers Championship with a 0:1 win over Ajex Amsterdam in the final. Retired since 1999, he was
the head coach at Betar in 2004. As of early 2010,
he was still coaching soccer in Israel.

■ ■ ■

OHRBACH, EYTAN (born January 12, 1977, in Israel–)
Swimmer. In 1993, he came in first place in the
100-meter backstroke at the Maccabiah Games. In
July 1994, he was first in the 200-meter backstroke
at the European Championships for youth held in
the Czech Republic. In February 1995, he came
in fourth place at the World Cup held in Sheffield,
England. He was 22nd at the Atlanta Olympics in
July 1996. He shared Israel's Sportsman of the Year
honors with Yoav Bruck in 1997. He came in second place in the 100-meter backstroke in the European championships in August 1997 held in Seville,
Spain. In January 1998, he came in seventh place in
the World Championships in Perth, Australia.

■ ■ ■

PE'ER, SHAHAR (born May 1, 1987, in Jerusalem,
Israel–) Tennis player. One of Israel's top tennis competitors, in May 2006 Pe'er made tennis
history at the Prague Open by taking the singles
and doubles titles on the same day. Following
those wins, her world ranking rose to number 32
in singles and number 49 in doubles. In February 2006, Pe'er gained her first career Women's
Tennis Association title at the Pattaya Women's
Open in Thailand, climbing to a career best of 33
(67 in doubles). At the 2004 Australian Open,
she had won the junior's championship, marking her for a bright future. In October 2005, she
was drafted into the Israel Defense Forces for a
two-year stint. "They're all surprised when I tell
them I've been trained to fire a rifle," Pe'er said,
alluding to her tennis colleagues. "They ask if it's
scary and I tell them not as scary as facing me on
the court." When she appeared at the IDF Induction Center near Tel Aviv, the press showed up in
large numbers, leaving an army spokeswoman
to say that even the chief of staff's visits do not
receive as much press attention. Pe'er reached her
career-high singles ranking of 15th on January 29,
2007. Her best Grand Slam singles result has been
reaching the quarter-finals at both the Australian
and U.S. Opens in 2007. She also reached the
women's doubles final at the Australian Open. In
January 2011 Pe'er was 11th in world rankings,
but she slipped to 23rd by June. As of June 6,
2011, she was ranked 29th in doubles.

■ ■ ■

PELED, PAULINA PEISACHOV (born April 20,
1950, in Vilnius, Lithuania–) Tennis. A junior

champion in her native Lithuania, she settled in Israel in 1966 at age 16. Peled made a meteoric rise, becoming number 20 in the world in 1974. When she won the Israeli Women's International Tennis Championship that year, she was the first Israeli woman to take the title in twenty years. Following five months of military service, Paulina did quite well on the American Virginia Slims women's pro circuit in 1975 but never again reached the ranking she had in 1974. By 1978 she had dropped to 102nd in the world rankings. She coaches tennis at a tennis club in Caesaria.

■ ■ ■

PISTOLESI, ANNA SMASHNOVA (born July 16, 1976, in Minsk, Belarus–) Tennis player. In 1994, four years after immigrating to Israel with her parents, Anna was named rookie of the year by *Tennis Magazine*, having completed her first year as a pro with a 347 ranking. Her highest singles rank came on February 3, 2003, when she was 15th in the world. Anna has won six career singles titles: in Tashkent, June 7, 1999; in Knokke-Heist, July 17, 2000; in Auckland, December 31, 2001; in Canberra, January 7, 2002; in Vienna, June 10, 2002; and in Shanghai, September 9, 2002. In December 2002, when she was ranked 16th in the world, Anna married her coach, Claudio Pistolesi. She won her ninth career title in 2004, and after divorcing Pistolesi, returned to play under her original surname, Smashnova. She retired from tennis in 2007.

■ ■ ■

RAM, ANDY. *See* **ERLICH, JONATHAN**

■ ■ ■

REVIVO, HAIM (born February 22, 1972, in Israel–) Soccer player. Along with Oded Katash, he was chosen Israel's 1998 Sports Figure of the Year. A highly talented competitor, he played in 32 games for the Israeli national soccer team scoring five goals. A star in the Spanish soccer league, he played for Selta Vigo there. In Israel, he played for the Bnei Yehuda team in Tel Aviv, Hapoel Tel Aviv, and Maccabi Haifa. Haim retired from soccer in April 2004. In 2006, after a brief stint playing in

Shoshana Ribner

Europe, he became owner of an Israeli soccer club named M.S. Ashdod.

■ ■ ■

RIBNER, SHOSHANA (born February 20, 1938, in Vienna, Austria–) Swimmer. One of Israel's best swimmers during the 1950s. Although her best stroke was the crawl, she also held records in the butterfly, medley swimming, and backstroke between 1950 and 1960. At the 1953 Maccabiah Games, she won gold medals in the 100- and 400-meter crawl. Shoshana participated in the 1956 Melbourne Olympics. That year she was Israel's Athlete of the Year. In 1957, she won two gold medals in the Maccabiah Games, one in the relay crawl, and the other in the mixed relay. She also won two silver medals in the 100- and 400-meter

Gershon Shefa

crawl. She now lives in Tel Aviv. Her son, Damon Fialkov, was the 200-meter backstroke champion in Israel in 1981. In May 1998, she was honored at a Tel Aviv University ceremony as one of Israel's top 50 athletes in its first 50 years.

■ ■ ■

SAKHNOVSKI, SERGEI. *See* **CHAIT, GALIT**

■ ■ ■

SELA, YOEL (born June 10, 1951, in Hadera, Israel–) and **AMIR, ELDAD** (born September 28, 1961 in Hadera, Israel–) Israeli sailors. They began sailing after the 1980 Moscow Olympics. They finished fourth in Flying Dutchmen class sailing at the Seoul Olympics in 1988, and might have won a medal had they not lost ground by staying out of a race on Yom Kippur. They were Sportsmen of the Year in 1984. Their greatest achievement came in 1990 when they earned fifth

place at the World Championships in Newport, Rhode Island. In 1991, they won the Italian Open at Garda, Italy, and came in second at the France Open in Toulon. They earned second place at the World Championships at the Olympic-class championships in Sam Remo, Italy. They placed only 20th at the Barcelona Olympics. Amir works in construction in Tel Aviv; Sela is a member of Kibbutz Sdot Yam.

■ ■ ■

SHEFA, GERSHON (born May 18, 1943, in Kibbutz Givat Haim, Palestine–) Swimmer. Shefa was the Israeli national swimming champion for nine years, from 1959 to 1968. His best stroke was the breaststroke; he also swam the individual medley. Gershon was Israeli Sportsman of the Year in 1962. He was the coach for the Israeli national swimming team six times between 1972 and 1980. He is world masters champion in the 200-meter breast stroke, having won that event in 1990 at the World Masters tournament in Rio De Janeiro, setting a record with a time of 2:46.45. He won two other breast stroke events in that tournament. Shefa coaches veteran swimmers at the kibbutz and manages its pool.

■ ■ ■

SHEZIFI, HANA (born November 5, 1943, in Iraq–) Track and field star. She participated in the 1968 Mexico City Olympics. Her main success was at the Asian Games—her outstanding achievements were at Bangkok (twice) and Teheran. She won three gold and one bronze medals in all. In the 800- and 1500-meter events she set Asian records. Hana won gold medals at the Maccabiah and Hapoel Games. She was Israel's Athlete of the Year in 1970. She won two bronze medals in the Asian championship in Seoul, South Korea, in 1975. Since 1996 she has been chairperson of the Israeli Bridge Federation in Tel Aviv and responsible for bridge instruction in Israeli schools.

■ ■ ■

SHMERKIN, MICHAEL (Born February 5, 1970, in Odessa, Ukraine–) Figure Skating. He immigrated to Israel on August 28, 1991. His figure

Hana Schezifi

skating has given Israel its first major international competitor in this sport. He lives in Kiryat Shemona and works at the Canada Center ice-skating rink in Metulla as a figure skating coach for children. In March 1994, he was 16th in the World Championships in Makuhari, Japan. In February 1994 at the winter Olympics in Lillehammer, Norway, he came in 11th. In March 1995, he was 15th in the World Championships in Birmingham, England. And in March 1996, he was 11th in the World Championships in Edmonton, Canada. In March 1997, he was 15th in the World Championships in Lausanne, Switzerland. Shmerkin coaches figure skating in Virginia.

■ ■ ■

SHMUELI, ZEHAVA (born May 19, 1955, in Rehovot, Israel–) Track and field star. She broke all the Israeli long-distance records between 1978 and 1992. Then the mother of two children, she finished 25th in the New York Marathon in October 1981 (out of 2,500 women runners) with the excellent time of 2:49.51, surpassing her own Israeli record by a large margin. She is also Israeli champion in the 5-, 10- and 25-kilometer distances. In 1981 *The Jerusalem Post* named her Israel Sportswoman of the Year. Running in the

annual Boston Marathon in April 1982, Zehava finished eighth among the hundreds of women entrants, setting an Israeli record of two hours, 44 minutes, almost six minutes better than her previous time. At the 1984 Olympics in Los Angeles, she finished 30th in the women's marathon with a time of 2:40.02. The following year, she gave birth to a daughter. She barely missed qualifying for the 1988 Olympics in Seoul. In May 1989, she set a new Israeli record, winning the 10,000 meter race for women in Tel Aviv in 34:40. She coaches long-distance running and is responsible for athletics at a combined junior high and high school at Ramat Hasharon.

■ ■ ■

SMADJA, OREN (born June 20, 1970, in Beersheba, Israel–) Judoist. Smadja captured a bronze medal in the men's 70-kilogram class at the Barcelona Olympics on July 31, 1992. He was only the second Israeli ever to win an Olympic medal. (Israeli judoist Yael Arad was the first, the day before). A surprise medal winner, Smadja won five contests with ippon (knock-out) moves. He came in second place in the World Championships (under 21 years of age) at Dijonne, France in 1990. He also won the Hungarian Open (under 21) that year. In 1991, Smadja came in third place in the European Championships (under 21) in Ankara, Turkey. By 1992 he appeared in adult competition, finishing third at the Prague Open, the English Open in London, and the European Championships in Paris. He did not compete again until 1995 when he came in second in the World Championships held in Makuhari, Japan. That year, he was named Israel's Sportsman of the Year. He suffered a serious knee injury in training ten days before the 1996 Atlanta Olympics, but competed anyway. In the summer of 1998, he trained again, this time for the 2000 Olympics in Sydney, Australia. He runs a children's sports program at Moshav Avihail. In February 1999, he won the silver medal at an event in Sofia, Bulgaria. He retired later that year.

■ ■ ■

Oleg Sodichov

SODICHOV, OLEG (born April 4, 1965, in Don-yetzk, former Soviet Union–) Weightlifter. In 1986, he won second place in the World Youth Championships in the 75-kilogram category. Oleg immigrated to Israel in 1991. In the European Championships in April 1992, he won a bronze medal in the 100-kilogram division (press and overall). At the 1992 Barcelona Olympics he placed sixth. He was a physical education instructor in the former Soviet Union.

■ ■ ■

SOHAR, URI (born January 14, 1937, in Petach Tikvah, Palestine–) Track and field athlete. He was an outstanding shot-putter. At the Asian Games in Tokyo in 1958, he won a bronze medal and then at the Asian Open Games he won a gold with an Asian record 15.05 meter throw. He was Israel's Sportsman of the Year in 1958. He participated in eight Maccabiah Games, winning a silver medal in 1957. His best achievement was 16.00 meters in Zurich in 1966 in the European Maccabiah Games. In January 1981, Sohar won second place in the shot-put with a throw of 14.72 meters in the World's Veterans

Games in New Zealand. Two years later, at those same Games in Puerto Rico, he came in third with a throw of 14.56 meters. In 1989, in Denmark, he was world champion in the shot-put for ages 50-55 at the World's Veterans Games with a throw of 13.97 meters. He owns a Haifa-based firm that cleans office buildings and factories and employs 250.

■ ■ ■

SPIEGLER, MORDECHAI (born August 19, 1944, in Azbest, former Soviet Union–) Soccer player. He joined the boys' team of Maccabi Netanya at age eight and grew up with the Maccabi Netanya team where he eventually became a soccer hero. He has participated in the largest number of international games (79) and scored the largest number of goals in those games (26) of any Israeli. Spiegler was the first and only Israeli soccer

Mordecai Spiegler

player to score a goal in World Cup play (1:1—against Sweden in Mexico in 1970). He also played professional soccer in France in 1972, 1973, and 1974; in 1975, he played for the New York Cosmos. He retired in 1977 and later coached Maccabi Haifa, Hapoel Haifa, and Betar Tel Aviv. Betar convinced him to come out of retirement and he played the last 14 games of the 1981-82 season for Betar Tel Aviv. Retired once again, he coached his home Maccabi Netanya club in 1982 for a year. For the next five years, he coached a number of other Israeli clubs. In 1990, he became manager of Maccabi Netanya. Spiegler served as an Israeli television commentator for the 1982, 1986 and 1990 World Cup games. On April 16, 1998, the Israeli newspapers *Yediot Aharonot* and *Ma'ariv* named Spiegler the outstanding soccer player in his nation's history. He called winning this recognition "the happiest and greatest of my career." In 2007, Spiegler was awarded a lifetime contribution award by the Israeli national team for his play in the 1970 World Cup competition.

Yuval Vishnetzir

■ ■ ■

STELMACH, NAHUM B. (born July 19, 1936, in Petach Tikvah, Palestine; died March 29, 1999) Soccer player. He was a member of the Israeli national team 61 times and scored 22 goals. In 1957 and 1959 he was named Israel's Sportsman of the Year. Stelmach scored his first international goal in 1956 in a game between Israel and the former Soviet Union in Ramat Gan. He later went into coaching. Stelmach was captain of the Israeli national team from 1958 to 1968 and captain of the Israeli army team in 1957. Stelmach was named the third most outstanding soccer player in his nation's history by the newspaper *Yediot Aharonot* in April 1998. As of the summer of that year, he was assistant coach of the national and junior soccer teams.

■ ■ ■

TSITIASHVILI, GOCHA (born November 7, 1973, in Tiblisi, Georgia, former Soviet Union–). Greco-Roman wrestler. He began wrestling at age 10 and immigrated to Israel on January 18, 1994.

After placing second in the European Championships in Athens, Greece, in April 1994, Gocha was named Israel's Sportsman of the Year for 1994. In September 1995, he came in third place in the World Championships held in Prague, putting him among the top four or five wrestlers in his weight class in the world. In April 1996, he was third in the European championships in Budapest, Hungary, and came in fifth place at the Atlanta Olympics in July 1996 in the 82-kilogram division. In April 1997, he came in seventh in the European Championships held in Thailand. Married with one son, he works as a sports coach for the municipality of Beersheba.

■ ■ ■

VISHNETZIR, YUVAL (born February 6, 1947, in Menahamiya, Palestine–) Track and field star. Holder of national records in long distance runs (1,500, 3,000, 5,000 and 10,000 meters). Yuval won a bronze medal in the 1970 Asian Games in Bangkok in the 5,000-meter race, and four years later won a silver medal in the 5,000-meter race

Edward Weitz

in the Teheran Games. He was among the 30 best runners in the world in the 1,500-meter race in 1975. He was Israeli champion 30 times and Israel's top sportsman in 1973. He was chosen as one of Israel's 50 top athletes and honored at a Tel Aviv University ceremony in May 1998.

■ ■ ■

WEITZ, EDWARD (born April 16, 1946, in Teshernigov, former Soviet Union–) Weightlifter. He was the Red Army champion in the 60-kilogram class and was ranked in the first five in the former Soviet Union in his division before immigrating to Israel. He won the Asian Games title in Bangkok in May 1976, for Israel, with a combined lift of 260 kilograms. At the 1976 Montreal Olympics he came in fifth out of 17 in the 60-kilogram class

with a total of 262.5 kilograms. Weitz had a series of lifts of 110 kilograms in the snatch and 152.5 in the clean and jerk. That was Israel's best placing in the Olympics. He was Israel's Sportsman of the Year in 1976. Weitz was honored in May 1998 as one of Israel's top 50 athletes.

■ ■ ■

YONASSI, ITZHAK (born October 18, 1962, in Ashkelon, Israel–) Shooter. As a youngster, Itzhak regarded an older cousin, an expert in marksmanship, as a role model. "I always wanted to be like him." Once Itzhak took up shooting, he decided, "I want to be better than him." He became better than most others. He became Israeli shooting champion in 1977 and won at least one of the three shooting categories every year through 1991. At the Los Angeles Olympics in 1984, he came in eighth in air rifle competition, scoring 582 out of a possible 600 points. At the Seoul Olympics four years later, he was 16th. A major in the permanent service of the Israel Defense Forces, Yonassi lives in Ramat Gan, is married, and has a son.

■ ■ ■

ZE'EVI, ARIK (born in 1977, in Israel–) Israeli judo champion. A three-time European champ, Ze'evi won an Olympic bronze medal in the under-100 kilogram judo competition at the Athens Olympics in August 2004. Prime Minister Ariel Sharon told Ze'evi: "We're very proud of you. You withstood the pressure like a true warrior." It was Israel's fifth Olympic medal ever and its third in judo. Ze'evi won the gold medal in the under-100 kilogram category at the European Championships for the second year in a row and for the third time in four years. At the 2008 Beijing Olympics he failed to win a medal. As of June 2010 Ze'evi was ranked 26th on the International Judo Federation's World Ranking List.

The Maccabiah Games

As a response to the religious oppression, po-groms, and isolation they suffered, the Jews of nineteenth century Eastern Europe formed self-defense groups for protection and gymnas-tic clubs to build their bodies. The athletic clubs appeared first in Constantinople in 1895 and then in Austria, Hungary and Germany. Taking Judas Maccabaeus, the Hebrew religious zealot and fighter from the second century B.C.E., as their role model, the clubs adopted the name Maccabi. By the eve of World War I, over 100 Maccabi-type clubs were in existence in Europe.

Selecting Judas Maccabaeus as their hero was not without irony. Although Maccabaeus, known as "The Hammer," was famous for his talents as a fighter, he had also opposed the Hellenization of Jewish life (Hellenization's most visible symbols were the Greek Olympiads and the cult of the physi-cal). But, despite this, Maccabaeus was a genuine hero, leading as he did a successful revolt against the Syrians, a triumph for religious freedom that led to the recapture, cleansing, and rededication of the Temple in Jerusalem on the 25th day of Kislev in 165 B.C.E. That date in Jewish history is commemo-rated on Hanukkah, the Festival of Lights.

After World War I, the European Maccabi movement organized international games. In 1929, the contests were held in Czechoslovakia; in 1930, Belgium; and in 1931, Germany. In 1929, a Maccabi World Congress met, and Yosef Yekuteli, the only delegate from Palestine, proposed some kind of convocation of Jewish athletes in Palestine. The delegates unanimously accepted the idea. They had been impressed with the 1928 Olympics in Amsterdam and thought the time ripe for a "Jewish Olympics."

The first Maccabiah in Palestine was held in March and April 1932 and 390 athletes from 22 nations participated.

The American delegation, 11 men and two women, did exceedingly well, winning 13 gold and numerous silver and bronze medals. One woman fencer from Palestine took a gold medal, the only gold medal won by Palestine in the first Games in *Eretz Yisrael* (The Land of Israel).

The second Maccabiah, in 1935 (with 1,700 athletes from 27 countries), was larger than the first, but it was equally primitive and disorganized. The stadium was a sandpit. The program, though broader than the first Games, was not followed precisely: for example, the 5,000-meter race was run twice! But, happily for the *Yishuv*, the Jewish community in Palestine, many athletes from other countries did not return to their country of origin. These 1935 Games were thus known as the "Aliya" Games.

A third Maccabiah was planned for 1938, but the shadow of war descending upon Europe caused the games to be canceled. By the time the next Games were held in 1950, in the new state of Israel, the Jewish people had witnessed the Holo-caust and Israel's War of Independence. For the first time in 1950, the athletes were housed to-gether in a military camp in Tel Aviv. Clubs from several countries that had participated in past Games, particularly those from the Arab states, did not attend, but South American countries were represented for the first time, as were Australia and India. Considering the pain and suffering endured throughout the war, even staging the games—though with only 20 countries and 500 athletes participating—was an achievement.

By 1977, 33 nations participated in the Mac-cabiah Games, with 2,276 athletes. That year the United States sent a contingent of 289 athletes. And, in July 1981, the number of countries in-volved was 35, with 3,500 athletes participating.

Some 4,000 athletes from 40 countries turned

out for the 12th Maccabiah in 1985, taking part in 28 sports. Mark Spitz, winner of seven gold medals in the 1972 Munich Olympics, lit the torch at the opening ceremonies. He was accompanied by three of the children of the Israeli Olympic athletes who were murdered by terrorists in 1972.

Seven men's and 14 women's records were broken in swimming with the U.S. team winning all but three of the gold medals in this category. And, 12 new men's records and seven women's records fell in track and field. In all, the U.S. team captured 109 gold, 90 silver, and 74 bronze medals, slightly less than half of those won by all other countries combined. A junior Maccabiah was held for the first time.

Then in 1989, at the 13th Maccabiah, 4,500 athletes participated from 44 countries. Jewish athletes from Russia and Hungary participated in the Maccabiah for the first time. The 1989 Games marked the "Bar Mitzvah" of the Maccabiah Games. Excellent performances were recorded in swimming, tennis and judo. American Ken Flax was among the stars at the Games, winning a gold medal in the hammer throw with a 78.86 meter toss. The closing ceremony was held at the Western Wall in Jerusalem for the first time.

For the 1993 Maccabiah Games, South Africa returned to the games after 20 years of political isolation, and after the fall of the Iron Curtain, many other Eastern European countries, among them Poland, Bulgaria, and Czechoslovakia, joined again for the first time since the establishment of the State of Israel. Athletes from eight Republics of the former Soviet Union also participated. In all, 5,100 athletes from 48 countries competed in 32 sports. The U.S. team numbered 639. Yael Arad, Israeli silver medal winner in judo from the Barcelona Olympics of 1992—Israel's first Olympic medal winner ever—lit the Maccabiah torch.

The 1997 Maccabiah Games came as Israel celebrated the 100th anniversary of the Zionist Movement and the start of the 50th anniversary of the State of Israel. A total 5,500 athletes from 50 states took part, competing in 34 sports. The Games were marred by a tragic accident at the opening of the Games when a bridge collapsed over the Yarkon River, over which delegations were streaming to get to the stadium, killing four Australian athletes and injuring 60 others.

For the 16th Maccabiah Games, held in July 2001, only half the number of athletes who had planned to participate actually arrived in Israel, the result of security concerns arising from Israeli-Palestinian violence. Some 2,000 athletes did take part. At the 2005 Maccabiah Games, nearly 8,000 Jewish athletes competed.

Some 9,000 athletes from 54 nations participated in the 2009 Maccabiah Games, considered by now the third largest sporting event in the world. Israel won the most gold medals with 138, and the most total—gold, silver, bronze—medals with 367. The United States followed with 44 gold, 146 total. Russia came in third with 12 gold and 34 total.

For the most part, the Maccabiah followed the Olympic model, but at times it initiated changes that the Olympics later adopted. One significant difference exists between Olympic rules and those of the Maccabiah Games: unlike Olympic athletes, a Maccabiah participant who lives in and competes for a given country can compete for another nation if and when he or she changes his or her country of residence. For instance, Tal Brody was a member of the American basketball squad that won a gold medal in the 1965 Maccabiah Games. He was also captain of the Israeli team that triumphed over the U.S. to win a gold medal in the 1969 Maccabiah Games.

American delegations to the Maccabiah Games have included such famous athletes as Isaac Berger (weightlifting), Lillian Copeland (track), Ernie Grunfeld (basketball), Mark Spitz (swimming), and Henry Wittenberg (wrestling).

The Maccabiah Games have witnessed some outstanding individual performances over the years:

RICK ARONBERG, United States, broke three swimming records in the 1989 Games: Won the 200-meter freestyle for men in 1:52.51 minutes, the 400-meter freestyle for men in 3:55.64 minutes, and the 1500-meter freestyle for men in 15:37.66 minutes.

ALEX AVERBUKH, Israel, set a new Maccabiah male pole-vault record (5.6 meters) in the 2001 Games.

MICKEY BAR YEHOSHUA, Israel, won the 200 meters in 21.63 seconds at the 2009 Games.

HILARY BERGMAN, United States, won the 200-meter freestyle swimming event in 1:55.91; the 400-meter freestyle in 4:04.34; the 1,500-meter freestyle in 16:20.55; the 400-meter individual medley in 4:39.31; the 400-meter freestyle relay in 3:34.36, and the 800-meter freestyle relay in 7:59.07. All these gold medals were won in the 1977 Games.

LIOR BIRKHAN, Israel, won a gold medal for swimming in the 1981 Games, setting a new Maccabiah mark in the 200-meter medley. In the heats she was only fourth best, but in the final she timed 2:29.96 minutes.

ADI BRANA, Israel, heavyweight class, won the snatch (117.5 kilograms), the jerk (142.5 kilograms), and the total (260 kilograms) in the 1977 Games.

MIRA BULVA, Israel, won the shot-put in the 1977 Games with a 42 foot, 10¼ inch (13.06 meters) throw; and the discus throw in the same Games with a 143 foot, 7½ inch (43.78 meters) throw.

WILLY CHEMBERLO, Israel, bantam weight class, won the snatch (82.5 kilograms), the jerk (90.0 kilograms), and the total (172.5 kilograms), in the 1973 Games.

LISA DOBY, United States, won four individual gold medals and three team ones in the relays in swimming in the 1993 Games.

ALON ELYAKIM, Israel, a 19 year-old soldier, became the first Israeli to win a Maccabiah gold medal in the 400-meter race in the 1981 Games.

DUSTIN EMRANI, United States, won the 800 meters race in 1 minute 50.05 seconds at the 2009 Games.

SHLOMO GLICKSTEIN, Israel, won the men's singles in the 1981 Games and thus became the first Israeli to win a Maccabiah tennis championship.

BRYAN GOLDBERG, United States, beat the Olympic gold medalist by almost a full second and broke the Maccabiah record by completing the 100-meter freestyle in 51.06 seconds in the 2005 Games.

SIGAL GONEN, Israel, set a record in the long jump for women with a jump of 6.13 meters in the 1985 Games.

ERAN GROUMI, Israel, set a record in the 200-meter butterfly for men with a time of 2:04.80 minutes in the 1989 Games.

GARY GUBNER, United States, won the shot-put in 1961 with a 60 foot, 1¼ inch (18.32 meters) throw.

YA'ACOV GUREVITZ, Israel, flyweight class, won the snatch (77.5 kilograms), the jerk (92.5 kilograms), and the total (170 kilograms) in the 1973 Games.

MICKEY HALIKA, Israel, won five individual gold medals and two team ones in the relays in the 1997 Games.

MARK HANDELSMAN, Israel, broke the record in the 800-meter run with a race of 1:49.29 minutes in the 1985 Games.

SIVAN JAN, Israel, 17, set Maccabiah records at the 2005 Games with a shot-put throw of 15.62 meters and a discus throw of 50 meters.

ORIT KOLDNI, Israel, set a record in the 400 meters for women with a time of 55.85 seconds in the 1985 Games.

LENNY KRAYZELBURG, United States, established a new Maccabiah record in the 2001 Games when he finished the male 100-meter backstroke in 0:55.24.

SHAUL LADANY, Israel, won the 3,000-meter walk in the 1969 Games in 13:35.4; the 20,000-meter walk in the 1973 Games with a 1:37.54 time; and the 50,000-meter walk in those same Games.

ANDREA LEAND, Israel, won the women's singles in tennis in the 1981 Games.

DANIEL MADWED, United States, won four gold medals in swimming at the 2005 Games, becoming the tournament's outstanding male junior swimmer.

LISA MARTIN, United States, won four individual gold medals and five team ones in the relays in swimming in the 1993 Games.

EDI PAPIROF, Israel, set two records in shooting in the Free Rifle (3 positions) for men (1153 points); and the Olympic Air Rifle for men (582 points) in the 1989 Games.

TERRY PERDUE, Great Britain, super-heavyweight class, won the snatch (142.5 kilograms), the jerk (170 kilograms), and the total (312.5 kilograms) in the 1973 Games.

JULIE ROSENFELD, Russia, 17, set a Maccabiah record in the hammer throw with a throw of 56.05 meters at the 2005 Games.

ESTHER ROTH, Israel, won the 100-meter race in the 1973 Games in 11.75; the 200-meter race in the 1977 Games in 24.03; the 100-meter hurdles in the same Games in 13.50; and the long jump in the 1969 Games with a 19 foot, ¾ inch (5.81 meters) jump.

ANDRES SALTZMAN, United States, set a new Maccabiah record of 52.33 seconds in the 1981 Games when he won the 100-meter freestyle swimming event, breaking Mark Spitz's 1969 52.90 Maccabiah mark.

JENNY SUSSER, United States, set two swimming records in the 1989 Games, winning the 50-meter freestyle for women with a time of 27.10 seconds, and winning the 100-meter freestyle for women with a time of 57.77 seconds.

DARIA UHARSKAYA, Russia, set a Maccabiah record in the 400-meter hurdles with a time of 01:00.03 at the 2005 Games.

WENDY WEINBERG, United States, won the 200-meter freestyle swimming event in 2:08.96; the 400-meter freestyle in 4:26.14; and the 800-meter freestyle in 9:03.46. She also won the 200-meter butterfly in 2:20.8. All these triumphs came in the 1977 Games.

EDWARD WEITZ, Israel, lightweight class, won the snatch 115 (kilograms), the jerk (150 kilograms), and the total (265 kilograms) in the 1977 Games.

ANITA ZARNOWIECKI, Sweden, won seven gold swimming medals and one silver swimming medal in the 1973 Maccabiah Games.

The
Hall of Fame

The Jewish Sports Hall of Fame was founded in 1979 to recognize Jewish men and women who achieve distinction in sports. Joseph M. Siegman, the Hollywood television producer who was the moving force behind the creation of the organization and is a former chairman, currently holds the post of Election Committee Chairman of the Jewish Sports Hall of Fame. R. Stephen Rubin serves as honorary chairman and Alan Sherman as chairman.

The Hall of Fame is located at the Wingate Institute for Physical Education and Sport, in Netanya, Israel, a thirty-minute drive north from Tel Aviv. In the first two years, it considered for admission only American athletes and sportsmen. As of 1981, however, the Hall of Fame allowed candidates from the entire world Jewish community.

The Selection Committee has tended to favor athletes who have set world records, won world championships, and won Olympic gold medals. American football, baseball, and basketball players, star athletes in other sports, coaches, and certain entrepreneurs and officials are among the exceptions who have been inducted. The Committee has sought to include athletes of all sports, major or minor. To be eligible, a candidate must have retired from sports competition.

HALL OF FAME MEMBERS

Harold Abrahams, Great Britain............................ 1981
Track & Field
Amy Alcott, USA.. 2000
Golf
Joseph Alexander, USA... 1985
Football
Mel Allen, USA 1980
Media
Lyle Alzado, USA.. 2008
Football
Yael Arad, Israel.. 2010
Judo
Ray Arcel, USA 1992
Boxing
Gerald Ashworth, USA 2001
Track & Field
Abe Attell, USA... 1983
Boxing
Arnold "Red" Auerbach, USA 1979
Basketball
Albert Axelrod, USA.. 1993
Fencing
Max "Maximillian" Baer, USA 2010
Boxing
Arthur Barr, Austria.. 1982
Soccer
Aron "Ali" Bacher, South Africa 1991
Cricket
William Bachrach, USA... 1994
Swimming

Sam Balter, USA.. 1994
Basketball
Viktor Barna, Hungary/Great Britain..................... 1981
Table Tennis
Herman Barron, USA... 1993
Golf
Istvan Barta, Hungary... 1998
Waterpolo
Harris Barton, USA... 2009
Football
Benny Bass, USA 1994
Boxing
Doug Beal, USA 2001
Volleyball
Adriana Behar, Brazil.. 2006
Beach Volleyball
Laszio Bellak, Hungary... 1995
Table Tennis
Carina Benninga, Holland 2000
Field Hockey
Senda Berenson, USA 1987
Basketball
Jackie "Kid" Berg, Great Britain 1987
Boxing
Isaac Berger, USA... 1980
Weightlifting
Samuel Berger, USA.. 1985
Boxing
Richard Bergmann, Austria 1982
Table Tennis

Jack Bernstein, USA	2000	**Lillian Copeland**, USA	1979
Boxing		Track & Field	
Kenny Bernstein, USA	2006	**Howard Cosell**, USA	1993
Auto Racing		Media	
Morris "Whitey" Bimstein, USA	2008	**Harry Danning**, USA	2000
Boxing		Baseball	
Arthur Bluenthenthal, USA	1997	**Pierre Darmon**, France	1997
Football		Tennis	
Walter Blum, USA	1991	**Massimo Della Pergola**, Italy	1989
Horse Racing		Official/Media	
Gyorgy Brody, Hungary	1982	**Umberto DeMorpurgo**, Italy	1993
Water Polo		Tennis	
Tal Brody, Israel	1996	**Barney Dreyfuss**, USA	1979
Basketball		Baseball	
Larry Brown, USA	1990	**Dutch Olympians**, 1928, Holland	1997
Basketball		Gymnastics	
Ellen Burka, Canada	2010	**Sam "Dutch Sam" Elias**, Great Britain	2011
Figure Skating		Boxing	
Angela Buxton, Great Britain	1981	**Nikolay Epshteen**, Russia	2001
Tennis		Ice Hockey	
Alain Calmat, France	1987	**Charlotte Epstein**, USA	1982
Figure Skating		Swimming	
Zefania Carmel, Israel	1982	**Laszlo Fabian**, Hungary	1996
Yachting		Canoeing	
Joe Choynski, USA	1991	**Jackie Fields**, USA	1979
Boxing		Boxing	
Robert Cohen, Algeria	1988	**Herb Flam**, USA	1992
Boxing		Tennis	

A gallery of mementos at the Jewish Sports Hall of Fame in Israel.

Wingate Institute for Physical Education and Sports in Netnaya, Israel.

Alfred Flatow, Germany 1981
Gymnastics
Gustav Flatow, Germany....................................... 1989
Gymnastics
Nat Fleischer, USA.. 1985
Media
Robert "Bobby" Frankel, USA............................. 2011
Horse Racing
Gal Friedman, Israel 2005
Sailing
Benny Friedman, USA 1979
Football
Max Friedman, USA... 1994
Basketball
Jeno Fuchs, Hungary.. 1982
Fencing
Tamas Gabor, Hungary... 1996
Fencing
Janos Garay, Hungary... 1990
Fencing
Mitch Gaylord, USA.. 1988
Gymnastics
Aaron "Okey" Geffen, South Africa....................... 1998
Rugby
Dr. Oskar Gerde, Hungary.................................... 1989
Fencing
Sid Gillman, USA.. 1991
Football
Marty Glickman, USA.. 1996
Media

Sir Arthur A. Gold, Great Britain............................ 1987
Contributor
Marshall Goldberg, USA.. 1980
Football
Charles "Buckets" Goldenberg, USA..................... 1993
Football
Israel Charley Goldman, USA............................... 1999
Boxing
Reuven "Ruby" Goldstein, USA 1995
Boxing
Margie Goldstein-Engle, US 2009
Equestrian
Sandor Gombos, Hungary 1997
Fencing
Aleksandr Gomelsky, USSR 1981
Basketball
Sidney "Sid" Gordon, USA.................................... 2010
Baseball
Maria Gorokhovskaya, USSR................................. 1991
Gymnastics
Brian Gottfried, USA 1999
Tennis
Eddie Gottlieb, USA.. 1980
Basketball
Milton Green, USA.. 1997
Track & Field
Hank Greenberg, USA.. 1979
Baseball
Abie Grossfeld, USA.. 1992
Gymnastics

Gary Gubner, USA 2001
Track & Field

George Gulack, USA 1984
Gymnastics

Boris Me. Gurevich, USSR 1987
Wrestling

Boris Mi. Gurevitch, USSR 1982
Wrestling

Bela Guttmann, Hungary 1981
Soccer

Sir Ludwig Guttmann, Germany/G. Britain 1981
Contributor

Alfred Hajos-Guttmann, Hungary 1981
Swimming

Hakoah-Vienna, Austria 1982
Soccer

Alphonse Halimi, France/Algeria 1989
Boxing

Sidney Halter, USA 2006
Football

William Harmatz, USA 1999
Horse Racing

Johann Harmenberg, Sweden 1997
Fencing

Harry Harris, USA 1996
Boxing

Sigmund Harris, USA 1994
Football

Cecil Hart, Canada 1992
Ice Hockey

Lew Hayman, Canada 2004
Football

Ladislav Hecht, Czechoslavakia 2005
Tennis

Gladys Heldman, USA 1989
Tennis/Media

Julie Heldman, USA 2001
Tennis

Ben Helfgott, Great Britain 1995
Weightlifting

Lilli Henoch, Germany 1990
Track & Field

Otto Herschmann, Austria 1989
Swimming

Victor Hershkowitz, USA 1991
Handball

Nikolaus Hirschl, Austria 1993
Wrestling

Marty Hogan, USA 1996
Racquetball

Marshall Holman, USA 2006
Tenpin Bowling

Nat Holman, USA 1979
Basketball

Ken Holtzman, USA 1995
Baseball

William "Red" Holzman, USA 1988
Basketball

Sarah Hughes, USA 2005
Figure Skating

Maria Leontyana Itkina, Soviet Union 1991
Track & Field

Joe Jacobi, USA 2005
Canoeing

Hirsch Jacobs, USA 1979
Horse Racing

Jimmy Jacobs, USA 1979
Handball

Irving Jaffee, USA 1979
Speed Skating

Allan Jay, Great Britain 1985
Fencing

Endre Kabos, Hungary 1986
Fencing

Rena "Rusty Glickman" Kanokogi, USA 2011
Judo

Louis "Kid" Kaplan, USA 1986
Boxing

Karoly Karpati, Hungary 1994
Wrestling

Gennadi Karponosov, Russia 2001
Ice Hockey

Elias Katz, Finland 1981
Track & Field

Agnes Keleti, Hungary 1981
Gymnastics

Irena Kirzenstein-Szewinska, Poland 1981
Track & Field

Abel Kiviat, USA` 1984
Track & Field

Traute Kleinova, Czechoslovakia 1994
Table Tennis

Ilana Kloss, South Africa 2010
Tennis

Bela Komjadi, Hungary 1992
Water Polo

Sandy Koufax, USA 1979
Baseball

Lenny Krayzelburg, USA 2005
Swimming

Solly Keriger, USA 1997
Boxing

Suzy Kormoczy, Hungary 2007
Tennis

Grigori Kriss, USSR 1989
Fencing

Lily Kronberger, Hungary 1983
Figure Skating

Alfred Kuchevsky, USSR/Russia 2011
Ice Hockey

Henry Laskau, USA 1996
Track & Field

Bowie Kuhn, with glasses, inducts Sandy Koufax into the Baseball Hall of Fame at Cooperstown, New York, on August 7, 1972. (Above right) Koufax's Baseball Hall of Fame plaque.

Entertainer Milton Berle (left) at the 1979 Jewish Sports Hall of Fame Inaugural Dinner with inductees Hank Greenberg and Jackie Fields.

Lydia Lazarov, Israel..............1982 Yachting	**Tatjana Lysenko**, Ukraine..............2002 Gymnastics
Karen Leibovitch, Israel..............2008 Swimming	**Joseph Magidsohn**, USA..............1999 Football
Benny Leonard, USA..............1979 Boxing	**Gyula Mandel**, Hungary..............1982 Soccer
Battling Levinsky, USA..............1982 Boxing	**Walentin Mankin**, USSR..............1987 Yachting
Edward L. Levy, Great Britain..............1988 Weightlifting	**Al McCoy**, USA..............1989 Boxing
Marv Levy, USA..............1998 Football	**Hugo Meisl**, Austria..............1981 Soccer
Fred Lewis, USA..............2011 Handball	**Fania Melnik**, USSR..............1984 Track & Field
Harry Lewis, USA..............2002 Boxing	**Daniel Mendoza**, Great Britain..............1981 Boxing
Ted "Kid" Lewis, Great Britain..............1983 Boxing	**Dr. Ferenc Mezo**, Hungary..............1986 Contributor
Jason Lezak, USA..............2006 Swimming	**Mark Midler**, USSR..............1983 Fencing
Mort Lindsey, USA..............1997 Bowling	**Walter Miller**, USA..............1983 Horse Racing
Alexandre Lippmann, France..............1984 Fencing	**Ron Mix**, USA..............1980 Football
Harry Litwack, USA..............1980 Basketball	**Ivor Montagu**, Great Britain..............1984 Table Tennis
Benny Lom, USA..............1996 Football	**Samuel Mosberg**, USA..............1985 Boxing
Sid Luckman, USA..............1979 Football	**Armand Mouyal**, France..............1988 Fencing

The 1980 inductees into the Jewish Sports Hall of Fame include (left to right) Isaac Berger, weightlifting; Mel Allen, sportcasting; Ron Mix, football; Marshall Greenberg, football; Al Rosen, baseball; and Henry Litwack, basketball.

Charles "Buddy" Myer, USA 1992
Baseball

Lon Myers, USA 1980
Track & Field

Alfred Nakache, France 1993
Swimming

Paul Neumann, Austria 1984
Swimming

Edward Newman, USA 1995
Football

Harry Newman, USA 1992
Football

Tzvi Nishri, Israel 1981
Contributor

Sidney Nomis, South Africa 1999
Rugby

Grigori Novak, USSR 1985
Weightlifting

Fred Oberlander, Canada 1991
Wrestling

Tom Okker, Holland 2003
Tennis

Bob Olin, USA 2008
Boxing

Ivan Osiier, Denmark 1986
Fencing

Victor "Young" Perez, Tunisia 1986
Boxing

Attila Petschauer, Hungary 1985
Fencing

Philadelphia Sphas, USA 1996
Basketball

Lipman Pike, USA 1985
Baseball

Zhanna Pintussevich, Ukraine 2009
Track & Field

Maurice Podoloff, USA 1989
Basketball

Daniel Prenn, Germany 1981
Tennis

Myer Prinstein, USA 1982
Track & Field

Bela Rajki-Reich, Hungary 2000
Water Polo

Mark Rakita, USSR 1988
Fencing

Marilyn Ramenofsky, USA 1988
Swimming

Mauri Rose, USA 2007
Auto Racing

Al Rosen, USA 1980
Baseball

Mel Rosen, USA 2004
Track & Field

Harry "Coon" Rosen, USA 1993
Softball

Allen Rosenberg, USA 1994
Rowing

Charlie Phil Rosenberg, USA 1990
Boxing

Wilf Rosenberg, South Africa 1994
Rugby

Maxie Rosenbloom, USA 1984
Boxing

Leonard Rosenbluth, USA 2003
Basketball

Albert Rosenfeld, Great Britain 2006
Rugby

Fanny Rosenfeld, Canada 1982
Track & Field

Barney Ross, USA 1979
Boxing

Victor Ross, USA 1995
Lacrosse

Mark Roth, USA 1992
Bowling

Emilia Rotter, Hungary 1995
Figure Skating

Leon Rottman, Romania 1981
Canoeing

Angelica Rozeanu, Romania 1981
Table Tennis

Louis Rubenstein, Canada 1981
Figure Skating

Mendy Rudolph, USA 1989
Basketball

Abe Saperstein, USA 1979
Basketball

Miklos Sarkany, Hungary 1990
Water Polo

Richard Savitt, USA 1979
Tennis

Dolph Schayes, USA 1979
Basketball

Jody Scheckter, South Africa 1983
Auto Racing

Corporal Isidore Schwartz, USA 1998
Boxing

Barney Sedran, USA 1989
Basketball

Eugene Selznick, USA 2002
Volleyball

Sergei Sharikov, Russia 2003
Fencing

Ylena Shushunova, USSR 2005
Gymnastics

Michael Sigel, USA 2011
Billiards

Al Singer, USA 2006
Boxing

Anna Sipos, Hungary 1996
Table Tennis

Irina Slutskaya, Russia	2009	**Sid Tannenbaum**, USA	1997
Figure Skating		Basketball	
Harold Solomon, USA	2004	**Eliot Teltscher**, USA	2009
Tennis		Tennis	
Jack Solomons, Great Britain	2004	**Lew Tendler**, USA	1992
Boxing		Boxing	
Moe Spahn, USA	1993	**Leah Thall-Neuberger**, USA	1999
Basketball		Table Tennis	
Frank Spellman, USA	1983	**David "Pep" Tobey**, USA	1995
Weightlifting		Basketball	
Don Spero, USA	1993	**Allan Tolmich**, USA	2002
Rowing		Track & Field	
Mark Spitz, USA	1979	**Shaun Tomson**, South Africa	1995
Swimming		Surfing	
David Stern, USA	1998	**Dara Torres**, USA	2005
Basketball		Swimming	
Georges Stern, France	1993	**Eduard Vinokurov**, Kazakhstan, SSR Republic	2007
Horse Racing		Fencing	
Steve Stone, USA	2004	**Richard Weisz**, Hungary	1983
Baseball		Wrestling	
Joel Stransky, South Africa	2009	**Matt Wells**, Great Britain	2007
Rugby		Boxing	
Earl Strom, USA	2008	**Sylvia Wene**, USA	1979
Basketball		Bowling	
Kerri Strug, USA	2000	**Lajos Werkner**, Hungary	1999
Gymnastics		Fencing	
Miklos Szabados, Hungary	1987	**Henry Wittenberg**, USA	1979
Table Tennis		Wrestling	
Eva Szekely, Hungary	1981	**Chagai Zamir**, Israel	1998
Swimming		Volleyball	
Laszio Szollas, Hungary	1996	**Max Zaslovsky**, USA	1983
Figure Skating		Basketball	

(Left to right) Red Auerbach, Jerry Saperstein (Abe's son), Dolph Schayes, Irving Jaffee, Dick Savitt, Sylvia Wene Martin, Hank Greenberg, Nat Holman, and Joe Leonard (Benny's brother).

Index